Shalom Rav

Insights on the Weekly *Parasha*

Rabbi Shalom Rosner

INSIGHTS ON THE WEEKLY PARASHA

BERESHIT • SHEMOT

COMPILED AND EDITED BY
Marc Lesnick

OU Press
Maggid Books

Shalom Rav
Insights on the Weekly Parasha

First Edition, 2019

Maggid Books
An imprint of Koren Publishers Jerusalem Ltd.

POB 8531, New Milford, CT 06776-8531, USA
& POB 4044, Jerusalem 9104001, Israel
www.korenpub.com

The publication of this book was made possible
through the generous support of the *Jewish Book Trust*.

ISBN 978-1-59264-530-5, *hardcover*

A CIP catalogue record for this title is
available from the British Library

Printed and bound in the United States

This book is dedicated to our dear parents

Rabbi David and Eileen Lesnick
Shaya and Rhona Bar-Chama

Each of whom has served as a role model
for us and our children as individuals dedicated
to Torah, Avoda and Gemilut Hasadim.

And to our dear children

Ariel and Rinat, Ori and Noam
Adena
Sarit and Yonatan
Rami
Amichai

Each of whom has brought us tremendous nahat,
by following in the path established by their grandparents.

Tamar and Marc Lesnick

אשר זעליג וייס

כגן 8
פעיה"ק ירושלם ת"ו

בס"ד

ידיד נפשי הרה"ג ר' שלום רוזנר שליט"א רב קהילת נופי השמש בבית שמש
ידוע ומפורסם בשערי תורה בשיעוריו הנפלאים והמרתקים, ואלפים הם שומעי
לקחו תמידין כסדרן. אך עד עתה ידענו רק את תורתו שבע"פ, ועתה זכה יקר לבבי
איש תורה דעת וחסד ר' שי לזניק נ"י ללקט, לכתוב, ואף לערוך לקט פנינים יקרים
מפז ומפנינים מדרשותיו של הרב על פרשיות השבוע ולהגיש אותם לפני ציבור
שוחרי התורה בלשון צחה ונקיה, ערוך בטוב טעם ודעת השוה לכל נפש.

בטוחני שרבים יתענגו על ספר יקר זה ויפיקו ממנו תועלת רבה.

ברכתי להרה"ג הרב רוזנר שליט"א ואתו עמו ר' שי שזכות התורה תעמוד להם
להתברך בכל משאלות לבם, ויזכו תמיד להגדיל תורה ולהאדירה בבריות גופא
ונהורא מעליא.

באהבה יתירה

אשר וייס

My dear friend, HaRav HaGaon Rav Shalom Rosner *shlit"a*, the Rav of Kehillat Nofei HaShemesh in Beit Shemesh, is well-known in the Torah world for his wonderful and fascinating *shiurim*, with thousands of loyal followers who listen to his *shiurim*. Until now, we were familiar with his *Torah Shebe'al Peh*, and now, my dear friend Rav Shai (Marc) Lesnick, a man of Torah, wisdom and *hesed*, was privileged with writing down and editing the pearls of wisdom from the *derashot* of Rav Rosner, given weekly on *parashat hashavua*, and making them available to the Torah community in a clear and concise style, and edited in a judicious and accessible manner.

I am certain that all will enjoy this valuable book and will derive much benefit from it.

I express my best wishes to HaGaon HaRav Rosner and Rav Shai (Marc) Lesnick, that the *zekhut* of the Torah shall protect them, and may they be blessed with health and the ability to continue to spread and encourage the study and observance of Torah.

With great love,
Asher Weiss

Rabbi Hershel Schachter
24 Bennett Avenue
New York, New York 10033
(212) 795-0630

הרב צבי שכטר
ראש ישיבה וראש כולל
ישיבת רבינו יצחק אלחנן

מכתב ברכה

עברתי על כמה מהמאמרים שבספרו של כב' יקירי הר"ר שלו' נ"י על
הפרשיות ונהניתי מאוד מהרעיונות וגם מאופן סידור הדברים,
וברכתי להרב המחבר שימצא הספר חן בעיני התלמידים וילמדו בו.
ויפה עשה ידידי הר"ר שלו' שהמתין מלהדפיס ספרו זה בעניני
השקפה עד לאחר שיצא שמו והתפרסם בעולם התורה כבעל הלכה,
ואשר ממילא דבריו בעניני השקפה יתקבלו ביותר.

בכבוד,
צבי שכטר

ENGLISH TRANSLATION OF
RAV HERSHEL SCHACHTER'S LETTER
OF RECOMMENDATION

I reviewed several of the *divrei Torah* that appear in the book of my dear
friend Rav Shalom Rosner on the *parshiyot,* and I very much enjoyed
the thoughts and the manner of presentation. My warmest wishes to the
author that the book will be enjoyed and studied by his students. My
friend Rav Shalom acted wisely and waited to publish a work on *hashkafa* until after he became well known as a halakhic scholar, so that his
words of *hashkafa* would be accepted more readily.

With respect,
Tzvi (Hershel) Schachter

Contents

Preface

Sheheheyanu vekiyemanu vehigiyanu lazeman hazeh!

I have been listening to Rav Rosner's *parasha shiurim* for years. Each morning I would download a *shiur* and listen to it during my drive to work. It felt like Rav Rosner was sitting in my passenger seat. From these *shiurim* I would always find inspirational words that I could share at our Shabbat table. I believe that these *divrei Torah* truly inspired my family, and on several occasions, I have heard my children repeat these thoughts, which to me is the greatest testimony that their message is pertinent.

Several years ago, I was approached by a group of young adults in Beit Shemesh who had just entered the army after learning in *yeshivot hesder* and *mekhinot*, and they requested a Shabbat *shiur*. I began delivering a weekly class on the *parasha,* and many of the sources that I used were from Rav Rosner's *shiurim*. After witnessing how people were so inspired by these *divrei Torah,* I decided that these pearls of wisdom had to be written and shared with Klal Yisrael. I owe a tremendous debt of gratitude to the amazing boys and girls in that weekly *shiur* that continues even after many of the participants have completed their army service and some have even married. They were one of the main catalysts for this *sefer*.

Rav Rosner's style is unique. He usually references ten to fifteen thoughts on each *parasha* cited from a wide spectrum of *hashkafot*, including Hassidic Rebbes, Rav Yosef Soloveitchik, Rav Shimshon Refael Hirsch, Nechama Leibowitz, classic *Rishonim* like the Ramban and Rambam, and modern commentaries such as Rav Asher Weiss and Rav Avigdor Nebenzahl.[1] Rav Rosner provides a clear and concise synopsis of various commentaries highlighting inspirational messages throughout each *parasha*. His classes are given each Wednesday night. They began in his community in Woodmere, and after Rav Rosner moved to Beit Shemesh they were given at his home until the shul for his *kehilla* was completed, where the weekly *shiur* is currently held.

In preparing this *sefer*, I reviewed every *shiur* that Rav Rosner gave in his weekly *parasha* series from 5769 through 5778 (ten years). In total there are approximately 150 *divrei Torah* per *parasha*. First, I would listen to each recording and then review the actual written sources.[2] I then selected what I felt were the most inspirational *divrei Torah* from each *shiur*, seeking to incorporate only a few *divrei Torah* from each *parasha*. There is much material that is included in Rav Rosner's *shiurim* that do not appear in this book. I apologize if I left out material that others feel should have been included, and I welcome constructive criticism so that we can improve future volumes and publications. Rav Rosner reviewed all of the *divrei Torah* included in this *sefer*.

I considered publishing Rav Rosner's *shiurim* for many years, and I can't express the feeling of gratitude that I have to HaKadosh Barukh Hu now that the first volume is finally going to print. Rav Rosner's inspirational thoughts have had a tremendous impact on my life and my family and I hope that we are able to properly relay these messages in this *sefer* so that its readers can be inspired as well. Our hope is that these *divrei Torah* can be shared at the Shabbat table and at *semahot* so they can enlighten our children, family, and community.

---

1. A bibliography is included at the end of the book so that the reader can identify each source quoted.
2. These *shiurim* are available on www.outorah.org. Some of the earlier shiurim (5769 and 5770) also appear on www.yutorah.org, and if a recording from one of those years is not downloadable on the OU site it can be retrieved at the YU site.

I want to take this opportunity to thank Rav Rosner for serving as a tremendous role model for my family and many families in the Beit Shemesh community and in the diaspora. May *Hashem* grant Rav Rosner many healthy years so he can continue to be *marbitz Torah*!

I also want to thank my father, from whom I learned and continue to learn not only *divrei Torah* but love and appreciation of Torah. As I mentioned above, on my way to work I listen to Rav Rosner's *shiurim*. However, on my way home from work, I speak with my father and we share *divrei Torah*. I now understand the meaning of *uvelekhtekha baderekh* – to try to be involved in Torah while on the road. My father is a true role model. He received *semiha* from Rav Gustman, and although he runs a business during the day, he learns each night and teaches several classes on Shabbat and during the week. My father taught me the meaning of *Torah veAvoda*. May Hashem grant my parents many healthy years so that they can continue to share their thoughts and insights with the family and with their community.

This work would not have been possible without the assistance of several individuals who assisted with transcribing many *shiurim*. In particular, Daliya Shapiro and Miriam Schlussel, who transcribed most of the selected lessons. I also owe a debt of gratitude to Rabbi Elli Fischer, who assisted with editing and did a tremendous job in helping me get the messages across in a clear and concise fashion. Yehoshua Paltiel contributed by preparing the biographies of various sources at the end of the volume so that the reader can better understand the background of each source quoted. I am grateful for the support and assistance that the entire Maggid staff has provided, in particular, Rabbi Reuven Ziegler, Ita Olesker, Elisheva Ruffer, and Aryeh Grossman.

I want to thank each of my dear children (Ariel and Rinat; Adena; Sarit and Yonatan; Rami and Amichai) for being the initial audience with whom I shared many of these thoughts on a weekly basis and for their insights that continuously enhance the discussions at our Shabbat table. It brings me tremendous *nahat* when they share these inspirational messages with their colleagues in the army, in yeshiva, in university, at *Bnei Akiva*, and at *semahot*. May they each be *zokhe* to the *nahat* that they bring to me and *Ima* from each of their own children.

Most importantly, I want to thank my dear wife Tamar. Without her patience and support I would not have been able to publish this *sefer*. Each night after returning from work, on Friday afternoons and Saturday nights, I would be preoccupied with preparing this *sefer*, and the precious time we spend together had to be compromised. I truly appreciate her support and understanding of the importance of this project. Tamar is a true *ezer kenegdo* – always encouraging me to accomplish what I consider impossible. Tamar continuously amazes and inspires our family with the many *hesed* projects she undertakes and her tremendous contribution to the community. May Hashem grant us many more happy and healthy years together.

I am forever indebted to Rav Rosner whose inspirational thoughts and *shiurim* have had an everlasting impact on my life and provided me with fascinating material to share with and inspire others.

We decided to name the *sefer* "Shalom Rav," which is a play on the name Rav Shalom Rosner. It is also a *pasuk* in *Tehillim* (119:165) that is quite appropriate: *Shalom rav le'ohavei Toratekha* – which means, "There is abundant peace to those who love Your Torah." Many of the *divrei Torah* incorporated in this book highlight the importance of *shalom bayit*, Jewish unity, mutual respect, and acceptance.

For a list of the audio files on which these chapters are based, see https://www.korenpub.com/media/productattachments/files/s/h/shalom_rav_audio.pdf

My hope is that the readers enjoy these *divrei Torah* as much as I do. May we be able to internalize Rav Rosner's meaningful messages and share them with others so that we can enhance our spiritual lives and the lives of those around us. *Hazak ve'ematz*!

Marc (Shai) Lesnick
Beit Shemesh
Tamuz 5779

Introduction

We recite in the Haggada:

ברוך שנתן תורה לעמו ישראל, ברוך הוא. כנגד ארבעה בנים דברה
תורה...

Blessed is He who gave the Torah to His people Israel, blessed is
He. The Torah is parallel to (*keneged*) four sons...

The Torah is "*keneged*" the four sons. What does this word connote? How
is the Torah "opposite" or "parallel" to the four sons? The Beit HaLevi
suggests that there is a magic and uniqueness to Torah, unparalleled in
the world of general wisdom. In biology or in mathematics, there are
beginning, intermediate, and advanced textbooks. The novice child will
not be studying the same material as the high school student, who in
turn will not be sharing studied content with the doctoral level profes-
sor. Torah, by contrast, affords all levels of learners equal opportunity.
The same Rashi that is studied by the first grader, is also studied by the
gadol hador. Yes, each understands it on his own level, but the Torah is
keneged all students, all types of sons and daughters, all colors of Jews.
This, then, is the magical nature of Torah.

We also believe that each and every Jew has his or her special, unique connection to the Torah. *Tosafot* (Berakhot 11b) ask why is it that with mitzvot a *hefsek* breaks the effect of the *berakha*, with the exception of learning Torah, where it does not? For example, entering a sukka after an extended break demands a new *berakha*, while learning Torah on the same day, after a break, does not require another *berakha*. *Tosafot* answer: A Jew is always connected to Torah, even when he is not actively learning at that moment. Hashem places within each one of us a spark of holiness (Nidda 30b) that is in constant connection with Him and His Torah.

Thus, not only does Torah have a magical mystique and relevance to it, but each Jew has that "*pintele yid*" that is yearning and thirsting for that connection with the Torah, the world of the Infinite.

This volume is a reflection of this ideal and thirst. It tries to cull inspirational nuggets from the vast world of Torah commentaries, from the *Rishonim* to the *Aharonim*, from the *pashtanim* to the *darshanim*, from the esoteric to the down-to-earth. Just as I tried to accomplish during the live *shiurim* themselves, I attempted to glean from the sources something for us to take with us into our lives, some *lemaase* spark that we can put into practice. The oral and written word are very different worlds, and committing ideas to writing runs the risk of losing the excitement, vitality, and energy of each of these offerings. My prayer, though, is that the reader allow themselves to be drawn into the source, as if the respective authors were orally transmitting their ideas in person, with all the vigor and excitement that each source engenders.

As I write these words of introduction, I am overcome by feelings of gratitude and the inability to properly express those feelings. Hashem has afforded me the opportunity to present the ideas of His holy Torah, through *shiurim* both to live audiences as well as to many virtual *talmidim* throughout the world. Be it through the *parasha shiur, daf yomi,* or the mitzva and *navi shiurim,* He has constantly given *siyata dishmaya* every step of the way. All I can pray for is the continued opportunity for spreading His Torah to so many of our thirsty brethren.

This *sefer* would not have become a reality had it not been for the diligence and superhuman effort of my friend Marc Lesnick. He single-handedly arranged all of the conversion from the oral to the written word, spent days and nights editing and rearranging the various thoughts, as well as keeping me up with all the deadlines. I am indebted to him for his help in this partnership to spread the *devar Hashem* to an even wider audience.

Rabbi Ziegler and Maggid Books have been a pleasure to work with, and I hope that our teamwork can continue for a very long time, in both the English and Hebrew realms.

To Rabbi Steven Weil and all the staff at the OU, I feel a deep sense of respect and gratitude for the opportunity to partner with you, in helping spread Torah to the four corners of the globe. You have created a platform for eager *lomdim* to access *shiurim* and elevate themselves in their *avodat Hashem*. May Hashem grant the entire organization great success in all of its endeavors on behalf of the Jewish people.

Hashem has allowed me to learn and teach in various illustrious rabbinic institutions, and I can truly state that all that I have gained is a tribute to my rebbeim and yeshivot. Mori VeRabi HaRav Michael Rosensweig, HaRav Herschel Schacter, HaRav Mordechai Willig, HaRav Yonasan Sacks, HaRav Asher Weiss, and HaRav Yechezkel Yacovsen have all shaped the Jew that I am, and I am merely a branch from their illustrious roots. May Hashem give them all many more years of spreading Torah throughout Am Yisrael.

My in-laws, Drs. Robert and Susan Schulman, have been a constant inspiration to me, both in deed and by example. They are known as pillars of Torah and hesed in their community, and we wish them many more years of tremendous contributions to Klal Yisrael, as well as to their family.

My father, Dr. Fred Rosner, was my first rebbi, learning Rambam with me on Friday nights at a very young age, as well as modeling what it means to be a public spreader of Torah, with the awesome opportunity of *kiddush Hashem* that that entails. He, along with my mother, have inculcated in me a love of Torah, a love of all Jews, and a love for the Land of Israel. May Hashem grant them many more years of health, nachas, and fulfillment in all their endeavors.

Finally, to my life-long partner, Tamar. You are behind each one of my accomplishments, and you are the greatest gift that Hashem has given me. May we be *zoche* together to continue to do His will to the best of our abilities, and may our dear children, Yehoshua, Avigayil, Avraham, Naama, Michael, Eliyahu, and Chananya, always be excited to follow the illustrious legacy of Torah which we have tried to inculcate into our home.

Shalom Rosner
Beit Shemesh
Rosh Hodesh Tamuz 5779

Bereshit

Parashat Bereshit

Life Doesn't Always Go as Planned: Turning Plan B into Plan A

At the completion of the six days of creation, the Torah tells us:

וירא א-להים את כל אשר עשה והנה טוב מאד. (בראשית א:לא)

> And Hashem saw all that He had made, and behold, it was very good. (*Bereshit* 1:31)

Notwithstanding the fact that the six days of creation were characterized as "very good," reading through the opening chapters of *Bereshit*, we are struck by the fact that it consistently seems as though various incidents didn't work out well or, at least, as planned. The first two people in the world, Adam and Chava, transgressed and were removed from the Garden of Eden. Their child, Kayin, murdered his brother Hevel. Hashem commanded the earth to bring forth trees that would taste like fruit. The trees sprouted fruit but the trees did not taste like the fruit. Hashem created the sun and moon relatively the same size and after the moon complained it was diminished.

Why does the Torah start in this way? Hashem could have created a perfect world. What are these stories, which seem like mistakes or surprises, supposed to teach us?

Rabbi Yisroel Reisman, in his book *Pathways of the Prophets*, cites Rav Pam,[1] who explains that the Torah begins with things that did not turn out as planned to teach us that when things do not go as planned in life, we must respond to these imperfections by creating an alternative plan. The Torah is teaching us how to move to "Plan B." So often, we establish a plan and prepare to execute it when, for some unfortunate reason beyond our control, we are unable to achieve it. The car didn't start. There was traffic. The store sold out of the items I needed. HaKadosh Barukh Hu is hinting to us to consider Plan B.

Man was originally supposed to dwell in the Garden of Eden. Adam sinned and was banished from the Garden of Eden. It seems as if Hashem's original plan failed and He had to initiate an alternative plan: Plan B. Ten generations later, man's actions brought destruction upon an immoral world and only Noach's family survived. What did Hashem do? He started over. Again, the initial plan seemed to fail and Hashem had to make alternative accommodations, what we refer to as Plan B.

Rabbi Reisman says in the name of Rav Pam that the message here is that life rarely follows Plan A. The most successful people are those who can adjust to and work with Plan B. This is not easy. It involves disappointment and a need to reevaluate and lower expectations.

Rabbi Reisman then quotes a famous story:

Childhood polio had handicapped one of the world's most famous violinists (Itzhak Perlman). He walks with braces and crutches. When he plays at a concert, the journey to the center of the stage is long and slow. Yet, his playing transcends his personal challenges. Once, in the middle of a challenging concerto, one of the strings of his violin snapped, with a loud popping sound.

---

1. Rabbi Yisroel Reisman, *Pathways of the Prophets* (New York: Mesorah Publications, 2009), 83.

The orchestra stopped abruptly, and everyone waited with bated breath to see what would happen. After a brief pause, he set his violin under his chin and signaled to the conductor to begin. With great brilliance, he improvised, modulating and adjusting the melody in a way that compensated for the missing string.... When he finished, there was an awed silence, followed by thunderous applause. The violinist silenced the crowd. Then he said, "Sometimes, it is the musician's job to find out how much music he can make with what he has left."[2]

That's Plan B. Strings break. Things don't happen as planned.

We often have expectations of ourselves, our children, and others, and our plans do not materialize. Hashem teaches us that rather than agonizing over what could have been, we need to be able to quickly adapt and make the best of Plan B. That is what the beginning of *Bereshit* teaches. We need to be agile and flexible. Life is not always a smooth ride. We need to make the best of what comes our way. Rather than fantasizing about what *could have been* and agonizing about missed opportunities, we need to make the best of what *is*. At the beginning of the Torah, we are taught that in life, you have to roll with the punches and turn Plan B into Plan A.

---

2. Ibid., 84–85.

Create and Recreate

Many commentators seek to uncover what we are intended to learn from *maase bereshit*. We know that all of Torah is meant to teach us something. However, *maase bereshit* seems so unique and divine that it is hard to know what we can learn from it. How does the creation of the world teach me something that can impact my daily life?

Says Rav Yosef Soloveitchik in *Reflections of the Rav*:[1] Perhaps this elaborate emphasis in *Sefer Bereshit* on creation was meant to be converted into a moral challenge to man: that just as God created, so too should man create.

As we know, we are enjoined to mimic HaKadosh Barukh Hu. *Ma Hu rahum, af ata tehei rahum* – "Just as He is compassionate, so too, you must be compassionate."[2] Just as He is kind, visits the sick, buries the dead, and comforts mourners, so too, we must do the same. Moreover, just as God is creative, so too, must man be creative and contribute what he can to this world.

---

1. Rabbi Abraham R. Besdin, *Reflections of the Rav: Lessons in Jewish Thought Adapted from Lectures of Rabbi Joseph B. Soloveitchik* (Jerusalem: Alpha Press, 1979), 26.
2. Shabbat 133b regarding *middot* and Sota 14a regarding actions; see also the Introduction of the Hafetz Hayim to *Ahavat Hesed*, where he notes that the mitzva to imitate Hashem appears eight different times in the Torah, perhaps alluding to the metaphysical character of this mitzva.

As individuals, we each have to be creative in the world around us. In the physical realm, a doctor who is faced with an ill patient should take all necessary measures to cure the patient. That is an act of creation. Any assistance we extend to others calls on us to create, whether one works in law, architecture, or any other profession. We each have to use the talents HaKadosh Barukh Hu bestowed upon us to come up with creative solutions to overcome challenges. In addition, we also have to be creators in the spiritual realm (*ruhniyut*). That is one of our major purposes in life. We must make ourselves better people spiritually. We need to constantly recreate ourselves, moving up the spiritual ladder. But that is not all. In addition, as Rav Soloveitchik explains, we must help shape the spirituality of our children. This is also an act of creation.

As Rav Soloveitchik states:

> There is also a mandate to be creative in the spiritual realm.... Indeed, education in fulfillment of "And you shall teach them diligently to your children" (*Devarim* 6:7) is creativity par excellence. A formless, undirected child is transformed into a refined Torah scholar. An undisciplined child, without any identity, a *tohu vavohu*, is gradually changed into a spiritual personality.[3]

A child starts off empty and formless (*tohu vavohu*). We have to remember that. Slowly, like the many days and stages of creation, he is then formed and refined. Parents need to facilitate their children's spiritual growth as well as their physical growth.

Along these lines, Rav Soloveitchik continues by offering a beautiful explanation of the midrash (*Bereshit Rabba* 3:9) that states that Hashem created worlds and then destroyed them, and then He created other worlds and destroyed them too. There were many different worlds created before this one (maybe that's why there are dinosaur fossils in this world). What does that midrash teach us? That He didn't get it right the first time? *Has veshalom*! What does it mean that God created worlds over and over again?

---

3. Besdin, 26.

What does Rabbi Abbahu teach? Surely it makes no sense to ascribe to an omniscient God, the *En Sof* (Infinite), the need to experiment before achieving His ideal. God could immediately have created a *ki tov* (worthy of His approval) world. Only man needs experiment because of his difficulty in translating mental conceptions into physical realities. Like Edison and other scientists in their experiments, He tries various approaches before He achieves satisfactory goals....

Rabbi Abbahu apparently wanted to teach the concept of multiple creations: that our world came into being in various stages. His description of the process, however, of God's displeasure with previous worlds and His final satisfaction with this world was intended to provide man with a moral lesson and was not to be understood literally. As God creates and recreates (actually refashions, i.e., *yetzira* and not *beri'a*), so too, should man be ready to rebuild and reconstruct, even as previous structures collapse. Thus, even a rabbinic concept of faith may be translated into a norm of human behavior.[4]

Why does it say that God recreated? To teach us that we will create, and we will fail – many times. We will put time into a project, and it will go nowhere. This midrash is teaching us to start again. Build another world. God built another world, so you can also build another world. *Ma Hu, af ata*. God didn't have to build another world. What we learn from His act is that we can rise after we fall and start over again.

As the Rav so beautifully explains:[5]

To build is initially difficult, but to rebuild is even more challenging. One can erect structures if one has the basic talent, commitment, and raw materials, but to reconstruct after the destruction of previous achievements is most difficult. Energies, resources, sleepless nights, and endless devotion, painstakingly expended, are all wasted.

---

4. Ibid., 27–28.
5. Ibid., 28.

In the prayer of *Uva LeTziyon*, we pray that we won't have to toil for naught: *lemaan lo niga larik*. But sometimes, it happens, and building a business after bankruptcy is much harder than building it initially. This is the history of the Jewish people, on an individual level as well as a national level. For the past 2,000 years, we have been in a constant state of destruction and of rebuilding, of falling and of reviving. Even in the last generation, the return of Jews en masse to our homeland and the massive growth in Torah learning worldwide following the tragedy of World War II are a testament to our nation's ability to rebuild.

Rabbi Akiva's 24,000 disciples were taken away from him,[6] and what did he do? He said, "I'm going to start again, with another five students." And that's why we're here today. The Oral Torah survived because Rabbi Akiva learned *Parashat Bereshit*: God created, destroyed, and started again, and so did Rabbi Akiva.

The lesson, then, of the first chapter of *Bereshit* is twofold. First, we need to be creative and contribute to the world, both physically and spiritually, starting with ourselves and our families and extending to the wider community. Second, *ma Hu, af ata*. Just like God creates and rec-reates, so too, we must not be afraid of recreating after setbacks. Human beings make mistakes and experience failures. We must create, not fear failure, and then be ready and able to successfully recreate.

---

6. Yevamot 62b.

Torah Begins with a *Beit*: Learning Is Step Two

The Torah begins with the letter ב of בראשית, *bereshit* – "in the beginning," which prompts a well-known question that is addressed in many midrashim. The Hebrew alphabet begins with א, and yet the Torah starts with a ב. Why?[1]

One suggestion is that the Torah begins with a ב and ends with a ל (combining the two letters forms the word לב – heart). The Lubavitcher Rebbe[2] takes this concept a step further and explains the significance of the Torah beginning with a ב and the specific message to each of us: "The fact that the Torah begins with the second letter of the Hebrew alphabet, *beit*, indicates that reading the text is actually the second phase of Torah study."

When we open up the Torah to learn, we have to realize that it's step two. Step two is learning. What's step one? Recognizing God's existence and the fact that the Torah is God's gift to us.

---

1. Perhaps this is the real reason why there's no *daf* (page) *alef* in the Babylonian Talmud. If it's good enough for the Written Torah, then it's good enough for the Orah Torah as well. There are other homiletic answers, but perhaps this is the simplest.
2. *Chumash: The Gutnick Edition, Parashat Bereshit.*

If I don't realize that I'm connecting to Hashem, then I'm not going to connect to Him fully. On the other hand, if I spend the time that I am devoting to learning thinking about Hashem, I'm not going to understand anything or be able to focus on my learning, because I'm going to be focusing on "ah, I'm connected to God." I'm not going to understand the *Tosafot*. *Talmud Torah* is supposed to bring us close to Hashem, but we are not supposed to be focusing on the experience of connecting to Hashem while we are learning.

So how do we address this challenge? *Before* we begin, we focus on God. We're supposed to realize the experience we're about to be involved in, before we open the Humash, before we open the Gemara. The Gemara even has a special prayer to say before one begins learning. We have to appreciate what we're about to do. A person should take a few moments before he begins learning to reflect that he is about to study God's wisdom that has been condensed into a form that is intelligible by humans. He is about to bind his mind into a total union with God. While he's learning, though, he should try to figure out what Rashi is saying. That's not the time to focus on how his learning is actively bringing him closer to HaKadosh Barukh Hu.

The Torah starts with a ב – *bereshit* – because it's step two. א is *Hashem ehad*; א is thinking about Hashem and His oneness.

The Lubavitcher Rebbe doesn't quote it, but this idea can help explain a perplexing Gemara found in Nedarim 81a. The Gemara asks why the *Beit HaMikdash* was destroyed. There is a well-known Gemara (Yoma 9b) that tells us that the first *Beit HaMikdash* was destroyed because of the "big three" sins (idolatry, murder, and illicit sexual unions), and the second *Beit HaMikdash* was destroyed because of baseless hatred (*sinat hinam*).[3]

The Gemara in Nedarim, however, offers a different explanation for the *Hurban*: *Shelo birkhu baTorah tehila* – "They didn't say the blessings over the Torah prior to studying Torah." Many commentators are puzzled by the Gemara's statement and ask (a) Why didn't they recite

---

3. Bava Metzia 30b provides another reason for the destruction of the *Beit HaMikdash*: that the people followed the letter of the law rather than acting *lifnim mishurat hadin* – "beyond the letter of the law."

the blessings over the Torah? and (b) Even if they didn't recite the blessings over the Torah, is that so terrible? They still learned! They just didn't articulate the blessings over the Torah. Maybe they were in a rush.

Perhaps we can suggest, based on the Lubavitcher Rebbe's insights, that *shelo birkhu baTorah tehila* means that they didn't do step א. They only started at ב. They started with *bereshit bara Elokim*, "In the beginning God created." The fact that the Torah is not just an intellectual pursuit but that it connects me to HaKadosh Barukh Hu, who is א, is not even written in the Torah. Knowing it is a prerequisite for learning. Prior to opening a Humash, we have to have an appreciation of what we are about to read and experience.[4]

On a similar note, the Bahag (*Sefer Halakhot Gedolot*), from the period of the *Geonim*, does not count belief in Hashem as one of the 613 commandments. Asks the Rambam: How could one not count belief in Hashem as a commandment?[5] It's the most important commandment in the world! The *Rishonim* defend the Bahag and explain that belief in Hashem is a prerequisite for everything else.[6] You don't come to the concept of a commandment, which implies a Commander, unless you already believe in God.

Likewise, appreciating Torah and its magical ability to connect us to Hashem is a prerequisite for studying Torah.[7] And that's why the

---

4. See Ran on Nedarim 81a in the name of Rabbenu Yona. Rabbi Asher Weiss, in *Minhat Asher: Sihot al HaMo'adim*, vol. 2, ch. 44, provides a similar explanation of what was so terrible about not making a blessing prior to learning Torah. Rabbi Weiss asserts that the fault was that they did not make a blessing on the Torah *prior* to learning; however, they may have made a blessing *after* having learnt Torah. If they were satisfied with what they had learnt, they made a blessing of praise, as one would recite a blessing after a meal. This was their grave error. We need to make a blessing *prior* to learning, similar to the blessing we recite prior to eating. By reciting a blessing prior to learning, we express our appreciation and understanding that we are about to study something holy, whether or not it is enjoyable. We study for the purpose of studying itself.

5. See Rambam, *Sefer HaMitzvot*, 1.

6. See Ramban, *HaSagot LeSefer HaMitzvot*, 1.

7. There is a story told about Rabbi Yehezkel Levenstein that highlights the significance of appreciating the Torah. Years ago, in order to attract customers, banks gave out gifts for opening accounts. One of his *talmidim* told him that he had received a toaster from a bank as a gift, and he demonstrated how it works. You insert the bread here,

Hurban occurred, because the people of that generation did not appreciate the opportunity they had: *Shelo birkhu baTorah tehila*.

May we preface our learning with a clear declaration of appreciation to Hashem for granting us the Torah and for selecting us as his chosen nation.

---

push this button, and after a few minutes, the toasted bread pops up. The rabbi nodded, indicating that he understood how to operate the new electronic device. The rabbi then noticed a large booklet that was in the box with the toaster and inquired about it. His *talmid* explained that it was the users' manual, which described how to use the toaster, provided warnings about misusing the toaster, and gave suggestions about what could be wrong if the toaster was not working properly. These instructions, moreover, appeared in several different languages. The rabbi began dancing in joy and explained that if this simple toaster, which just requires one to push a button, comes with a detailed instruction manual, then certainly HaKadosh Barukh Hu had to provide us with an instruction manual on how to act in this world, which is infinitely more complicated. If only we really understood that the Torah is that manual and that we follow its instructions, what a perfect world this would be! Understanding the importance and significance of the Torah before we study it provides us with the necessary perspective to carefully understand all its intricacies and treasures.

Let "Us" Make Man?

ויאמר א־להים נעשה אדם בצלמנו כדמותנו. (בראשית א:כו)

And God said, "Let us make man in our image, after our likeness..." (*Bereshit* 1:26)

When the Torah describes the steps leading up to the creation of man,
ambiguous language is used. Hashem appears to be consulting with
angels and suggests "let **us** make man in **our** image," using the plural
rather than singular terms, which may cause one to infer that Hashem
did not create man alone.

The Gemara in Megilla cites this verse as one of the verses that
miraculously was revised by all seventy rabbis in the Septuagint translation to אעשה – "I will make" in the singular, so that the translation
would not be misunderstood.[1]

Rashi quotes *Hazal*'s explanation that Hashem purposely consulted with the angels:

ענותנותו של הקדוש ברוך הוא למדנו מכאן: לפי שאדם בדמות
המלאכים ויתקנאו בו, לפיכך נמלך בהם.

---

1. Megilla 9a.

We learn Hashem's humility from here: Since man is created in the image of angels, they may get jealous; therefore, He consulted with them.

The reason Hashem consulted with the angels was so that they would not be envious of humans. This action portrays Hashem's humility, as if it were a joint decision.

The Ramban offers a different approach:

נתייחד בעשיית האדם מאמר בעבור גודל מעלתו כי אין טבעו כטבע החיה והבהמה.... אמר באדם "נַעֲשֶׂה" כלומר אני והארץ הנזכרת נַעֲשֶׂה אָדָם שתוציא הארץ הגוף מיסודיה כאשר עשתה בבהמה ובחיה.... ויתן הוא יתברך הרוח מפי עליון ואמר "בְּצַלְמֵנוּ כִּדְמוּתֵנוּ" כי ידמה לשניהם במתכונת גופו לארץ אשר לוקח ממנה וידמה ברוח לעליונים שאינה גוף ולא תמות....לספר הפלא אשר נפלא בו משאר הנבראים.

A [separate] proclamation was designated for the creation of man because of his stature, since his nature is not like the nature of animals and beasts... [and] with man, He said, "let us make." That is to say, I and the earth (that was mentioned), let us make man: The earth will bring forth the body from the elements as it did with the beasts and the animals..."and He blew into his nostrils, a living soul." And it stated, "in our image, in our likeness," since he would be similar to both of them, in the configuration of his body, to the earth from which he was taken; and he would resemble the higher ones in his soul, which is not a body and does not die...to tell of the miraculous wonder which separates him from all the creatures.

The Ramban explains that a separate proclamation was designated for the creation of man because of his stature. Man is not like animals and beasts. Hashem uses the terminology of "let us make" in the plural, as if to say, "I and the earth." The earth will contribute to the creation of the body, as is stated: "Man was formed from the dust of the earth."[2]

---

2. Bereshit 2:7.

Furthermore, man's soul was created with a breath of the Almighty, as it is stated: "and He blew into his nostrils, a living soul."[3] Man is a combination of *ruhani* (spiritual) and *gashmi* (physical). Man was the first creature to comprise a synthesis of spiritual and physical elements. This is a miraculous wonder!

The *Shulhan Arukh* cites several understandings of the term: *asher yatzar et ha'adam behokhma* – "that man was created using great wisdom."[4] The Rama explains that we thank Hashem for the miracle of creating man with a synthesis of both physical and spiritual elements.[5] The genius of that creation is a sensational phenomenon. That combination that was used in the creation of man is evidence of Hashem's great wisdom, and we express our appreciation when we witness the awesome functioning of the physical body each time we use the washroom.

A story is told that one of the sons of Rabbi Aaron Soloveitchik expressed that the blessing of *Asher Ge'alanu*, recited during the Pesah Seder, is one of the most beautiful blessings. Rav Aaron Soloveitchik differed with his son and told him that in his humble opinion, the greatest blessing is one we recite on a daily basis: the blessing of *asher yatzar et ha'adam*, recited after one uses the washroom. It is about the uniqueness of man. Unlike other creatures who were created from dust alone, man is a being that comprises both physical and spiritual characteristics. He is infused with the breath of Hashem and is created in His image. May we recognize the wisdom that went into the creation of man and live up to Hashem's expectations of us.

---

3. Ibid.
4. *Shulhan Arukh, Orah Hayim 6.*
5. Ibid.

The True Meaning
of *Ezer Kenegdo*

ויאמר ה' א-להים לא טוב היות האדם לבדו אעשה לו עזר כנגדו.
(בראשית ב:יח)

And the Lord God said: "It is not good for man to be alone, I will make a helpmate for him." (*Bereshit* 2:18)

This *pasuk* is an amazing contrast with the first chapter of *Bereshit*, which repeatedly states, "and God saw that it was good." Everything is good: All of creation is good, the animal kingdom is good, and the whole universe is good. This culminates in Hashem surveying all He created and saying that it is not only good, but *very* good. Now, all of a sudden, we have something that's not good: It is not good for man to be alone.

Hashem declares, "I will make a help mate for him" – an *ezer kenegdo*. However, over the next ten *pesukim*, Hashem then brings Adam all the animals, which he names. Only then does Hashem remove a rib from Adam, from which he forms Eve. What are these *pesukim* about the animals doing here? The simple explanation is that Hashem is informing Adam, "You can't mate or pair with any of these or any other creatures, so I have to create somebody new."

What is the meaning of *ezer kenegdo*? It seems like a self-contradictory juxtaposition: An *ezer* is a help. *Keneged* means "opposite." Rashi, quoting *Hazal*, highlights this contradiction: "If one is worthy, she is a help; if one is not worthy, she opposes him." In a marriage, each spouse must live up to the other, must be worthy of the other. Otherwise, there will be tension.

The Netziv offers a different idea based on the simple understanding of the words. Individuals comprise many elements. People relate differently to situations and have diverse strengths and attributes. There are so many diverse elements to each person and gender. Husbands and wives have to be connected and help each other on so many different levels – *kenegdo*, complementing all the different elements in their specific personalities.

The Netziv then offers a second explanation. The opposition and tensions with one's spouse is designed to help them – that's the key. Sometimes, being opposites could be the greatest help. The greatest critic in the world should be our spouse, and we should be able to hear it from them, because we're one. It is often hard to accept criticism, but if we are being criticized by a spouse, we should appreciate it. Knowing there is unconditional love and commitment, such criticism is only being shared so we can improve ourselves. That partnership is true *ezer kenegdo*.

Two people, man and woman, husband and wife, are not the same person. They're different beings that come together. If a husband and wife both possess a penchant for anger, the result could be disastrous. Rather, each weakness should be offset by a corresponding strength. That's why spouses so often each have different strengths, specifically opposites, to balance out the relationship of the family. Even children know this sometimes – if they want A, they'll go to parent A. If they want B, they'll go to parent B. Even the children know the differences, because parents aren't exactly alike, and they aren't meant to be alike.

Many *Aharonim* (Rav Soloveitchik and Rabbi Aviner, among others) suggest that this could help explain the Gemara (Berakhot 61a) that describes two stages in the creation of man.[1] Hashem thought to

---

1. This is reflected in the *sheva berakhot* recited at a wedding and during the week following a wedding, which have two blessings that end with a reference to the creation of man (*yotzer ha'adam*).

create mankind as two, but then decided to create man as one.[2] Then He separated "them" and eventually brought them back together. How are we to understand those different "stages"? What is the message of man and women being created together or in two stages? Perhaps the idea is that each man and woman, husband and wife, are so different, with distinct backgrounds and interests, that they could never be expected to join together as one. Therefore, Hashem created them initially as one unit, one *neshama*, and then split them into two beings so that the event of marriage will represent a reunion. Each partner thereby brings their respective strengths and abilities to the relationship, creating a perfect, complementary, wholesome family.

---

2. Obviously, Hashem did not change His mind. This idea expressed is to provide insight into differing values.

Parashat Noach

A *Tzaddik* in a Fur Coat

Noach may very well be the most enigmatic figure in the entire Torah. It is usually easy to decipher whether a particular character in the Torah is a righteous or evil figure. In connection with Noach, however, there seems to be much ambiguity. The opening *pasuk* of the *parasha* states that Noach was a righteous person (*tzaddik*) in his generation:

אלה תולדת נח, נח איש צדיק תמים היה בדרתיו. (בראשית ו:ט)

These are the generations of Noach. Noach was in his generation a man righteous and whole-hearted. (*Bereshit* 6:9)

Rashi comments on this as follows:

בדורותיו: יש מרבותינו דורשים אותו לשבח, כל שכן שאלו היה בדור צדיקים היה צדיק יותר, ויש שדורשים אותו לגנאי, לפי דורו היה צדיק, ואלו היה בדורו של אברהם לא היה נחשב לכלום. (רש״י בראשית ו:ט)

Some of our sages explain this verse in a praiseworthy manner: Had Noach lived in a generation of *tzaddikim*, he would have been

even more righteous. Other sages explain this verse in a derogatory manner: In comparison to his generation he was righteous.
Had Noach lived during Avraham's generation, he wouldn't have
been anything special. (Rashi on *Bereshit* 6:9)

Due to the addition of the word "in his generation" certain commentators infer that Noach was only righteous as compared to his colleagues.
The simple reading of the *pasuk* leads one to conclude that Noach was a
tzaddik. Why do we need to search for a hidden meaning that may lead
one to derive an opposite conclusion?

What could be negative about Noach? Rabbi Adin Steinsaltz[1]
raises an intriguing question. It took Noach 120 years to build the ark,
and during that time, he was unable to inspire even one person. We see
that Avraham influenced many in his generation. How is it that Noach
was unable to persuade even one other individual to repent? Where
did Noach go wrong?

Rabbi Steinsaltz explains as follows: When a difficult situation
arises, there are two typical types of possible reactions. For example,
when it's cold outside, there are two ways in which a person can achieve
warmth. He can either put on a coat, or he can light a fire. Either choice
will achieve the same result vis-à-vis the individual. The difference is
that if there are others in the room, only a fire will warm them all. One
coat will only provide warmth to the individual that wears it; lighting a
fire, though, will comfort everyone in the room.

When Noach built the ark for his family, it was the result of the
first reaction: to prevent destruction, to save himself. That's why he
built the ark.

Noach was the first example of what's called in Yiddish *a tzaddik
in peltz* – "a righteous man in a fur coat," who chooses the option that
addresses his own concerns and does not necessarily take into account
the welfare of others.

In contrast, when Avraham is told that Sodom is going to be
destroyed, he kept bargaining with Hashem. He requested that Hashem

---

1. Rabbi Adin Steinsaltz, *Hayei Olam* (Jerusalem: Koren Publishers, 2011), 13.

save the city in the merit of 50, 40, even 10 righteous people. Noach doesn't bargain!

This is the key difference between Noach and Avraham. Do their actions take into consideration the welfare of others, or only their own well-being? The lesson we need to learn from Noach is that it is not enough to be a *tzaddik* in our own four *amot*. We need to be concerned about the well-being of others. We cannot be selfish. We must be considerate and caring to others and be proactive in providing solutions for the welfare of others, both in the physical and spiritual domains.

Other commentators defend Noach, explaining the "derogatory manner" in which he is described by some sages differently.[2]

Rabbi Yisrael Moshe Fried, in his *sefer Yam Simha*,[3] takes an interesting approach, explaining that the term *legnai* (derogatory) does not have the same meaning here as it does elsewhere. The emphasis on Noach being a *tzaddik* in his generation means that Noach's *avoda* and what he accomplished were specific to his generation. If Noach would have lived in Avraham's generation, he would not have been able to accomplish his unique mission (*tafkid*), which was to rise above society's collapse and serve HaKadosh Barukh Hu despite all that was transpiring around him. He would not have been as great in another generation; not in comparison to Avraham, but in comparison to himself in another generation. It was specifically in his generation that he was able to stand up to all those mocking him and observe Hashem's command to build the ark. He was able to resist the corruption of his society and remain righteous. Facing challenges made Noach stronger. If he would have lived in a different generation, without these challenges, he would not have achieved such great heights. [4]

---

2. Sforno favors such an approach and suggests that the opening *pasuk* tells us that only now, at the age of 500, did Noach have children. It was only once Noach began to reprove others for their wrongdoing that he merited having children.
3. Rabbi Yisrael Moshe Fried, *Yam Simha* (1997), Parashat Noach.
4. Rabbi Kook in *Siddur Olat Re'iyah* (Jerusalem: Mosad Harav Kook, 1989), 356, explains the passage recited on the High Holy Days, "My God, before I was created, I was unworthy." There is a reason why one was born in the twenty-first century rather than in another century. Each of us has a unique mission in life: to fulfill a specific purpose in a specific generation. We would have been useless in another generation,

Noach's *avoda* would not have been as beloved to HaKadosh Barukh Hu in a different generation, and that is the *genai* of the word "in his generation." If he would have lived in another generation, he would not have been as great as he became in the generation of the Flood. He rose to the challenge specifically during a difficult period when he was surrounded by non-believers. This interpretation does not view Noach negatively in any way. He was a true *tzaddik* and completed his mission to the fullest, which could have only been achieved in that specific generation.

---

but we are essential in this generation. Each of us has to look into ourselves to identify our purpose and mission and to do what we can to fulfill that mission.

Using Time Productively

In *Parashat Noach*, we are introduced to a world replete with theft, promiscuity, and corruption. How could the behavior of mankind sink so low so quickly? What was at the root of their evil behavior? Rav Pam explains that the answer to this question may be provided by understanding a particular midrash.

We are introduced to Noach at the end of last week's *parasha*. Why was he named Noach?

> ויקרא את שמו נח לאמר: זה ינחמנו ממעשנו ומעצבון ידינו מן האדמה
> אשר אררה ה'. (בראשית ה:כט)

> They called him Noach because they saw that he would help them, that he would save them from all their agricultural difficulties. (*Bereshit* 5:29)

What led the people to think that this newborn child would provide some sort of salvation to mankind? Were they prophets?

The midrash explains that Noach was the first human to be born with separated fingers. Prior to Noach's birth, all humans were created with webbed fingers. This was not an issue, since before Adam sinned, man was not supposed to have to work the land. His punishment was "by the sweat of your brow shall you eat bread."[1] For an individual with webbed hands, this was indeed a harsh punishment. How is someone with webbed hands supposed to hold a shovel or other tools needed to plow the land? Then, suddenly, a child is born with separate fingers, making it much easier to hold tools and to be able to more easily utilize tools. This newborn child, with independent fingers, displayed a clear advantage over all other humans, which led others to believe that he would contribute much to mankind. Thus, when people saw his fingers, they knew that he would usher in a new, more productive era.

At first, the people did not know whether this was a mutation or something that would become a new reality. Quickly, it became apparent that it was a "game changer." Noach's birth brought about unbelievable technological advancement in the world. Fingers! What an amazing creation! Suddenly, people could work the land more efficiently! With this newfound dexterity, tasks that seemed difficult and nearly impossible were accomplished quickly, efficiently, and with precision. Tasks that took hours could now be completed in minutes. Rav Pam[2] states:

> Noach was a great inventor who created the first basic tools to ease the backbreaking labor of farm work. According to the *Midrash Tanhuma* (11), he invented the plow to seed the earth, the scythe to cut wheat, and the ax to fell trees. As amazing as it may seem, until then, all such work was done by hand! Imagine the agony and frustration of plowing a field with one's fingers.... These basic tools were absolutely revolutionary in the times of Noach and brought about a radical improvement in the task of earning one's daily bread.

Getting back now to our question (how did mankind turn so evil so as to deserve to be destroyed?), the simple answer is that innovation led to leisure hours. People became much more efficient and suddenly had

---

1. *Bereshit* 3:19.
2. Rabbi Shalom Smith, *The Pleasant Way: Adapted from the Teachings of Horav Avrohom Pam* (Lakewood, NJ: Israel Book Shop, 2002), 30–31.

a lot of free time on their hands. Free time in and of itself is not problematic. What is problematic is when that time is used in the wrong way.

When there is free time, when we have freedom to do whatever we want, we can use that time productively and accomplish great things, or we can use it in an unproductive and wasteful manner that can lead to destruction. As we know, what transpired among the generation of the Flood was corruption, crime, and violence. Society degenerated at a shocking pace, and the worst forms of immorality took hold. There was an epidemic of absolute wickedness that the world had not seen in more than fifteen centuries of its existence.

As we know, we are always better off when we're busy than when we're not. The more work we have, the more productive we become. This idea helps illuminate the last mishna in Makkot (3:16), which states, "HaKadosh Barukh Hu wanted to bring merit to Israel, so he increased the Torah and commandments for them." Several commentators ask: Hashem wanted to give us merit, so He provided us with 613 commandments? Give us ten! How is it meritorious to have so many commandments?[3] An answer might be that the busier we are, the better off we are. When a person does not occupy his time with constructive activities, it leads to boredom, which can be destructive. The reason for this is that boredom brings on mental instability and a desire for immorality. When a person has nothing with which to fill his time, he gets into trouble.[4]

What led to the destruction of the generation of the Flood was the way they misused their free time.

There is a famous saying: "If you want something to get done, give the task to the busiest person in the room." It is easy to turn down a job or forgo an additional responsibility because we are "too busy" to learn for half an hour at night or attend a *shiur* once a week. One important

---

3. Also see Rambam and Maharal's commentaries on that mishna for different approaches.
4. See Rambam in *Hilkhot Isurei Bia* 22:21, who states that illicit thoughts only occupy those whose minds are empty of *hokhma* (knowledge).

lesson we need to learn from the generation of the Flood is to be as productive as we can and to utilize our time properly.[5]

---

5. I was once passing by Madison Square Garden in New York City, where there was a huge digital clock displaying the hour, minute, second, and milliseconds. I was amazed at how quickly time was passing. Although in actuality, time was not moving any quicker than it had done in the past, by watching the milliseconds pass so quickly, I felt as if I wanted to stop the clock. It made me feel rushed. It made me realize the value of every second. Time is in our hands, and we have to make sure we don't waste it. A lost second is something we can never recover.

   A story is also told (see *Parashat Hayei Sara*, "Making Every Day Count") of the Hafetz Hayim, who was approached by a *talmid* who explained that Rabbi Naftali Tropp, a Rosh Yeshiva in Radin, was very ill, and *talmidim* were undertaking to donate time from their lives toward Rabbi Tropp. This *talmid* asked the *Hafetz Hayim* how much time he was willing to donate: a day, a week, a month? The Hafetz Hayim thought for a few moments and said, "I will donate one minute." The *talmid* was puzzled. The Hafetz Hayim explained, "Do you not realize how much one can accomplish in a minute?" This was the Hafetz Hayim, who wrote *Mishna Berura*, *Shemirat HaLashon*, and many other great books. He utilized and maximized every second of his life productively. See also Sforno on *Shemot* 12:2, where he explains that the gift given to Israel as we left Egypt was *time*: "From now on, the months are yours, to do with as you please. During your bondage, your days were not yours. Rather, they were for the work and pleasure of others. Therefore, 'this is the first of the months of the year for you,' for this is when the reality of you doing as you wish began."

Taking the First Step

עשה לך תבת עצי גפר קנים תעשה את התבה וכפרת אתה מבית ומחוץ
בכפר. וזה אשר תעשה אתה: שלש מאות אמה ארך התבה חמשים אמה
רחבה ושלשים אמה קומתה. (בראשית ו:יד-טו)

Make for yourself an ark of gopher wood; you shall make the
ark with compartments, and you shall caulk it both inside and
outside with pitch. And this [is the size] you shall make it: three
hundred cubits the length of the ark, fifty cubits its breadth, and
thirty cubits its height. (*Bereshit* 6:14–15)

The Torah provides the dimensions of the ark: 300 x 50 x 30 *amot*. However large that may seem, realistically, it could not have fit samples of
every species of animal. Ramban and his *talmid*, Rabbenu Bahya, both
acknowledge that it was obviously a miracle.

This begs the question: If it was going to be a miracle anyway since
all these animals would not fit in one ark with these dimensions, why
couldn't Noach just build a sailboat? What was the purpose of building
a large structure if he would have really needed several of these structures to house the requisite species?

Furthermore, Hashem could have saved Noach and the animals
without an ark. Hashem could have made them fly! He could have made
them float on water. There are many ways He could have saved them.

The entire event was a miracle, so why did Hashem command Noach to spend so much time and effort building an ark? Rabbenu Bahya offers a solution to this question.

והתשובה בזה דרך התורה לצוות על האדם שיעשה כל יכלתו בדרך הטבע ומה שיחסר הטבע בהן ישלים הנס.

The answer is that the way of the Torah is to command man to do his best naturally, and what is insufficient in nature, will be completed miraculously.[1]

God always demands that we do the most we can. Hashem always wants us to take the initiative and then he will do His part. *Ein somhin al hanes* – "we must not rely on miracles."

All miracles require that some act is performed by a person. We can't just sit back and expect things to spontaneously occur. We have to do our part and then Hashem does the rest. When we conquered Jericho, we had to encircle the city for seven days, and we had to blow the shofars and horns. We had to do something. We could not break down the walls, but we had to take the initiative and implement some action so that Hashem could complete the task.

Every war we fight and win is based on miracles, but we still need an army. In *Sefer Yehoshua,* the Jewish army is commanded to ambush the enemy, because we couldn't just rely on miracles; we have to do our part. This is why, says Rabbenu Bahya, we have to go through the motions just like the other nations.

We find this on the individual level as well. When Pharaoh's daughter sees Moshe's basket floating in the Nile, the Torah tells us:

ותרד בת פרעה לרחץ על היאר ונערתיה הלכת על יד היאר ותרא את התבה בתוך הסוף ותשלח את אמתה ותקחה. (שמות ב:ה)

Pharaoh's daughter went down to bathe, to the Nile, and her maidens were walking along the Nile, and she saw the basket in

---

1. Rabbenu Bahya, *Bereshit* 6:15.

the midst of the marsh, and she sent her maidservant, and she took it. (*Shemot* 2:5)

According to one opinion in Sota (12b; quoted by Rashi on this *pasuk*), her hand stretched out many *amot* in order to reach Moshe's basket. The same question can be asked: If a miracle would be needed in any case for Pharaoh's daughter to reach Moshe, why did she have to do anything? Let Hashem have the basket float ashore adjacent to where she was standing! Rabbenu Bahya's reasoning above applies here as well: Hashem waits for man to take the first initiative and do his utmost, and then Hashem will complete the task by means of a miracle.

That is why Noach had to build a large ark, even if it would not have been large enough to house all the species. Noach had to do the maximum that he could, and Hashem would take it from there. We always need to give it our all. We can dream the impossible, but we should not sit idly by, hoping it will miraculously become a reality. We need to take the initiative, to take the first step, and only then will Hashem do His part.

The Symbolism of the Rainbow

In *Parashat Noach,* we are introduced to the rainbow. HaKadosh Barukh Hu promises that He will never destroy the world again and uses a rainbow as a reminder of this covenant. Why was this specific natural phenomenon selected as the symbol and covenant that the world will not be destroyed by a flood? Several commentators seek to explain the symbolism.

The Ramban suggests that the rainbow is perhaps symbolic of a backward bow. When you fight someone with a bow and arrow, you pull back the bow to shoot the arrow. When the parties make peace, they proceed with a backward bow; the bow faces themselves rather than the enemy, symbolizing that they will no longer aim the bow in the other party's direction. The Ramban suggests that a rainbow, which similarly faces upwards, is a message of peace from HaKadosh Barukh Hu that He will never again destroy the world as He did in the time of the *Mabul.*

Rabbi Avraham Rivlin,[1] among others, provides a different understanding of the symbolic meaning of the rainbow. One of the unique

---

1. Rabbi Avraham Rivlin, *Iyunei Parasha* (Old City Press, 2010), 45.

and beautiful aspects of a rainbow is its spectrum of colors. What do all the different colors of the rainbow symbolize?

It stands as a lesson to all mankind about the sin of the generation of the *Mabul*. In that generation, everyone lived for themselves, without considering others or including themselves in the collective. The Torah tells us that the world was filled with theft, fraud, and injustice. People cared for themselves and lacked concern and compassion for other people and their property. The rainbow symbolizes unity. What a beautiful sight when all of the colors come together and form a rainbow. What a beautiful world it would be if people of different persuasions, of different *hashkafot*, would respect each other and come together. If we do not want to be deserving of another *Mabul*, then we have to be a united people. Each person can be an individual, but that individual has to be within the spectrum. The rainbow symbolizes diversity within unity.[2]

The midrash tells us that in some generations, a rainbow never appeared because of the special merits of the rabbinic leaders of the generation. For example, in the generation of Rabbi Yehoshua ben Levi, no rainbow appeared.[3] How are we to understand this midrash?

When there's a *tzaddik* who binds all Jews together, then there is no need for a rainbow to remind us of our divisions. We are all unified, like the color white.

We each need to do our share in being accepting of others, respectful of the ideas of others, and tolerant of differing opinions. We can live together in harmony, even with opposing views, as long as we can live side by side within the same spectrum. What a truly beautiful and colorful world that would be!

Rav Meir Shapiro asks another question about the rainbow. It took Noach several hundred years to build the ark, so how is it that he was unable to influence even one individual? Apparently, Noach's heart was not in the task. He gave up on the people of his generation. When a teacher (*rebbe*) does not have faith in his students, they will certainly not succeed. The rainbow is a bright burst of color on an

2. Also see the explanation of Rabbi Yaakov Kamenetzky, in *Emet LeYaakov* on *Parashat Bemidbar*, regarding the flags of the tribes.
3. *Bereshit Rabba* 35:2.

otherwise dreary, rainy day. It is symbolic of *not* giving up on others no matter how dark the situation may seem, If we keep trying, we might be able to suddenly see our influence on our students and witness them beginning to shine. We need to believe in them and encourage them to expose their true colors.

Hashem's Descent to Observe Mankind

In this week's *parasha,* we are told the story of the tower of Babel, *Migdal Bavel.* The *pasuk* tells us that Hashem "descended" to see what was transpiring.

וירד ה' לראת את העיר ואת המגדל אשר בנו בני האדם. (בראשית יא:ה)

Hashem descended to see the city and the tower that the people had erected. (*Bereshit* 11:5)

Hashem, as it were, descended from the heavens to witness the tower being erected. Whenever there is anthropomorphism like this in the Torah, Onkelos changes the literal meaning, because he can't accept such terminology that relates to Hashem in such human-sounding terms. In this case, Onkelos interprets Hashem's "descent" as a revelation: *ve'itgalei.* Hashem appeared. He didn't "descend."

Sforno offers a different explanation. Whenever this term "descend" is used with respect to God, it means Hashem is about to perform an act of retribution that on the surface appears like a stricter form of punishment than is deserved. It means Hashem sees beyond the action at hand and focuses on the ramifications and repercussions of such action. As occurs in the instances of a *ben sorer umoreh* and with the people of Sedom. Hashem sees what the action will lead to, and He judges accordingly. In this context, Sforno explains that Hashem saw what *Migdal Bavel* was leading to, and that is why He punished the people.

The term "descend" appears several other times in the Torah, and we see that this interpretation is applicable in those instances as well. The Torah begins the story of the destruction of Sodom with Hashem saying *erda na ve'ere* – "I will descend and see." What did Hashem "see" there? He saw that they were a cruel nation, that *hesed* was outlawed throughout the city, and that this lack of *hesed* would ultimately affect the entire world. Hashem didn't just look at the current actions of Sodom; rather, He considered the results and ripple effects of their actions.

Likewise, when *Hazal* discuss why the wayward and rebellious son, *ben sorer umore*, is punished so severely, they use the term "descend": "the Torah descended to the implications of his thinking."[1] The Torah considers the ultimate impact of his current actions on his future, and for that reason, he is punished at this juncture.

Rav Yeruham Levovitz expounds on this point and concludes from Sforno's thesis that we must be careful to not just think of the short term, of the here and now.[2] We must contemplate the impact our decisions and actions can have on other people and on our future.

Throughout our lives, we cannot have tunnel vision and be focused only on what's in front of our eyes. We have to think about the potential consequences of our actions before we make a move. The Gemara (*Yoma* 9) states that the first *Beit HaMikdash* was destroyed because of the three cardinal sins of idolatry, bloodshed, and immorality, *gilui arayot*, whereas the second *Beit HaMikdash* was destroyed due to baseless hatred, *sinat hinam*. A murder is horrifying, but the effects of *sinat hinam* can be even greater. We are still in the same *galut*, thousands of years later, because of *sinat hinam*. The reason is that such rampant *sinat hinam* affects all of society, and the ramifications are unbelievable. We cannot even fathom the ripple effects of hatred, though our drawn-out *galut* gives us an inkling of how terrible it is.

---

1. Sanhedrin 72a.
2. Rav Yeruham Halevi Levovitz, *Daat Torah, Bereishit* (Jerusalem, 2001), 67.

The Hafetz Hayim gave a powerful *mashal* that brings this points home. Someone once came to him and asked for advice on how to do *teshuva* for all the *lashon hara* he had spoken.

The Hafetz Hayim asked for a pillow. He ripped it open and sent the feathers flying in every direction. He then asked the man to please collect all the feathers and return them.

"But that's impossible!" replied the shocked man.

Said the Hafetz Hayim, "That's *lashon hara*. Once the words leave your mouth, they can never be retrieved."

This is what *Hazal* are teaching us: to consider all the consequences of our actions. As *Hazal* tell us in Masekhet Tamid:[3] "Who is wise? One who anticipates consequences."

Everything we do affects others. It behooves us to consider the ramifications of our speech and our actions on those around us. We should take into account every nuance, every side effect, every opportunity for a *kiddush Hashem* that could come out of our actions, so that Hashem can "descend and see" and be proud of our actions.[4]

---

3. Tamid 32a.
4. We are told that on Rosh HaShana, the book of the living and the book of the dead are open before Hashem. It is easy to comprehend that God is judging those who are alive and evaluating their deeds. However, why would the book of the dead be open? These individuals have already passed on. What new acts are being evaluated? Notwithstanding that a dead person is absent physically from this world, the impact he had on others still remains long after he departs from the world. If Torah is transmitted in his name, or if his bad influence continues to cause others to sin, it can still be attributed to him. That is why our impact on others is so significant. It can truly have an everlasting effect. (Based on Rosh HaShana 17b and Rama, *Hilkhot Yamim Noraim*.)

Mixed Language

ויהי כל הארץ שפה אחת ודברים אחדים. (בראשית יא:א)

Now the entire earth was of one language and uniform words. (*Bereshit* 11:1)

The end of *Parashat Noach* contains the episode of the generation that built a tall tower in an attempt to reach the heavens.

The Talmud Yerushalmi (*Megilla* 1:9) quotes an opinion that the people in the world at that time spoke all seventy languages. How does this opinion fit with the above *pasuk* that says they all spoke one language? Wasn't their punishment that they would all speak different languages?! Moreover, Hashem said, "Let us descend and mix up (*hava nerda venavla*) their language."[1] What exactly do the words *havah* and *nerda* connote? Finally, the verb used to describe Hashem mixing up the languages, *navla*, is the same verb used to describe a mixture or blend. What was being mixed or blended?

Rav Shimon Schwab[2] answers these three questions.

Language is a convention that is accepted by a group of people and shaped by its sages. Languages are constantly changing and being

---

1. Bereshit 11:7
2. *Maayan Beit HaShoeva* (New York: Mesorah Publications, 2001), 20.

differentiated from one another based on events and circumstances. Even before the builders of the tower, there were many languages unique to specific families and clans. There were also, no doubt, many different dialects, inflections, pronunciations, and accents. However, because they had a unity of purpose, they were intelligible to one another. Just as parents understand the "language" of a preverbal baby, so too did all of the people of that generation understand one another. Language was no barrier to communication. When the *pasuk* states that the people all spoke "one language," this is what it means.

But this unity led to a problem. They were so reliant on one another that they figured they did not need HaKadosh Barukh Hu. That was their mistake. They used their unity to rebel against Hashem. They felt themselves to be self-sufficient.

Rav Schwab continues and explains that whenever the Torah describes Hashem as "descending," it represents Hashem showing His involvement. It's His reminder that we need Him and cannot survive on our own. Hashem did not punish the people of this generation as much as He showed them that the world cannot exist without Him. He came down and created a mixture: He mixed some of Himself within the world so that the people would realize that there is more than just them, and that they need to connect to Hashem, too. Then, Hashem separated them, because just being a unit without Hashem in the picture was not going to work.[3]

Unity, *ahdut,* is a wonderful trait, but we have to make sure we use it correctly. Nowadays, people sometimes believe that "my strength and the power of my hand accomplished this for me."[4] Self-reliance sometimes makes people less dependent on Hashem. We must take care in remembering the source of our success.

---

3. See the Ramban at the end of *Parashat Bo*. This was the purpose of the *makot*.
4. *Devarim* 8:17.

Parashat Lekh Lekha

Introductions

In *Parashat Lekh Lekha* we are "introduced" to Avraham Avinu. The Torah does not tell us much about Avraham (that void is filled by many midrashim). Rather, we are immediately thrown into the first command directed to Avraham, enjoining him to go forth from his homeland:

> ויאמר ה' אל אברם, לך לך מארצך וממולדתך ומבית אביך אל הארץ
> אשר אראך. (בראשית יב:א)

And Hashem said to Abram, "Go forth from your land and from your birthplace and from your father's house, to the land that I will show you." (*Bereshit* 12:1)

Is this really an introduction? There is a stark contrast between Avraham's introduction and the introduction to Noach in last week's *parasha*. The Torah immediately gives some color to Noach's personality when he is first introduced to us:

> אלה תולדות נח נח איש צדיק תמים היה בדורותיו את האלוקים התהלך
> נח. (בראשית ו:ט)

> These are the generations of Noach: Noach was a righteous man, perfect in his generations; Noach walked with God. (*Bereshit* 6:9)

The Torah introduces Noach as a *tzaddik*, a righteous man. That's an introduction! We are immediately informed of his greatness. Yet, Avraham's introduction is absent. There are no adjectives that describe Avraham's greatness. In fact, it appears as if there is no introduction to Avraham whatsoever. The Torah just introduces "Avraham," with his command from Hashem to leave his current location. How are we to understand this contrast with respect to the distinct introductions of Avraham and Noach?

The Gemara (Taanit 21a) tells a story about Rav Yochanan and Ilfa. The two were learning together in yeshiva and were very poor, so they decided it was time to return home to start families and earn a living. On their way home, they stopped near a rickety wall to eat lunch. While they were there, Rav Yochanan heard an angel say, "The walls should collapse on these individuals, since they are abandoning eternal life for temporal life." The other angel responded that they couldn't do that because one of them was destined for greatness in Torah. Rav Yochanan turned to Ilfa and asked if he heard the dialogue among the angels. Ilfa was puzzled, as he did not hear any such dialogue. Rav Yochanan understood that if he heard the dialogue, they must have been referring to him. Rav Yochanan immediately decided to return to yeshiva to continue to dedicate all his time to learning Torah. Subsequently, Rav Yochanan becomes a renowned scholar.

Several times, the Gemara cites Ilfa as saying that had he returned to yeshiva, he could have become the leading Torah sage of the generation. The Gemara seems to fault Ilfa for not returning to yeshiva. Is that really fair? Is it Ilfa's fault? He didn't hear the conversation between the angels. Had he heard the conversation, perhaps, like Rav Yochanan, he would have headed back to the yeshiva as well.

The commentators explain that both Ilfa and Rav Yochanan *could* have heard the voice, but only Rav Yochanan was tuned into the divine frequency. He heard the voice loud and clear. So often in life does HaKadosh Barukh Hu speak to us in so many different ways. But do we hear what He is saying? Do we hear Hashem guiding us, instructing us, and hinting to us which path to choose? The greatest introduction that we can give to someone is that they heard God's voice. Avraham is introduced as someone who hears the voice and follows through on that first command that he receives from Hashem. The first Jew heard the voice, understood it without questioning it, and immediately acted upon it, without hesitation. We need to "tune in" so we can hear Hashem's voice and act accordingly as well.

Age, Maturity, and Growth

ואברם בן חמש שנים ושבעים שנה בצאתו מחרן. (בראשית יב:ד)

And Avram was seventy-five years old when he left Haran.
(*Bereshit* 12:4)

Rav Nebenzahl points out that it seems intriguing that the Torah and
Hazal focus an unusual amount on Avraham's age.[1] At various stages of
Avraham's adventure the Torah informs us of his age. All the forefathers,
avot, have their age mentioned a couple of times, but none get as much
emphasis as Avraham.

According to many, Avraham was three when he discovered
Hashem based on the *pasuk* עקב אשר שמע אברהם בקלי – "because Avraham listened to My voice" (*Bereshit* 26:5). The *gematria* of עקב (*ekev*) is
172. We know Avraham lived to the age of 175, but he listened to Hashem's
voice only for *ekev* – 172 years. The missing three years are the years that
Avraham hadn't yet recognized Hashem. Some claim Avraham was fifty
when he recognized Hashem, others say he was forty-eight, and yet others suggest he was forty.[2] *Tosafot* and the Rosh suggest that Avraham was
seventy when he left Haran, but then he returned, only to leave again at

---

1. Rav Nebenzahl, *Sihot Al Sefer Bereshit* (Jerusalem, 2004), 73.
2. See Rambam and Raavad at the beginning of *Hilkhot Avodat Kokhavim.*

seventy-five.[3] At the end of the *parasha*, it mentions how old Avraham was when he circumcised himself.

Why do *Hazal*, based on the Torah, discuss Avraham's age more than that of any other Jew? Rav Nebenzahl explains: How old was he when he recognized Hashem, exactly? Avraham Avinu, at various stages in his life, had a new recognition of HaKadosh Barukh Hu. At three, forty, forty-eight, fifty-two, seventy, and seventy-five years old, he appreciated and recognized Hashem more than he had done previously.

Avraham was the first person to connect with God, the first one to create a relationship with Him. Adam and Noach may have spoken to Hashem, but not in the same way as Avraham. Avraham was the first one who developed the *avoda* of commitment and action, and he spent his entire life constantly strengthening his faith and rediscovering Hashem on deeper levels.

The different opinions on Avraham's age do not constitute a dispute, *mahloket*, about history. The various ages teach us that recognizing Hashem was a step-by-step process for Avraham. It was and is a developing path. Yes, Avraham was three when he discovered Hashem, but he continued to recognize HaKadosh Barukh Hu when he was forty as well, and through all his years, this recognition became deeper. Avraham underwent a process as the first Jew, and as such, he was the prototype for all future Jews. We are to constantly work on our *emuna* (belief) so that our spirituality constantly grows.

There's a story told about Rav Saadia Gaon that a student once saw him rolling around in the snow.[4] The student called out, "Rebbe, what are you doing?"

Answered Rav Saadia, "HaKadosh Barukh Hu is unbelievable!"

"True," replied the student, "but why are you rolling around in the snow?"

"I'll tell you why," said the Gaon. "I just returned from my travels, and at one point I stayed at an inn. The innkeeper was very nice to me, and gave me everything I needed. I had no complaints.

---

3. *Tosafot*, Shabbat 6b and the Rosh, Yevamot 6:12.
4. Others suggest it was some other self-affliction, as snow is not too common in Iraq.

"When I was about to leave, someone entered the inn, recognized me, and called out, 'Rav Saadia Gaon!' The innkeeper was mortified and began apologizing, 'If I had known who you are, I would have treated you better.' I didn't understand; he had given me everything and treated me so respectfully. 'Yes, but had I known that you are Rav Saadia Gaon, I would have given you super treatment!'

"I thought to myself, every single day I have a deeper appreciation of HaKadosh Barukh Hu; therefore, every single day of my life I should spend doing *teshuva* because I didn't realize yesterday how great Hashem really is."

Hence, Rav Saadia Gaon was rolling in the snow as a form of *teshuva* for his previous ignorance regarding HaKadosh Baruch Hu's unfathomable greatness.

If we would appreciate every single day, we would rush to accomplish more, and we would be in a constant state of *teshuva*.

Rav Nebenzahl explains this further with a *mashal*. When we are young, we are introduced to the Rambam. We are told he was a great man, a brilliant philosopher, and that he wrote many *sefarim*. At the time that we initially become acquainted with the Rambam we believe we understand who he was. Then, when we get a little older, we find out that he wrote *Mishneh Torah* and *Moreh Nevuhim*, and we develop a greater appreciation of who he was. "Now I understand who the Rambam was," we think.

Then we begin learning, and suddenly we realize, wow! The Rambam! How did he categorize and organize the Written Torah and Oral Torah in such a clear way? How amazing and brilliant he was! Then, we learn for another ten years, and now we realize how one of his words clues us into a whole *sugya*. We're in awe of the Rambam, and now we think we understand who the Rambam was.

That is what occurred with Avraham Avinu. When he was three years old, he thought he had it. He saw the sun and the moon, and he realized that statues made of stone are not gods. There must be a God with supernatural ability that rules the world. Then, when he was forty and forty-eight, he realized in a much deeper and more meaningful way the greatness of the Omnipotent.

The first Jew went through a process, and we too have to go through that process at every age and every stage of our lives.

Through the years, Avraham Avinu wasn't only recognizing HaKadosh Barukh Hu on a different level. Through recognizing Hashem, he learned more about himself. He became aware of his inner strength. Every time he deepened his relationship with Hashem, he uncovered more of himself, until the pinnacle of it all: the *Akeda*. He reached such a level of connection with Hashem that he was ready to sacrifice his own son for that connection.

As we mature, our spirituality grows as well. As we gain life experience, our appreciation of Hashem is constantly strengthening. We have to grow as individuals and as spiritual beings. That will enable us to reach our full potential.

Avraham's Love
for *Eretz Yisrael*

ויהי רעב בארץ וירד אברם מצרימה לגור שם כי כבד הרעב בארץ...
ויהי כאשר הקריב לבוא מצרימה ויאמר אל שרי אשתו הנה נא ידעתי
כי אשה יפת מראה את. (בראשית יב:י-יא)

And there was a famine in the land, and Abram descended to
Egypt to sojourn there because the famine was severe in the
land. Now it came to pass when he drew near to come to Egypt,
that he said to Sarai his wife, "Behold now I know that you are a
woman of fair appearance." (*Bereshit* 12:10–11)

In the opening *pesukim* of *Parashat Lekh Lekha*, Hashem commands
Avraham Avinu to leave his current location and to journey to a new,
unknown destination. When Avraham arrives in *Eretz Yisrael*, he is
promised that he will be blessed in this land and that here, his children
will prosper. Ironically, however, soon after Avraham arrives, there is a
famine in the land. This phenomenon seems to contradict Hashem's
promise that Avraham will be blessed in the land. What type of blessing is it to be left without any food?

Notwithstanding this difficulty, Avraham does not question
Hashem. Avraham is forced to leave *Eretz Yisrael* and descend to Egypt

due to *pikuah nefesh* (it was a matter of life and death). The Torah describes Avraham's approach to Egypt and the charade he plans with his wife, Sarah, to save her from the immoral Egyptians.

ויהי כאשר הקריב לבוא מצרימה...

Now it came to pass when he drew near to come to Egypt...

Why does the *pasuk* use *lashon hifil* (the causative tense) to describe his approach? Why is *hikriv* used and not *karav*? The form of the root the *pasuk* uses means "to draw near" rather than "to approach." Rashi doesn't comment on this issue, but Rabbi Dovid Feinstein suggests an answer based on another instance in the Torah where the word *hikriv* is used.

In *Parashat Beshallah*, as the Egyptians are chasing after Am Yisrael as they head toward the Reed Sea, the Torah uses the word *hikriv*, and Rashi comments on the word usage there. Rabbi Dovid Feinstein[1] explains: that this word is also used in *Parashat Beshallah* to describe how Pharaoh approached the Jews at the Reed Sea. In explaining what Pharaoh drew near, Rashi comments that this unusual form indicates that Pharaoh "pushed himself" to be at the forefront of the Egyptians' attack on the Jews – even though he was afraid.

It's unclear why Rashi does not comment here in *Parashat Lekh Lekha* on the word *hikriv*, but we can perhaps apply Rashi's interpretation in *Parashat Beshallah* to that case as well.

Pharaoh was afraid to chase the Jews. He couldn't possibly have forgotten the ten plagues he had just experienced. Yet, he pushed himself. He forced himself to overcome these feelings and do what he had to do. That's what *hikriv* suggests there. He brought himself close. He had to force himself.

Rabbi Dovid Feinstein suggests that if we apply that Rashi here, we can have a deeper understanding of what Avraham was *hikriv* in *Parashat Lekh Lekha*. This suggests that in our narrative, also, Avraham had

---

1. Rabbi Dovid Feinstein, *Kol Dodi Al HaTorah* (New York: Mesorah Publications, 1992), 32.

to push himself to overcome something. In the preceding verse, Rashi points out that Hashem brought famine only on the land of Israel and nowhere else in order to test Avraham. Hashem had told Avraham to leave his home and go to a foreign land, promising to provide Avraham with wealth and success in Israel and then soon after his arrival, the situation is grave. There is a famine, and he is forced to leave the country to survive.

What was the *nisayon*?

Would he jump at the opportunity to leave a country which did not live up to his expectations, in spite of Hashem's promises, or would he be reluctant to forsake the land that Hashem had told him would be his, and whose spiritual superiority he had surely already recognized?

Avraham was going to have to leave. He had no choice. But *how* was he going to leave? That was the *nisayon*. Would his attitude be, "Awesome! I don't have to be here anymore!" or "I really don't want to leave. This is such an amazing land. It's so spiritual. I feel so connected to God here, but there's a famine, so I have to leave."[2]

According to Rashi on *Parashat Beshallah*, we can understand *hikriv* to mean that Avraham had to overcome internal feelings in order to leave *Eretz Yisrael*. What were these internal feelings? He had to battle his intense love, *havivut*, for *Eretz Yisrael* that had been implanted in him from when Hashem said "to the land I will show you" and rise above this love in order to take his next step.

Avraham resisted leaving Israel every step of the way. When he finally reached the point where there was no choice, he still had to push himself to leave. From this, we see how great was Avraham's love of the land of Israel and how strong was his desire to fulfill Hashem's wishes.

We are all descendants of Avraham Avinu. Every year, *Parashat Lekh Lekha* should serve as a reminder for us to deepen our feelings of

---

2. The Gemara (Avoda Zara 3b) cites a request by the other nations to give them another chance at receiving the Torah. Hashem provides them with a sukka. Upon experiencing extreme weather conditions, they exit the sukka and kick it down. The Gemara comments that although the halakha states that one who experiences discomfort in the sukka is exempt from the mitzva, and one is therefore not obligated to sit in the sukka in bad weather conditions, the attitude of kicking down the sukka upon exiting was not justifiable.

love for *Eretz Yisrael*. Wherever we live in the world, we have to recognize that *Eretz Yisrael* is God's land, the land He chose as the land of the Jewish nation. We *daven* for the day that all of us will be here; but until then, we must recognize the fact that this is the chosen land, and we need to love it more than anywhere else in the world.

Unfortunately, today, many nations attack Israel on unfounded moral and ethical grounds. Each of us is an ambassador of *Eretz Yisrael* and we have to do everything in our power to defend our country and ensure that we act in a way that serves as a light unto the other nations of the world.

The Promised Land

Each of the *avot*, separately, was promised *Eretz Yisrael* as an inheritance. In fact, this promise was mentioned in the first conversation that each of the *avot* had with HaKadosh Barukh Hu.

Hashem said to Avraham Avinu:

שא נא עיניך וראה מן המקום אשר אתה שם צפנה ונגבה וקדמה וימה. כי את כל הארץ אשר אתה ראה לך אתננה ולזרעך עד עולם. (בראשית יג:יד-טו)

Please raise your eyes and see, from the place where you are, northward and southward and eastward and westward. For all the land that you see I will give to you and to your seed for eternity. (*Bereshit* 13:14–15)

Hashem tells Avraham to raise his eyes to see the surroundings in the promised land. What did Avraham see at that point? He didn't see yeshivot and *shuls*, he didn't see spiritual centers or buildings. He didn't see anything except the land itself. Hashem instructed Avraham: Put on your spiritual glasses and look north, south, east, and west – I'm giving you all this land forever. It doesn't matter what any other nation says – *Eretz Yisrael* belongs to the children of Israel, and the proof is here, in this promise that Hashem made to Avraham Avinu.

Rav Shimshon Pincus wonders why Hashem's promise to Avraham and later to Yitzhak and Yaakov relates to the land and not to providing their offspring with Torah and mitzvot.[1]

We have been exiled from *Eretz Yisrael* for two thousand years. We've been disconnected from the land for so long, and yet, we're still alive. If we think about it, we know a Jew cannot live without Torah. A Jew can live without *Eretz Yisrael*, but not without Torah. To live in *Eretz Yisrael* is a major mitzva, but our defining characteristic is the Torah. So why is *Eretz Yisrael*, and not Torah or mitzvot, what Hashem promises to the *avot*?

Rav Pincus explains with a parable.

We bless every bride and groom: "May you be *zokhe* to build a *bayit ne'eman beYisrael,* a faithful house in Yisrael."

Why do we say a "house"? Why do we focus on the *bayit*? A house is not a necessary component of a marriage. Some of the greats in past generations didn't have enough money to live in a house. They lived with the in-laws – for years! What do we mean when we bless the newlyweds with building a *bayit ne'eman*?

It is true that the house is not the essence of the marriage. Rather, it's what's inside the house that matters most. However, the house, with everything that's inside, defines the marriage. We are blessing the young couple with a house *full* of Torah and mitzvot and *hesed,* because the house is the glue that holds it all together. The house is the context to hold all the content. In Rav Pincus's words:

הדבר החשוב ביותר בחיי הנישואין הוא הפרטיות ו"בית" מבטא פרטיות זו בהיותו מקום סגור - ארבע קירות וגג.

זו היתה הבטחתו של הקב"ה לאבות הקדושים - בניהם ייכנסו לארץ ישראל ויחיו יחד עם הרבש"ע בפרטיות, ללא שכל גורם זר יתערב ביניהם.

הדבר שבעצם מגדיר את כל ה'אידישקייט' - את הקשר בינינו לבין הרבש"ע, היא ארץ ישראל! ודאי שהמהות והתוכן של ה'אידישקייט' הן התורה והמצוות...אבל האוירה, הסביבה שמגדירה את אותו קשר מופלא טמונה אך ורק בארץ ישראל...[2]

---

1. Rav Shimshon Pincus, *Tiferet Shimshon* (Jerusalem: Yefe Nof, 2009), 138.
2. Ibid.

The most important facet in a marriage is privacy – and a house sets the closed environment that provides a private domain within four walls and a roof. This was Hashem's promise to our forefathers – your children will enter Eretz Yisrael and will dwell with Hashem in privacy, without any other foreigners intervening. Essentially what characterizes our religion – our special relationship with Hashem is Eretz Yisrael. Obviously, the essence is Torah and mitzvot, but the proper environment that establishes our relationship with Hashem is only I Eretz Yisrael.

What defines us as a nation? What's the context for all of our content? *Eretz Yisrael!* Obviously, it's Torah and mitzvot, but it's Torah and mitzvot within the context of *Eretz Yisrael.* That's the ultimate plan. That's where it started, and that's what we yearn for every day.[3]

This was Hashem's promise to each of the *avot.* He promised the context, the definition and framework for everything that would happen in Jewish history. He promised us a land that would serve as a platform in which Torah and mitzvot could be fulfilled in their ultimate form.

---

3. The Semak (*Sefer Mitzvot Katan*) counts belief in Hashem as the first mitzva. He derives an amazing expansion of this mitzva related to the Gemara (Shabbat 31a) that lists six questions that are asked to individuals after 120 years. One of them is "Did you anticipate redemption?" There's a problem with this question: Where do we find that there is a mitzva to anticipate redemption? The Semak explains that the first of the Ten Commandments is not only a mitzva to believe in Hashem, but it is also a mitzva to believe that He took us out of Egypt and therefore that He can be relied upon to redeem us once again.

To Be Rich or to Enrich?

ויהי כאשר הקריב לבוא מצרימה ויאמר אל שרי אשתו הנה נא ידעתי
כי אשה יפת מראה את. כי יראו אתך המצרים ואמרו אשתו זאת והרגו
אתי ואתך יחיו. אמרי נא אחתי את למען ייטב לי בעבורך וחיתה נפשי
בגללך. (בראשית יב:יא-יג)

Now it came to pass when he drew near to come to Egypt, that he
said to Sarai his wife, "Behold now I know that you are a woman
of fair appearance. And it will come to pass when the Egyptians
see you, that they will say, 'This is his wife,' and they will slay
me and let you live. Please say [that] you are my sister, in order
that it go well with me because of you, and that my soul may live
because of you." (*Bereshit* 12:11–13)

Just a little while after Avraham arrives in Eretz Yisrael, a famine overtakes
the land, and he is forced to depart to Egypt. As Avraham approaches
Egypt, he says to his wife, Sarah, "I'm nervous that when the Egyptians
see you, they will want you. If they know you're my wife, they'll kill me
and keep you. Please, say you're my sister, so that it will be good for me
in your merit, and my soul will live because of you."

Rashi explains that what Avraham meant by the words *lemaan
yitav li baavurekh* was "they will give me presents."

Rav Yosef Zvi Salant asks in his commentary the *Be'er Yosef*:[1] What is Avraham talking about? He's worried about wealth? And at a time like this? There must be a deeper idea here.

The *Be'er Yosef* suggests that Avraham should not have been worried that they would kill him, because Avraham Avinu had a tremendous, hidden, secret weapon, a weapon that they couldn't take away from him: his *ko'ah hadibbur* – the strength of his speech. Avraham was an unbelievable orator. If they surrounded him, he could just say, "Hey, wait a second, guys, can we just talk for a minute?" And he would get them into conversation, and he would be able to convince them.

Avraham was worried that they would not even give him a chance to open his mouth, and then he would be a goner. They would see this beautiful woman, kill Avraham Avinu on the spot, and then ask questions later. Therefore, Avraham requested that Sarah claim that she was his sister so it would at least give Avraham a chance to engage with the locals in dialogue.

What does *lemaan yitav li baavurekh* really mean? It is not referring to gifts. Avraham wanted Sarah to say that she was his sister so that he would be able to convince the Egyptians not to kill him. Avraham knew and appreciated what makes humans unique. As the *Kuzari* points out, man is above all other beings, as he can express himself through speech.[2] Avraham wanted to use the gift of speech to have a positive impact on others.

Avraham Avinu's purpose in life was to bring people closer to Hashem. He wanted his life so he could continue to fulfill his mission in this world of bringing people closer to HaKadosh Barukh Hu. That is the benefit he desired; not riches, but to be able to enrich others. May we all be blessed with the ability and desire to positively impact others.

---

1. Rav Yosef Salant, *Be'er Yosef* (Jerusalem, 2009), 27.
2. The *Kuzari* ranks life in this order: inanimate matter, plant life, animal life, and human (speaking) life. In fact, when explaining why Bilaam's donkey spoke to him, Rav Shlesinger (*Eile Hem Mo'adai* [Jerusalem 2002], Sefirat Haomer, 473) suggests that as Bilaam misused his speech to curse Am Yisrael, then he was no greater than a talking donkey, i.e., an animal.

On Account of My Spouse

אמרי נא אחתי את למען ייטב לי בעבורך וחיתה נפשי בגללך.
(בראשית יב:יג)

Please say [that] you are my sister, in order that it go well with
me because of you, and that my soul may live because of you.
(*Bereshit* 12:13)

Rav Yitzhak Zilberstein questions Avraham's request in this *pasuk*.[1]
What can Avraham possibly mean when he says the words *lemaan yitav
li baavurekh*? Does Avraham actually care about receiving gifts? That
doesn't seem to match the character we know. After being victorious
in his battle with several kings to free Lot, Avraham refused to partake
of any of the loot.

Rav Zilberstein suggests that we focus on the word *baavurekh* in the above *pasuk*. He cites a Gemara (Bava Metzia 59a) that
declares:

אמר ר' חלבו, לעולם יהא אדם זהיר בכבוד אשתו, שאין ברכה מצויה
בתוך ביתו של אדם אלא בשביל אשתו, שנאמר: "ולאברם הטיב
בעבורה". (בבא מציעא נ"ט)

---

1. Rav Yitzchak Zilberstein, *Aleinu Leshabe'ah*, vol. 1 (Bnei Brak: Zoran, 2000), 179.

> Rav Helbo said: Man should be careful with respecting his wife, for blessing in the home is present only in the merit of one's wife, as is stated, "And Avraham benefited because of her." (Bava Metzia 59a)

The Gemara tells us that a man must be very careful with the honor and respect he shows his wife, since all *berakha* in one's household is in the merit of one's wife. The Gemara's source is actually our context.

When Avraham told Sarah *lemaan yitav li baavurekh*, he wanted to show the world and emphasize that he received presents from Egypt *because of Sarah*. He wanted the world to know that all the *berakha* a man will ever see in their life is due to their wife.

The *pasuk* doesn't say only *lemaan yitav li*, it says *baavurekh*, so that every man would recognize the centrality of the existence of his wife in their home and thus honor her and show her proper respect. Avraham didn't want the presents for himself. He wanted the presents to show the world forevermore the real source of all things good in one's life – is his wife! A person can think that if he learns and puts in the hard work, he's going to have *siyatta dishemaya*, but really, it's all due to the wife. The wife, the mother, is the pipeline for good things to flow into a home, and she is the cause of bountiful *berakhot* in the home.

Avraham did not accept gifts from the King of Sodom because he did not want people to think that it was the King of Sodom who enhanced Avraham's wealth. Pharaoh, the king of Egypt, is not credited with enhancing Avraham's wealth either, even though he was the one who provided the gifts. All the credit goes to Sarah, his wife.[2]

As we know from a famous midrash on *Parashat Hayei Sara*, as long as Sarah was alive, there was *berakha* in the dough, the candles stayed lit, and the *Shekhina* hovered over her tent. When Sarah died, those three *berakhot* disappeared. One might wonder: Didn't Avraham

---

2. This reminds us of the Gemara (Ketubot 64a), wherein Rabbi Akiva declares to his students that all of his Torah and his students' Torah are on account of his wife. In addition, before Rav Eliezer Ben Azarya accepts the appointment of Rosh Yeshiva, he tells those around him that he first needs to obtain his wife's consent, as this job will clearly impact her life as well (Berakhot 27b).

light Shabbat candles? Avraham did every mitzva! This midrash teaches us that there was no *berakha* in the home after Sarah left this world, and it stayed that way until Rivka married Yitzhak and brought the *berakha* back.

Avraham wanted presents: to teach the world and to future generations, forever, that what he received was due to his wife Sarah. May we always show great appreciation to our spouse, our partner in life, and together partake in the blessings that Hashem has in store for us.[3]

---

3. See Rambam, *Hilkhot Ishut* 15:19–20 for an idyllic description of the relationship between a husband and wife.

Avoiding Disputes

וגם ללוט ההלך את אברם היה צאן ובקר ואהלים. ולא נשא אתם הארץ
לשבת יחדו כי היה רכושם רב ולא יכלו לשבת יחדו. ויהי ריב בין רעי
מקנה אברם ובין רעי מקנה לוט... ויאמר אברם אל לוט אל נא תהי מריבה
ביני וביניך ובין רעי ובין רעיך כי אנשים אחים אנחנו. (בראשית יג:ה-ח)

And Lot, who went with Abram, also had flocks and cattle and
tents. And the land did not bear them to dwell together, for their
possessions were many, and they could not dwell together. And
there was a quarrel between the herdsmen of Abram's cattle and
between the herdsmen of Lot's cattle... And Abram said to Lot,
"Please let there be no quarrel between me and between you and
between my herdsmen and between your herdsmen, for we are
kinsmen." (*Bereshit* 13:5–8)

We are told that due to the abundant cattle that belonged to Avraham
and Lot, a disagreement broke out among their shepherds regarding
the territory. Rashi on this verse explains that the argument among the
shepherds was over Lot's shepherds allowing their animals to graze on
any land, while Avraham's shepherds protested that such activity was
stealing and thus forbidden. Lot's shepherds argued that the land was
given to Avraham, but because Avraham had no descendants, the land
belonged to Lot, as he was the next of kin.

To avoid the disagreement leading to a dispute, Avraham suggested that Lot choose a location in which to settle, and Avraham would head in the opposite direction.

The Alshikh identifies a nuance and asks why the word for dispute changes between *pasuk* 7 and *pasuk* 8. In the first *pasuk,* the term used is *riv*, while in the second *pasuk,* the term used is *meriva*. What is the difference between a *riv* and a *meriva*?

The Alshikh, quoted in *Sefer Lehitaneg BeTaanugim,*[1] explains that whenever we get into an argument with someone else, there is a cause or a reason for the argument. It may not be a good reason, but there is something upon which to place blame. Once the argument starts, however, it is often blown out of proportion, and both sides start adding fuel, throwing in details and events that occurred in the past that have nothing to do with the argument at hand. The argument starts out as a little thing, but then both sides keep adding more and more, and it blossoms in a terrible way, until both parties are suddenly arguing about anything and everything. That's what *mahloket* causes.

That is why the dispute between Avraham and Lot is originally called a *riv*, which is the masculine form of the word. But once it expands and multiplies, the feminine form, *meriva*, is used to symbolize the reproduction of the *mahloket*.

That's what Avraham was saying to Lot. Right now, it is a *riv,* a small dispute between our shepherds. Let's do what we can now to prevent having this dispute snowball into something much larger.

The *Sefer HaHinukh*[2] suggests a simple yet very challenging way for us to diffuse many disputes and even prevent our getting to the stage of *meriva*. In the context of helping strategize how to not violate the sin of revenge, *nekama,* he suggests that all Jews live in two realms: object and subject. We are subjects with free choice, and we will be rewarded and punished for each of our decisions. But we are also objects, recipients of whatever is out of our control. If we miss the bus or are insulted, the perpetrator as a subject will be punished, but as an object, we must accept that this was an act that was destined to happen. Hashem used

---

1. Y. Greenboim, *Lehitaneg BeTaanugim* (Jerusalem, 2016), 32.
2. *Sefer Hahinukh*, Mitzva 247.

the other individual as a vehicle through which this act was to transpire. This is a very challenging task, but if we really condition ourselves, we can even prevent ourselves from *riv* and *meriva*.[3]

In *Pirkei Avot,* there is a distinction between a dispute for the sake of heaven, *mahloket leshem shamayim,* and a dispute that is not for the sake of heaven, *mahloket shelo leshem shamayim.* A *mahloket leshem shamayim* is the *mahloket* between Hillel and Shammai. An example of a *mahloket shelo leshem shamayim* is the *mahloket* of Korah and his band.[4]

How can one tell when a dispute is *leshem shamayim*? If you are upset at the *situation* and not the *person,* it is *leshem shamayim.* Hillel and Shammai argued quite often, but it was not personal. They argued in order to reach the truth. They were not angry at each other.

In the Gemara, Torah scholars are called *baalei trisin,* those who wield shields:

א"ל המתן עד שיכנסו, בעלי תריסין לבית המדרש (ברכות כז:)

He said to the other, wait until they enter, the *baalei trisin,* into the *beit midrash.* (Berakhot 27b)

Rav Kook in *Ein Aya*[5] explains that a *tris* is a shield. Sages don't win arguments by merely finding fault in the other side's argument; rather, they do so by defending, shielding, their position. When one seeks the truth, he does not need to attack another. However, he must be able to defend his ideals and beliefs.

---

3. I heard from Rabbi Mayer Twersky that this is also the hidden meaning of Yosef's calming words to his brothers when he assured them that he was sent to Egypt as part of Hashem's plan (*Bereshit* 45:8): As subjects, yes, you might be culpable, but as objects, I see no grounds for revenge; you were just tools in the hand of God.

4. It is interesting to note that it is not referred to as a *mahloket* between Korah and Moshe, since Moshe was not a party to the dispute. It was only Korah who was arguing.

5. Rav Kook, *Ein Aya,* Berakhot 27b.

We should always do what we can to increase peace and avoid conflicts. As it is stated: תלמידי חכמים מרבים שלום בעולם – Wise men spread peace in the world.[6]

---

6. Berakhot 64a.

Parashat Vayera

Guests Come First

At the beginning of the *parasha*, Avraham sees travelers approaching from afar. He runs toward them and invites them into his tent. He addresses them using the word *adonai*, my master:

ויאמר אדני אם נא מצאתי חן בעיניך אל נא תעבר מעל עבדך.
(בראשית יח:ג)

And he said, "My master, if only I have found favor in your eyes, please do not pass on from beside your servant. (*Bereshit* 18:3)

It is not clear whether this word is a reference to the Almighty (as this is one of the names used to refer to Hashem) or a reference to the three travelers. Rashi offers two explanations. The first answer suggests that Avraham used the word to address the leader of the group. According to this opinion, the word need not be treated as God's name in this case. The second explanation suggests the opposite: Avraham was addressing Hashem, asking Him to wait while he ran to greet the guests. In this case, it must be treated as a holy name.

If we follow the second approach, that Avraham was talking to God, then this *pasuk* is the source for the Gemara in Masekhet Shabbat that states that "hosting guests is greater than receiving the *Shekhina*."[1] Avraham was in the middle of speaking with Hashem, and he interrupted this divine experience in order to greet guests who appeared to simply be traveling merchants.

We learn of the great significance of the mitzva of *hakhnasat orhim* (welcoming guests) from Avraham, but how did Avraham know that he was permitted to leave God's presence in order to fulfill this mitzva? Imagine standing before a king and suddenly ignoring the king's presence to engage in conversation with another individual. It is most disrespectful.

I once heard Rabbi J. J. Schachter answer this question based on a famous Rambam. In his introduction to *Perek Helek* (the last chapter of *Mishna Sanhedrin*), the Rambam lays out the thirteen principles of faith, which later formed the basis for *Ani Maamin*. The seventh principle concerns the prophecy of Moshe Rabbenu, specifically how he was unique and the greatest prophet who ever lived. The Rambam writes that Moshe was the greatest prophet. No one preceding or following him in the history of the world reached his level of prophecy. All of them were at least a notch lower: This is one of the principles of *Ani Maamin*! Moshe was different! He was the chosen one. There was no *mehitza* (wall) between him and the Divine. He was at the highest level of prophecy a human could reach.

The Rambam explains that there were four differences between the level of prophecy of Moshe Rabbenu and all other prophets.

The first difference is that with respect to all other prophets, there was some type of mediation between the prophet and HaKadosh Barukh Hu. They did not speak directly to Hashem, like speaking to a friend. It was more distant. Moshe, however, spoke to Hashem directly, as is stated in *Parashat Behaalotekha*, Hashem spoke with Moshe face to face.

Second, says the Rambam, all prophets, including Avraham, Yehoshua, Eliyahu HaNavi, and Elisha, were asleep or in some type of

---

1. Shabbat 127b.

trance when they received prophecy. But Moshe was awake and completely cognizant during prophecy.

Third, he explains, all prophets other than Moshe would shake, as if from fear, while receiving a prophecy.

The final difference that the Rambam lists is that with respect to all other prophets, Hashem initiated the meeting. It wasn't up to them, and it wasn't their choice if and when a conversation would transpire. Hashem could speak to a prophet once in forty years or a few times. It wasn't the prophet's choice. Moshe, on the other hand, could speak to Hashem at any time he wished, and he could initiate the conversation.

According to this reasoning, we can answer our question regarding Avraham. Moshe was the only one awake during a prophecy, meaning that Avraham Avinu, included among other prophets, was sleeping or in a trance while in conversation with Hashem. Says Rav Schachter: We know Avraham was allowed to leave the *Shekhina*'s presence to greet guests, but how did Avraham know? Well, how did he see the guests if he was in a trance or sleeping? Didn't he lose all of his faculties? It must be that this time was an exception. Usually, he was in a trance while speaking with Hashem, but this time he wasn't, or at least not to the extent that he was unable to see his guests.

Avraham realized this phenomenon and thought: "Why do I see these guests? Why is Hashem giving me the ability to see them while He is speaking with me? It must be that He wants me to see them and care for them."

That's how Avraham understood the importance of *hakhnasat orhim*. May we be *zokhe* to invite, greet, and host guests and fulfill this important mitzva to its maximum.

Another approach to the same question is offered by Rav Wolbe[2] in his commentary on the Humash:

> How could Avraham leave the presence of Hashem in order to welcome guests? Isn't there a principle that if one is performing a mitzva, he is exempt from other mitzvot? Isn't our highest goal

---

2. Rav Shlomo Wolbe, *Shiurei Humash* (Jerusalem, 2009), 138.

to bask in the glory of the *Shekhina*? How could Avraham voluntarily forgo remaining in Hashem's presence?

Rav Wolbe suggests the following. What is our goal in life? What is our purpose? Not to bask in the glory of Hashem, but rather to be an *oved Hashem,* servant of Hashem. If I am a good *eved,* servant, then I will be worthy of being close to the *Shekhina* in the next world. It is important that we set appropriate priorities in this world. If one is sitting on a bus and learning and an elderly person boards the bus, one should stand up and offer their seat to the elderly person, even if he won't be able to learn as well while he is standing. That is selecting *avdut,* service to Hashem, over all else.

Rav Yisrael Salanter was once reciting the *Shema* when he overheard two individuals from the *hevra kadisha* arguing over who should have the privilege of burying a particular deceased individual. Rav Yisrael Salanter immediately interrupted his *keriat Shema* and ran outside to bury the deceased person. That is what a true *eved Hashem* does. Burying the dead takes precedence over *keriat Shema* and *kabbalat ol malkhut Shamayim,* accepting the yoke of the kingship of Heaven.

Avraham recognized that when faced with a choice of doing an act of *hesed* by serving as an *eved Hashem* or remaining in the presence of Hashem, the former was the proper choice.

Genuine Hospitality

וירא אליו ה' באלני ממרא והוא ישב פתח האהל כחם היום. וישא עיניו
וירא והנה שלשה אנשים נצבים עליו וירא וירץ לקראתם מפתח האהל
וישתחו ארצה. (בראשית יח:א ב)

Now Hashem appeared to him in the plains of Mamre, and he
was sitting at the entrance of the tent when the day was hot. And
he lifted his eyes and saw, and behold, three men were standing beside him, and he saw and he ran toward them from the
entrance of the tent, and he prostrated himself to the ground.
(*Bereshit* 18:1–2)

The opening *pesukim* in this *parasha* depict how Avraham was sitting at
the entrance to his tent seeking travelers whom he could invite inside,
when he suddenly *saw* three individuals approaching. The word *vayar*,
he saw, appears twice. The first time it means simply that he saw, and
the second instance implies that he understood. He understood that
these individuals were in need of hospitality. Despite recuperating from
his *brit mila*, Avraham ran to greet them and invite them into his home.

As we know, this is the source in the Torah for the mitzva of
hakhnasat orhim.

Avraham wasn't the only one in this *parasha* who performed the
mitzva of *hakhnasat orhim*. In the next chapter, we find Lot performing

this mitzva when he invites the angels who came to Sodom into his home. Lot later takes extreme measures to protect these angels from attempted assault by the malicious people of Sodom.

Why do *Hazal* emphasize and magnify the *hakhnasat orhim* of Avraham, yet they hardly comment on Lot's hospitality?

Rabbi Levi Yitzchak of Berditchev, cited in *Lahazot BeNoam Hashem*,[1] suggests the following:

Both Avraham and Lot engaged in *hakhnasat orhim*, but there is a qualitative difference in the way each of them performed this mitzva. When describing Lot's actions, the *pasuk* says, "The two angels came toward Sodom."[2] Here, they are explicitly identified as *malakhim*, angels, whereas with respect to Avraham, they were called *anashim*, men. Rabbi Levi Yitzchak explains that Avraham thought they were men, simple nomads traveling in the desert. Lot saw that his guests were angels – important, dignified individuals – and so he was prepared to host them. Lot performed the mitzva only because he thought they were important people. Avraham, *ish hahesed*, the man of kindness, ran toward his guests even though he thought they were just a group of simple desert wanderers.

The essence of *hakhnasat orhim* is not for our pride or *kavod* – to be able to brag about who we are hosting. It's a great thing to host important figures and rabbis, but the real message of *hakhnasat orhim* is to perform the mitzva even for simple, unfamiliar people who need hospitality.

We have to contemplate this point when we perform mitzvot. How much is our *hesed* really about the recipient, and how much is it about me as the provider? Our *hesed* has to be focused on the recipient and their needs.

There's a story told about Rabbi Levi Yitzchak.[3] Once, he arrived in Lvov and went to the house of one of the wealthy individuals in the city. He requested a room in which he could spend the night. This was in the days before photography, so Rabbi Levi Yitzchak's appearance

---

1. Shaltiel Meir ben Rav Shlomo Hacohen (Jerusalem, 2013), 144.
2. *Bereshit* 19:1.
3. Some ascribe this story to the *Beit HaLevi*.

was not known to all. The wealthy individual apologized and said, "I'm sorry, I don't have room for travelers."

Rabbi Levi Yitzchak pressed, "Just a small room. I won't bother you."

The landlord answered, "I really wish I had room for you, but I have no space. Down the road is a teacher who always finds room for guests in his house." This rich man knew that this schoolteacher would never turn away a stranger.

Rabbi Levi Yitzchak went to the teacher's home and was welcomed with great warmth. After a little while, word got out that Rabbi Levi Yitzchak was in town, and everyone ran over to the teacher's house to catch a glimpse of him. The rich man ran along as well and begged forgiveness. "I didn't know it was you! I wish I had known! I can't believe I turned you away!" he lamented.

Rabbi Levi Yitzchak asked, "How can I grant you *mehila* (forgiveness)? Are '*hakhnasat* Rabbi Levi Yitzchak' and '*hakhnasat orhim*' two different things? The mitzva is to honor the guest, no matter who it may be." We have to learn from Avraham Avinu to respect every Jew, no matter who he is – not just our friends or other familiar people. Obviously, this doesn't mean we have to bring into our homes people who might have a negative spiritual influence on us or our family members. However, we have to look out for other people and realize that the mitzva is about them, not about us.

Humility Coupled with Confidence

ויען אברהם ויאמר הנה נא הואלתי לדבר אל א דני ואנכי עפר ואפר.
(בראשית יח:כז)

"I have just begun to speak to my Master, yet I am dust and ashes."
(*Bereshit* 18:27)

What is the meaning of this *pasuk*? Rav Yosef Soloveitchik explains that
to be a truly humble person requires two ingredients to be ingrained
in us. It is not only awareness of being "dust and ashes." It also requires
saying "I have just begun to speak." In Rav Soloveitchik's words:[1]

> This phrase has become a foundation of our worldview. The hal-
> akha built the laws of modesty on the dichotomy of importance
> and worthlessness. On the one hand, modesty derives from "I
> am aware that I have just begun to speak to the Lord," the con-
> sciousness of man's importance due to his perpetual standing in
> the presence of the Infinite. We must never forget God's constant

---

1. *Humash Masoret HaRav* (New York: OU Press, 2013), 124.

presence, and this knowledge will always give us worth and importance.

Often, we believe that self-worth and self-confidence are antitheses of humility. However, being a humble person doesn't mean we think we are nothing and can't accomplish anything in life. That is not humility, because if it was, Moshe would not have accomplished anything in his life, and Moshe was *anav mikol adam,* the humblest of all men. If he only believed "I am dust and ashes," he wouldn't have become Moshe Rabbenu.

Moshe and Avraham became great people because they had humility coupled with "I have just begun to speak." They recognized their power and strengths, but they also realized that it all came from Hashem. Every Jew must recognize his *kohot,* strengths, but he must acknowledge that they are all from Hashem.

Rav Tzadok HaKohen of Lublin[2] writes that the ultimate tragedy is not when we don't recognize our faults, but rather when we don't recognize our *strengths:* the potential of what we can accomplish.

Hazal tell us that Aharon HaKohen motivated people to do *teshuva* by being an *ohev shalom verodef shalom,* a lover and pursuer of peace. He used to go over to people just to say hello and befriend them. People became so overwhelmed that Aharon wanted to be their friend that they felt they had to shape up and do mitzvot to be worthy of his companionship.

Knowing that HaKadosh Barukh Hu is my Friend and is always with me, *sheviti Hashem lenegdi tamid,* is the first step of recognition. It means developing self-worth in the presence of Hashem. This is perhaps the hardest aspect of becoming humble, as it means balancing the recognition of my finitude with my relationship with the Infinite. This was the amazing feat of Avraham and Moshe, and it is what we strive to fulfill.[3]

---

2. Rav Tzadok Hacohen of Lublin, *Pri Tzadik* (Jerusalem: Yerid HaHasidut, 2017), 145.
3. On a similar note, there is a well-known *mahloket* between the worldviews of the great *musar yeshivot* Novardok and Slabodka. Novardok believed that man, *adam,* derives his name from *adama,* earth. This point constantly reminds us that we were created from the dirt of the earth. Slabodka believed that *adam* is related to *adame:* "I will resemble" Hashem. This interpretation reminds man that he was created in Hashem's image. Perhaps the resolution of this argument is to combine both of these understandings into a balanced approach, as suggested by Rav Soloveitchik above.

Ethics from Sinai

ויאמר אבימלך אל אברהם מה ראית כי עשית את הדבר הזה ויאמר
אברהם כי אמרתי רק אין יראת אלקים במקום הזה והרגוני על דבר
אשתי. (בראשית כ:יא)

And Abraham said, "For I said, 'Surely, there is no fear of God
in this place, and they will kill me over my wife.'"
(*Bereshit* 20:11)

In this week's *parasha*, we are told of an episode involving King
Avimelekh of Gerar, which parallels a similar, earlier event with the king
of Egypt. In both instances, Avraham informs the locals that Sarah is his
sister rather than his spouse out of fear that he would be killed in order
to enable another to marry his wife. King Avimelekh of Gerar, relying on
Avraham's testimony, takes Sarah into his palace. Immediately, Avimelekh
and his household are stricken with an illness and are informed that it
is a punishment for having taken Avraham's wife. Avimelekh is furious
at Avraham for not admitting to him that Sarah is his wife. Avraham's
response to Avimelekh is: "Surely there is no fear of God in this place;
and they will kill me over my wife."

Rabbi Elchanan Wasserman is puzzled by the inclusion of the word *rak*, only.[1] What is it meant to emphasize? Rabbi Elchanan gave a *derasha* before World War II on this question, and it is quoted in *Lekah Tov*.

Avraham was explaining to Avimelekh that a nation can be so polite and civilized, extremely enlightened and well mannered, but if their behavior is not based on *yirat Shamayim*, fear of God, the people can turn into the most abominable, lowly, and animalistic nation in minutes. That was Rabbi Elchanan's understanding of this *pasuk*.

Avraham was concerned about revealing that Sarah was his wife because people like Avimelekh who have no basis for their manners and societal rules can redefine what is acceptable in society and justify killing someone so that his wife can be permissible to the king.

It goes without saying that what Rabbi Wasserman said at that time proved to be true of the Germans. They may have been considered the most civilized and enlightened people, but history showed how prophetic Rabbi Elchanan's words were.

Perhaps this can be connected to a fundamental thought expressed by Rav Ovadiah of Bartenura.[2] He asks why *Pirkei Avot* begins with a description of the transmission of the Torah from Moshe at Sinai to the time of the *Tanna'im*. This would have been appropriate for the beginning of the first tractate, Masekhet Berakhot, to illustrate the transition from the Written Torah to the Oral Torah, but not for *Pirkei Avot*, which is at the end of *Seder Nezikin* and contains no mitzvot! Rav Ovadiah suggests that this is exactly the point.

It is not necessary to be told that Moshe received the Torah from Sinai at the beginning of Eiruvin or Temura. Where else would such laws come from? One may hypothesize, however, that ethics, such as those that are found in *Pirkei Avot*, are from humans. The grave danger with such a belief is that man can redefine ethical and moral behaviors and adapt them to societal norms. It is critical for us to understand that the ethical and moral precepts of *Pirkei Avot* were God-given, received by

---

1. Rav Yaakov Yisrael Hacohen Bifus, *Lekah Tov* (Rekhasim: TShB"R Harav, 1991), 93. See also, *Kovetz Ma'amarim*, vol. 1 (Jerusalem: Machon Or Elchanan, 2001), 80.
2. *Pirkei Avot* 1:1.

Moshe at Mount Sinai, and transmitted to subsequent generations. These are precepts that cannot be adapted or compromised on. As we have witnessed all too often, leaving morality to be defined by mortal beings can lead to tragedy. When defining moral and ethical principles and behaviors, it is our duty and obligation to answer to a Higher Authority.

The *Akeda*

Akedat Yitzhak was a defining moment in Jewish history and is something we reference in our prayers often, particularly during the period of *selihot* and on Rosh HaShana. It was a very significant event in Avraham's life that had eternal repercussions.

Let us explore various aspects of the *Akeda* to better understand its importance and significance.

Question one: Why is *Akedat Yitzhak* referred to as one of Avraham's *nisyonot*? A mishna in *Pirkei Avot*[1] tells us:

עשרה נסיונות נתנסה אברהם אבינו, ועמד בכולם, להודיע כמה חיבתו
של אברהם אבינו. (פרקי אבות ה:ג)

There were ten tests with which Avraham Avinu was tested, and he passed all ten, to teach us how much he loved Hashem and how much Hashem loved him. (*Pirkei Avot* 5:3)

Why is it called Avraham Avinu's test if Yitzhak was a major player in the event? After all, he was the one being sacrificed. He willingly let himself be roped down! He could have run away. And yet, it's called

---

1. *Pirkei Avot* 5:3.

the test of Avraham Avinu. Even the Torah begins the episode by saying that "Hashem tested Avraham."

Question two: Despite the varying opinions of different *Rishonim* regarding what exactly the ten tests of Avraham were, almost everyone agrees that number ten was the *Akeda*. It was the pinnacle, the highest point one could reach in their *avodat Hashem*. The question is, what exactly did the *Akeda* symbolize? What more did Avraham have to prove to God? He had already jumped into the furnace, already smashed his father's idols (endangering his life by doing so), and risked his life to save Lot. He had seemingly proven himself as a complete servant of Hashem already! What more did he have to prove?

In other words, what was it about the *Akeda* that made it unique? We focus on it so much in our davening, in *selihot*, on Rosh HaShana, on Yom Kippur. The *zekhut* has lasted thousands of years. We're still talking about it centuries later, more than almost any other event in our history! So what exactly was Avraham's battle, and what was his victory?

First let's explore several answers provided by the commentaries with respect to question one: Why is the *Akeda* a greater test for Avraham than for Yitzhak?

MAHARIT: YITZHAK WAS UNAWARE

The Maharit,[2] an early *Aharon* who lived in the 1500s and was the son of the Mabit, suggests that Yitzhak was not aware of what was about to transpire. If he wasn't cognizant of the fact that he was climbing Mount Moria in order to be sacrificed, then it obviously could not be considered a test of his faith.[3]

Avraham Avinu, amazingly, accepted the commandment immediately. He had three days during his journey to the mountain to ponder it, let it sink in, and come up with every excuse not to do it. As we know, the more time we have, the more we usually rationalize why we don't have to do something – whether to get out of a certain responsibility, to push off a dreaded meeting – the more time we have, the more excuses

---

2. Responsa Maharit 2:6.
3. According to Rashi, Yitzhak was aware of what was transpiring, although it is not explicitly mentioned in the Torah.

we are able to conceive. Yet Avraham Avinu didn't change his mind, but kept moving forward to fulfil Hashem's command.

According to the Maharit, the question doesn't really get off the ground. It was Avraham's test and not Yitzhak's because Avraham was the only one who knew about it! Yitzhak only realized what was happening after he was tied down.

MAHATZIT HASHEKEL: HARDER TO LIVE
A LIFE OF KIDDUSH HASHEM

The *Mahatzit HaShekel*, a commentary on the *Magen Avraham* that appears in the *Shulhan Arukh*, suggests a different answer.[4]

Getting burned is painful for a moment – just until the person dies. On the other hand, to slaughter a son, in this case a son for whom Avraham had prayed for a hundred years, would leave behind lifelong pain. Pain for a lifetime is greater than a one-time tragic event. Yitzhak would die, there would be pain, but he would have closure. He would do it. He'd sacrifice his life, and that would be it.

it was possibly a greater test for Avraham because he would have to live with the *Akeda* every single day for the rest of his life. Hashem didn't promise him another son in Yitzhak's place, and that's why Avraham takes center stage in the view of *Hazal*.

Rabbi Bernard Weinberger, in his *sefer Shemen HaTov* (*Mo'adim*), comments on the *pasuk* "Avraham returned to his youths" (*Bereshit* 22:19) and questions what happened after the *Akeda*. It says in the Torah that Avraham went back to his *naarim*, Yishmael and Eliezer, and he casually returned to life. In next week's *parasha*, he buries his wife, takes care of finding a wife for Yitzhak, and so on. Regarding Yitzhak, there is no word of his whereabouts. He disappears until the end of *Parashat Hayei Sara*. Where'd he go? We know from *Hazal* that after the *Akeda*, he went to learn in the *beit midrash* of Shem and Ever.

We can ask the obvious question: Didn't Yitzhak just willingly allow himself to be offered as a sacrifice? What more could he possibly have to learn? What more did he have to accomplish in his life after being *moser nefesh* on an altar like that?

---

4. *Mahatzit HaShekel* on sec. 591.

Yes, it's hard to be *moser nefesh*; however, it's one level to die *al kiddush Hashem*, but it's an even higher level to know how to *live al kiddush Hashem*, day in and day out. To ensure that every action one does is proper and in accordance with the will of Hashem.

We experience *nisyonot* every single day, which is harder than going through a one-time act of *mesirut nefesh*. Yitzhak knew how to die *al kiddush Hashem*. It's much harder to live *al kiddush Hashem*.

HATAM SOFER: INDIRECT COMMAND IS GREATER

The Hatam Sofer offers a third approach, which differs from the previous two, in that he believes Yitzhak's role is more admirable.[5]

If Hashem tells us to do something, we're going to listen. If a *bat kol* comes down from the heavens and commands us to do something, there's no way we're not going to do it. But Yitzhak didn't hear a *bat kol*. Yitzhak willingly went onto the altar and allowed his father to slaughter him because he heard the command from his father, and he believed in him. He had complete *emunat hakhamim*, faith in Torah scholars.

The Hatam Sofer compares Avraham Avinu and Yitzhak Avinu to the Written Torah and the Oral Torah. Avraham Avinu corresponds to the Written Torah, the direct word of Hashem. Yitzhak Avinu, on the other hand, was based on Oral Torah, *emunat hakhamim*, the deepest level of *emuna*. He was willing to sacrifice his life not because Hashem told him directly, but because Avraham told him that was Hashem's request. Yitzhak heard it secondhand. Therefore, the Hatam Sofer believes that the *Akeda* was an even greater test for Yitzhak than for Avraham, who heard the command directly from Hashem.

Our second question was: What was the purpose of the *Akeda*? Why did Hashem have to further test Avraham? What did he still have to prove?

RASHBAM: DON'T RELY ON OTHERS

The Rashbam points to the phrase which introduces the *Akeda*, "after these events," and comments: Wherever the Torah uses the term "after

---

5. Responsa Hatam Sofer, end of *Orah Hayim*.

these events," the subject at hand is directly connected to the previous topic. What preceded the *Akeda*?

Right before the *Akeda*, Avraham entered into a peace treaty with Avimelekh. The *Akeda*, according to the Rashbam's radical view, was a punishment to Avraham Avinu for making a treaty with a non-Jewish king over a piece of *Eretz Yisrael*. "You made a treaty because you're worried about your child's future? Well, now go take him up to the mountain and sacrifice him to Me," said Hashem, so to speak. "I'm in charge of the future. Don't rely on treaties with other nations."

RAMBAN: PERSONAL RECOGNITION OF INNER STRENGTH

The Ramban explains the purpose of the *Akeda* based on his view of *nisyonot* in general. The purpose of a test is for the one being the tested, not the Tester. In other words, Hashem did not need to know anything. He knew Avraham's character, his personality. He knew Avraham was the perfect *eved Hashem*. Hashem of course even knew the end result. So why test Avraham? Hashem provided the *nisayon* because he wanted Avraham to *recognize his own greatness*, to see how much potential he had and how high he could soar to get close to HaKadosh Barukh Hu.

For example, a very difficult teacher might test his students not because he's strict, but to show them how much they know. The students get upset about the exams, but after they take them and pass, they're so surprised and pleased. They are amazed at how much they learned and what they accomplished.[6] Similarly, Hashem knew how great Avraham could be, but he wanted Avraham to know it as well.

RABBENU BAHYA: PORTRAY STRENGTH AND BELIEF TO AVRAHAM'S GENERATION

Rabbenu Bahya agrees with the Ramban that the purpose of the nisayon was not to prove anything to Hashem, but he believes it was

---

6. See the Maharal's explanation of the mishna at the end of Makot, which states that Hashem gave us so many mitzvot in order to give us more opportunities to accrue merit.

not necessarily to prove anything to Avraham either. The purpose of the nisayon was to illustrate to his generation the *gadlut*, greatness, of a *tzaddik*, to show everyone else what one person could do, what level each person can reach.

RADAK: PORTRAY STRENGTH AND
BELIEF TO FUTURE GENERATIONS

The Radak also suggests that it was for other people. But which other people does he mean? The *nisayon* wasn't meant to prove anything to Avraham's generation. After all, how would they have known? If Avraham would have told them, nobody would have believed him! Avraham, the opponent of human sacrifice, the first monotheist, killed his own son? Therefore, it couldn't have been for that generation. Instead, it was for us, the later generations. We believe the story written in the Torah, and we'll learn *ahavat Hashem* from it.

The Irony of the *Akeda*

Many commentators believe that the *Akeda* was one of Avraham Avinu's greatest achievements. To enhance our appreciation of what Avraham encountered, Rav Dessler[1] cites three inherent contradictions within Hashem's command to Avraham to sacrifice his son.

First, Avraham realized that by fulfilling this command he would be uprooting and nullifying every single thing that he had worked for his entire life. He had broken Terah's idols, preached about monotheism, shown people the ethical way to live, taught them to engage in acts of *hesed*, and preached against idolatry. Suddenly, he had to go kill his own child, which completely contradicted his entire outlook and teachings.

Second, the command to perform the *Akeda* went against HaKadosh Barukh Hu's explicit statement that Yitzhak was the fulfillment of the promise that Avraham would have descendants. He finally received his long-awaited son, and then Hashem gave him this command.

Third, the *Akeda* went against his infinite love for Yitzhak.

This *nisayon* was unlike any other. We cannot fathom what it was like for a hundred-year-old man, who had everything except for one thing he so desperately desired, a son, to finally have that child after all that yearning and despair. Avraham waited for *one hundred years*!

---

1. Rav Eliyahu Eliezer Dessler, *Mikhtav Me'Eliyahu*, vol. 4 (Jerusalem, 1991), 190.

We can't even begin to imagine the love he had for Yitzhak! And with each passing year, that love grew. At the time of the *Akeda*, Yitzhak was thirty-seven years old. The father and son had a relationship for thirty-seven years, and then the command came to Avraham to slaughter his son. And yet, Avraham doesn't say a word in protest.

Thus, the *Akeda* represented Avraham giving up his life's work, his understanding of God's promise, and his infinite love for his son. All three challenges make the *Akeda* the most monumental of Avraham's tests.

RAN: "PLEASE" – IT'S YOUR CHOICE

The Ran offers a further insight into the uniqueness of the *Akeda*. The *pasuk* says: קח נא את בנך, "*Please* take your son."[2] Asks the Ran: What is the word "please" (*na*) adding? The Ran notes that *Hazal* suggest in numerous places that *na* introduces a request, not a command. The implication is that there was never a command to sacrifice Yitzhak! Avraham wasn't commanded by Hashem to do it. Hashem only communicated his will to Avraham, and Avraham went ahead and fulfilled it. That one word, says the Ran, teaches us that real love means performing an act for another without being commanded to do so. It's the highest level of love because it shows that you know what the other person wants before they have to ask for it.

And that made the test so much harder, because Avraham performing the *Akeda* wasn't fulfilling a command of Hashem, but just fulfilling a will of Hashem. Avraham could have said, "This one is too tough! I can't do it!" But he didn't. He went ahead with the *Akeda* out of his love for Hashem.[3]

Let us conclude with a final point on one of the most amazing and underappreciated *pesukim* in all the Torah. The *pasuk* says:

וישכם אברהם בבקר. (בראשית כב:ג)

And Avraham woke up early in the morning. (*Bereshit* 22:3)

---

2. *Bereshit* 22:2.
3. The first time that the word *ahava*, love, appears in the Torah is in connection with the *Akeda*.

He got up early in the morning for the *Akeda*. What do we infer from this line? That Avraham Avinu slept the night before the *Akeda*. Often in life, if we have *anything* that we're even a little worried about, we can't sleep the night before. We toss and turn and cannot be relaxed. Yet, Avraham was able to sleep the night before he was scheduled to sacrifice his son, because he knew that it was what Hashem wanted from him.

As we go through life and have our *Akedas*, our *nisyonot*, and we feel like everything is on the line, we have to realize that HaKadosh Barukh Hu knows what's best for us and that He's right there with us. If we have that *emuna*, that belief and trust, then we too will be able to sleep soundly knowing we are in God's hands.

Parashat Hayei Sara

Sarah's Concern
with the *Akeda*

ויהיו חיי שרה מאה שנה ועשרים שנה ושבע שנים שני חיי שרה.
(בראשית כג:א)

And the life of Sarah was one hundred years and twenty years
and seven years; [these were] the years of the life of Sarah.
(*Bereshit* 23:1)

At the beginning of *Parashat Hayei Sara,* we are informed of the death
of Sarah. Although the Torah does not specify the cause of her death,
Rashi derives an explanation based on its juxtaposition to the previous
parasha (*semikhut parshiyot*).

ונסמכה מיתת שרה לעקידת יצחק, לפי שעל ידי בשורת העקידה
שנזדמן בנה לשחיטה וכמעט שלא נשחט, פרחה נשמתה ממנה ומתה.
(רש"י בראשית כג:א)

And this *parasha* follows the *parasha* of the *Akeda,* because hearing the news of her son almost being slaughtered caused her death.
(Rashi on *Bereshit* 23:1)

After hearing that Yitzhak was almost slaughtered on Mount Moria, Sarah dies from severe shock.

Asks Rabbi Moshe Sternbuch:[1] It seems a bit surprising that Sarah, who was considered such a *tzadeket*,[2] would have such a reaction. How are we meant to understand this reaction?

Rabbi Sternbuch suggests an idea based on an insight from the *Maggid Meisharim*, a *sefer* written by the Beit Yosef, Rabbi Yosef Karo.[3]

Rabbi Karo writes that the *Maggid* promised that he, Rabbi Karo, would merit *a death al kiddush Hashem*. At the end of his days, Rabbi Karo wondered why it had not happened, and he was upset that he couldn't fulfill *bekhol nafshekha* by giving his life to sanctify Hashem's name.

The *Maggid* replied, "You were *zokhe* to a higher calling for the end of your life: that of living *al kiddush Hashem*." Dying *al kiddush Hashem* takes one moment in time, but to keep living *al kiddush Hashem*, every single day, that is an even higher level then sacrificing one's life in a moment *al kiddush Hashem*.

We can apply this idea to why Sarah was upset over Yitzhak's near death: Sarah was in shock that her son was almost not able to live *al kiddush Hashem*, which is a higher level than dying *al kiddush Hashem*.

Based on this idea, perhaps we can understand why Avraham did not consult with or share the news of the *Akeda* with Sarah. Maybe Avraham thought that Sarah would daven for Yitzhak to remain alive so he could live a life *al kiddush Hashem*. Avraham, however, with his simple faith, just wanted to fulfill the wish of Hashem and perform the *Akeda*.[4]

---

1. Rabbi Moshe Sternbuch, *Taam VeDaat* (Bnei Brak, 1983), 95.
2. *Hazal* tell us that Sarah's level of prophecy was even greater than that of Avraham. See Rashi on *Bereshit* 21:12.
3. Rabbi Yosef Karo was also the author of the *Shulhan Arukh* and *Beit Yosef*. The *sefer Maggid Meisharim*, written in Aramaic, is compiled of conversations Rabbi Karo had with a *malakh*, angel. Every night when Rabbi Karo went to sleep, he would pose to the *malakh* all of his questions from the day. In the morning, he would write down all the answers.
4. See *Parashat Vayera* for a further discussion on this point.

The Circle of Life

As we open up this week's *parasha*, we detect a sharp contrast between *Parashat Vayera* and *Parashat Hayei Sara*. In *Parashat Vayera*, unbelievable, cosmic, world-changing events occurred, whirlwinds that would make headlines. Angels visited Avraham, Sodom was destroyed, Lot's wife turned to salt, and Avraham nearly sacrificed his son. Each awesome event made an impression on the entire world.

Then comes *Parashat Hayei Sara*, which seems to deal with very different events. In contrast to *Parashat Vayera*, this *parasha* does not deal with earth-shattering events. Avraham buries Sarah and seeks to find a wife for Yitzhak – down-to-earth, everyday activities.[1] Yes, obviously there were miracles, like Eliezer's *kefitzat haderekh* when traveling to Haran and the water rising up to Rivka, but in contrast to *Vayera*, the types of occurrences are drastically different. The events in *Parashat Vayera* would never happen to us. Fire and brimstone raining down on a city like in Sodom? The *Akeda*? *Malakhim* coming for a meal? These things don't happen in every generation. The stories in *Hayei Sara*, conversely, are not dramatic like those recounted in *Parashat Vayera*.

---

1. There are some commentaries that even refer to this as a *nisayon* for Avraham. After being on such a spiritual high, he had to deal with the mundane negotiation with Efron the Hittite over a burial plot.

What's the message of the juxtaposition of these two *parshiyot*? Rav Adin Steinsaltz suggests the following.[2]

Throughout our lives, we experience hectic times that require a lot of effort, action and physical and emotional strength, while at other times, life is quiet, peaceful and even boring. No matter which life cycle we are experiencing, we need to serve HaKadosh Barukh Hu to the best of our ability.

There's one lifecycle that is full of extremes, on a personal level and a national level. For example, Tishrei is an extreme time period: There are *selihot*, Rosh HaShana, *Aseret Yemei Teshuva, Tzom Gedalya,* Yom Kippur, and Sukkot. Something is always happening, and emotions take a front seat. We often experience a spiritual high during this period. Similarly, on a personal level, we all have moments of excitement and of *simha,* and God forbid, sometimes the opposite. We experience emotional ups and downs. That's one lifecycle type.

The second type of life cycle is that of the day to day, when things are routine and seem uneventful. There are always bumps in the road, but they can be little speed bumps. These are days with no major detours: just life as usual.

Even the cycle of the year can follow this rule. For example, in the spring and summer, life is busy. From Passover, it's exciting: Passover, *Sefirat HaOmer, Pesah Sheini, Lag BaOmer,* Shavuot. Then the High Holy Days: Rosh HaShana, Yom Kippur, Sukkot, Shemini Atzeret, and Simhat Torah. Then, suddenly, as winter approaches, things quiet down and Marheshvan enters.

On an individual level, we waver between these two types. Sometimes we are extremely busy and preoccupied with significant events, and at other times, we continue with our uneventful daily routine.

These are the different stages and time periods of our life, and they parallel *Parashat Vayera* and *Parashat Hayei Sara. Parashat Vayera* represents the extreme events and feelings, while *Parashat Hayei Sara* signifies the day-to-day activities. We have to realize, though, that the extremes go in both directions. Life is like a seesaw. Sometimes, if we have a big high, we swing the other way right afterward. Sometimes

---

2. Rav Adin Steinsaltz, *Hayei Olam* (Jerusalem: Maggid Books, 2011), 43.

we feel empty after a Yom Tov ends, or after a family *simha,* or perhaps even after Shabbat, because we have to return to our normal work week.[3]

In life, we must recognize that there are sometimes *Parashat Hayei Sara* days, and other days are *Parashat Vayera* days. Sometimes, we are on a high, and at other times, we are going with the flow. Our duty is to fulfill our mission as an *oved Hashem* in both situations. We have to make the day to day exciting and to try to normalize extreme events. Avraham flourished in both scenarios, and we should emulate his example.

---

3. *Arukh HaShulhan, Orah Hayim* 297:1, states that we use spices at Havdala because our *neshama* feels let down after Shabbat.

Making Every Day Count

ואברהם זקן בא בימים וה' ברך את אברהם בכל. (בראשית כד:א)

And Abraham was old, advanced in days, and Hashem blessed Abraham with everything. (*Bereshit* 24:1)

What do the words *ba bayamim* – "advanced in days" – in this *pasuk* mean? Says the midrash:

אמר רבי אחא: יש לך אדם שהוא בזקנה ואינו בימים, בימים ואינו בזקנה, אבל כאן זקנה כנגד ימים וימים כנגד זקנה.

Rav Acha said: You have certain people that are old but don't have days, that have days yet are not old, but here old age and days join together.

Some people have old age, *zikna*, but don't have days, and some have days, but don't have *zikna*. Avraham had both. What does that mean, and what message is the midrash trying to give us?

The *Sefer Peninei HaTorah*[1] quotes the following intense yet insightful *mashal*, which is cited in various *sefarim*:

A man went to a very distant city where every person was a tremendous *yirei Shamayim*. He went all around the city and visited the holy places and the cemetery. While he was in the cemetery, he noticed something strange about all the gravestones. On the stones was written the age of the deceased, which is unusual, as gravestones usually just list the date of the death or *yahrzeit*, and sometimes, perhaps, the date of birth. But the strangest part was how young the ages were: Not a single stone said an age over forty years old. He was very curious about this oddity. "Is this a city that consumes its inhabitants?" he wondered. "I myself saw old people here!" He ran back to the elders of the city and asked, "What's going on? In the cemetery, no one lived over forty, but all of you look much older." The head of the *Hevra Kadisha* answered him: "The *minhag* of our town is to record only the years that we were servants of Hashem. We write on the *kever* the amount of time that we served HaKadosh Barukh Hu, because, after all, what are we here for? To be *ovdei Hashem*." They record only the "net" not "gross" years, representing the actual time they engaged in serving Hashem. Those are the ages written on the gravestones.

Returning to the *pasuk,* we can now understand its wording. Avraham was physically old, *zaken, and* he was *ba bayamim*, which literally means "coming with days." He came with all his days. His days were full. There was no difference between net and gross in Avraham Avinu's life. From the moment he recognized Hashem, every day counted.

The *Peninei HaTorah* then quotes a story from the Hafetz Hayim. Rabbi Naftali Tropp, the *rosh yeshiva* in the yeshiva of Radin, was very sick toward the end of his life. The *talmidim* wanted to do something for him, and they decided to donate some of their life to their ailing *rosh yeshiva*. They went around collecting donations of time from everyone.

---

1. Rav David Hadad, *Peninei HaTorah* (Beer Sheva, 1992), 35.

When they went to the Hafetz Hayim to ask if he would donate time from his life for Rabbi Naftali, he thought a bit and then answered, "One minute." The *talmidim* were stunned. The Hafetz Hayim was willing to donate only a minute?

"Do you know what you can accomplish in a minute?" the Hafetz Hayim explained to them. We need to be productive and be careful not to waste even a minute. Rather, we should make every minute count.[2]

A similar message is derived from a midrash on the first *pasuk*:

רבי עקיבא היה יושב ודורש, והצבור מתנמנם בקש לעוררן, אמר: מה ראתה אסתר שתמלוך על שבע ועשרים ומאה מדינה? אלא תבא אסתר שהיתה בת בתה של שרה, שחיתה מאה ועשרים ושבע, ותמלוך על מאה ועשרים ושבע מדינות. (בראשית רבה נח:ג)

Rabbi Akiva was once giving a shiur when his talmidim began to fall asleep. He wanted to wake them up, so he asked his students: What made Esther think she could rule over 127 countries? He then explained that Esther got the power from Sarah, who lived for 127 years. (*Bereshit Rabba* 58:3)

What exactly is the connection between Sarah's years and Esther's ruling over 127 countries?

Hazal tell us that Torah can only be mastered by those who "kill themselves" and toil to comprehend it. We must work hard and diligently in our pursuit of Torah. Rabbi Akiva was trying to inculcate in his students the value of time. If each year was a country, then each week was a state, each hour a village. When you sleep in shiur, you are missing out on so much. This was a tactic that Rabbi Akiva utilized to portray the value of time.

---

2. Rav Zevin in *LaTorah VeLaMo'adim* on *Parashat Emor* has a similar thought about the value of time. He explains that nothing in the world is eternal, although it may exist for centuries. Time, however, is something that virtually never exists, since a second passes instantaneously. Interestingly, however, we can make time eternal by utilizing it productively. The time we spend attending a *shiur* or conducting an act of *hesed* remains with us forever. See also the section in this *sefer* on *Parashat Noach* called "Using Time Productively."

Rav Chaim Kanievsky is known to make a *siyum Shas* each year before Pesach. One year, he made an additional *siyum Shas* that was not around Pesach, and he showed tremendous happiness at this *siyum*. When his *talmidim* asked him about the additional *siyum* that year, he responded, "This *siyum* I made not by completing *Shas* in a set *seder*, but from all the times I learned while I was sitting and waiting for a bus or at the bank or at the doctor." By not wasting a minute, Rav Kanievsky was able to make an additional *siyum Shas*.

Rabbi Akiva, who taught his *talmidim* the value of time, lived by this principle. *Avot DeRabbi Natan* (6:2), describes how Rabbi Akiva once saw how water made its mark on stones and realized that it was not too late for him to begin to learn Torah. If water can make indentations on the hard surface of the rocks, then Torah can penetrate the human heart. At the age of forty, Rabbi Akiva began to learn the *alef-beit* in a first-grade class and rose to greatness. He realized that it is never too late to accomplish anything. All it takes is perseverance and an ability to utilize time efficiently. This is the individual who internalized the midrash about Sarah's 127 years and Esther's 127 countries.

The Gemara (Avoda Zara 18a) tells the tragic story of Rabbi Hanina ben Teradyon, one of the ten martyrs. Rabbi Chanina was sentenced to death for learning Torah. The Romans wrapped his body in a Torah scroll and set it aflame. They also placed wet wool on his heart to make the fire burn more slowly and increase his pain and agony. Witnessing this catastrophe, Rabbi Hanina's *talmidim* begged him to open his mouth to expedite the end and minimize his suffering. Rabbi Hanina replied that they should be concerned with the Torah and not him. He explained that he saw the words of the Torah rising to the heavens. The executioner was astonished by Rabbi Hanina's *emuna* throughout this ordeal and asked if he would remove the wool to alleviate the suffering, would he receive a portion in the world to come? Rabbi Chanina responded affirmatively. The executioner immediately removed the wool and then jumped into the flame and died. A *bat kol* was heard asserting that both Rabbi Chanina and the executioner were admitted into the next world. Upon hearing this, Rebbe began to cry, and he said:

יש קונה עולמו בשעה אחת ויש שקונה עולמו בשנים.

There are those who are worthy of meriting the world to come in an hour and others that must work to achieve it over years.

Rebbe now realized the power of a moment. How careful we need to be to maximize our productivity in every moment!

The Eleventh Trial

Parashat Hayei Sara begins with the death of Sarah and with Avraham's eulogy and weeping. This account comes on the heels of the *Akeda*, and Rashi makes the connection between the end of *Parashat Vayera* and the beginning of *Parashat Hayei Sara*. Her death, Rashi says, was caused by the news that her son was on the altar and he had almost been killed.

According to most *Rishonim*, the *Akeda* was the pinnacle of Avraham's life. It was the tenth test, after which Hashem said, "Now I know you are a *yarei Elokim*."[1] However, there are some *Rishonim* who claim that Avraham's tests didn't end there. There was one more *nisayon* – that of burying Sara.

Rav Dessler teaches us a lesson that should serve as a message to us every day of our life.[2] First, we have to fix our *middot,* and only then can the Torah rest properly upon us. If someone learns a lot of Torah but doesn't exemplify proper *middot*, the Torah cannot rest on him, and his Torah will be crooked and warped because there's no appropriate receptacle within which the Torah may reside. The way to strive in Torah, says Rav Dessler, is through proper *middot*. And this is how we learn which was the greatest test experienced by Avraham.

---

1. *Bereshit* 22:12.
2. Rav Eliyahu Eliezer Dessler, *Mikhtav Me'Eliyahu*, vol. 4 (Jerusalem, 1991), 245.

What was his greatest test? The *Akeda* was number nine. The tenth was his return from the *Akeda* to find his wife dead. Imagine the emotional rollercoaster that Avraham experienced. He had three days as he walked up the mountain to rehash the thought that he was about to kill his son. Then, he arrived and had to tie up his beloved son. He lifted the knife, the tears streamed from his eyes, and the *malakh* stopped him at the last second. His emotions were at a climax, and then they were abruptly interrupted. He returned home, only to find that Sarah was no longer there, or anywhere. She had died while he was gone. And he may have felt that it was his fault and because of what Hashem told him to do.

On top of this turbulent whirlwind of emotions, Avraham then had to go through the whole process with Efron the trickster, who appeared helpful in the beginning, but then changed his colors. He went through all this just to bury Sara.

When Avraham Avinu approached Efron to purchase Me'arat HaMakhpela and then had to deal with his trickery, Sarah was newly deceased. Her body lay before Avraham, awaiting burial. Imagine his pain and anguish at that moment. Yet, despite everything he was going through, Avraham acted toward Efron and the Hittites with the utmost respect. His *middot* were exemplary.

We learn from Avraham Avinu that just because we're having a bad day, doesn't mean we have the right to spread it to those around us. Our face is a public space (a *reshut harabim*) and one is prohibited from placing a stumbling block in a *reshut harabim*.

Avraham was having a more emotional day than maybe anyone in history ever had, and even so, he acted cool, calm, and collected with the Hittites, even though he knew they weren't very straight and forthright.

We have to learn from Avraham the way in which *bnei Torah* must act. Even if we are going through a difficult or challenging time, we have to be careful not to take it out on others. Always treat others with the proper respect and patience.

His Will Comes First

ויבא אברהם לספד לשרה ולבכתה. (בראשית כג:ב)

Abraham came to eulogize Sarah and to bewail her. (*Bereshit* 23:2)

The *pasuk* states: Avraham *came* to eulogize Sarah and weep for her. The Torah does not explicitly mention from where Avraham came.

A midrash posits that Avraham came from Mount Moria, from the *Akeda*.

This midrash seems to ignore several *pesukim* that appear between the *Akeda* and *Parashat Hayei Sara*. At the end of *Parashat Vayera*, we are told that Avraham returned to Be'er Sheva. The *parasha* then ends with Rivka's birth. It appears that Avraham wasn't coming straight from Mount Moria to bury Sarah. He was coming from Be'er Sheva, as the *pasuk* relates![1]

---

1. The Hizkuni suggests that Avraham came from Be'er Sheva, although Sarah was in Hevron, for the following two reasons: First, Avraham didn't want Sarah to be in the house the morning he left for the *Akeda*, so he sent her to Hevron and told her he would meet her there and bring with him all of their belongings. Second, Sarah was ill, so she went to Hevron for the fresh mountain air.

Perhaps the intention of the midrash is to express that the act that Avraham was about to do was a continuation of the act he performed at the *Akeda.*

SHALHEVET YOSEF: FROM WHERE
DID AVRAHAM ARRIVE

Another thought on the same *pasuk* with respect to identifying from where Avraham came to eulogize Sarah appears in *Shalhevet Yosef*[2] (a book written by a talmid of Rav Ovadia Yosef), which quotes a midrash in *Yalkut Shimoni* that provides a different perspective.

The midrash cites two opinions: Rav Levi suggests that Avraham was coming from burying his father, Terah. Rav Yosi disagrees, since there was at least a two-year gap between Terah's death and Sara's death. So how could Avraham have been returning from burying Terah? Rav Yosi offers an alternative solution, suggesting that Avraham was returning from the *Akeda*, from Mount Moria. There is thus a *makhloket* in the midrash regarding whether Avraham came from burying Terah or from the *Akeda.*

The *Shalhevet Yosef* cites Rav Shach's explanation of this *makhloket.* The midrash is not providing geographical suggestions, nor is it suggesting an actual location from which Avraham departed. Rather, the midrash is focusing on the content of the eulogy. Which attributes of Sarah were the main focus in Avraham's eulogy? Where was he coming from? Which facet of Sara's amazing life was Avraham going to focus on in his eulogy of her?

Rav Levi's opinion that Avraham was coming from burying Terah symbolizes the following. Burying Terah meant burying that part of Avraham's life. Avraham had originally been an *oved avoda zara.*[3] What gave Avraham the *ko'ah* to see the truth? Of course, it came from within him, but it was also his partner in life, Sarah Imenu, who encouraged his greatness.

---

2. Yosef Hai Siman-Tov, *Shalhevet Yosef* (Jerusalem, 1995), 54.
3. See the Rambam at the beginning of *Hilkhot Avodat Kokhavim.*

Avraham's eulogy, according to this opinion, came from the recognition that so much of what he was able to achieve in life was because of his wife. His eulogy focused on the burial of Terah, which symbolized the burial of Avraham's past. This is similar to the famous story of Rabbi Akiva, where he attributed all of his and his *talmidim's* Torah to his wife.

Rav Yosi offers a different view and suggests that Avraham was arriving from Mount Moria, from the *Akeda*. What's the message of Rav Yosi's approach? What does Sarah have to do with the *Akeda*?

Says Rav Shach: The *Akeda* was only able to happen, and Avraham and Yitzhak were able to pass the test of the *Akeda*, only because of Sara's influence throughout their earlier years. How did Yitzhak, this robust young man, have the courage and strength to literally stretch out his neck for Hashem, the strength to willingly sacrifice his life? Because of the upbringing he received from his mother. Sarah was the one who protected Yitzhak from Yishmael's influence by having him removed from their home. The greatest litmus test of a parent's success, says Rav Shach, is what the children become. Which angle did Avraham focus on in his praise to Sarah? The *Akeda*, which symbolized the greatness of her child that she nurtured.

Avraham could have spoken about anything: Sara's great righteousness or the fact that she never sinned. But he chose this, her child's greatness, because the success of Yitzhak was so much dependent on her. We see from here how much we have to invest in our children. One of the greatest testimonies to a person is the achievement of his or her children. Avraham surely believed that was one of Sara's greatest contributions.

We can learn from these opinions two important aspects of a relationship. According to Rav Levi, a spouse is there to strengthen and bring out the best in their mate. Based on the opinion of Rav Yosi, a couple must work together to bring out the best in their children. We should try to combine both concepts and do the utmost to facilitate enabling our spouse to be the best they can be, while working with our spouse to provide the proper education and establish the ideal environment for our children so they can flourish and grow as God-fearing *bnei Torah*.

On this same *pasuk* the *Be'er Yosef*[4]adds a further question. From the *pesukim,* it seems as though Avraham acted in the opposite manner of how we would have expected. Usually, as soon as a person dies, there's an immediate cry: an emotional, uncontrollable weeping. After that comes the eulogy, the intellectual evaluation of the relatives trying to capture into words the life and values of the deceased. Here, it's the opposite: The *pasuk* says Avraham first eulogized her and then cried, and even his crying was muted, as we know from the way the word is written in the Torah with a small "כ". Let's explore several opinions regarding Avraham's behavior.

BE'ER YOSEF: OVERCOMING NATURAL REACTION

The *Be'er Yosef* explains: Why are there normally three days of weeping and seven of eulogy when someone passes away? Initially, when a close relative or friend dies, a person feels the pain of the emotional and physical bond being severed. After that feeling of weeping, once things calm down somewhat, then the mourners are ready to offer a eulogy on behalf of the deceased.

Avraham Avinu, on the other hand, was able to overcome his natural emotions because he realized what had to be done for the nation at this point: He had to buy Me'arat HaMakhpela.

Avraham conquered the natural reaction of crying out in pain upon experiencing the loss of a loved one so he could engage in the acquisition of her burial site.

Asks the *Be'er Yosef*: What happened at the *Akeda*? The same thing! Avraham overcame his natural feelings of love for his son in order to follow the word of Hashem. When the *pasuk* says that Avraham came from Mount Moria, it means he came from the same place *figuratively.* Just like at Mount Moria, when he conquered his natural inclinations in order to follow the word of Hashem, here too, he knew what the word of Hashem was: He had to bury his wife. He had to be in control of himself to deal with Efron the trickster. Once Sarah had been buried, he would have his time to mourn.

---

4. Rav Yosef Salant, *Be'er Yosef* (Jerusalem, 2009), 67.

Avraham overcame his natural reaction in order to fulfill what had to be done at that time.

KEHILLAT YAAKOV: NO REGRETS

The Kehillat Yaakov (cited in *Lekah Tov*)[5] suggests another explanation for why Avraham first eulogized and then cried:

Just as an act of *teshuva* wipes out a transgression, so too, if one regrets having performed a mitzva, it nullifies the act of the mitzva. When we perform mitzvot, we experience two *nisyonot*. Initially, the *Satan* tries to prevent us from performing the mitzva. If he is unsuccessful, then he tries somehow to make us regret having fulfilled the mitzva due to a negative result connected to the performance thereof (loss of money, another opportunity, etc.).

The *Satan* was unable to prevent Avraham from fulfilling the *Akeda*, so he then tried to get Avraham to regret having performed the *Akeda*, since that was the cause of Sara's death (as the midrash states). To show that Avraham did not at all regret having fulfilled this mitzva, he first gave the eulogy and only later cried. Had he cried immediately, it may have been perceived as regret for having performed the *Akeda*.

Perhaps that is also why the word *velivkota* (to cry) is written in the Torah with a small "כ": to highlight that the crying was minimized and secondary. His main concern was to speak of her good deeds and only thereafter to cry over the loss of his wife. That crying was in no way to be interpreted as remorse over having fulfilled the mitzva of the *Akeda*, which caused her death.

Sometimes we work so hard to fulfill a mitzva and then not even realize a negative connotation that we associate with that mitzva. For example, when there is a three-day Yom Tov, we work so hard to prepare for it so that everyone can enjoy it together. Then, we complain about how difficult it is. We can't let the *Satan* win after all our hard work. It is not enough to fulfill the mitzvot. We have to be happy that we fulfilled them as well.

---

5. Rav Yaakov Yisrael Hacohen Bifus, *Lekah Tov* (Tasher Harav, 1991), 107.

NETZIV: MOURNING THE LOSS OF THE MASSES

The Netziv[6] suggests that since Avraham arrived from a distant location, the crowds had already gathered in anticipated of Sara's funeral and so Avraham had no time to engage in personal mourning. He had to immediately proceed to eulogize his wife before the awaiting crowd. Perhaps we can add, that Avraham considered that Sara was like a mother to many and so he addressed their sorrow prior to his own in order to comfort them.

---

6. Naftali Tzvi Yehuda Berlin, *Haamek Davar, Bereshit* 23:2.

Learning from Eliezer's Example

The Torah dedicates sixty-seven *pesukim* to describe Eliezer's mission to obtain a wife for Yitzhak. Rashi (*Bereshit* 24:42) is bothered by how much press is given to this event and by the fact that it's not only written once, but twice. The whole incident is written in the Torah as it occurred, and it's repeated in its entirety with slight changes when Eliezer reported what happened to Lavan. Rashi quotes:

אמר רבי אחא יפה שיחתן של עבדי אבות לפני המקום מתורתן של
בנים, שהרי פרשה של אליעזר כפולה בתורה, והרבה גופי תורה לא
נתנו אלא ברמיזה... (רש"י בראשית כד:מב)

Rav Aha says: The conversation of the servants of our forefathers are greater before Hashem than the Torah of later generations, which is derived from the fact the conversation with Eliezer is repeated and much of the Torah was provided with hints. (Rashi on *Bereshit* 24:42)

Rashi quotes a statement by *Hazal* that the ordinary conversations of the servants of the *avot* are greater than the Torah of the later generations. As proof, our *parasha* is mentioned, where Eliezer's conversation is repeated. What exactly is the message that *Hazal* are trying to convey here?

Rabbi Aharon Kotler suggests that the reason the *pesukim* tell us so much about what Eliezer thought, what he did, and what he said is because there's so much *derekh eretz* and *middot* that we can learn from the event.[1] It therefore had to be lengthy and detailed. He explains that when it comes to halakha, the Torah can be concise. But in matters of character it is much harder to get a handle on what to do in every situation. When I wake up in the morning, I know I have to put on my *tzitzit* and *tefillin*. I have to *daven* and make *berakhot*. But when I meet my friend on the street, how do I approach him? What am I supposed to say? It's not always so clear when it comes to *derekh eretz*, to acting outside the world of formal mitzvot. It's a much grayer area.

Says Rabbi Aharon Kotler: That's why the Torah has to spend so much more time on this topic. When it comes to *middot* and *derekh eretz*, we need more input, more teaching – and it's still not enough.

Every single situation calls for different behavior. Just from this one story of Eliezer searching for a wife for Yitzhak, we learn so many varied ideas and *middot*. We learn who is worthy of being one of our matriarchs: one who embodies *hesed*. We learn about *hashgaha* from Eliezer's deep belief that HaKadosh Barukh Hu would help him. We see how Eliezer listened to Avraham and followed his command even though he had his own daughter who he'd hoped would marry Yitzhak. We learn modesty from how Rivka got off her camel. There's so much *musar* and *middot* and *derekh eretz* in this *perek*! Let us delve deeper into this idea.

FIND A MENTOR

Areas outside the world of formal mitzvot also need to be governed by a Torah perspective, which is not always so simple. That is exactly why the Gemara says in Berakhot[2] that serving, apprenticing, and being around a *rebbe* (*shimush*), is greater than Torah study. Just being in a car together with a *rebbe* is sometimes more valuable than listening to three hours of a shiur, because even the everyday speech of a rabbi is so powerful.

---

1. Rabbi Aharon Kotler, *Mishnat Rav Aharon* (Israel, 2001), 50.
2. Berakhot 6b.

I heard in the name of Rav Yosef Soloveitchik that the Gemara (Berakhot 47b) defines what an uneducated person, an *am ha'aretz*, is according to halakha. We're not talking about the colloquial, derogatory term. Rather, in the days of the Gemara, there was someone who was officially classified as an *am ha'aretz*. It was an important distinction to make, since in some cases they couldn't be trusted with certain mitzvot. They couldn't be part of a *zimun*, for example.

The Gemara provides a number of opinions as to the definition of an *am ha'aretz*. One opinion is that an *am ha'aretz* is someone who doesn't recite *Shema*. He is not accepting the yoke of the kingship of Heaven, and that's a stain on his *neshama*. Rav Yehoshua suggests it is someone who doesn't wear *tefillin*. Ben Azzai said that it is a person who doesn't wear *tzitzit*. Rav Natan explains that an *am ha'aretz* is someone who doesn't have a mezuza on his doorpost. These are major mitzvot. We can understand that people who reject these fall into the category of an *am ha'aretz*.

Rav Natan bar Yosef argues that an *am ha'aretz* is a person who has children and doesn't give them a Jewish education. The mitzva of be fruitful and multiply doesn't end at birth. It starts at birth. The mitzva is to raise *bnei Torah*, not just to have children.

The last opinion brought in the Gemara suggests that an *am ha'aretz* is someone who may even sit and learn three *sedarim* a day, but he has not served a *rebbe*. Rav Soloveitchik explains: One can know every mitzva and every halakha and every halakhic explanation of the *Shulhan Arukh*, but if he doesn't have a *rebbe* to know how to apply it, then he could very well be an *am ha'aretz*.

DO WHAT IS RIGHT AND GOOD

The Ramban comments on the *pasuk* in *Parashat Va'ethanan*:

ועשית הישר והטוב בעיני ה' למען ייטב לך ובאת וירשת את הארץ
הטבה אשר נשבע ה' לאבתיך. (דברים ו:יח)

Do what is right in the eyes of Hashem, so that you shall experience goodness, and inherit the land of Israel that was promised to your forefathers. (*Devarim* 6:18)

The Torah tells us to do what is right and good in the eyes of Hashem. The Ramban asks: The Torah gives us 613 mitzvot to do; isn't this *pasuk* superfluous? What can it possibly be adding? Just do the mitzvot! Isn't that all Hashem wants?

The Ramban explains that it is impossible for the Torah to detail how we should act in every single situation. The Torah can't delineate every possible scenario in business, in personal relationships, and in life in general. At times, it is not so clear to us how to act. Therefore, the Torah provides us with basic guidelines – 613 of them. We are commanded to follow these, and if a situation arises that's not clearly covered by these 613 mitzvot, a person should apply what they think should be done in such cases. Determine what the proper mode of action is in the given situation.

One can even think: "If my *rebbe* were here, would I be doing this, watching that, saying this?" Imagine your *rebbe* in the room with you. We all have to have that *rebbe*, like Yosef HaTzaddik had his father. That's what it means to do the "right and the good." This is the proverbial "fifth" section of *Shulhan Arukh*.

Rav Shlomo Zalman Auerbach was particularly meticulous about attending the wedding of any orphan or a widow, however far it was.[3] Once, a couple got married, and both the *hatan* and *kallah* were orphans. Rav Shlomo Zalman was very involved in the wedding, which took place in Tel Aviv. After the wedding, to the surprise of everyone, Rav Shlomo Zalman did not return to Jerusalem, where he lived, but rather slept over in Tel Aviv, which was very, very unusual for him. Nobody understood why.

Years later, the rabbi who had accompanied Rav Shlomo Zalman that night was involved in the wedding of an orphan, and Rav Shlomo Zalman called him over to tell him something. Said Rav Shlomo Zalman, "Do you remember years ago, when I slept over in Tel Aviv after a wedding?" "Yes," replied the rabbi. "I'll tell you why I did that, because I want you to be cognizant of a crucial sensitivity. What happens the day after a wedding? The *hatan* and *kallah* begin to open all their presents,

---

3. Eliyahu Nave, *Hiko Mamtakim*, vol. 1 (Jerusalem, 2008), 12. This is a collection of stories and *hanhagot* of Rav Shlomo Zalman Auerbach.

and what's the first thing they want to do? They want to run to show their parents the presents they received. Well, this couple's parents were no longer alive. I wanted them to have someone to run to, so I slept over and went there the next day to fill that void for them."

Rav Shlomo Zalman was full of these stories, which show his tremendous greatness not just in abiding by strict halakhic principles, but in exemplary *middot* and *derekh eretz*.

Rabbi Hanoch Teller recounts another story.[4] There was a young woman who lost her husband. She went to Rav Shlomo Zalman to ask where to bury her husband, with his family or with her family. Without batting an eyelash, Rav Shlomo Zalman replied that he should be buried in his family's plot. Why? Because if he would be buried in her family plot, how soon would she get remarried? She would be too stuck on the past, on her first husband, and Rav Shlomo Zalman knew that she had to move on. The woman had to live her life and move forward.

This is why, says Rabbi Aharon Kotler, the Torah spent so much time on the story of Eliezer: because it's not halakha! It's *middot*! It's *derekh eretz*! It's thinking about the other person, even beyond what we would normally think. That can't be explained in shorthand, but only through real-life examples.

---

4. Rabbi Hanoch Teller, *And from Jerusalem: His Word* (Jerusalem, 1991).

Parashat Toledot

Biological and Ethical Offspring

ואלה תולדת יצחק בן אברהם: אברהם הוליד את יצחק. (בראשית
כה:יט)

And these are the generations of Yitzhak the son of Avraham;
Avraham begot Yitzhak. (*Bereshit* 25:19)

This *pasuk* is unusual. It begins as an introduction, ready to list Yitzhak's
toledot, offspring, when it veers off track and mentions that Avraham
fathered Yitzhak. The following *pesukim* return to Yitzhak, his marriage,
and the subsequent birth of his children. Why the repetition of the fact
that Avraham was Yitzhak's father?

Rashi explains this emphasis on Yitzhak's lineage as a hint to their
physical similarity: Avraham and Yitzhak physically resembled each
other so that people would know that Yitzhak was the son of Avraham.
The scoffers of the generation claimed that Sarah had become pregnant
from Avimelekh and that Yitzhak was his child. Yitzhak looked exactly
like Avraham so that people would have no doubt that Avraham was
Yitzhak's father.

Rav Shlomo Zevin,[1] in his classic style, suggests that there are two types of offspring in this world: natural offspring and intellectual offspring. Natural offspring are the biological extension of the father, but intellectual offspring are the logical extension.

Rav Zevin offers two examples of the concept of having a logical extension within a halakhic framework. In Talmudic terms, it is referred to as *avot* and *toledot*. For example, with respect to the prohibitions of Shabbat, the *av melakha* of planting, *zorei'a,* is planting a seed in the ground. A derivative, *tolda,* of *zorei'a* is watering the ground. Does watering the ground flow naturally from the act of seeding? There's nothing natural about that connection. They're two different activities. But logically, there is a connection between the two. The *toledot* in *hilkhot Shabbat* don't flow naturally from the *avot melakha;* rather, they are based on the logic of the *melakha.* You can learn the *tolda* from the *av* because there is a logical connection. This is the logical kind of offspring.

Within the halakhot of impurity, the *toledot* flow more naturally from the *avot,* and the connection is more natural. For example, if A touches B, B becomes impure. When B touches C, C becomes impure. The *av* is so clearly the source of the *tolda.* The "offspring" of the impurity come into existence from the source, like a natural *tolda.*

Rav Zevin applies this idea to people. We have parents, we have ancestors, and we have descendants. We have natural, biological children, and we have halakhic, intellectual descendants. Who are those? Students! If you teach someone Torah, it is as if you are the parent, and the student is your child.

A story is told about an incident that occurred between Rav Shach and Rav Shlomo Zalman Auerbach once at a wedding. Rav Shlomo Zalman was an uncle of the *hatan,* who was learning in Ponovezh. Rav Shach and Rav Shlomo Zalman were arguing over who should be the *mesader kiddushin.* Finally, Rav Shach said, "You're the uncle! You have to be!" to which Rav Shlomo Zalman responded, "But you're the *rebbe,* and a *rebbe* is a father. And a father is closer than an uncle!"

---

1. *LaTorah VeLaMo'adim* (Jerusalem: Kol Mevaser Publishers, 2002), 39.

Says Rav Zevin, a true father has to try to be both a natural and halakhic, Talmudic parent. Avraham was both Yitzhak's biological father and the one who extended the relationship externally by teaching Torah.

The difference between these two categories of offspring is that wherever there is a natural connection, the offspring cannot reject that connection. It's definitive. You can't get out of it. If something is biological, like impurity, the connection can never be broken. The second category, the intellectual, spiritual connection can, if the recipient so desires, be severed.

Avraham tried to be both, but it was Yitzhak's choice to be receptive to the next level of relationship, to receive the Torah from Avraham. Yitzhak, as well, served as a father and *rebbe*, yet only one of his children accepted it: Yaakov.

This is what this first *pasuk* teaches us: These are the *toledot* of Avraham, and Avraham gave birth to Yitzhak, not Yishmael (in the sense of the *rebbe*-father/*talmid*-son relationship). Yitzhak was the one who uniquely accepted what Avraham wanted to transmit.

May we be *zokhe* to serve as biological and intellectual parents, transmitting the tradition to willing recipients, building a legacy to last for generations!

The Importance of
One's Surroundings

ויתרצצו הבנים בקרבה ותאמר אם כן למה זה אנכי ותלך לדרש את
ה'. (בראשית כה:כב)

And the children struggled within her, and she said, "If [it be]
so, why am I [like] this?" And she went to inquire of Hashem.
(*Bereshit* 25:22)

After being barren for years, Rivka finally becomes pregnant, but she suffers a difficult pregnancy. The *pasuk* tells us that the fetuses struggled
within her. Rashi quotes the famous midrash on this verse:

רבותינו דרשוהו לשון ריצה, כשהיתה עוברת על פתחי תורה של שם
ועבר יעקב רץ ומפרכס לצאת, עוברת על פתחי עבודה זרה עשו מפרכס.
(רש"י בראשית כה: כב)

The Rabbi's interpret it as referring to "running": when she would
pass the entrance to Shem and Ever's house of Torah, Yaakov
would run and try to escape; when she would pass the entrance
to a house of idolatry Esav would seek to escape. (Rashi on
Bereshit 25:22)

Hazal explain that Yaakov and Esav were running to get out (*veyitrotzetzu* is related, they suggest, to the verb meaning to run, *ritza*). When Rivka would pass the *beit midrash* of Shem and Ever, Yaakov, *in utero*, felt the *kedusha* and reacted by wanting to exit to the *beit midrash*. When Rivka passed a *beit avoda zara*, Esav wanted to exit.

Yaakov was trying to get out when Rivka passed Shem and Ever. But could he possibly get a better *havruta* than the one he already had? We know the Gemara (Nidda 30a) tells us that everyone learns all of Torah with a *malakh* during gestation. So why, asks Rav Chaim Brisker, did Yaakov want to get out? What could the *beit midrash* of Shem and Ever offer that he didn't already have?

Rav Chaim answers in the name of his father, the Beit HaLevi:

> דכיון שהיה בחברת עשו הרשע, העדיף להפסיד הלימוד עם המלאך,
> העיקר שלא להתחבר לרשע.

> Since he was in the presence of the wicked Esav, it was preferable to forgo learning from the angel. Of utmost importance is not to remain connected to a wicked person.

A person can have the best *rebbe*, the best *havruta*. However, if he is in a negative setting or doesn't have a proper social environment, then it doesn't matter how great the *havruta* is. The pernicious elements of his surroundings will harm him.

A mishna in *Pirkei Avot* tells us not to connect to the wicked – *al tishaber larasha*.[1] The version in *Avot DeRabbi Natan* adds two words: *ve'afilu leTorah* – even for Torah. That is, if in order to acquire Torah, one would have to place himself in a compromising environment, the Torah is not worth it.

Therefore, even if your *havruta* is a *malakh*, if you're sitting right next to Esav, you won't succeed. Yaakov realized this problem, and he preferred to give up his learning with a *malakh* to get away from Esav's company. One's surroundings clearly influence one's outlook, in particular during one's most formative years.

---

1. *Pirkei Avot* 1:7.

A story is told about a Jew from Lodz, who as a young boy during World War I wanted to leave yeshiva and enter the business world. His father objected to him leaving yeshiva at that age and stage of life.

The Hafetz Hayim was in Lodz at the time, so the father suggested that they go seek advice from him. The father was worried that his son would be negatively influenced in the business world, while the boy protested that his father went out to work every day and didn't seem to be getting ruined. "If it's good enough for my father, it should be good enough for me!" the boy objected. "I may be a little younger, but I'll be working eventually, so why can't I just start now?"

The Hafetz Hayim heard the argument and explained to the boy: "We find in *Tanakh* the mention of a cruel bird called the *bat yaana*. What about this bird is so cruel?" He explained: The *bat yaana* has a fierce personality and a hot temperament, to the extent that she can eat even glass. She doesn't think, and assumes her young can also digest glass, so she gives it to them as food. The glass cuts their throats and kills them.

The Hafetz Hayim explains that the same applies here. "Your father is already set. Obviously, a proper social environment is important at every stage in life, but we have to be especially vigilant in our youth. Like the *bat yaana*, a certain environment may be acceptable for a parent, but not for the child. Your father can handle the negative influences of the marketplace, but you're still young and easily influenced, so it's not yet time for you to enter the workforce."

Yaakov preferred to learn in the *beit midrash* of Shem and Ever to learning with an angel because he didn't want to be in the company of Esav.

It is so important for us to consider the impact our surroundings can have on us, especially on our children, and ensure that the proper environment is provided for ourselves and our children to flourish in Torah and *middot*.

Patience Is a Great Virtue

The very first time Yaakov and Esav step on the scene is before they are born. There, the Torah tells us that the fetuses battled each other inside Rivka. Eventually, we see that Yaakov is the chosen child, and Esav is rejected.

What lesson can we learn from these two individuals? What is it about Esav that we want to reject, or avoid in our lives, and how is Yaakov different from him that we choose to emulate Yaakov?

Pirkei DeRabbi Eliezer[1] fills us in on some details regarding the story of the *bekhora* (firstborn): When they were *in utero*, Yaakov said to Esav, "There are two worlds in front of us: Olam Hazeh – this world is about eating, drinking, marrying, and business. But Olam Haba the world to come is different. Olam Haba does not contain those delicacies. Let's make a deal: You take Olam Hazeh, this world, and I'll take Olam Haba, the world to come."

Upon Esav's return from a long day in the field, he enters the house, tired and hungry, when he sees Yaakov preparing soup. He demands some soup, and Yaakov agrees on condition that Esav sell him the birthright. Esav responds, "I'm going to die anyway, why do

---

1. *Pirkei DeRabbi Eliezer,* chapter 32.

I need the birthright?"[2] Who exactly is Esav, and what lesson can we learn from his character?

Rabbi Avishai David, in his *sefer Shai LeAvi*,[3] explains that Esav is all about the here and now. He had no patience. He wanted physical fulfillment, pleasure. "Give me *now*," says Esav, "I don't want to think about the future, about the implications of my actions. I just want this now." His name, Esav, is from the root *asui*, meaning complete. There's no process when it comes to Esav. He was born fully formed, with hair. In contrast, Yaakov has a worldview. He can see the long term. Yaakov appreciates that actions taken today will have future implications. That's the difference between Yaakov and Esav: Olam Haba vs. Olam Hazeh, *bekhora* vs. soup.

He quotes Rav Soloveitchik, who further elaborates: What happened to the descendants of Esav and Yaakov? Esav received his inheritance of Mount Seir immediately. [4]

Yaakov goes to Egypt, not to *Eretz Yisrael*. Yaakov initiates the process of building his nation. He has to go down before he can go up. It is a process to form a nation and return to Israel. Esav can't deal with processes. If he doesn't get it right now, he's not interested. Yaakov understands there is much to gain from the journey.

Yaakov has patience. He's able to wait out the process in order to build a future. He planted trees[5] in Egypt to be used in the *mishkan*. He can see far in advance and plans ahead.

Finally, there is the story in *Parashat Vayishlah*, in which there is a conversation between Yaakov and Esav after their long years of separation, and Yaakov uses the term *na* (please) when asking Esav to accept his gift. What's the meaning of all these "*na*"s? Another meaning of *na* is "raw," which symbolizes the here and now, not waiting for food to be

---

2. *Bereshit* 25:32
3. Rabbi Avishai David; *Shai LeAvi* (Jerusalem: Miskan Publishers, 2017), 142.
4. See *Yehoshua* 24:4.
5. See Rashi on *Shemot* 25:5, that quotes a midrash on the words *atzei shitim* – acacia wood. Rashi asks how did the Jews find these tall trees in the desert? R. Tanchuma explains that Yaakov saw that in the future his descendants would build the *Mishkan* in the desert, so he brought acacia trees to Egypt and planted them there. Yaakov planned for the future.

cooked. In *Parashat Vayishlah*, Yaakov's "*na*"s mean "now," just like in *Tanakh* we have *ana Hashem hoshi'a na* – Please, Hashem, save us "now."

Na suggests immediacy. That's what was going on in their conversation. Yaakov knew what Esav was about, that their *hashkafot* were different. He was telling Esav, "You run ahead, I'm going slow – things take time. There's a Master Artist Who is drawing the tapestry of history. We need to have a long-term view. Esav, you want to get to the end already, so just go on ahead without me."

Esav's *hashkafa* was one of *na* – immediate fulfillment. Soup vs. birthright, this world vs. the world to come, Mount Seir vs. Egypt, running ahead vs. taking the time to do it right. All four events reflect their two diametrically opposed worldviews.

Rabbi David concludes that this is an illness of our generation. We're all guilty of this. We have a sickness that we must have immediate satisfaction. That's Esav's influence, the need for immediate fulfillment – having it "now." People want to know the whole Torah now. They want all success, whether material or spiritual, *right now*.

All too often in *Tanakh*, a lack of patience leads to disastrous ramifications. For example, because people thought Moshe was late in returning from Sinai, they became impatient and built the Golden Calf. Shaul lost his kingship partially because he didn't wait for Shmuel before offering sacrifices.

We need to be more patient, to advance gradually and to at times forgo immediate satisfaction for a better future. Esav's downfall was caused by his desire for immediate gratification. Yaakov's patience and consideration of the future lead him to great success. We have to prevent Esav's attitude from leaking into our lives and strengthen Yaakov's *hashkafa*. May we always be cognizant that patience is a great virtue.

Of Salt and Straw

ויגדלו הנערים ויהי עשו איש ידע ציד איש שדה ויעקב איש תם ישב
אהלים. (בראשית כה:כז)

And the youths grew up, and Esav was a man who understood
hunting, a man of the field, whereas Yaakov was an innocent man,
dwelling in tents. (*Bereshit* 25:27)

The simple meaning of this *pasuk* is that the Yaakov and Esav grew up,
and Esav became a hunter while Yaakov sat in the tents of Torah.

Rashi quotes a deeper level of interpretation of this *pasuk*. *Hazal*
say that Esav hunted and trapped animals *and* people:

לצוד ולרמות את אביו בפיו, ושואלו אבא היאך מעשרין את המלח
ואת התבן, כסבור אביו שהוא מדקדק במצות... (רש"י בראשית כה:כז)

Esav trapped his father with his mouth, by asking "Father, how
does one tithe salt and straw?" So his father reasoned that he was
careful in fulfilling mitzvot. (Rashi on *Bereshit* 25:27)

Esav deceived his father, Yitzhak, through shrewd speech. Hence, Yitzhak
favored Esav and decided to provide Esav with certain *berakhot* over
Yaakov.

How did Esav trick Yitzhak into favoring him? He asked his father a deep, seemingly intelligent question: How does one tithe salt and straw? Esav pretended he cared so much about every mitzva that he took *maaser* even from items like salt and straw, from which *maaser* need not be taken.

What was Esav really suggesting by asking this question? Rav Zevin explains:[1] Salt and straw represent diametrically opposed substances. Straw is less than food. It's what is removed from food. Kernels of grain are removed from their stalks, and the remaining straw is disposed of. That's why it's used as fodder, animal food. Salt, on the other hand, is above food. We use salt to enhance food. It preserves food and it improves its flavor. Salt also enhances meat by extracting blood from it.

There's a lot of straw out there in the world. Straw is what is beneath us, what we have to try to rid ourselves of. Ideas and values we see in the streets or encounter in our lives need to be rejected. The trickery and sin that lurks out there is the straw we have to extract from our lives. What is the salt? We have to take the salt, the Torah, and sprinkle it into our lives to make our lives "tasty" to HaKadosh Barukh Hu. Symbolically, no *korban* was ever brought without salt, and our Shabbat table must have salt on it. We have to salt our lives and dispose of all the straw.

When we salt our lives, we become eternal. As we know, the only eternity is our connection to Torah and mitzvot. There's nothing eternal in this world. Everything eventually ceases to exist. We have to use the Torah as a preservative: "Salting" our lives brings us eternity.

Based on these understandings of salt and straw, what did Esav intend when he questioned the proper way to take *maaser* from these items?

Teruma and *maaser* sanctify and fix the item under discussion. Before one separates *teruma* and *maaser*, the item is called *tevel* – no one is allowed to eat it. After taking *teruma* and *maaser,* what remains becomes permissible.

Straw and salt don't need such separation. Why? Straw is pure garbage. You have already separated the food from it, and the remaining

---

1. Rav Shlomo Zevin, *LaTorah VeLaMo'adim*, 40.

straw is garbage. It must be disposed of, as there's no fixing it. Our job is to separate the garbage.

What about salt? Salt doesn't require any "fixing" by us. As we said, salt is above food. It fixes other foods! And salt is a symbol of the Torah. It's not up to us to "fix" the Torah or "sanctify" the Torah or enhance the Torah. We have to use what is there to sanctify and fix *ourselves*.

Now, we can understand Esav. When he asked his father about separating *teruma* and *maaser* from salt and straw, he was saying that he wanted to separate the garbage straw so he could bring utter evil into his life. He was saying, "We can bring the garbage into our lives. We can fix it." Instead of agreeing that there are some things that are not fixable and that we just have to stay away, he wanted to use those bad things, to attempt to separate them and make them usable. Furthermore, he wanted to *maaser* the salt, the Torah. Esav's plan was to try to "fix" the Torah, to adapt it.

In every generation, there are Esavs in different forms. They want to fix the "straw," to use the evil and negative. At other times, they want to change the Torah. We have to understand what requires disposal and what is to be preserved. To distinguish the straw and salt from other substances.

Defining Character

ויגדלו הנערים ויהי עשו איש ידע ציד איש שדה ויעקב איש תם ישב
אהלים. (בראשית כה:כז)

And the youths grew up, and Esav was a man who understood
hunting, a man of the field, whereas Yaakov was an innocent man,
dwelling in tents. (*Bereshit* 25:27)

The *pasuk* describes Esav as a hunter, a man of the fields, and Yaakov as a
"simple man, a tent-dweller." Rav Pincus wonders about the terminology
of the *pasuk*. *Hazal* tell us what a terrible individual Esav was and about
his many transgressions (Bava Batra 16b), and yet, the Torah chooses to
capture his essence by calling him "a hunter, a man of the field." Yaakov,
who must have performed many mitzvot, is characterized by the Torah
as a simple tent-dweller.

Does "a man of the field" capture all of Esav's flaws, the depth of
his wickedness? And does the fact that Yaakov dwelled in tents really
define his greatness?

Rav Pincus, in *Tiferet Shimshon*,[1] suggests that the true litmus
test of a person's greatness is what he does during his free time. When
it comes to what we must do, there's no choice, so we do it. So where

---

1. Rav Shimshon Pinchus, *Tiferet Shimshon* (Yefe Nof, 2009), 285.

do our true colors show? When we choose our extracurricular activities, how we fill our free time.

Before I made *aliya* with my family, I had to go to the Israeli consulate in New York. I blocked a couple of hours out of my schedule for it, because it usually takes a lot of time. When I got there, though, it was almost empty. It was unbelievable! As I filled out the paperwork, I overheard a guy who was sitting across from me on the benches. He was on his phone talking to his friends, saying, "You're not going to believe it! I blocked out the entire morning to come to the Israeli consulate. I thought I would be here all morning! And you know what, I'm finished here, and I don't have to go back to work for three hours! Isn't that unbelievable? I have this whole morning free!" Then he called another person. Then another. He spent two hours, the entire time I was there, calling people to tell them how much free time he had because he had blocked out the whole morning for the consulate trip and had finished earlier than expected.

"Killing time" is not a Jewish perspective. What did Esav do in his spare time? NOTHING. He hung out in the fields, and that led him to perform transgressions, as doing nothing often does. Yaakov used his time to sit and learn. That's what we have to want to do: *use* our time and not waste it.[2]

The most valuable gift Hashem gives us is time, and as we get older, we realize how valuable every second of our life is. Hopefully, each year of life gives us a greater perspective and recognition of the value of using our time productively.

We have to be able to account for every minute of our lives. Our relaxation time should be built into our schedules and not define our day or life. How we use our time defines the kind of person we are, as we learn from the *pasuk* that describes Yaakov and Esav.

---

2. See *Parashat Noach,* "Using Time Productively."

A Lesson in Education

ויגדלו הנערים ויהי עשו איש ידע ציד איש שדה ויעקב איש תם ישב
אהלים. (בראשית כה:כז)

And the youths grew up, and Esav was a man who understood
hunting, a man of the field, whereas Yaakov was an innocent man,
dwelling in tents. (*Bereshit* 25:27)

Rav Shimshon Refael Hirsch comments on this *pasuk* with an explanation that could seem a little controversial, but its basis is among the
Rishonim.

We know that our forefathers and mothers were not perfect, and
that's what makes them role models for us. Perfection doesn't speak to
us, says Rav Hirsch, and knowing that our great leaders were imperfect
is instructive for us. Based on the way in which the Torah formulates
certain behaviors, we can gain instruction for ourselves. It is not up to
us, *has veshalom*, to ascribe any sins to the *avot* and *imahot* that *Hazal*
did not. Based on what *Hazal* teach us, though, there are messages for
us to learn.

While Rav Hirsch goes one step further than *Hazal* do, he has a
suggestion we can all learn from even if we don't necessarily agree with
Rav Hirsch ascribing it to the *avot* and *imahot*.

The *pasuk*, says Rav Hirsch,[1] provides us with the impression that Yaakov and Esav received the same education.

> As long as they were little, no attention was paid to the slumbering differences in their natures; both had exactly the same teaching and educational treatment, and the great law of education, *hanokh lena'ar al pi darko* – bring up each child in accordance with their own way – was forgotten, that each child must be treated differently, with an eye to the slumbering tendencies of his nature.... The great Jewish task in life is basically simple, one and the same for all, but in its realization is as complicated and varied as human natures and tendencies are varied.

The goal of life is to bring up our children to be good *ovdei Hashem*. How to do that is different for each child. Rav Hirsch suggests, based on the *pesukim* and based on a *Hazal* that comments on Yaakov Avinu's favoritism of Yosef which led to problems, that a similar issue could have occurred here. Yitzhak and Rivka may have, in some small way, caused Esav to become who he was. Esav may have been a *rasha* from the day he was born, but perhaps their educational philosophies and the way they conducted their *hinukh* contributed to his character. The message for us here is to be so careful and vigilant to know the qualities and strengths and weaknesses of each of our children, because that can really contribute to their behaviors and who they will be as an "end product." One cannot teach all children using the same methods. While some can read and understand immediately, other children require visual aids or need to have material repeated over and over in order to grasp an idea. Some children flourish outside the classroom and have difficulty sitting and concentrating for hours. We must take into consideration the strengths and weaknesses of each child so that we can properly address their needs and maximize their abilities.

---

1. *The Pentateuch, Translated and Explained by Samson Raphael Hirsch,* Bereshit (Gateshead: Judaica Press, 1989), 425.

Rav Hirsch adds another thought as well. It is dangerous for children when parents give mixed messages, when the father and mother are not on the same page in how they express their views to their children. Parents have to be a strong front, united, and they must love all their children equally, even those who are not so righteous – and especially those.

Parents have to share values and have a similar hierarchy of what's important in life. Parents don't always see eye to eye, but they have to talk about disagreements in private, not in front of their children, and then come to an agreement about how to proceed.[2]

The message for us is the message of parenting: having a strong, united front and educating each child in a way that enables him to utilize his strengths.[3]

---

2. Perhaps this is why the Torah in *Parashat Ki Tetzeh* describes the *ben sorer umoreh* at first as not listening to "his father's voice and his mother's voice." Because they have two different voices, they are saying two different things. Later, when the parents appear before the *Beit Din*, they say "he does not listen to our voice." Now, they have a united voice. It is critical for parents to have a unified message so as not to confuse children.

3. The Piaseczno Rav, in his classic book *Hovat HaTalmidim*, defines the word *hinukh* to mean an "initiation," the beginning of the utilization of potential (as in *hanukat habayit*, when the *Beit HaMikdash* is inaugurated). A proper education is one in which the child is able to learn to maximize his or her potential.

Yitzhak's Love for Esav: Not Blind Love

ויאהב יצחק את עשו כי ציד בפיו ורבקה אהבת את יעקב. (בראשית כה:כח)

And Yitzhak loved Esav because [his] game was in his mouth, but Rivka loved Yaakov. (*Bereshit* 25:28)

The Torah tells us, "Yitzhak loved Esav because he had entrapment in his mouth, and Rivka loved Yaakov" (*Bereshit* 25:28). Interestingly, the Torah expresses the reason for Yitzhak's love of Esav, but not for Rivka's love of Yaakov. The wording of the *pasuk* seems to suggest that Rivka's love was different from Yitzhak's, that it wasn't contingent on anything.

What is the meaning of "entrapment in his mouth," and why is it a reason to love Esav? Rashi on this verse comments: Esav had traps in his mouth. As *Hazal* tell us, he used to ask fake halakhic questions that he didn't really mean in order to trick Yitzhak into thinking he was learned.

Many commentators point out that it's very hard to assume that Yitzhak was really fooled. Everyone in the world knew Esav was a *rasha*. Even Leah knew, as we see in *Parashat Vayeitzeh*. It is difficult to imagine that Yitzhak, one of the *avot*, was duped and did not realize who Esav was. Moreover, it stands to reason that Rivka recognized her son for what he was and would have communicated it to Yitzhak.

The *Peninei HaTorah*[1] suggests that Yitzchak knew full well what Esav was. That's why he was so surprised when Yaakov, posing as Esav, used *shem Hashem*. He *knew* Esav would not use God's name!

The *Peninei HaTorah* informs us of an educational reality here. When a child leaves the fold of Torah, as long he or she maintains a relationship with either parent or a teacher, it's the parent or educator's job to do whatever they can to continue that relationship as much as possible, as tenuous as it is. Therefore, when the child is ready to come back, the relationship will be there. As long as the child has a little respect for the parent or teacher, focus on the relationship and give it some time and patience. If, however, the child cuts off all relationship from his parents, then most hope is lost, and the child is in a very worrisome place.

As we know, the one mitzva Esav did excel in was honoring his father and mother. He put on his Shabbat clothes whenever he wanted to see his father. Therefore, suggests the *Peninei HaTorah*, maybe Yitzhak showed Esav love not despite his evil inclination but *because* of it – because he wanted to try to bring Esav back.

Rabbi Meir Premishlaner would tell a story about his *rebbe*, Rabbi Haim Czernowitz, author of *Be'er Mayim Hayim*, who had a child who wasn't going in the *derekh hayashar*. Rabbi Czernowitz didn't throw his son out even though he had left the fold. He did what he could to treat the child properly. He used to throw up his hands to the heavens and say, "Please, Hashem, show us compassion, like a father shows to a wayward son. And even if, HaKadosh Barukh Hu, we turn away from you, please show us mercy like I show to my child."

Rabbi Meir Premishlaner then added that maybe the *pasuk* alludes to something the Gemara (Shabbat 89b) teaches: Hashem asked each of the *avot* if they could defend Klal Yisrael. Avraham said no, Yaakov said no, and only Yitzhak said yes. He was the one to beg Hashem to have mercy on Klal Yisrael. Maybe the words "because entrapment was in his mouth" allude to this point: Yitzhak loved Esav because this love for the evil son gave Yitzhak something with which to defend Klal

---

1. Rav David Hadad, *Peninei HaTorah* (Beer Sheva, 1992), 42.

Yisrael before Hashem. "HaKadosh Barukh Hu, you're upset at Klal Yisrael because they left you? My son left me, and yet I had mercy and tried to be *mekarev* him. So please have patience for us, have mercy on your children."

Through Yitzhak loving Esav despite his shortcomings, Yitzhak was able to defend Klal Yisrael in the future. May we learn this lesson from Yitzhak, be patient, and be able to positively influence even the most challenging children.

Yitzhak's *Gevura*

Unlike the other *avot*, Yitzhak Avinu hardly gets any coverage in the Written Torah.[1] In the one *perek* that is devoted to Yitzhak, most of what Yitzhak does is exactly parallel with Avraham's life. Both Avraham and Yitzhak experienced a famine, had to leave to seek food, had dealings with a man named Avimelekh, and had to claim their wife was their sister.

Later, Yitzhak re-digs all the wells Avraham had dug and the Philistines covered over, and he names the wells with the same exact names that his father did! The Torah continuously emphasizes that Yitzhak did everything the same as Avraham Avinu. Yitzchak built an altar and he made a treaty. It seems that Yitzhak didn't do a single original act.

The Rambam, at the beginning of *Hilkhot Avodat Kokhavim*, discusses the history of paganism. He explains that in the times of Enosh, people believed in God, but then they started to believe in Hashem's servants, such as the sun, moon, and stars. People began to venerate them, thinking it was an honor to HaKadosh Barukh Hu to honor His servants. Eventually, over time, they forgot that those beings were just servants, and they started worshipping those entities. This continued until Avraham Avinu came along. Avraham questioned how these servants, i.e., the

---

1. *Parashat Lekh Lekha, Parashat Vayera,* and *Parashat Hayei Sara* are about Avraham, and *Vayetzeh* and *Vayishlah* are about Yaakov.

natural and spiritual forces, could operate without a Higher Power controlling them. When he came to the conclusion that there was a God in control, he announced it to everyone. He went from city to city proclaiming
monotheism and teaching people about Hashem. The Rambam writes:

והודיעו ליצחק בנו. וישב יצחק מלמד ומחזיר ויצחק הודיעו ליעקב
ומינהו ללמד, וישב מלמד ומחזיר כל הנלוים אליו. ויעקב אבינו למד
בניו כולם.... (הלכות עכו"ם א:ג)

Avraham taught his belief to Yitzhak, Yitzhak sat and taught and
reviewed, and Yitzhak transmitted to Yaakov, who sat and taught
and reviewed and Yaakov taught all his children…. (Rambam,
Hilkhot Avodat Kokhavim 1:3)

The historical reference to Yitzhak in the Rambam encompasses but five
words. Why such scarcity with respect to Yitzhak? Considering all we
know of Yitzhak is that he learned and reviewed what Avraham taught
him, what are we supposed to learn from him? The Torah hardly tells
us anything about him – what exactly is the message?

I heard the following idea in the name of Rabbi Yaakov Medan.
The first *pasuk* of *Parashat Toledot* is:

ואלה תולדת יצחק בן אברהם אברהם הוליד את יצחק. (בראשית כה:יט)

And these are the generations of Yitzhak the son of Avraham;
Avraham begot Yitzhak. (*Bereshit* 25:19)

Rashi comments on the apparent redundancy of this verse and explains
that Hashem made the *panim*, appearance, of Yitzhak look like that of
Avraham. *Panim* means face, but it also means *penimiyut*, the inside, the
essence.

Avraham was an innovator. He was a revolutionary who started
a religion. As the first generation of a movement, his whole life was full
of innovation. He came up with the idea and got everybody going. That
was who he was. He was a man of *hesed*, which requires reaching out.
He went out and spread the word. That's what his purpose was: to be a
revolutionary, to spread monotheism.

How does a legacy, a movement, continue? It must be given time to develop roots before it can grow. The second generation of any movement has to be a group of people who don't change anything, who do exactly as the first generation did, so that the movement can take root and become strong. The movement needs that second generation of followers who just accept and follow so that it can then further develop. Once the third generation comes, the movement is already something serious, it has roots. At that point, people can branch off and add a little or change some things. It's only natural that we want to add on our own. It's a tendency of people to want to be innovators.

What was Yitzhak's greatness? That he was *not* an innovator! His whole innovation was that he was not an innovator. He was the *av* who was supposed to serve as a conduit, the conduit that gave time for this new idea of monotheism to take root and for people in the world to get used to it. If he were to change the idea right away, it wouldn't give people time to grasp and absorb it totally. Yitzhak's whole purpose in life was to do exactly what Avraham Avinu did. The only thing we know from the Torah about Yitzhak is that he did exactly what his father did, because that is what he was supposed to do. That was his whole purpose.

Avraham was *hesed*, and Yitzhak was *gevura*. A strong person, *gibor*, is someone who conquers his own tendencies to do something new. To quash that desire is much harder than anything else. Yitzhak conquered his personal desires for the good of the nation, of the religion, and that's why we don't have much written about him.

What does the Rambam say about Yitzhak? That he reviewed, because that's what he was supposed to do. That was Yitzhak Avinu.

Truth or Trickery

Probably the most difficult and challenging section to understand in this *parasha* is the behavior of Yaakov and Rivka with regard to the *berakhot*. Did Rivka and Yaakov lie? What was the purpose of their charade? Why didn't Rivka just go over to Yitzhak and say, "Honey, you chose the wrong son. You need to give the *berakhot* to Yaakov"? She knew that Yaakov was the righteous one and Esav was the evil one, and she had received the prophecy that "the greater shall serve the younger." Whether or not she told Yitzhak about this prophecy, which we can assume she did, she definitely knew which of her sons was the good one.

What was Yaakov's whole role in this story? Simple: an obedient son. His mother told him what to do and didn't give him much of a choice in the matter. Yaakov isn't really the focus of this story, says Rav Shimshon Refael Hirsch. He just followed orders. Even though Yaakov probably knew who he was and who Esav was and that it wasn't a good idea to give the *berakhot* to Esav, he can't be at fault here for not opposing his mother's plan. Rivka knew Yaakov wouldn't want to trick Yitzhak, but she also knew that Yaakov would listen to her because of the mitzva of honoring parents.

But what was Rivka's intention?

Right before the whole story of the *berakhot,* as if by introduction, there are two seemingly randomly placed *pesukim* that say:

ויהי עשו בן ארבעים שנה ויקח אשה את יהודית בת בארי החתי ואת
בשמת בת אילן החתי. ותהיין מרת רוח ליצחק ולרבקה. (בראשית
כו:לד-לה)

And Esav was forty years old, and he married Yehudit, the daugh-
ter of Beeri the Hittite, and Basemath, the daughter of Elon the
Hittite. And they were a vexation of the spirit to Yitzhak and
Rivka. (*Bereshit* 26:34–35)

Esav married two Hittite women and caused Yitzhak and Rivka pain, to
the point where, Rashi tells us, Yitzhak became blind from the smoke of
the *avoda zara* of these women. Yet, Yitzhak still desired to give the *berakhot* to Esav. When Yitzhak called Esav in and instructed him to bring
food and then receive the *berakhot*, Yitzhak opens up the conversation
with the words "I am old." This must mean that Yitzhak had wanted to
give these *berakhot* to Esav for a long time, but each time he attempted
to do so, Rivka pushed him off, trying to convince him that he had the
wrong son. This must have been going on until Yitzhak said, "I'm old
already. It's now or never."

This spurred Rivka to action. She asked herself, "How do I prevent this from happening? How do I convince Yitzhak that Esav is an
evil person who has been masquerading as a pious son and fooling his
father all these years?"

There was only one way to do that, says Rav Shimshon Refael
Hirsch,[1] and that was by taking the *ish tam* and masquerading him as
the *ish tzayid*! The only way to prove to Yitzhak that he'd been wrong
all this time was to show him that Rivka could trick him in the exact
opposite way. According to this view, Rivka's whole point was to trick
Yitzhak so he would realize that if he could be tricked in this direction,
then Rivka was right all along, and Esav could have tricked him the
other way around!

Rivka's act was successful. Because what does the *pasuk* say happened right after Yitzhak realized that he had been fooled into giving

---

1. *The Pentateuch*, Bereshit (Gateshead: Judaica Press, 1989), 443.

Yaakov the *berakhot*? Yitzhak said to Esav that Yaakov will be blessed. Yitzhak didn't take it back.

The *pasuk* says:

ויחרד יצחק חרדה גדלה עד מאד. (בראשית כז:לג)

And Isaac shuddered a great shudder. (*Bereshit* 27:33)

Yitzhak was overcome with a trembling fear. Rav Hirsch explains that Yitzhak wasn't overcome because he thought he gave the *berakhot* to the wrong person. Rather, this fear was his realization that he had been tricked his entire life, and all that Rivka had been saying was true. That's why he didn't switch the *berakhot* afterward, and he didn't regret giving them to Yaakov.

This is the amazing explanation Rav Hirsch suggests concerning why Rivka specifically *tricked* Yitzhak into giving the *berakhot* to Yaakov – not to hide anything from Yitzhak, but to prove to Yitzhak that he was capable of being duped into loving Esav his whole life. In the end, Rivka's scheme was successful, and Yaakov received Yitzhak's blessing.

Shalom Bayit

ותאמר רבקה אל יצחק קצתי בחיי מפני בנות חת. (בראשית כז:מו)

And Rivka said to Yitzhak, "I am disgusted with my life because of the daughters of Heth. If Yaakov takes a wife of the daughters of Heth like these, from the daughters of the land, of what use is life to me?" (*Bereshit* 27:46)

At the end of the *parasha*, Rivka turns to Yitzhak and says, "I've had enough. I'm disgusted by these women. We have to let our son Yaakov find a wife elsewhere." And Yaakov is sent away.

Rav Yitzhak Zilberstein, in *Tuvkha Yabiu*,[1] asks a question on this *pasuk*: Rivka made up a story here and claimed that the need to send Yaakov away from home was to find a wife. Her true intention was to protect Yaakov from Esav, who was intent on murdering him. Why didn't she just say straight out that they had to get Yaakov out of there before Esav could kill him?

Rav Zilberstein asks: How did Rivka know that Esav intended to murder Yaakov? We can assume that she knew through *ruah hakodesh* what was going on in Esav's mind. Rivka would not tell her husband

---

1. Volume 1 (Bnei Brak: Tzoran, 2000), 148.

something that he didn't know himself, because that would basically be stating that she had a higher level of *ruah hakodesh* than Yitzhak. While that may have been true (indeed, Sarah had a higher level of *ruah hakodesh* than Avraham did), Rivka didn't want to say or do something that could make her husband feel inferior (whatever that means on Yitzhak's level).

Rivka instead fabricated a story, and the sensitivity she showed toward Yitzhak is a tremendous lesson to us with regard to how we treat and speak to our spouse. Rivka altered the truth for the sake of *shalom bayit* and her husband's honor.

May we emulate Rivka's sensitivity toward Yitzhak by being careful in the way we communicate with our spouses, always showing our utmost respect and avoiding any act or statement that could be perceived as offensive or degrading. We should always keep in mind the Rambam's classic words of how spouses should treat each other:

וכן ציוו חכמים שיהיה אדם מכבד את אשתו יותר מגופו, ואוהבה כגופו ואם יש לו ממון, מרבה בטובתה כפי הממון. ולא יטיל עליה אימה יתרה ויהיה דיבורו עימה בנחת, ולא יהיה עצב ולא רוגז.

וכן ציוו חכמים על האישה שתהיה מכבדת את בעלה ביותר מדיי, ויהיה לו עליה מורא, ותעשה כל מעשיה על פיו, ויהיה בעיניה כמו שר או מלך: מהלכת בתאוות ליבו, ומרחקת כל שישנא. וזה הוא דרך כל בנות ישראל ובני ישראל הקדושים, הטהורים בזיווגן ובדרכים אלו, יהיה יישובן נאה ומשובח.

Our Sages commanded that a man should honor his wife more than his own person and love her as he loves his own person. If he has financial resources, he should offer her benefits in accordance with his resources. He should not cast a superfluous measure of fear over her. He should talk with her gently, being neither sad nor angry.

And similarly, they commanded a woman to honor her husband exceedingly and to be in awe of him. She should carry out all her deeds according to his directives, considering him to be an officer or a king. She should follow the desires of his heart and shun everything that he disdains.

This is the custom of holy and pure Jewish women and men in their marriages. And these ways will make their marriage pleasant and praiseworthy.[2]

2. *Hilkhot Ishut* 15:19–20.

Parashat Vayetzeh

Spiritual Protection

וידר יעקב נדר לאמר: אם יהיה אלקים עמדי ושמרני בדרך הזה אשר
אנכי הולך ונתן לי לחם לאכל ובגד ללבש. ושבתי בשלום אל בית אבי
והיה ה' לי לא־להים. והאבן הזאת אשר שמתי מצבה יהיה בית אלקים
וכל אשר תתן לי עשר אעשרנו לך. (בראשית כח:כ-כב)

And Yaakov uttered a vow, saying, "If Hashem will be with me,
and He will guard me on this path, upon which I am going, and
He will give me bread to eat and clothes to wear; and if I return
in peace to my father's house, and Hashem will be my God; then
this stone, which I have placed as a monument, shall be a house
of God, and everything that You give me, I will surely tithe to
You. (*Bereshit* 28:20–22)

When Yaakov awoke from his sleep after the dream, he erected a headstone
and made an unusual vow. He asked for protection from Hashem, food
to eat, and clothing to wear. Yaakov promised to donate *maaser* in return.

The *Keli Yakar*,[1] the great Prague Darshan, raises a number of
questions on this *pasuk*, the first being: Why did Yaakov make a vow if

---

1. *Keli Yakar, Bereshit* 28:20.

Hashem had just promised him protection, the very thing that Yaakov is requesting? Why did Yaakov seek to obtain further reassurance of Hashem's protection? Second, this *pasuk* is very wordy and there are redundancies, e.g., "bread to eat and clothes to wear." What else would one do with bread and clothing?

Additionally, the *Keli Yakar* picks up on a slight difference between the wording of Yaakov's vow and Hashem's promise. Hashem said, "I will return you to this land," whereas Yaakov said, "I will return safely to my father's house." Yaakov's wording sounds like he is taking the credit for his safe return.

The *Keli Yakar* suggests that Yaakov was requesting spiritual rather than physical protection. He proves his assertion from Hashem's promise: "I will guard you wherever you go." Yaakov had said, "and protect me on *this path* that I (*anokhi*) am walking ... and I will return safely." From these words we learn that Yaakov's interest was his *ruhniyut*, which is dependent on a person. Our spiritual strength is in our control. Physical protection is out of a person's control. It's entirely up to God.

Yaakov realized that his *ruhniyut* was up to him. While every Jew has free choice, we need divine help to succeed even in that area. We need divine help to defeat the *yetzer hara*, and that is what Yaakov was requesting.

As David HaMelekh says in *Tehillim* (119:37): "Prevent my eyes from seeing falsehood." He realized he needed Hashem's help even in the spiritual realm.

This explains the apparently superfluous wording of the *pasuk*. Hashem promised to guard Yaakov from everything in His control, but Yaakov's "path" is an individual path, the *derekh* of his life, the path he had to choose. Yaakov requests: *ushmarani baderekh hazeh,* "and guard me on this path." The word *zeh,* "this," usually connotes something specific that can be indicated directly (see Rashi on *Shemot* 12:2). It is as if Yaakov was pointing to his *derekh* in life, that of Torah and mitzvot, of serving Hashem. Yaakov emphasized this point, which is why the *pasuk* is so wordy and why this request was appropriate. He was asking for something that Hashem had not promised: help in the spiritual realm.

Regarding his request for "bread to eat" and "clothes to wear," the *Keli Yakar* explains that wealth is a major challenge to our spiritual existence, as it blinds the eyes of those who have it. *Hazal* tell us that the challenge of wealth is even greater than the challenge of poverty. If we don't have, we know we have to pray to HaKadosh Barukh Hu. If we have wealth, we feel less of a sense of urgency to *daven*. As *Hazal* tell us, rebellious feelings against God only emerge when we feel like we have everything.

Yaakov was asking Hashem to satisfy his physical needs and no more: clothing to wear and food to eat, no extras. That's the message. We should have what we need and recognize that everything comes from HaKadosh Barukh Hu, realizing that sometimes, having more is a great *nisayon*.

Yaakov's whole request then, had to do with his spiritual life, and that is why it was appropriate. We need to learn from Yaakov and pray that we, too, should be worthy of Hashem's guidance and protection in the spiritual as well as the physical realm.

Rav Shimshon Refael Hirsch[2] makes a similar point when he notes that this *pasuk* is in the exact opposite order of *Birkat Kohanim*. In *Birkat Kohanim*, we ask for the *berakha* first, and then we ask for protection:

יברכך ה׳ וישמרך. (במדבר ו:כד)

Hashem will bless and guard you. (*Bemidbar* 6:24)

Here, the opposite order is given:

ושמרני בדרך הזה אשר אנכי הולך ונתן לי לחם לאכל ובגד ללבש. (בראשית כח:כ)

He will guard me on this way, upon which I am going, and He will give me bread to eat and a garment to wear. (*Bereshit* 28:20)

Yaakov first asks for protection and then for bounty. Why? His answer is required reading for anyone about to enter the business world, and for all of us.

---

2. *The Pentateuch*, Bereshit, 100.

Yaakov, at this point in the *parasha*, was about to enter the "outside" world for the first time. Until now, he had been a *yoshev ohalim* – a "tent dweller." Upon leaving yeshiva for the first time, he immediately asked for protection, because when we go out into the big wide world, we need it.

He was not asking for protection for his physical possessions. In *Birkat Kohanim*, we ask for possessions, *berakha*, and then we ask for protection of those possessions. Here, however, Yaakov was referring to his spiritual state. He desperately needed protection from spiritual dangers. From the time Adam was thrown out of Gan Eden, the curse of "by the sweat of your brow shall you eat bread" (*Bereshit* 3:19) prevailed. The curse does not just refer to the physical difficulty in sustaining a living. Included in the curse are spiritual dangers. It's going to be hard for us spiritually. "We'd be much safer if we didn't have to go out to work. But we have to go out." It's a mitzva to support our family. Part of the curse is that it will be physically challenging, and very often spiritually as well.

Therefore, before anything, Yaakov asked for protection from potential spiritual dangers as he embarked on his journey to the house of Lavan.

A House and a Gate

וַיִּירָא וַיֹּאמַר מַה נּוֹרָא הַמָּקוֹם הַזֶּה: אֵין זֶה כִּי אִם בֵּית אֱלֹקִים וְזֶה שַׁעַר
הַשָּׁמָיִם. (בראשית כח:יז)

And he was frightened, and he said, "How awesome is this place!
This is none other than the house of God, and this is the gate of
heaven." (*Bereshit* 28:17)

Yaakov awoke from his dream in which he visualized angels ascending and descending a ladder, and he immediate realized this was not
an ordinary occurrence; he exclaimed: "How awesome is this place!"
"This place" where Yaakov was located, was the site where the two *Batei
HaMikdash* stood and where the third will stand. Yaakov refers to this
location as both a house (*bayit*) and a gate (*shaar*). These are two different descriptions of the same location.

I once heard Rav Aharon Lichtenstein explain as follows: A *bayit*
is an ultimate destination, an end. We embark on a journey and we arrive
at our destination – a house.

A *shaar* (gate), on the other hand, is not a place we go *to*, but
something we go *through*. A gate is a means, not an end. The *Beit HaMikdash* was both a house and a gate. It was a *bayit* in that it was a place we
went to, on the *Shalosh Regalim*, to bring offerings and to see the *kohanim*. But it was also a gate. We *used* the experience of having been at the

139

bayit as a means to get even closer to HaKadosh Barukh Hu, to bring the inspiration back home with us. In that sense, the *Beit HaMikdash* was a gate, a *shaar*. It is meant to be both an end, a *bayit*, and a means, the gateway to heaven.

When we experience any spiritual high, during *davening*, at a *shiur*, doing an act of *hesed*, accomplishing that experience may be an end within itself, yet we need to take it with us. We must internalize it and utilize it as a means to enhance our spirituality in other areas as well. As Yaakov began his journey to the house of Lavan, he understood that he needed to carry with him the spiritual sensation he was experiencing at that location.

This is how we should view each station of life's spiritual journey: as both a *bayit* and a *shaar*.

Like the Dust of the Earth

והנה ה' נצב עליו ויאמר אני ה' א-להי אברהם אביך וא-להי יצחק הארץ אשר אתה שכב עליה לך אתננה ולזרעך. והיה זרעך כעפר הארץ ופרצת ימה וקדמה וצפנה ונגבה ונברכו בך כל משפחת האדמה ובזרעך. (בראשית כח:יג-יד)

And behold, the Lord was standing over him, and He said, "I am the Lord, the God of Abraham your father, and the God of Isaac; the land upon which you are lying to you I will give it and to your seed. And your seed shall be as the dust of the earth, and you shall gain strength westward and eastward and northward and southward; and through you shall be blessed all the families of the earth and through your seed." (*Bereshit* 28:13–14)

Yaakov experienced an unbelievable prophecy while he was sleeping. Hashem appeared in front of the ladder on which the angels were ascending and descending, and He made a promise to Yaakov. Hashem told Yaakov that the land he was currently lying on would be given to him and his children. His descendants would be as numerous as the dust of the land, they would spread out in all directions, and through them would be the *berakha* of all families of the earth.

Rabbi Aaron Lewin, in his *HaDerash VeHaIyun,* notes that *Bnei Yisrael* are compared to three different entities in the different promises to the *avot,* and one of them is listed in the above *pasuk.*

ישראל נמשלו לעפר לחול ולכוכבים.

Bnei Yisrael are compared to dirt, to sand, and to the stars.

Rabbi Lewin explains the significance and symbolism of each of these.

Stars: Every star is its own world and is lightyears away from the next one. Stars travel in their own orbits, sometimes getting close to another star, and sometimes further. Each star is its own separate entity that does not combine with another star. When Am Yisrael is not united and each individual follows his own path and does not focus on the next person, then we are compared to stars.

Sand: What is the next level? Sand particles stick close together, but if you lift up sand in your hand the grains of sand can slip through your fingers. Sand is not one solid unit, but rather several independent particles. It comprises individual grains of sand that can come together but that can easily slide into separation. Sometimes we act together for a common cause although we are not a single unit. There is solidarity but not unity. That is when we are compared to sand.

Dirt: When you clump together a bunch of dirt, it becomes one unit, to the point where you would have to work hard to separate the dirt particles from each other. If we are ultimately so connected to each other, as we should be, and we are all like one body, then we're like dirt, which is the ultimate of these three depictions of Am Yisrael.

We have had a long and arduous exile. We're tossed and turned from exile to exile and from tragedy to tragedy. The only way to survive is by staying together. If we separate, we aren't going to make it.

Hazal interpret a phrase from *Sefer Amos* (9:6): "and founds its vault on the earth" – *ve'agudato al eretz yesada* – to mean that the earth is founded on *agudot,* which generally means "groups." A *mashal* is given of a man who lifts a pile of twigs and attempts to break it. He finds it impossible. When he lifts one twig, however, he easily snaps it in two. When there is *sinat hinam,* we are very breakable and fragile. When things are joined together, they are unbreakable, and the same can be applied to us as a nation.

This explains the *pasuk* further: If we are like dirt, then we will spread all over the world. Only if we are like the dirt, with an internal connection to every fellow Jew, will we merit true *berakha*.

Sand and stars, while they are lower levels than dirt, are still *berakhot*, as the *avot* were blessed. There are times when the other forms of unity are appropriate. Hashem does not desire for us all to be homogenous and all exactly the same *ovdei Hashem*. As Rabbi Yaakov Kamenetsky[1] says, *shalom* means having *different* parts that come together. We are each a different star of HaKadosh Barukh Hu.

Sometimes, we have to be like the sand, standing at each other's side, but leaving room for independence. At other times, we need to be strong in our belief and shine like stars, remaining independent. However, the greatest *berakha* is when there is an unbreakable bond, like in the composition of dirt. May we be able to achieve such levels of unity in our generation.

1. Rav Yaakov Kamenetsky, *Emet LeYaakov, Bemidbar.*

My Dear Brothers

ויאמר להם יעקב אחי מאין אתם ויאמרו מחרן אנחנו. (בראשית כט:ד)

And Yaakov said to them, "My brothers, where are you from?" And they said, "We are from Haran." (*Bereshit* 29:4)

ויאמר הן עוד היום גדול לא עת האסף המקרה השקו הצאן ולכו רעו. (בראשית כט:ז)

And he said, "The day is yet long; it is not the time to take in the livestock. Water the sheep and go, pasture." (*Bereshit* 29:7)

Yaakov encounters a group of shepherds gathered around a well, and he strikes up conversation with them. He asks them why they are just sitting around wasting time when they should be busy caring for their sheep. The shepherds reply that they are waiting for additional shepherds to gather at the well so that together they can remove the heavy rock that covers the mouth of the well.

Their answer is somewhat surprising. Yaakov was traveling from another town and his conversation with these shepherds began with rebuke. One would have expected these shepherds to be somewhat disturbed with Yaakov. The expected reply should have been: "Who do you think you are, coming to our town and immediately giving us *musar?*" Instead, they actually heeded his question and answered him normally! Lavan wasn't the nicest guy; Haran obviously didn't breed the nicest people, and yet, these shepherds just took Yaakov's *musar* in stride and didn't get upset. Why?

The Ponovezher Rav, quoted in the *Yagdil Torah,*[1] explains why the shepherds took so well to Yaakov's *musar.* He tells us that the secret lies in one word Yaakov used. The *pasuk* tells us, "Yaakov initiated his communication with the shepherds by calling them: 'My brothers...'" He began the conversation with a word of affection, connoting that they were equals, in it together, one and the same. If the receiver of your words feels like you're really interested in his well-being, he'll accept your *musar.* It's all in the attitude. Often, it is not what you say, but how you say it.

The Ponovezher Rav was known to have a *ko'ah* in bringing people who were so distant from Torah back to *Yiddishkeit.* How was he so successful? He would say that the magical words to open anyone's heart are "dear brothers."

We should be careful to address others with a phrase of affection, a phrase that shows we are together with them, in order to successfully transmit our constructive criticism and maximize its effectiveness.[2]

1. Rav Moshe Menachem Ludmir, *Yagdil Torah* (Jerusalem: Genesis Press 1991/2008), *Vayetzeh.*
2. Rabbi Ahron Soloveichik, in *Logic of the Heart, Logic of the Mind* (Jerusalem: Genesis Press, 1991), 87, notes that the word for rebuke, *hokhaha,* can also mean "demonstration" or "evidence." He thus explains that the purpose of rebuke is to "prove" to another that they can improve and to enable them to reach their true self. Interestingly, in English, too, the related terms "prove" and "reprove" correspond to these meanings of *hokhaha.*

Leah's Gratitude

ותהר עוד ותלד בן ותאמר הפעם אודה את ה' על כן קראה שמו יהודה
ותעמד מלדת. (בראשית כט:לה)

And she conceived again and bore a son, and she said, "This time,
I will thank Hashem! Therefore, she named him Yehuda, and
[then] she stopped bearing. (*Bereshit* 29:35)

Leah gave birth to her fourth son and named him Yehuda to acknowl-
edge her gratitude to Hashem. The Gemara (Berakhot 7b) states that
Leah was the first person to thank Hashem. This is surprising: Did Adam,
Noach, and Avraham never express gratitude to Hashem?

Another Gemara (Shabbat 118) states that one who recites *Hallel*
every day is a blasphemer. Most commentators explain that this refers to
the *Hallel* of *Tehillim* 136, *Hodu LaShem*, which we recite each Shabbat
morning and which is also known as *Hallel HaGadol*. What is so wrong
with reciting Hallel every day? The *Ketav Sofer*[1] explains that in reality,
we should be thanking Hashem for *everything*, for every breath we take.
Saying Hallel is a show of recognition of Hashem's miracles. If you recite
Hallel HaGadol every day, it means you recognize that Hashem is in
charge of the miracles in the world. To praise Hashem each and every

---

1. *Ketav Sofer Al HaTorah* (Edison, 1991), 90.

day for the miracles He performs is recognizing the great events, while disregarding the "small things." Highlighting the great miracles, belittles what we take for granted on a daily basis, like the sun rising, flowers blooming, and us walking. That is why, says the *Ketav Sofer*, reciting *Hallel* every day is not something *Hazal* enacted.[2]

The *avot* certainly praised and thanked Hashem, but they lived a life of tremendous miracles, so their praise may not be viewed as on the highest level of *hodaa*. Leah, on the other hand, gave birth to Yehuda in the usual, natural childbirth. Thousands of babies are born each day. What was the great miracle of Yehuda's birth? It was natural. No great miracle occurred. Leah recognized Hashem's greatness and kindness and thanked Him for what most of us view as natural. Leah was the first to thank Hashem for something natural, recognizing that there's nothing natural about it. To appreciate what appears mundane is often a great miracle performed by Hashem on our behalf. We have to internalize this message and remember it in our lives too.[3]

---

2. See also *Meshekh Hokhma,* beginning of *Parashat Behukkotai.*
3. Rav Yeruham Levovitz (*Daat Torah, Ki Tavo* 26:3) explains that we bring fruit as *bikkurim,* even though this seems like a small token of appreciation, to instill in us that we need to be appreciative for the little things in life and acknowledge that they come from Hashem.

   Rabbi Dovid Miller, a *rosh yeshiva* in the YU Gruss Kollel, mentioned in his eulogy of Rabbi Benny Eisner, *z"l,* that Rabbi Eisner was the *baal tokeia* in the Gruss Kollel for many years on Rosh HaShana, and Rabbi Miller was the *makri.* When Rabbi Eisner was very sick, Rabbi Miller didn't think Rabbi Eisner would be able to blow the *shofar* that Rosh HaShana morning, but when the time came, Rabbi Eisner said he would blow. He began the blowing. He did the first thirty, the second thirty, and then he couldn't do anymore.

   After davening, Rabbi Miller went over to Rabbi Eisner to see how he was feeling, and Rabbi Eisner said, "HaKadosh Barukh Hu is so good. All my life, I never thanked Him for every breath I was able to take. Now, every breath I'm able to take, I thank Hashem, because every breath is so obviously a gift from Hashem."

Do the Ends Justify the Means?

When Yaakov left Lavan's house with his family, ready to move on, Rachel stole Lavan's *terafim* (idols of some sort) to prevent her father from engaging in idolatry. Lavan chases after Yaakov and accuses him of stealing his idols. The *Shvilei Hayim*[1] addresses an age-old question: Do the ends justify the means? If one's goal is very holy and noble, what kind of means can one utilize to attain that goal? Can one use less-than-holy methods to achieve the goal?

It seems that Rachel felt that she could. She stole her father's idols in order to prevent him from worshipping *avoda zara*. *Hazal*, however, say she was punished for stealing them – she died while giving birth to Binyamin.

Based on Rachel's punishment, it would seem that ends do not justify the means, but rather the opposite: The means create the noble ends. We have to act properly in order to create a positive result.

The problem, says the *Shvilei Hayim*, is that we have another incident that seems to lead to the opposite conclusion. In *Parashat Vayera*,

---

1. Rabbi Chaim Elazary, *Shvilei Hayim* (Canton OH, 1947), 46.

Sarah laughed when she heard she would have a baby, thinking it absurd that she or her old husband could have a conceive a child:

ותצחק שרה בקרבה לאמר אחרי בלותי היתה לי עדנה ואדני זקן.
(בראשית יח:יב)

And Sarah laughed within herself, saying, "After I have become worn out, will I have smooth flesh? And also, my master is old." (*Bereshit* 18:12)

When Hashem relayed this event to Avraham, although Sarah stated that Avraham was old, Hashem altered the truth and informed Avraham that Sarah referred to herself as old. We derive from this that one is permitted to lie to maintain the peace, in certain instances.[2] This would suggest that the ends (not to embarrass Avraham or get him upset at Sarah) justifies the means (Hashem changing the truth).

To explain the contradiction, we have to understand a fundamental principle, which we learn from one major difference between these two cases: If getting to one's goal using questionable means will cause someone pain, that is *prohibited*. To lie for the sake of peace in a way that does not hurt anyone would be permissible. Rachel caused pain and agony to Lavan, so she was held accountable, whereas Hashem did not cause pain to anyone. On the contrary, He even increased *shalom* between a husband and wife.

We see a similar case with Hanah and Peninah. According to *Hazal*, Peninah made fun of Hanah's not having children in order to push her to turn to Hashem and to enhance her *tefilla*. Despite her good intentions, Peninah was held accountable for causing Hanah pain, so she lost her children.

On the other hand, when Shmuel HaNavi is asked to anoint David as king, he fears that if this plan is revealed, he could be killed Hashem tells Shmuel to tell people he is on his way to bring a sacrifice.

---

2. Yevamot 65b.

Here, a white lie was permissible to maintain the peace as it did not negatively impact anyone.[3]

In conclusion, one may use what may seem to be inappropriate means to achieve a positive result as long as it does not adversely impact anyone else.

---

3. Rabbi Aaron Levine, in his book *Economics and Jewish Law: Halakhic Perspectives* (Hoboken, NJ: Ktav, 1987), 12, uses this biblical story to explain that at times it is permissible to conceal one's primary motive and reveal his secondary motive to protect a business interest when it is no one else's business what his primary motive is and it can jeopardize his interests.

Parashat Vayishlah
We Are All *Sheluhim*

When one thinks of Chabad one thinks *sheluhim*, emissaries, and the Lubavitcher Rebbe[1] tells us that this concept stems from our *parasha*.

We all have a job to do while we are on this earth. We are "day workers," and we have to do everything in our power to accomplish what we can and utilize all the time we have effectively, like Yaakov Avinu did when he worked for Lavan every second.

The Rebbe explains that *shelihut* relates to us in two ways. The first element relates to what we do personally. We have to work on ourselves in order to influence those close to us – our families, our communities, and beyond. Sometimes, though, we cannot get to everyone directly, but we can still touch the lives of others who will then go out on a *shelihut* of their own. The second element concerns delegating and empowering others to play a role as a *shaliah*.

These two phases are alluded to in *Parashat Vayetzeh* and *Parashat Vayishlah*.

---

1. *Chumash: The Gutnick Edition* (NY: Kol Menachem, 2008), 223.

(1) *Vayetzeh* means "he departed." Yaakov left his homeland on a *shelihut* to influence an environment which was alien to Judaism.

(2) *Vayishlah* means "he sent," alluding to the second phase of *shelihut*, when a *shaliah* is not satisfied with his own ongoing achievements and he inspires others to be *sheluhim*.

Vayetzeh suggests each person going out to affect change and do what they can do to have a positive impact directly on others. That is followed by the second phase, *Vayishlah*, which is empowering others to positively impact third parties. As the children of Yaakov Avinu, we have this strength in our DNA. He set the tone for us. We have to follow his lead and fulfill our *shelihut* as well.

Rav Yosef Soloveitchik, in a different context, talks about the concept of *shelihut* and explains:[2]

האדם נברא בתור שליח. עצם היצירה, הלידה, מכילה בתוכה בהכרח את דבר מינוי השליחות.

Man is created as a messenger; creation itself incorporates within it an appointment of a mission.

Each of us is born with a mission, in fact several missions, which change throughout our lives. Just the fact that I exist means I have a purpose to fulfill. Hashem put me in the world now to be able to fulfill my purpose. Why else would I be born if not to fulfill a mission? The Gemara (Nidda 15b) explains that we all take an oath before we are born, vowing to fulfill our task, our mission on this earth. It's similar to the oath Eliezer took before he went out on his *shelihut* to find a wife for Yitzhak Avinu.

The fact that we all live right now, in a certain community, and that we weren't born in a different era proves this to us. Nothing is haphazard. HaKadosh Barukh Hu put us on this earth, specifically at this time, to fulfill a certain mission.

Hashem knows what we can fulfill, using all our strengths and weaknesses. Sometimes, overcoming our challenges and weaknesses is

---

2. Rav Yosef Soloveitchik, *Yemei Zikaron* (Jerusalem: WZO, 1998), 11.

part of what we need to accomplish. It's important to keep in mind that Hashem only gives us a mission that we can accomplish.

As we know, there's no one who fulfilled this better than the Lubavitcher Rebbe, creating literal *sheluhim*.

In this vein, Rav Soloveitchik offers a deeper insight into *Parashat Vayera*: When the *malakhim* came to Avraham Avinu, the *pasuk* says that there were three men, but when they came to Lot in Sodom, the *pasuk* calls them two angels. Rav Soloveitchik suggests: Avraham knew he had a *shelihut* to fulfill, which meant he was the greatest *malakh* of them all! What is a *malakh* if not a being that is created to serve a purpose? Thus, there was no difference between a *malakh* and Avraham Avinu. Both existed only to fulfill their potential. They were like colleagues, and so the *malakhim* were referred to as men by Avraham, because relative to him, they were all equals. They had a purpose, and Avraham had a purpose. Avraham wasn't surprised to see them because in his eyes, they weren't any different from himself. They were each doing what they were created to do.

Lot, though, never heard of such a thing. A purpose of existence? A *shelihut*? He didn't live for a higher purpose, and so for him, they were *malakhim*. He wasn't on their level. That's what the belief system was in Sodom: Everyone lived for their own good, not for any higher purpose.

Every individual has a mission in life. We all have a *shelihut*, and that's what we learn from *Parashat Vayishlah*. Rav Soloveitchik adds that sometimes our *shelihut* changes. At different stages in our life, our purpose may have different themes and focuses. But at every stage of our life, we have a *shelihut*. May we be able to identify and fulfill our *shelihut* at every stage of our life.

Fear of Missing Out

וַיִּירָא יַעֲקֹב מְאֹד וַיֵּצֶר לוֹ וַיַּחַץ אֶת הָעָם אֲשֶׁר אִתּוֹ וְאֶת הַצֹּאן וְאֶת הַבָּקָר
וְהַגְּמַלִּים לִשְׁנֵי מַחֲנוֹת. (בראשית לב:ח)

Yaakov became very frightened and was distressed; so he divided the people who were with him and the flocks and the cattle and the camels into two camps. (*Bereshit* 32:8)

Yaakov feared his confrontation with Esav. The *pasuk* uses two expressions of fear – *vayira* and *vayetzer*. Rashi addresses this double language and explains that the first expression of fear refers to Yaakov's fear of being killed, and the second to his fear that he may have to kill his brother.

Hazal suggest another reason for his fear. Rabbi Yaakov Neiman explains that Yaakov was afraid because there were two mitzvot that Esav was able to fulfill and that Yaakov was temporarily unable to perform.[1] These were the mitzvot of honoring parents and dwelling in *Eretz Yisrael*. Yaakov was scared that in the merit of those two mitzvot, Esav would be viewed in the eyes of Hashem more favorably than he.

---

1. Rabbi Yaakov Neiman, *Darkhei Musar* (Tel Aviv: Or Yisrael Press, 1979), 66.

Rabbi Neiman explains this concept on two levels: First, Esav committed the worst sins imaginable, while Yaakov learned Torah all day. Why was Yaakov scared that Esav would find favor in Hashem's eyes for having performed one mitzva better than Yaakov? Esav didn't even live in *Eretz Yisrael leshem Shamayim*! Why was Yaakov so afraid? Could Esav's dwelling in *Eretz Yisrael* override all his other transgressions?

Yes, says Rabbi Neiman, and we see from here the significance of dwelling in *Eretz Yisrael*. While we may not understand it, there's something special in the *neshama* of someone who lives in *Eretz Yisrael*, and Yaakov understood that. That's why he was scared.[2]

There is something else we learn from Yaakov's fear. A great person is one who sees a positive trait in another and respects the other person for that. The lesson here is, "Who is wise? One who learns from every person."[3] There is virtue in seeing the greatness in someone even if they are on a lower spiritual or religious level in most other areas. If there's something about Shimon that Reuven can emulate, he has to seize the opportunity. That's what we learn from Yaakov Avinu. He looked at Esav, a *rasha*, to see what he could learn from him. Esav honored his parents exceptionally, and despite the fact that Yaakov was so much greater than Esav in every way, he realized that he could learn from Esav. The message for us is to be open to learning from others.

That's the difference between a regular person and an outstandingly virtuous person: The latter always looks for what he can learn from every person, and from every *part* of every person, so that he himself can become a better person. As the Ramban writes in his famous letter to his son: If you see in another person an attribute that you don't possess, lower yourself in humility. We have to be able to respect others and be open to learning from people whom we think of as not being as righteous as us. A parent from a child, a rebbi from a student. It's always possible. It doesn't matter who the person is.

---

2. Sanhedrin 102b speaks of Omri being rewarded for building cities in *Eretz Yisrael*, although he was far from being a *tzaddik*.
3. *Pirkei Avot* 4:1.

Yaakov had a fear of missing out. He was afraid that he lacked certain positive characteristics that Esav possessed. May we be able to look beyond the surface and recognize the positive traits of others so that we can internalize them and improve upon ourselves.[4]

---

4. One can ask why the first thing a Jew says when he enters *shul* every morning is *ma tovu ohalekha Yaakov* – "How goodly are your tents, O Yaakov!" This is a quote of the wicked Bilaam. Is that how we start our day? Explains the Torah Temima (in his commentary on the *siddur, Barukh SheAmar*): Bilaam may have been a *rasha*, but we don't care who first uttered the words. We only care about the words themselves and what we can learn from them.

Save Me from My Brother, from Esav

הצילני נא מיד אחי מיד עשו: כי ירא אנכי אתו פן יבוא והכני אם על
בנים. (בראשית לב:יב)

Now save me from the hand of my brother, from the hand of Esav,
for I am afraid of him, lest he come and strike me, [and strike] a
mother with children. (*Bereshit* 32:12)

When reading this *pasuk*, one may wonder about the double language:
"Save me from my brother, from Esav." Why the repetition? We know Esav
is Yaakov's brother. Rashi explains that the word "brother" is dropped
because Esav did not act toward Yaakov like a brother.

The Beit HaLevi[1] offers a different explanation. He quotes the
Zohar that says when one *davens*, he must specify exactly what he's
requesting. What was Yaakov requesting? When Yaakov realized that
Esav was approaching, he understood that one of two things could happen, and he was not content with either option. Esav was approaching
with four hundred men. Yaakov realized that Esav was either going to
try to kill him or, just the opposite, that Esav would want to reconcile

---

1. *Beit HaLevi on Bereshit and Shemot* (Warsaw, 1888), 33.

and become friends. Yaakov was worried about both of these options. Neither was good. He was worried about "his brother," the possibility that Esav would embrace him as a brother, and about "Esav," that Esav would show his true colors. This can also explain Yaakov's use of two different words for fear, *vayira* and *vayetzer*. He was afraid Esav was coming to kill him and equally worried that Esav wanted to befriend him.

"Hashem," Yaakov begged, "save me from both of these Esavs – the cruel one and the friendly one." Hashem did save him. Yaakov wasn't killed by Esav, although that *was* Esav's initial plan. Upon seeing (and receiving gifts from) Yaakov, Esav had a change of heart. Later, when Esav asked to travel together, Yaakov excused himself by saying his family's slow pace would only slow Esav down, and thus he escaped from the "friendly" Esav as well. Yaakov understood that Esav is dangerous when he wants to kill him *and* when he wants us to be very close to him.

The Beit HaLevi goes on to explain that Yaakov Avinu is the archetype of the Jewish people; he's the patriarch who goes into exile and returns with his children. Throughout the years of the Edomite exile, the exile we're still in today, both sides of Esav's personality are apparent. So often in our history have our enemies tried to kill us, to exterminate us. Hashem, in His great mercy, continuously preserves the Jewish people.

But then, sometimes, our oppressors grant us freedom and allow us to assimilate, with the intention of spiritual annihilation. "Be like us!" they say, and like the Greeks, they want us to accept their religion and their beliefs. They claim to share some beliefs with us, such as believing in a *Creator* and in the afterlife, and they nudge us to give a little, to meet them halfway. This "friendliness" is as dangerous as their spears and guns. An offer of spiritual freedom may be an even greater *nisayon* than a Crusade or a Holocaust.

Yaakov was worried about both aspects of exile: the exile that destroys with hate and the exile that destroys us with an embrace. For that reason, Yaakov davened to Hashem to spare him from both the brother-exile and the Esav-exile.[2]

---

2. See *Minhat Asher: Rav Asher Weiss on the Haggada* (New York: Mesorah Publications, 2008), 130, which expresses a similar idea regarding Lavan's desire to "uproot everything."

Recognizing Hashem's Gifts

ויותר יעקב לבדו ויאבק איש עמו עד עלות השחר. (בראשית לב:כה)

And Yaakov was left alone, and a man wrestled with him until the break of dawn. (*Bereshit* 32:25)

In this week's *parasha*, we are told that Yaakov crosses over the river with his family then returns alone to retrieve some small containers he had left behind. The Gemara in Hullin[1] asks why Yaakov returned for such small items. It answers that to a *tzaddik*, his money is more cherished than his body. Yaakov went back for these negligible items because he was so careful about his money. Why is money so beloved to *tzaddikim*? Because they are so careful not to steal, everything they acquire is with effort.

Asks the *Be'er Yosef*:[2] What are *Hazal* telling us? Yaakov went back because *tzaddikim* are more careful about their monetary assets than they are with their physical body? Is that true? Do we really believe that? Isn't this world a temporary place? We're supposed to be sojourners

---

1. Hullin 91a.
2. Rav Yosef MiSalant, *Be'er Yosef* (Jerusalem, 1972), 93.

in this world, temporary residents, not settled inhabitants. It almost sounds like Yaakov was very focused on his *gashmiyut*.

Additionally, the next *pasuk* tells us that Yaakov wrestled with a man. The word *vaye'avek* meaning "wrestled" is derived from the word *avak*, "dust." Their wrestling brought up a lot of dust. *Hazal* say that there was so much dust, it reached all the way to Hashem's throne of glory. That's not such a common phrase. Where else do we have it? In *asher yatzar* we say, "It is revealed and known before Your throne of glory." Is there any connection between these two uses?

The *Be'er Yosef* explains how someone's money is more beloved to him than his body. He quotes the Vilna Gaon who explains that it doesn't mean a person would rather die than lose his money, because if he's dead, his money serves no purpose. It means he'd rather suffer physical pain than financial pain. *Hazal* don't mean that Yaakov focused on his money. They mean that he worked hard for his money, and the physical effort was worth it for him to obtain his money.

The Gemara tells us in Yoma[3] that a person cannot touch what has been designated for his friend, even a hairsbreadth. Nothing I have can go to someone else and vice versa. Every single item HaKadosh Barukh Hu provides for each of us is through precise *hashgaha*. Every dollar I make, as long as I earned it permissibly, was designated for me. So too, every deal that falls through and every dollar that is lost happens through Hashem's *hashgaha*.

If one receives a gift from a great person, wouldn't one do every-thing in their power to protect and guard it? Every single item we have is a gift from HaKadosh Barukh Hu, and that's why *tzaddikim* care so much even about their "small containers." They realize that HaKadosh Barukh Hu gave these gifts specifically to them. Waste a gift from Hashem? Never! Because every asset comes through *hashgaha peratit*.

Thus, Yaakov's money was more precious to him than his own body because his acquisition of every single item came through physical effort to avoid theft. Yaakov's action of returning for the small containers reflected his recognition that everything is from HaKadosh Barukh Hu.

---

3. Yoma 38b.

The angel of Esav came to fight with him, contesting this belief, trying to undermine Yaakov's *emuna*. He tried to argue with Yaakov: You think you received these small containers from Hashem? You think Hashem cares about these? No, you got them through a good deal, a bargain. Yaakov's fight with the angel was a battle with the *yetzer hara*, who tried to convince Yaakov that there is no *hashgaha peratit*.

The fight reaching all the way up to the throne of glory hints to what the fight was about: The *avak*, the small things, come from the throne of glory. Yaakov fought until he reached the throne of glory, arguing that even the small things come from Hashem. Hashem is involved in every little thing in our lives. Perhaps that's why we say these words in *asher yatzar*, after the most mundane, physical thing we do, to acknowledge that Hashem is involved even in the most minute physical functions.

Retzon Hashem

וְיַעֲקֹב נָסַע סֻכֹּתָה וַיִּבֶן לוֹ בָּיִת וּלְמִקְנֵהוּ עָשָׂה סֻכֹּת עַל כֵּן קָרָא שֵׁם הַמָּקוֹם סֻכּוֹת. (בראשית לג:יז)

And Yaakov traveled to Sukkot and built himself a house, and for his cattle he made booths; therefore he named the place Sukkot. (*Bereshit* 33:17)

After the long-awaited meeting between Yaakov and Esav, the Torah tells us that Esav returned to Mount Seir and Yaakov traveled to Sukkot, where he built himself a house and "booths (sukkot) for his cattle." The *pasuk* tells us that the place is called Sukkot *because* Yaakov built booths for his animals there.

Often in the Torah, a place is named for a significant event that occurred at that location. It is therefore a bit puzzling that this city was named Sukkot for... stables that Yaakov built? In addition, the *Tur*, in *Hilkhot Rosh Hodesh* (*Orah Hayim* 417), says that Avraham, Yitzhak, and Yaakov are connected to the *Shalosh Regalim*, and that Yaakov represents Sukkot, based on this *pasuk*.

This stable-building seems to be a defining point for Yaakov. What is so significant about building a stable for his animals?

The *Ohr HaHayim*[1] on this verse provides an interesting insight: Yaakov did something that no one else had done before. He was the first person who, given the choice (which Noach wasn't), chose to look out for his animals and have compassion on them.

Rav Asher Weiss, in his *Minhat Asher*,[2] expounds upon this idea. There is a halakha that we're not allowed to cause pain and suffering to animals (*tzaar baalei hayim*). The Gemara[3] even states that it is a biblical prohibition. However, it is not explicit anywhere in the Torah, nor does the Gemara provide a source. If we look into the commentaries, we are stunned to find at least eleven suggestions as to its source in the Torah.

Rashi on the Gemara in Shabbat (128b) suggests that we learn *tzaar baalei hayim* it from the mitzva of *perika*, removing a heavy load from an animal. The *Shita Mekubetzet*[4] suggests, based on the Raavad, that we learn it from the prohibition to muzzle an animal while it's working. Others say it's *halakha leMoshe miSinai*. The Rambam in *Moreh Nevuhim*,[5] quoting a *pasuk* from *Parashat Balak*, suggests that the source is from the fact that an angel appeared to reprimand Bilaam for striking his donkey three times. The *Sefer Haredim*[6] says the source is the mitzva to follow Hashem's ways (*vehalakhta bedrakhav*),[7] which includes being compassionate toward all living things. The Hatam Sofer[8] likewise says that Hashem has compassion on all his creatures, and so too, should we.

Rabbi Asher Weiss then tells us to take a step back for a minute. How could there be eleven sources for this prohibition? There aren't eleven sources for anything! Why is it so hard to find a source for this prohibition? Because, says Rabbi Asher Weiss, there is no source. There are some ideas in our lives that fall under the category of the will of Hashem (*retzon Hashem*) – the "fifth *Shulhan Arukh*," as we like to call

1. *Ohr HaHayim, Bereshit* 33:17.
2. *Minhat Asher, Parashat Vayera*, siman 21:4, p. 130.
3. Bava Metzia 32b.
4. *Shita Mekubetzet*, Bava Metzia 32a.
5. Rambam, *Moreh Nevukhim* 3:17.
6. *Sefer Haredim*, chapter 14.
7. *Devarim* 13:5.
8. *Hatam Sofer*, Bava Metzia 32a.

it. There are the 613 mitzvot, which create a framework for other ideas. If you fulfill the mitzvot and follow the Torah, it will be obvious that causing pain and suffering to animals is something HaKadosh Barukh Hu does not want us to do. It becomes obvious that this is a value in *Yiddishkeit*. While we may find a hint to it here and there, there really is no source, because the source is the whole Torah. That is the concept of the will of Hashem.

Rabbi Weiss suggests that this concept applies as well to the mitzva of *hinukh*, providing our children with a proper education. Most *Rishonim* are of the opinion that mitzva of *hinukh* is *derabbanan*. Does that mean that on a *de'oraita* level, I can let my children do whatever they want, but the rabbis came along and invented the idea of educating and training them? No! Obviously the mitzva of *hinukh* is *de'oraita*, says Rabbi Asher Weiss. It's the will of Hashem! The nitty gritty details might be *derabbanan*, but the idea is obviously from HaKadosh Barukh Hu.

Now we can understand the *Ohr HaHayim*'s words on a deeper level. The significance of Yaakov making booths for his animals reflected that Yaakov kept not only the 613 mitzvot, but he also did the will of Hashem. The first thing Yaakov did, even before buying land in Shekhem, which we read about in the next *pasuk*, was to set up his animals in comfort. His heart led him to act in a way that he knew would be pleasing to Hashem. That is how a *ben Torah* conducts his every move – *al pi retzon Hashem,* according to the will of Hashem.

The Crime of the People of Shekhem

In their comments on this *parasha*, several *Rishonim* discuss *dinim*, one of the seven Noachide laws: A justice system should be set up to judge cases. The Ramban (on *Bereshit* 34:13) cites the Rambam as explaining that the reason why Shimon and Levi were justified in wiping out the entire city of Shekhem was because Shekhem, the son of Hamor, abducted Dinah, and the townspeople did not bring him to justice.

According to the Rambam, the mitzva of *dinim* is to set up courts to judge the other six of the Noachide laws. Thus, when the city of Shekhem didn't judge him for his theft, the entire city became liable to receive the death penalty. The Ramban is bothered by this explanation. If it's so clear that they were right, says the Ramban, then Yaakov should have agreed with their action. Why was he angry at Shimon and Levi?

The Ramban explains *dinim* to mean setting up a viable, honest society. It's an all-encompassing command to establish a functional society that is safe, secure, and productive – paying workers on time, not cheating people, not stealing, etc. According to the Ramban, *dinim* does not refer specifically to judging the other six Noachide laws; rather, if anything is violated, then the people are not fulfilling the mitzva of *dinim*.

A discussion on the application of the seven Noachide laws would not be complete without highlighting the opinion of the *Sefer HaHinukh*. In *Parashat Va'ethanan*, mitzva 416, the mitzva that forbids coveting the possessions of others, is discussed. There, the *Sefer HaHinukh* states that this mitzva applies to all men and women, and it applies to non-Jews as well.

We all know our basics: There are only seven mitzvot for gentiles. Gentiles are commanded (1) not to eat the flesh of a live animal, (2) not to blaspheme, (3) not to steal, (4) not to engage in forbidden sexual unions, (5) to set up a justice system to judge cases, (6) not to kill, and (7) not to practice idolatry. Coveting is not one of them! However, the *Hinukh* explains that the whole world is obligated in this mitzva because it is an extension of theft. The *Hinukh* emphasizes that these seven mitzvot are seven *categories* of mitzvot. In other words, we should not think that non-Jews have seven mitzvot while Jews have 613, because each of those seven includes numerous mitzvot.[1]

The privilege of being a Jew, says the *Sefer HaHinukh*, is that Hashem made each of our mitzvot into a separate command so that we can get more reward. He did not just give us categories that encompass many more commandments within them; rather, he gave us 613 separate mitzvot, because:

רצה הקדוש ברוך הוא לזכות את ישראל לפיכך הרבה להם תורה
ומצוות. (משנה מכות ג:טז)

HaKadosh Barukh Hu wanted to give merit to Israel, so he gave them the Torah and many mitzvot. (Mishna Makkot 3:17)

---

1. See Hullin 92a, for an opinion that Bnei Noach accepted thirty mitzvot.

Parashat Vayeshev

What's Wrong with a Little Peace and Quiet?

וישב יעקב בארץ מגורי אביו בארץ כנען. (בראשית לז:א)

Yaakov dwelt in the land of his father's sojournings, in the land of Canaan. (*Bereshit* 37:1)

The *parasha* opens after Yaakov's return to Canaan. Rashi interprets the first *pasuk* as follows:

ביקש יעקב לישב בשלוה, קפץ עליו רוגזו של יוסף. צדיקים מבקשים לישב בשלוה אומר הקב"ה לא דיין לצדיקים מה שמתוקן להם לעולם הבא, אלא שמבקשים לישב בשלוה בעולם הזה. (רש"י בראשית לז:א)

When Yaakov sought to live in tranquility, Yosef's troubles appeared. The righteous seek to live in tranquility; Hashem says: Is what is waiting for the righteous in the next world not enough, that they request tranquility in this world as well? (Rashi on *Bereshit* 37:2)

Yaakov wanted a little peace. He had a challenging life and wanted to live out his golden years. But what happened instead? The troubles with

Yosef began. Rashi explains, *tzaddikim* wish for a little peace and quiet, and Hashem says, "*Tzaddikim* have the world to come, they don't need this world as well."

What was so wrong with Yaakov's desire to dwell in peace? After all that Yaakov had been through, first with Esav, then Lavan, then Dina, and then Esav again, his life was filled with trials and turmoil. What was so terrible about desiring a little peace and quiet?

There are a number of answers to this question, and we will explore several.

RAV MOSHE FEINSTEIN: HINUKH NEVER ENDS

Rav Moshe Feinstein, in his *Darash Moshe*, explains that the message of *Hazal* is about educating our children. Yaakov thought he was done with worrying about *hinukh*. His children were all grown up and on the right *derekh*. His children were the twelve tribes – he didn't have a Yishmael or an Esav to worry about, and he figured that his mitzva of *hinukh* was complete.

At the point when Yaakov felt content, he is reminded that even with grown and righteous children, the job of a parent never ends. The commandment of *hinukh* is lifelong. You can have a ninety-year-old parent and a seventy-year-old child, and it's still the parent's job to tell the child what to do and help the child fulfill his *derekh* in *avodat Hashem*. As parents, we can never rest on our laurels and feel as if we fulfilled our task. As children mature, the manner in which we educate them may change, but a parent's responsibility toward his child never ends. That is a lesson *Hazal* teach us from Yaakov Avinu.

RABBI NISSAN ALPERT: NO BREAK FROM SINAT HINAM

Rabbi Nissan Alpert, in *Limudei Nissan*,[1] offers a different explanation, suggesting that the Torah is teaching us a fundamental lesson. As long as there is internal strife among Jews, there is no *shalom* in the world. Until there's *shalom bayit* within the nation of Yisrael, no one has the right to sit back and relax in personal peace. From external enemies, Hashem will protect us, and maybe in that area we can experience peace

---

1. Rav Nissan Alpert, *Limudei Nissan* (New York: Otzar Hasefarim, 1991), 259.

and tranquility. However, from the troubles within our nation, the terrible hatred that causes exile and prevents tranqulity among our nation, there is no relief until we remedy it.

Yaakov wanted to relax, but when there's *sinat hinam* in the world, nobody can relax. We each have to do what we can to attain unity and only then can we earn our personal peace.

RAV SHIMON SCHWAB: NO BREAK
FROM COMMUNAL ACTIVITY

Rav Schwab, in *Maayan Beit Hashoeva*, explains that for Yaakov, as one of the *avot*, there was something wrong with his desire for some peace and quiet. Avraham had accepted the responsibility of publicizing Hashem's name in the world. His *avoda* was to teach the world that there is a Leader ruling the universe. He spread the belief in one God; that was Avraham's whole essence.

Yitzhak did the same thing. He spread the word of Hashem, and Yaakov did so as well. That was the *avoda* of the *avot* – to spread the message of HaKadosh Barukh Hu.[2] At this point, Yaakov wanted to do some internal work and focus on himself. While it is great to invest in self-improvement, that cannot come at the expense of focusing on public needs. It was fine for Yaakov to focus on himself and his family, but he could not ignore the rest of the world.

Yaakov wanted tranquility from public life, to enter into early retirement, and Hashem told him his plan was wrong. You're a public person, Yaakov, and you have to keep being a light unto the nations. Perhaps that is why the words *eretz megurei aviv* appear in the *pasuk,* hinting that this was the land in which his fathers converted people (*megurei* being related to *ger*). That was to be Yaakov's continued mission as well.

Instead, Yaakov ended up moving to Egypt, where he managed to inspire an entire nation. We need to care for the well-being of our families, but we must never cease to be involved in communal activities, be it in our *shuls*, day schools, yeshivas, *hesed* organizations, etc. Only through our continued contribution to the community may we reach true tranquility.

---

2. See Rambam, beginning of *Hilkhot Avodat Kokhavim*.

RABBI NISSAN ALPERT, PART TWO:NO FOURTH AV

Rabbi Nissan Alpert offers an alternative suggestion as well. Yaakov wanted Yosef to be the fourth *av*, and he wanted to appoint him in his own lifetime. Yaakov wanted it to be clear to everyone who was the chosen one, unlike what occurred between him and Esav. He thought Yosef as leader would be best for the continuity of the family, which would eventually become a nation. He thought this was needed. Yaakov's desire to dwell in tranquility means that he wanted to hand the reins of leadership to Yosef.

If Yosef would have been an *av*, what would his special *midda* have been? Each of the *avot* represented a trait: *hesed, gevura,* and *emet.* What would Yosef's attribute have been? Rabbi Alpert suggests that it would be *middat hamalkhut,* leadership. Up until this point, there was no need for a king because there was no nation. But now that the family had grown and Yaakov knew they would be a nation, there had to be a king to preside over them.

Hashem, however, disagreed. There wasn't supposed to be a fourth *av*, and it was not yet time for Yaakov to rest in peace.

Hatred or Jealousy?

וַיַּחֲלֹם יוֹסֵף חֲלוֹם וַיַּגֵּד לְאֶחָיו וַיּוֹסִפוּ עוֹד שְׂנֹא אֹתוֹ. (בראשית לז:ה)

And Yosef dreamed a dream and told his brothers, and they continued to *hate* him. (*Bereshit* 37:5)

וַיְקַנְאוּ בוֹ אֶחָיו וְאָבִיו שָׁמַר אֶת הַדָּבָר. (בראשית לז:יא)

So his brothers *envied* him, but his father awaited the matter. (*Bereshit* 37:11)

Yosef shared both of his dreams with his brothers. After he described his first dream to his brothers, their reaction was one of hatred, but after his second dream, the Torah describes the brother's reaction as one of envy and jealousy.

The Beit HaLevi[1] explains the reason for this shift. The focus of the first dream was with respect to physical wealth and success in this world. Yosef would be blessed with supporting not only his brothers but the entire region (as we know occurred in Egypt).

The second dream focused on spiritual superiority over his brothers. Based on the content of the dreams, we can understand the different

---

1. *Beit HaLevi on Bereshit and Shemot* (Warsaw, 1888), 38.

reactions of the brothers. When it came to wealth and riches, the brothers weren't jealous. That's not what they were after. If someone is rich, it doesn't reflect anything about their essence. Property is external and doesn't define who we are. Inherently, a wealthy person is no different from a poor person. They didn't like that Yosef said he was going to be richer than they, but they weren't jealous. They didn't care to be in the center of the physical world.

But when it came to the spiritual pursuits of Torah and *avoda*, they knew that someone who has more in those areas is inherently greater, and they were jealous of that. Someone who is deeper in Torah and mitzvot is inherently different and greater than others who are not. The Gemara (Bava Batra 21a) says:

קנאת סופרים תרבה חכמה.

One who is jealous of others in the field of Torah, will gain wisdom.

They wanted the spirituality for themselves and were thus jealous of Yosef after he relayed his second dream, which symbolized his higher level of spirituality.

The baalei musar suggest that when it comes to *ruhniyut,* we should seek to attain what others greater than us have achieved. When it comes to *gashmiyut*, we should admire people who make do with little.

We need to keep a proper perspective and not desire the home, car, or other material riches of our neighbors, but rather the Torah and spirituality attained by those on a higher level than us.

Who Sold Yosef?

ויהי כאשר בא יוסף אל אחיו ויפשיטו את יוסף את כתנתו את כתנת
הפסים אשר עליו. ויקחהו וישלכו אתו הברה והבור רק אין בו מים.
וישבו לאכל לחם וישאו עיניהם ויראו והנה ארחת ישמעאלים באה
מגלעד וגמליהם נשאים נכאת וצרי ולט הולכים להוריד מצרימה.
ויאמר יהודה אל אחיו: מה בצע כי נהרג את אחינו וכסינו את דמו. לכו
ונמכרנו לישמעאלים וידנו אל תהי בו כי אחינו בשרנו הוא וישמעו
אחיו. ויעברו אנשים מדינים סחרים וימשכו ויעלו את יוסף מן הבור
וימכרו את יוסף לישמעאלים בעשרים כסף ויביאו את יוסף מצרימה.
(בראשית לז:כג-כח)

Now it came to pass when Yosef came to his brothers, that they
stripped Yosef of his shirt, of the fine woolen coat which was
upon him. And they took him and cast him into the pit; now
the pit was empty there was no water in it. And they sat down to
eat a meal, and they lifted their eyes and saw, and behold, a caravan of Yishmaelites was coming from Gilead, and their camels
were carrying spices, balm, and lotus, going to take [it] down to
Egypt. And Yehuda said to his brothers, "What is the gain if we
slay our brother and cover up his blood? Come, let us sell him to
the Ishmaelites, but our hand shall not be upon him, for he is our
brother, our flesh." And his brothers hearkened. Then Midianite
men, merchants, passed by, and they pulled and lifted Yosef from

the pit, and they sold Yosef to the Ishmaelites for twenty silver [pieces], and they brought Yosef to Egypt. (*Bereshit* 37:23–28)

When we read through the *pesukim* describing the capture and sale of Yosef, the following story unfolds. The brothers throw Yosef into a pit and then enjoy a meal together. Next, the brothers see a caravan of Arab spice merchants passing through the area. Yehuda convinces his brothers that it would be better to sell Yosef to the Arab merchants rather than commit an act of murder. That leads us to infer that the brothers then sold Yosef.

The *pesukim*, however, continue to relay the events with the passing of Midianite merchants, who pull Yosef out of the pit and sell him to the Yishmaelites. The Rashbam[1] raises a shocking question: Who, in fact, sold Yosef to the Yishmaelites? What should be an obvious question is often overlooked!

This is an amazing example of how we can read the same *pesukim* for years and yet never stop to focus on the wording and analyze what the Torah actually states. If we look closely at the text, as the Rashbam stresses, the Torah does not explicitly state that the brothers actually carried out Yehuda's suggestion and sold Yosef. The *pesukim* portray that the brothers *decided* to sell Yosef to the Arabs, but then says, "*they* pulled Yosef up and sold him." It's a very ambiguous "they" – and we don't, in reality, know who actually sold Yosef.

The Rashbam claims that the basic *peshat*, the plain meaning, of the *pasuk* is that the passing Midianites pulled Yosef out of the pit and sold him to the Yishmaelites.[2]

The Rashbam explains that the brothers were eating their meal and they weren't quite next to the pit, because the Torah tells us, "Do not eat by the blood" (*Vayikra* 19:26), so they would not have eaten near the pit where Yosef was in danger. While engaged in their meal, the brothers gazed and saw an Arab convoy approaching from a distance. The brothers

---

1. Rashbam on *Bereshit* 37:28.
2. In his first comment on *Parashat Vayeshev*, the Rashbam states that Rashi, his grandfather, told him later in life that he would have rewritten some of his commentary to better reflect the *peshat*.

remained where they were (perhaps higher up on a mountain) and completed their meal while awaiting the Yishmaelite convoy to approach the area from below so that they could then transact business with them. In the interim, the Midianites came across the pit, pulled Yosef out of it, and then sold him to Yishmaelites without the brothers' knowledge. Based on the simple reading of this chapter, the brothers may have intended to sell Yosef, but in actuality, Yosef was sold by another party prior to the brothers being able to fulfill their intended plan.[3]

The Rashbam, who seeks to stick to the *peshat*, provides us with a very interesting insight that differs from what seems to be "common knowledge" with respect to the story of the sale of Yosef. His approach should remind us to always read the text carefully so we can familiarize ourselves with the simple facts portrayed in the source before we delve into the deep blue sea of the commentaries.

---

3. The Rashbam continues to explain the *pasuk* in *Parashat Vayigash* where Yosef reveals himself to his brothers and says: "I am the brother you sold" (Bereshit 45:4). The Rashbam explains that the word "you sold" really means "you caused the sale." Perhaps Yosef believed that the brothers arranged the sale that was conducted by the Midianite merchants or blamed them for leaving him in a situation where he was vulnerable to such a transaction.

Hidden, Yet Present

וישבו לאכל לחם וישאו עיניהם ויראו והנה ארחת ישמעאלים באה מגלעד
וגמליהם נשאים נכאת וצרי ולט הולכים להוריד מצרימה. (בראשית לז:כה)

And they sat down to eat a meal, and they lifted their eyes and saw, and behold, a caravan of Yishmaelites was coming from Gilead, and their camels were carrying spices, balm, and lotus, going to take [it] down to Egypt. (*Bereshit* 37:25)

The brothers throw Yosef in the pit, and then they sit down to eat. Soon enough, they see a caravan of Yishmaelites passing, carrying sweet-smelling, aromatic spices. Of course, *Hazal* wonder about this – since when do Yishmaelite merchants carry aromatic spices? They were actually known to sell foul-smelling products. So, why this time did they carry pleasant merchandise? Rashi on this *pasuk*, suggests that it was out of respect for Yosef. He was being exiled to Egypt. The least he could have was a pleasant journey.

The *Otzrot HaTorah*[1] explains: Yosef was thrown into a pit by his own brothers, which according to some, was filled with snakes and scorpions. Then, he was removed, sold to Yishmaelite merchants, brought to Egypt, and had no idea whether his father was in on the whole plot

---

1. Rabbi Eliyahu Chaim Cohen, *Otzrot HaTorah* (Bnei Brak, 2006), 233.

(after all, Yaakov had sent him to Shekhem in the first place to look for his brothers). He was undoubtedly lonely and depressed. So, a little spice was going to make him feel better? How would pleasant merchandise make any difference to Yosef in his situation? Rashi adds that this illustrates the reward of *tzaddikim*, but that just raises a further question: Is this really all *tzaddikim* can expect?

The *Gedulat Mordekhai*, quoted in *Otzrot HaTorah*, brings a *mashal*. A man going through a terrible illness has to undergo surgery. After the surgery, the patient is under anesthesia, completely unconscious. His family members surround his bed, wondering about him, hoping for a sign of life. Suddenly, they see his eyes flicker, his fingers twitch, a little movement, and they cry out in joy. Why? What is so exciting about a little movement when the patient is still unconscious and not yet out of the woods? The family doesn't even know if the surgery was successful!

The little movements are a sign that salvation is on the horizon, and the promise of better days to come fills the family with joy.

Yosef was going through terribly trying times. The pleasant-smelling spices were a slight movement on Hashem's part, a wink, so to speak, to show Yosef that Hashem was at his side. That small notion from Hashem gave Yosef the strength and the optimism to continue.

When Klal Yisrael go through difficult times, there's often a wink from Hashem, reminding us that He is with us. Perhaps He is hidden, but He is definitely present. Many times, it's only the people going through the tragic times who can comprehend the hidden blessings. We have to look for and find the little notion from Hashem hidden within the challenge. That's the message of the spices. Within every difficult challenge, Hashem threads a glimmer of hope, a silver lining around the cloud. It is up to us to recognize this communication from Hashem and to comprehend that He is with us throughout our challenges and triumphs.

Yaakov's Mourning

ויקרע יעקב שמלתיו וישם שק במתניו ויתאבל על בנו ימים רבים.
ויקמו כל בניו וכל בנתיו לנחמו וימאן להתנחם ויאמר כי ארד אל בני
אבל שאלה ויבך אתו אביו. (בראשית לז:לה)

And all his sons and all his daughters arose to console him, but
he refused to be consoled, for he said, "Because I will descend
on account of my son as a mourner to the grave"; and his father
wept for him. (*Bereshit* 37:35)

The brothers dipped Yosef's coat into blood, and they returned to Yaakov
and showed it to him. Yaakov understood that Yosef had been killed by
an animal. He tore his clothes and mourned. The Torah tells us that he
would not accept any comfort.

Why didn't he accept any comfort? Everyone in life accepts comfort when tragedy strikes, and the pain gradually softens. So why couldn't
Yaacov be comforted? Rashi on this verse comments:

אין אדם יכול לקבל תנחומין על החי.

A person cannot be comforted with respect to someone who
is alive.

However, if Yaakov thought Yosef was dead, why couldn't he be comforted? The answer is based on a Hatam Sofer, who points out a Gemara (Taanit 30b) that declares:

כל המתאבל על ירושלים זוכה ורואה בנחמתה.

Whoever mourns over Yerushalayim merits seeing its comfort.

The problem, points out the Hatam Sofer, is that this Gemara is in the present tense, when it really should be in the future tense. We don't see the comfort presently, while we're still in exile. Explains the Hatam Sofer, we know that Tisha BeAv is called a *mo'ed*, and on that day we don't recite *Tahanun*. How is it a *mo'ed* if the *Beit HaMikdash* was destroyed on that day?

Another question can be asked: Is there any other religion in history that still mourns over something that took place two thousand years ago? Who thinks about anything that happened even five years ago? We don't only think about it, we act on it – we relive it, and we conduct ourselves in accordance with acts of mourning. The fact that we mourn, says the Hatam Sofer, proves that it's not dead. That's the biggest proof that the *Beit HaMikdash* is alive in *Shamayim* and will come down when Hashem says the time is right.[1] That's why the Gemara uses the present tense. The fact that we mourn is the greatest proof that the *Beit HaMikdash* still exists and will return.

A story is told about Napoleon, who saw Jews mourning on Tisha BeAv and inquired about it. He was told that the Jews were mourning the destruction of their Temple. Napoleon was puzzled, since he did not hear of any recent destruction of a Jewish Temple. Upon hearing that the crying and weeping was in connection with a Temple that was destroyed centuries ago, Napoleon responded, "If this Temple is so ingrained in the people that it cannot be forgotten, it will surely be rebuilt in the future."

Yaakov tried to be comforted, he *wanted* to be comforted, but it just didn't work. He kept crying and mourning. The fact that he kept mourning was the proof that Yosef was still alive.

---

1. See Rashi on Sukka 41a.

Being a True
Oved Hashem

ויהי ה' את יוסף ויהי איש מצליח ויהי בבית אדניו המצרי. (בראשית לט:ב)

Hashem was with Yosef, and he was a successful man, and he was
in the house of his Egyptian master. (*Bereshit* 39:2)

The word *vayehi* – "and it was" appears three times in this short verse.
Why all this repetition?

Lahazot BeNoam Hashem[1] suggests that a true *eved Hashem* has
to serve Hashem under all circumstances, whether we're "feeling it" or
not. Often, we only turn to Hashem when things are difficult. That is
when we remember to have *kavana*, focus well, perform mitzvot carefully, recite *Tehillim*, and seek *segulot*. But when things are going well,
we have a harder time recognizing Hashem in our lives. This scenario is
referred to in a *pasuk* in *Devarim* (32:15) that describes how Am Yisrael
rebel we have everything that leads usto forget from where it all came.

But then there's the opposite case, too. Some people only remember Hashem when everything is going well, but when things are difficult,

---

1. Shealtiel Meir Ben Harav Shlomo Hacohen (Jerusalem, 2013), 355.

they get angry, lose their focus and can't concentrate during *davening*. Neither of these extremes is called real commitment to HaKadosh Barukh Hu.

Yosef HaTzaddik was a real *eved Hashem*. He served Hashem in all situations. The first *vayehi* is the title, so to speak, of the *pasuk*: Hashem was with Yosef. This is followed by two explanations: Yosef was successful, meaning that everything was going well, and throughout that period he served Hashem. Later the *pasuk* tells us that Yosef served his master, meaning that he was a slave, and throughout that period he served Hashem. He was connected with Hashem in all circumstances. The Torah is teaching us the true meaning of service. It's not always easy, but it's always our job.

Interestingly, the *pasuk* in *Parashat Ki Tavo* says:

תחת אשר לא עבדת את ה' א-להיך בשמחה ובטוב לבב מרב כל. (דברים כח:מז)

Because we didn't serve HaKadosh Baruch Hu with simchah, He held us accountable. (*Devarim* 28:47)

Isn't it interesting that within the rebuke, where this *pasuk* is positioned, Hashem demands *simha* from us? That is exactly what Hashem wants from us: that even when things aren't going well, we have to be connected with Him and be happy to serve Him.

A story is told that the Lev Simha told his Hassidim to have special *kavana* when reciting the words "*ana Hashem*" during Hallel. There was an argument among the Hassidim as to whether the Rebbe was referring to *ana Hashem hoshia na* or *ana Hashem hatzliha na*? The *rebbe's* son approached the *rebbe* to resolve the debate among the *hasidim*. The *rebbe* responded that it was neither: It was when he said *ana Hashem ki ani avdekha* – "Please Hashem, for I am your servant." This is the key to being a Jew, understanding that we are here to serve Hashem.[2]

May we be able to fully appreciate what it means to be an *oved Hashem* in all circumstances.

---

2. Rav Asher Weiss (*Shiur Parashat Yitro* 2011, www.torahbase.org) adds that when the word "*ana*" ends with an *alef* (אנא ה' הושיע נא) it connotes "pleading"; while when "*ana Hashem*" is spelled with a *heh* (אנה ה' כי אני עבדך) it connotes "gratitude."

The Secret to Success

וירא אדניו כי ה' אתו וכל אשר הוא עשה ה' מצליח בידו. (בראשית לט:ג)

And his master saw that Hashem was with him, and whatever he (Yosef) did Hashem made prosper in his hand. (*Bereshit* 39:3)

Potifar saw that Hashem was always with Yosef. Rashi explains that this means that Yosef was always invoking Hashem's name. *Midrash Tanhuma*[1] expands on this: When Yosef walked in to serve his master, he'd be whispering, "Ribbono Shel Olam, help me be successful in all that I do." Potifar asked Yosef what he was whispering, and Yosef answered that he was asking Hashem for assistance.[2]

The *Shomer Emunim*[3] states that the closer we bring ourselves to Hashem, the nearer Hashem brings Himself to us. The more we believe in *hashgaha*, the more *hashgaha* we will merit. Hashem repays us measure for measure. As it says in *Tehillim*,[4] "Hashem is our shadow"; He

---

1. *Midrash Tanchuma, Bereshit* 37:8.
2. *Emet LeYaakov* (41:17) points out that every phrase uttered by Yosef in the Torah mentions Hashem.
3. Rav Yosef Irgas, *Shomer Emunim*, Essay on *Hashgaha Peratit*, ch. 23.
4. *Tehillim* 121:5.

moves according to our movements. However we act, HaKadosh Barukh Hu reciprocates.

A story is told about a rich man who gave a lot of *tzedaka*, but didn't believe that his wealth was from God. He attributed his success to his own acumen. Hashem sent Eliyahu HaNavi on a mission. The man went out to the market one day to buy oxen, when he bumped into Eliyahu. Eliyahu asked him, "Where are you going?" to which the man answered, "To the market, to buy oxen."

Eliyahu said, "Say '*im yirtzeh Hashem.*'" The businessman was confused. "What does God have to do with this? The money is in my wallet; it's up to me to make the purchase." Eliyahu responded, "Okay, have it your way..." The rich man continued on his journey, during which his wallet fell out of his pocket. Eliyahu hid it on a rock in the forest. The man arrived at the market, found amazing oxen, but when he reached for his wallet, he discovered that it was gone. He left the market dejected and upset.

After some time, the same scenario repeated itself. The businessman went out to buy some goods, and he bumped into Eliyahu HaNavi in the form of an old man. Eliyahu told him to say *im yirtzeh Hashem*, but the man refused. Eliyahu made the man fall asleep, whereupon his money was stolen, and finally the man realized that something was going on. At long last, he attributed everything to Hashem. He decided that from then on, he'd always say *im yirtzeh Hashem*.

The next time the wealthy man went out to the market, he encountered Eliyahu HaNavi in the form of a poor young man seeking work. Eliyahu asked him where he was headed, and he responded that he was heading out to the market to buy oxen, *im yirtzeh Hashem*. Eliyahu blessed him to find oxen without too much effort, to which the businessman replied, "If I find good oxen, I'll come back and hire you." He bought the oxen, which suddenly escaped him and ran into the forest. He chased after them and reached the rock where all his money was resting.

We have to bring HaKadosh Barukh Hu into our lives and remember to keep Him close to our hearts and on our lips always – and we will, with Hashem's help, succeed like Yosef, the man of success (*ish matzliah*).

Yosef's Two Dreams and Lights of Hanukka

Yosef had two different types of dreams in *Parashat Vayeshev*; one was related to the heavens, the other to the earth. These two dreams complement each other. It's impossible to gather your bundles if you're not looking up at the stars. Similarly, it's impossible to be in the stars if you don't have your feet planted firmly among your bundles. We need both areas of leadership, *ruhani* (spiritual) and *gashmi* (physical).

There's a *makhloket* in the Gemara (Shabbat 23a) whether the conditions of the mitzva of the menorah have to be fulfilled at the time of the lighting or when the menorah is placed into position. The conclusion is: at the time of lighting.

However, Rav Shlomo Zevin[1] posits that the message of both applies to Hanukka. One element we celebrate on Hanukka is the lighting up of the souls that took place at the time of Hanukka. The Greeks made decrees to restrict our observance of mitzvot, but we defeated them and were again able to fulfill our mitzvot. We were able to kindle our inner flames and enlighten ourselves spiritually.

---

1. *LaTorah VeLaMo'adim*, 73.

But there was also *hanaha,* a placement. We were able to become strong and set up a Jewish government for the next centuries. There was a physical war and victory, when we became firmly planted, and that's symbolized by *hanacha,* placement.

The two miracles that we celebrate symbolize these two elements. Lighting symbolizes the spiritual victory, and *hanaha* the physical one.

Those are also Yosef's two dreams. Yosef represents Klal Yisrael. We have to make sure we are perfected in both areas of lighting and *hanaha,* spiritual and physical. We have to raise our physical lives and connect them to our spiritual lives. Our sheaves need to have an eye toward the stars. We need both elements as we seek to fulfill the mitzvot to the best of our ability.

The Power of Hope

Hanukka, the last Yom Tov established by *Hazal*, is a holiday of lights at the darkest time of year. These lights represent the hope that should take us through this long and dark exile, a message further brought out in *Parashat Vayeshev*.

Tamar, the hero of this *parasha*, represents this concept of darkness, the idea of retaining hope throughout a seemingly hopeless ordeal.

Rav Yosef Soloveitchik, in *Days of Deliverance*,[1] points out that that the *Mashiah* is descended from a past of questionable relationships: Lot and his daughters, Yehuda and Tamar, and others. Both Tamar and Lot's daughters were in a state of hopelessness – they saw only darkness and could easily have given up. However, they resisted such thoughts and instead persevered, intent on building a future. In the Rav's words:

> A pair of vulgar, unwitting young girls, the daughters of Lot, were the sources of the power to begin everything anew. They believed that the whole world had been destroyed, and it was up to them to recreate it. True, they did it in a horrible way; but their primitive intention was good and demonstrated a remarkable strength of spirit. That same strength is a foundation of the kingdom of the

---

1. Rabbi Joseph B. Soloveitchik, *Days of Deliverance* (Hoboken, NJ: Ktav, 2007), 151.

House of David, of the eternity of Israel: The belief in tomorrow and in a kingdom of justice.

This is the root of the kingship of the House of David – no matter how dark the present is, we must always hope for a brighter future.

In a similar vein, at a burial, as soon as the body is buried, we recite the *kaddish* of the resurrection of dead. As soon as dirt is tossed over the body of the deceased, we exclaim and declare that we believe in the resurrection. That is who we are. If not for the belief in the future, exemplified by Lot's daughters, the idea of the kingdom of the House of David could not have been realized.

We see this concept played out with Tamar as well. Tamar, showed the strength of waiting and hoping, of having faith even when she became the subject of mockery. We are all Tamars. The *ko'ah* to realize beyond hope and logic that something will evolve out of the darkness stems from Tamar.

What gave the Hashmonaim confidence despite being vastly outnumbered and surrounded by darkness? Their strength and belief came from Tamar and from Lot's daughters. This belief in a bright future despite the present darkness was in their blood from their ancestors.

Throughout our years in the darkness of the exile, we must retain the hope that Tamar had and that empowered the Hasmonaim. This is the root of the kingdom of David and must remain strong in our hearts at all times.

Parashat Miketz

Rise or Fall, It's All about Focus

A brief but powerful thought with respect to the transition between last week's *parasha* and this week's: In last week's *parasha, Parashat Vayeshev*, the Torah depicts Yosef as the favored son. He receives a special garment from his father, and his brothers are jealous of him. By the end of the *parasha*, though, Yosef is in prison. He starts on top of the world and ends with hitting rock bottom. Conversely, in this week's *parasha*, Yosef starts off in prison and ends up the viceroy of Egypt. In one *parasha*, he falls all the way down, in the next, he springs all the way up. What transpired that caused this contrast?

In *Parashat Vayeshev*, Yosef occupied himself with telling everyone else his dreams. He was the focal point of his own thoughts and conversations. When one is self-centered, it will lead to downfall. Transitioning into *Parashat Miketz*, however, Yosef occupies his time listening to and interpreting other people's dreams (the cupbearer, baker, and Pharaoh himself). When one focuses on assisting others, it will lead to greatness.

We can apply this lesson to our own lives. When we are busy talking about our own dreams, and aspirations – when we are the focus – then even if we are at the top of the world right now, we are heading down. That's not a successful way to live. We should rise to the occasion and learn to listen to other people's dreams, difficulties, and situations and focus on their needs. That is the way to attain greatness.

First Impressions

ושם אתנו נער עברי עבד לשר הטבחים ונספר לו ויפתר לנו את חלמתינו:
איש כחלמו פתר. (בראשית מא:יב)

And there with us was a Hebrew youth, a slave of the chief slaughterer, and we told him, and he interpreted our dreams for us; [for] each [of us], he interpreted according to his dream. (*Bereshit* 41:12)

When Pharaoh was disturbed by the dreams he had and could not find someone to interpret them correctly, the royal butler suddenly remembered Yosef, whom he had met in prison. Rashi comments on the words the butler used: "a Hebrew youth, a slave":

ארורים הרשעים שאין טובתם שלמה. מזכירו בלשון בזיון.

The wicked should be cursed because their goodness is never complete. He [the butler] referred to [Yosef] in a derogatory manner.

Rashi classifies the butler as a wicked man. But did the butler really do such a terrible thing that it warrants that he should be labeled a wicked person? The *Lekah Tov*[1] quotes the *Mahazeh Eliyahu*, who asks: How did the butler have the gall to depict Yosef in such a derogatory manner? After all, Yosef interpreted his dream and predicted his return to glory.

The *Mahazeh Eliyahu* explains that the *pasuk* doesn't say that the butler straight out called Yosef a fool. Rather, he called Yosef a youth. He knew that Pharaoh's impression of such people (lads, Hebrews, and servants) is that they're from the lowest classes of society. The butler's intention was to provide Pharaoh with a negative first impression of Yosef because he knew that it's very hard to overcome a first impression.

What was the wickedness of the butler? He didn't say anything evil outright; rather, he wanted to plant a negative perception about Yosef into Pharaoh's head. He knew Yosef could do great things, and he didn't want Yosef to succeed.

That's the pernicious nature of an evil word about someone else. No amount of convincing can rid a person of their first impression. This is the power of the spoken word.

The Alshikh[2] compares this to *lashon hara* – once we hear something, it burns in us forever. It's impossible to uproot or forget it. He compares a negative word to *rotem* wood, which burns forever. Our bad word sits like *rotem* wood in our listener's heart, so it can never be forgotten.

This is even the basis for a halakha. Says Rav Chaim Shmuelevitz,[3] it is forbidden for a judge to hear one side of a case before both parties are present, because the judge may be influenced by the first side he hears, and then it will be nearly impossible for him to change his initial perception.

We need to be extremely careful not to defame someone or provide a negative first impression about someone that will taint another's perception. Such damage is hard to undo.

---

1. *Lekah Tov*, 259.
2. Ibid.
3. Ibid.

Pharaoh's Acceptance of Yosef's Interpretation

ויהי בבקר ותפעם רוחו וישלח ויקרא את־כל־חרטמי מצרים ואת כל
חכמיה ויספר פרעה להם את־חלמו ואין פותר אותם לפרעה. (בראשית
מא:ח)

Now it came to pass in the morning that his spirit was troubled;
so he sent and called all the sorcerers of Egypt and all its sages,
and Pharaoh related to them his dream, but none could interpret
it for Pharaoh. (*Bereshit* 41:8)

Pharaoh awoke from his sleep very troubled over his dreams. He called
for all his sorcerers, yet none could interpret his dreams correctly. Rashi
picks up on an extra word in the above *pasuk*: Why does the *pasuk* say
"none could interpret it for Pharaoh" instead of "none could interpret
it"? "For Pharaoh" seems superfluous.

Rashi explains this word to mean that while there *were* interpretations, none were to Pharaoh's satisfaction. He wasn't content with
the explanation that he would have seven daughters and then bury all
seven. When Yosef interprets the dream, however, Pharaoh was pleased
with his interpretation. What made Pharaoh reject all the others and
accept only Yosef's? Let us focus on three suggestions provided by the

commentators that explain the difference between the interpretations provided by the wise men of Egypt and Yosef's interpretation.

MESHEKH HOKHMA[1]

Regarding Pharaoh's first dream of the cows, the *pasuk* states:

והנה שבע פרות אחרות...ותעמדנה אצל הפרות על שפת היאר. (בראשית מא:ג)

> And behold, seven other cows... and they *stood next to the cows* on the bank of the river. (*Bereshit* 41:3)

There were seven fat cows, and then skinny cows, and they stood next to each other. However, when Pharaoh relays his dream to Yosef, he neglects to make any mention of the fact that the cows stood near each other. What does this difference in wording symbolize?

It hints at an action that Pharaoh would have to take during the years of plenty in order to help him survive the years of famine. While the fat cows stood there, the skinny cows were already standing next to them. This symbolized that already during the good years Pharaoh would have to think about the bad years. He would have to plan for the famine by saving up food during the years of plenty. When Yosef related to this small detail that Pharaoh knew he had left out, Pharaoh saw that Yosef knew it all and that his interpretation was correct. Pharaoh exclaimed, "Is there any man like this, in whom is God's spirit?" (*Bereshit* 41:38), because Yosef even interpreted parts of the dream that Pharaoh had omitted.

NAHLAT TZVI

The *Nahlat Tzvi* offers a different explanation as to why Pharaoh accepted Yosef's interpretation over all the others.[2]

Pharaoh always had dreams, but never the same one twice, with the same message. He inferred from this that this dream must somehow

---

1. *Meshekh Hokhma, Bereshit* 41:3.
2. Meshulam Gross, *Nahalat Tzvi* (NY: Sentry Press, 1942), 101.

be of national importance, that it was different from his usual dreams that just applied to himself. He understood that if the dream was just about him, one would have been enough, so in this case, the two dreams with one message must be bigger than him. Thus, when only Yosef's interpretation affected national destiny, it made sense to Pharaoh that his was the true interpretation.

RAV SHLOMO ZEVIN

Rav Zevin provides a third explanation.[3] He says that even though the same *lashon* was used in both dreams, there was a significant difference between the two dreams. There are three types of dreams according to Rav Zevin:

Some dreams are total nonsense.

Other dreams are a clear vision. Instead of being a metaphor or *mashal*, the dream is a message from God, a clear vision (like the dreams the prophets experienced).

The third type of dream is somewhere in the middle: It carries a true message, but it requires interpretation. It's like a *remez*, a hint, and it needs explanation.

Within this third category, there are two subcategories. The dream can either be clear-cut information about what is going to happen, so that when the dream is interpreted, the message is clear. Alternatively, the dream can require the dreamer to act upon the information to actualize the dream.

Pharaoh's dream was of the third type: a message clothed in a metaphor. Based on all the interpretations he received, he realized that only Yosef's could be correct. His reasoning was that Hashem wouldn't tell him something that was out of his control, and only Yosef's interpretation was a message with direction, telling him what Hashem wanted from him.

This concept applies to life too, not just to dreams. There are three outlooks on life that a person can have, explains Rav Zevin, and these three parallel the three types of dreams:

---

3. Rav Shlomo Zevin, *LaTorah VeLaMo'adim*, 75.

There's the attitude that the whole word is nonsense and there's no point to it. Life is without rules.

Other people take the world as it is: This is the world, there's nothing I can do about it.

The Torah, however, doesn't believe in either of these extremes.

The type of dream from which we should learn is the dream that requires interpretation. It is for us to contemplate our actions. The world wasn't created for nothing. The world needs interpretation and then action to be taken.

No matter what life brings, we need to internalize and act upon it.

The Significance of the Names of Yosef's Children

ויקרא יוסף את שם הבכור מנשה: כי נשני אלקים את כל עמלי ואת
כל בית אבי. ואת שם השני קרא אפרים: כי הפרני אלקים בארץ עניי.
(בראשית מא:נא-נב)

Yosef named his firstborn son Menashe, because "Hashem has
helped me forget all of my difficulties and my father's house."
His second son he called Efraim, because "Hashem has helped
me multiply and become great in this land." (*Bereshit* 41:51–52)

Rav Yosef Nehemia Kornitzer,[1] the last prewar Rabbi of Krakow, is
bothered by these *pesukim*. Why did he name his sons in that order of
gratefulness? Shouldn't Yosef have named his first son as a thanks to
Hashem for making him succeed in the land and bear children, and only
because of that would he name his second son in honor of healing him
from all the trials he'd been through? It seems like his firstborn should
have been named Efraim, and his second son Menashe.

---

1. Rav Yosef Nehemia Kornitzer, *Hidushei Rav Yosef Nechemia* (Jerusalem: Chemed,
   1998), 101.

Another question one can ask is: Was Yosef actually happy that he forgot his father? We know that he *did not* forget his father at all. The memory of his father is what protected him from Potifar's wife. Obviously, something much deeper is meant here.

The Gemara[2] tells us that the more successful one is, the greater his *yetzer hara* becomes. The greater I feel about myself, the more credit I want to take for myself. Even worse, Yosef was submerged in a land of abominable actions, a lowly land where everyone was involved in all that is forbidden. He was the only person in Egypt who had not sunk into the quagmire of evil. Imagine the difficulty and *nisyonot* he went through on a daily basis! And yet, he was successful. Even though he was so successful, he still didn't succumb to his growing *yetzer hara*.

How does one succeed in life as Yosef did? How does one take precautions to protect himself? What can one conjure up in his mind to help him remember to control himself in difficult situations?

There are two areas one can focus on to protect himself from the *yetzer hara* as he continues in his successes. First, one must always remember the days when it was harder. When someone has success financially, he should always remember when times weren't as good, when life wasn't so easy. Only if one remembers the earlier times can he be successful. That's why at the Pesah Seder we start by discussing our degradation and only then move on to the praise: because we don't want it to go to our heads, to think we were redeemed from Egypt through our own strength.

The second way to protect oneself spiritually is to always remember his forefathers and what they lived for. He should ask himself what they would want him to do in the situation he finds himself in. One must always ask himself: When will I reach the level of the previous generations, of the great people in my lineage and the *gedolim* of Klal Yisrael? One should always look at the generations gone by and see how great they were and then reach for the stars.

We find that Yosef did exactly these things. When Yosef was being seduced by Potifar's wife, he envisioned his father's face in the window and was thus able to prevent himself from sinning.

---

2. Sukka 52b.

Such protection is necessary when one is on his own. When alone, conjuring up the image of a holy ancestor is a way to overcome a challenge. But once someone is *zokhe* to have a child, it becomes much clearer to him why he has to stay true to his tradition. He realizes that if he isn't strong, then there's no hope for his children. A person is much more careful with his actions and *ruhniyut* once he has children. Every father wants his children to have true fulfillment and reach even greater heights and exceed his own achievements. Once we have children, the aspect of remembering one's ancestors is less crucial.

People who believe they can leave all *hinukh* up to the school and that what is done in the home doesn't matter are mistaken. A school has to partner with the parents in order to bring to fruition the potential of a child.

Therefore, we can finally understand our questions on the above *pesukim*. Yosef, as we know, was very successful and had a tremendous *yetzer hara* against him. Throughout his life, he focused on his down days, his earlier stages of lowliness, when he was being sold by his brothers, when he was in the pit, when he was in jail. He recalled all and realized that it wasn't his doing that had subsequently made him great. He recalled his father, whom he needed to help escape the clutches of Potifar's wife. That's why his first son was named Menashe, because at that point he needed his father's memory. While he was alone, he needed to remember his lowliness and recall his father's greatness.

But once he had a child, he didn't need that any longer. He had the strength to remain steadfast in his ways because he had children. He would stay pure in order to be a good role model for his children.

Yosef's children became his greatest motivation for maintaining and improving his spiritual level, and hopefully our children will be that for us as well.

Another explanation of the significance of the names of the sons of Yosef is provided by Rav Shlomo Zevin,[3] whose thought is connected to Hanukka, which usually falls on *Parashat Miketz*. Rav Zevin points out that these two names are not just about one individual and his two children. We know that the actions of the fathers portend for their

---

3. *LaTorah VeLaMo'adim*, 78.

descendants; in this case, these two children represent *middot* that we all have to have. We're referred to as *she'erit Yosef* and *haben yakir li Efraim*. We are all Yosef's children, so we are all Menashe and Efraim. They represent two of our *kohot*: Menashe represents turning from evil – help me root out my pain, my difficulties, the negative. Efraim represents doing good, gaining the positive.

Klal Yisrael is never referred to as Menashe's children because turning from evil is not the *ikar*. We are called the children of Efraim because the *ikar* is the obligation, the doing good, the light of Torah. Focusing on doing good will get rid of the evil and the difficulties.

And maybe these two *middot* are exactly the *middot* that Hillel and Shammai argued about. In general, they had different *middot*, but at this time of year, we talk about the *makhloket* they had regarding how many candles we light on each night of Hanukka (Shabbat 21b).

What's the root of this *makhloket*? Rav Zevin explains that fire does two things – it destroys and removes, and it illuminates and shines. Both aspects are necessary. We have to root out our *yetzer hara* and our negative tendencies, and of course, we have to focus on the positive, to spread the light of the Torah.

The Maccabim did both. They had to burn out the Greek mentality, the Hellenistic nature of some Jews, and then they had to purify the *Beit HaMikdash* and rekindle the menora's lights and the light of Torah and mitzvot.

What was the Maccabim's primary objective? Which aspect do we remember? That's the *makhloket* between Hillel and Shammai. Shammai posits that we descend from lighting eight candles to one, because the main objective is to root out the negative, symbolized by this descending kindling of the menorah. Hillel believes that the main objective is the light, and the darkness will automatically disappear with the addition of light, so we are to increase the light by increasing a candle each night.

Efraim and Menashe are both *middot* of Klal Yisrael, but the main objective is the element of Efraim (spreading the light) over Menashe (extinguishing evil).

The Purpose of
Yosef's Charade

When Yosef's brothers appear in Egypt in search of food during the famine, we are told that Yosef recognized his brothers, but they did not recognize him (likely because his appearance had changed over the twenty-two years that transpired). Two major questions can be raised regarding Yosef's behavior while he was viceroy in Egypt: First, why didn't he ever send a message to his father that he was alive, especially since he *knew* his father would be agonizing over his disappearance? He was gone for more than two decades, and he didn't even send a postcard! Second, when he finally meets his brothers, why didn't Yosef reveal himself to them immediately rather than conducting a charade and conspiracy scheme?

Let's explore several commentaries that address these issues and provide differing opinions.

RAMBAN

The Ramban recognizes a *pasuk* that seems to be out of context.

ויזכר יוסף את החלמות אשר חלם להם ויאמר אלהם מרגלים אתם
לראות את ערות הארץ באתם. (בראשית מב:ט)

> And Yosef remembered the dreams that he had dreamed about them, and he said to them, "You are spies; you have come to see the nakedness of the land." (*Bereshit* 42:9)

In the middle of the *pesukim* describing Yosef meeting his brothers, the Torah seems to randomly note that Yosef remembered his dreams from previous years, and then he accused the brothers of being spies. The Ramban's thesis is based on this one *pasuk*, which he believes sheds light on the entire episode. The Ramban initially cites Rashi's interpretation and refutes it. Rashi claims that Yosef recalled the dreams because his dreams had just been fulfilled right before his eyes as his brothers bowed down to him. The Ramban disagrees and argues that in the dream all of the brothers bowed down to him. Now, though, one brother, Binyamin, was absent. Therefore, the dream had not yet been fulfilled in its entirety.

The Ramban suggests, therefore, that Yosef's goal became to devise a plan that would result in Binyamin descending to Egypt so that he too would bow down to Yosef, thereby fulfilling the dream. That is what prevented Yosef from revealing himself "prematurely" to his ten brothers, prior to having the eleventh brother present to bow down to him and fulfill his dream.

Were it not for this explanation, claims the Ramban, Yosef would be considered a sinner for causing his father so much pain and anguish (over his "death," Shimon being imprisoned, and Binyamin being taken to Egypt). If Yosef's actions had been purely for revenge or any other reason, he would have been taken to task for hurting his father.

However, a question that begs asking is, why was it so necessary for Yosef that all aspects of his dream come true, especially at the expense of his father? Some suggest that Yosef understood his dreams to have been prophetic. Since his dreams were prophecies, he took it upon himself to make sure that they came true.

ABARBANEL

The Abarbanel takes a different approach, suggesting that Yosef was testing his brothers to see if they had changed at all over the twenty-two years that had passed. Did they regret their actions? If he revealed himself would they try to kill him? He wanted to be sure that they did complete *teshuva*.

What is *teshuva*? Real *teshuva* is when a person finds himself in exactly the same situation he was in when he transgressed, yet this time he holds himself back from sinning.[1] Yosef thought, "I have to figure out a way to get all of my brothers here and then take away Binyamin, the other son of Rachel and the other one who is beloved to our father, and see what they do. Do they let him go, like they did with me, or do they count him as one of them and stand up and protect Binyamin."

That was why he did not reveal himself to them.

The Abarbanel's answer still leaves us with a difficulty: Was it Yosef's place to get his brothers to do *teshuva*, especially at the expense of his father's pain? Isn't this very concept of trying to get his brothers to become better individuals (to give them *musar*)[2] what got Yosef into trouble in the first place? Abarbanel does not specifically address this issue, but as we will see in a moment, Rav Shimshon Refael Hirsch offers a logical explanation.

RAV SHIMSHON REFAEL HIRSCH[3]

Rav Hirsch offers a third approach.

Rav Hirsch explains Yosef actions as altruistic: He wanted his brothers and himself to be a family unit once more before returning to their father. He didn't want to give his father back one son (himself) but take away the other ten (by their being jealous or unforgiving). He was attempting to figure out a way from both his point of view and that of his brothers' to create a unit of brotherhood, and in that way return all of Yaakov Avinu son's to him.

All of Yosef's actions were for the sake of their father. He needed a plan that would ensure that he didn't feel any hatred toward his brothers, nor they toward him. He had to be sure that they had done *teshuva*, as that would enable Yosef to wholeheartedly forgive them. Yet, he also

---

1. Rambam, *Hilkhot Teshuva* 2:2.
2. *Abarbanel* (Tel Aviv: Hapoel HaMizrachi Publishers, 5744), 400.
3. *The Pentateuch*, Bereshit, 591.

had to be able to ensure his brothers that he held no hard feelings toward them. Yosef's only goal in trying to ensure that they had done *teshuva* was so that they could all become one family unit again.

Furthermore, since the original hatred of the brothers toward Yosef stemmed from Yosef seeming better than them – from the love Yaakov showed Yosef and Yosef's dreams – the real test would be now, when they stood in front of Yosef who actually *was* in a greater position than they were, as viceroy of Egypt. There was so much opportunity for them to be jealous at this point, so he needed to show them how much he loved them.

Yosef needed his brothers to realize that he had always acted *leshem Shamayim*, and the only way to do that was to get them into a situation where he could really hurt them, and then, instead of harming them, say, "I'm Yosef, and I love you." At that point they would realize that all along he was acting *leshem Shamayim*.

Yosef's whole charade and his silence for twenty-two years served a purpose: to get the brothers to do *teshuva* and realize that he had always acted *leshem Shamayim* and that he was not out to hurt them. This would reunite the family and bring true peace to his father Yaakov.

All of My Troubles

ויאמר אלהם יעקב אביהם אתי שכלתם יוסף איננו ושמעון איננו ואת
בנימן תקחו עלי היו כלנה. (בראשית מב:לו)

And their father Yaakov said to them, "You have bereaved me –
Yosef is gone, and Shimon is gone, and you want to take Binyamin! All these troubles have come upon me." (*Bereshit* 42:36)

When the brothers returned home from Egypt to obtain Binyamin so
they could return with him to Yosef, Yaakov firmly objected. "You have
made me bereaved," he said. "Yosef is no longer with us, nor is Shimon.
Now you want to take Binyamin?" Yaakov then ends his sentence with
the words *alai hayu kulana* – "all these troubles have come upon me."
What exactly does this phrase mean?

Rav Asher Weiss[1] quotes the Vilna Gaon, who offers a very creative interpretation of this phrase. The word *alai* appears in another
context earlier in *Sefer Bereshit*. When Yaakov Avinu feared that Yitzhak
would recognize that he was disguised as Esav, Rivka reassured him that
he had nothing to fear. Rivka told him: *alai kilelatkha beni* – "your curse
will be upon me" (*Bereshit* 27:13). The Gaon explains:

---

1. *Rav Asher Weiss on the Haggadah* (New York: Mesorah Publications, 2008), 130.

הכוונה היא, כי רבקה הודיעה ליעקב בזה, שלא יבואו עליו צרות נוספות,
כי אם שלש אלו הרמוזות במלת "עלי", היינו עלי בראשי תיבות, צרת
עשו, צרת לבן, וצרת יוסף.

The intention is that Rivka informed Yaakov that trouble will only
come to Yaakov from three things, which are hinted to from the
acronym *alai* – Esav, Lavan, and Yosef.

Rivka was expressing to Yaakov that he had nothing to fear with respect
to tricking Yitzhak because only three specific troubles were supposed
to affect Yaakov in his life: Esav, Lavan, and Yosef, represented by the
rashei teivot of the word *alai* (עלי = עשו לבן יוסף). When the brothers
requested to take Binyamin to Egypt, Yaakov said, "What are you talking
about? I am only supposed to agonize due to three people: Esav, Lavan,
and Yosef. Not Binyamin. You can't take Binyamin. This is not meant
to be." That's how the Gaon understands the *remez* (hint) connecting
the words in these two *pesukim*.

Rav Asher Weiss develops this idea further, suggesting that these
three troubles of Yaakov represent something much larger. Since *maase
avot siman lebanim* – the deeds of our forefathers prefigure the history
of the Jewish people – these three troubles represent the three types
of troubles that Klal Yisrael suffer throughout exile. The troubles that
happened to Yaakov are the troubles that happen to us, his descendants.

Esav represents those who want to annihilate us physically, like
Esav wanted to physically kill Yaakov. There are "Esavs" throughout the
generations that want to annihilate the Jewish people: Hamans and Hit-
lers, *yemah shemam*.

The second type of trouble is that of Lavan. His goal was not to
kill Yaakov; rather, Lavan wanted to destroy Yaakov spiritually. Thus,
Lavan represents our enemies who wish to do the same, people like
Antiochus and Stalin, *yemah shemam*.

Then we have the troubles of Yosef, which is the problem of *sinat
hinam*, the inner fighting within Klal Yisrael. That's the worst trouble, the
one we still suffer from today. It is the trouble that we bring upon ourselves out of a lack of respect for our fellow Jew. The actions of the Esavs
and Lavans are not in our control. We just react to them. However, the

trouble of Yosef is one that we can prevent. Each and every individual has to do his part to spread *ahavat Yisrael* so that we can bring an end to the difficulty of Yosef, the *sinat hinam* that caused our exile and prevents our redemption.[2]

---

2. This idea also relates to the *minhag* of *karpas* at the beginning of the Seder. What is the meaning of the word *karpas*? The word *karpas* appears in Rashi at the beginning of *Parashat Vayeshev*, which refers to the muilticolored garment that Yaakov gave to Yosef (as royal garments are depicted in Megillat Esther – *hur, karpas, tehellet ve'argaman*). At the beginning of the Seder we take the *karpas* symbolizing Yosef's garment and dip it in salt to symbolize the brothers that dipped Yosef's garment in blood (see Rabbenu Manoach on Rambam, *Hilkhot Hametz UMatzah* 8:2). Before we discuss the *geula* from Egypt, we first need to understand what brought us into exile. It was the hatred between brothers that led to the exile and something that has repeated itself throughout history. May we learn our lesson and unite so we can be worthy of a complete redemption.

Binyamin's Silence

Sometimes we are missing an important detail from a biblical story, and because of that, we get a warped and incomplete understanding of the story we're reading. Often, the missing detail concerns the age of a character of the story. There are various stories in *Tanakh* where, when we don't recognize the age of a character, we may not fully appreciate what is transpiring. The greatest example of this is *Akedat Yitzhak*.

When we're young, we think Yitzhak was a little boy who had no idea what was going on at any point in the story. We think he innocently followed his father because he didn't know any better. We don't realize that Yitzhak was thirty-seven years old when the *Akeda* took place, and he surely could have overtaken his father, who was very old. By not realizing his age, we lack appreciation of Yitzhak's true sacrifice and *mesirut nefesh*.

Another example is from *Sefer Shmuel*, in the *perek* that describes the anointing of Shaul as king.[1] How old was Shaul when he was anointed? The *pasuk* calls him a *bahur*,[2] and so we imagine he was around fifteen to twenty years old. But if you do the math, with the knowledge that Shaul was king for only two years, Shaul was at least fifty, and

---

1. *I Shmuel*, chapters 9–10.
2. *I Shmuel* 9:2.

probably even sixty, when he was anointed because he had a forty-year-old son when his kingship ended. The word *bahur* in the *pasuk* therefore can't mean young, but rather, it means *nivhar*, chosen.

So, we see that when we're missing the age, we're missing a big aspect of the story.

Based on this, Rabbi Rivlin[3] asks, how old was Binyamin in this week's *parasha*? How old was this "little brother" whom everyone was worried about, whom everyone was busy discussing? Throughout the *pesukim*, he's called "little brother" twelve times! We imagine he's three or four years old!

However, when they go down to Egypt just a short while later, the *pasuk* tells us that Binyamin goes with his *ten sons*! The Torah doesn't tell us exactly how old he is, but he had to be at least thirty in this week's *parasha* for the rest of the story to make sense. Therefore, *katan* here doesn't mean baby; it means the youngest.

That's Rabbi Rivlin's first message: Always make sure you have all the relevant facts.

If Binyamin was in fact around age thirty, isn't it amazing that he didn't open his mouth even once during this entire episode? He didn't say a word in *Parashat Miketz* or *Parashat Vayigash*! Not to his father to appease him, not about being accused of stealing the goblet. He was completely silent the entire time. As an adult, he very well could have stood up for himself, so why didn't he?

There's a deep message to be learned here. Binyamin wasn't speechless. He just held his tongue. It's not that he didn't have anything to say, but rather that he practiced his *midda* of *shetika*, silence, that he inherited from his mother, Rachel.

Binyamin had two famous descendants who also practiced *shetika*: Esther HaMalka kept her identity private and didn't reveal where she was from (*Esther* 2:20), and Shaul didn't tell anyone he was king even after he was anointed because he was such a humble man.

Binyamin's stone on the High Priest's breastplate is called the *yashpeh*, which spells *yesh peh* – "he has a mouth"! It symbolizes that

---

3. Rav Avraham Rivlin, *Iyunei Parasha* (Kerem B'Yavneh, 2000), 256.

while Binyamin had what to say, he overcame it with his *midda* of *shetika*.[4]

The lesson for us is that sometimes, even if we have something to say, it's better to keep quiet.

---

4. Perhaps Binyamin learned to keep quiet after witnessing that his older brother Yosef's speech is what got him into trouble.

Bli Ayin Hara

There is a gemara in Berakhot[1] that tells us that *ayin hara*, the evil eye, has no control over the tribe of Yosef:

אמר להו אנא מזרעא דיוסף קא אתינא דלא שלטא ביה עינא בישא
דכתיב בן פורת יוסף בן פורת עלי עין ואמר רבי אבהו אל תקרי עלי
עין אלא עולי עין.

He said, "I am from the seed of Yosef and the evil eye does not control me, as is stated: 'A charming son is Yosef, a son charming to the eye.'" Rav Avahu says don't read it charming to the eye, rather above the [evil] eye.

Why is Yosef above the evil eye? The Gemara provides one idea: The eye that didn't want to take from something that wasn't his (Potifar's wife), cannot be affected by the evil eye. He controlled his eye, so "the eye" has no control over him.

Perhaps we can say something deeper, based on another question on the *parasha*. If we look at Pharaoh's words to Yosef when he asked Yosef to interpret the dreams, Pharaoh says:

---

1. Berakhot 20a.

וַיֹּאמֶר פַּרְעֹה אֶל יוֹסֵף חֲלוֹם חָלַמְתִּי וּפֹתֵר אֵין אֹתוֹ וַאֲנִי שָׁמַעְתִּי עָלֶיךָ
לֵאמֹר תִּשְׁמַע חֲלוֹם לִפְתֹּר אֹתוֹ. (בראשית מא:טו)

I have dreamed a dream but have not found an interpretation,
and I heard about you, that you can interpret my dream. (*Bereshit*
41:15)

Yosef responded that his gift was from Hashem and not his own power.
Pharaoh's immediate response is introduced with the word *vayedaber*,
whereas he had initially addressed Yosef with the word *vayomer*. There
is a big difference between these two words. Rashi tells us that *vayedaber* is a harsher form of speech than *vayomer*. Why did Pharaoh start off
softly and then move on to harsher speech?

Says Rabbi Imanuel Bernstein in his *sefer* on aggada:[2]

> The individual who represents immunity from the evil eye is Yosef.
> How was he able to achieve this? A quality which stands out
> about Yosef is his determination to do the right thing regardless
> of the reaction it will provoke from those around him. Initially,
> this gets him into trouble as he insists on telling his brothers the
> dreams he has had where they all bow down to him. Later on,
> his resistance to Potiphar's wife is a classic example of this trait.
> She is the only other person present in that situation...as the lady
> of the house, she wields great authority over him...yet for every
> day over the course of a year, he makes himself more and more
> unpopular with her.

Yosef would say and do what he felt was right, even if it would endan-
ger him. Once Yosef decided something, he didn't focus on the consequences of following through with his decision. Sometimes, we have
to focus on the consequences; as we know, all *middot* have a middle
ground and have to be balanced. But there are certain personalities in

---

2. Rabbi Immanuel Bernstein, *Aggadah: Sages, Stories and Secrets* (Beit Shemesh: Mosaica Press, 2015), 96.

Tanakh who highlight certain extreme *middot* in order to teach us about the *midda*, and then our goal is to balance it.

While we have to think about the consequences of our actions, there's also an idea that if we focus on them too much, we'll be too paralyzed to do anything.

Rabbi Bernstein continues:

> Twelve years later, when he is taken out of jail to see if he can interpret Pharaoh's dreams, we see this trait express itself in a rather extreme form. Pharaoh greets Yosef and says, "I have dreamt a dream, and there is no one to interpret it, and I have heard about you that you are able to hear a dream and interpret it." This itself is quite remarkable; Pharaoh is bestowing a compliment on an insignificant slave who has spent the last dozen years rotting in jail.[3]

Pharaoh has just complimented Yosef, a lowly slave. His life hinged on finding favor in Pharaoh's eyes. Yosef should have answered accordingly, yet what did he say? "Yosef said, 'It is not me; God will respond with Pharaoh's welfare.'" Yosef rebuffs Pharaoh's compliment and corrects his mistake!

He corrected Pharaoh, however dangerous that would be. He told Pharaoh that he was wrong! How could he do that? No one spoke to Pharaoh that way!

After Yosef's rebuff, Pharaoh's attitude toward Yosef changed and his speech became harsher. The mood changed from *vayomer* to *vayedaber*. But Yosef didn't care. He only cared about saying and doing what was right.

That's why *ayin hara* doesn't affect him, because his eye for truthfulness is loyal and sharp and not affected by anything around him. Now we understand why Yosef represents immunity from the evil eye. His sense of whether or not he is doing the right thing does not come from his surroundings. It is generated from an internal sense of right and

---

3. Ibid.

wrong. Hence, the negative vision of those around him does not lead to negative self-vision.

This little nuance in the *pasuk* gives us a whole insight into what Yosef did, the risk that he took, and what we can learn from him.

Sometimes we just have to take action. One of the cities *Bnei Yisrael* had to conquer on their way into *Eretz Yisrael* was called Heshbon. I heard in the name of Rav Kook that sometimes we have to conquer our own *hesbonot*, calculations, in order to do the right thing. He was referring specifically to moving to *Eretz Yisrael*, but the concept applies to all areas.

Lessons from the Rambam about Hanukka

The Rambam starts *Hilkhot Hanukka* with history, which is very unusual for him. The fact that he puts history into the *Mishneh Torah* means that the history is relevant to the halakha. The Rambam tells the story of the Greeks and how the Hashmonaim overcame them, and he ends off by saying that Jewish autonomy returned for at least two hundred years, until *Hurban Bayit Sheni*.

בית שני, כשמלכי יון גזרו גזרות על ישראל, ובטלו דתם, ולא הניחו אותם לעסוק בתורה ובמצוות ופשטו ידם בממונם ובבנותיהם, ונכנסו להיכל, ופרצו בו פרצות, וטמאו הטהרות וצר להם לישראל מאד מפניהם, ולחצום לחץ גדול. עד שריחם עליהם א-להי אבותינו, והושיעם מידם והצילם, וגברו בני חשמונאי הכהנים הגדולים, והרגום, והושיעו ישראל מידם והעמידו מלך מן הכהנים, וחזרה מלכות לישראל יתר על מאתים שנים, עד החורבן השני.

During the period of the second Temple, when the Greek kings were in power, they proclaimed decrees against the Jewish people, abrogating their religion and forbidding them to study the Torah or to perform the divine precepts. They laid their hands on their wealth and their daughters; they entered the Temple and broke through it, defiling the things that were pure. The people of Israel were sorely distressed by their enemies, who oppressed them ruthlessly until the God of our fathers took pity, saved, and rescued them from the hands of the tyrants. The Hasmonean great priests won victories, defeating the Syrian Greeks and saving Israel from their power. They set up a king from among the priests, and Israel's kingdom was restored for a period of more than two centuries, until the destruction of the Second Temple.[1]

Asks Rabbi Yehuda Amital, why does the Rambam, in relating the story of Hanukka, include the point about our autonomy?[2] Why does he emphasize this point when the *malkhut* and the leadership of the time were far from remarkable in their righteousness?

Rabbi Amital quotes Rav Kook, who says there are different stages and levels to the return of Jews to *Eretz Yisrael*, and the ultimate level of Jewish government in *Eretz Yisrael* is one that is based on Torah and halakha. Says Rabbi Amital, the government in the times of the Hashmonaim was most certainly *not* acting at this ultimate level to which Rav Kook refers. In fact, it was far from it. They didn't follow Torah and halakha, especially as time went on. So why does the Rambam add this detail as if it is something to celebrate?

Rav Amital gleans a crucial halakhic nugget based on this comment of the Rambam. He explains that the obligation of *hallel vehodaa* is not based on having the ultimate end result of our exile with *Mashiah's* arrival. Just having a life in *Eretz Yisrael* where a Jew can live as a Jew, even if the government is far from perfect, fulfills the obligation of *hallel vehodaa*. The *pasuk* from *Zechariah* that describes the days of redemption and how life will be when the *Mashiah* arrives states:

כה אמר ה' צ-באות עד ישבו זקנים וזקנות ברחבות ירושלם ואיש משענתו בידו מרב ימים. ורחבות העיר ימלאו ילדים וילדות משחקים ברחבתיה. (זכריה ח:ד-ה)

---

1. Rambam, *Hilkhot Megilla VeHanukka* 3:1–3.
2. *Be'er Miriam: Hanukka* (Tel Aviv, 2013), 182–85.

So said the Lord of Hosts: Old men and women will yet sit in the streets of Yerushalayim, each with his cane in his hand because of old age. And the streets of the city will be filled with boys and girls playing. (*Zechariah* 8:4–5)

"Is this the vision of redemption that we yearn for?" asks Rabbi Amital. Kids playing in the street? Seniors taking walks? That's our vision of the future? And he answers yes, because normal, regular life in Yerushalayim is redemption. It's not the full redemption, and we pray for the ultimate redemption, but even just being able to function in Yerushalayim, in *Eretz Yisrael*, that is fulfilling the mitzva of *hallel vehodaa*. This is a message that we learn from Hanukka. That's why the Rambam includes the point about autonomy in *Hilkhot Hanukka*.

It wasn't the greatest *malkhut* in the post-Hanukka era, but it was a *malkhut* nonetheless, and we have tremendous gratitude to HaKadosh Barukh Hu for that *malkhut*.

We have to have tremendous gratitude to HaKadosh Barukh Hu when, in our day, children play freely in the streets of Yerushalayim, and there are elders sitting on benches in Yerushalayim. Seventy years ago this was not the case, and *barukh Hashem,* we are *zokhe* to have that today.

Rabbi Amital continues and quotes Rabbi Menahem Ziemba, who discussed the problems with going to *Eretz Yisrael*. We have to recognize that even if the government of Israel is not a perfect, ideal *malkhut,* and Israel is not a country based purely on Torah and halakha, it still serves as a homeland for us. Imagine if Israel had existed as a country before World War II – how many refugees could have entered its borders? Obviously, HaKadosh Barukh Hu did not deem it appropriate for that time, but we have to appreciate that we have it now.

The message of Hanukka, says Rabbi Amital, is that every stage of redemption is something to be grateful for, and we have to recognize that it is a stage in the redemption. Especially in our generation, Hanukka is a reminder of the modern-day miracles we experience in *Eretz Yisrael* today.

Parashat Vayigash
Revealing Hidden Strength

At the end of the previous *parasha*, *Parashat Miketz*, Yehuda was help-less, speechless:

ויאמר יהודה מה נאמר לאדני מה נדבר ומה נצטדק. (בראשית מד:טז)

And Yehuda said, "What shall we say to my master? What shall we speak, and how shall we exonerate ourselves? (*Bereshit* 44:16)

Suddenly, at the start of *Parashat Vayigash*, he has a new tone of voice, one of strength:

ויגש אליו יהודה ויאמר בי אדני ידבר נא עבדך דבר באזני אדני ואל
יחר אפך בעבדך: כי כמוך כפרעה. (בראשית מד:יח)

Then Yehuda approached him and said, "Please, my lord, let now your servant speak something into my lord's ears, and let not your wrath be kindled against your servant, for you are like Pharaoh. (*Bereshit* 44:18)

The *pasuk* states, *vayigash elav Yehuda:* Yehuda approached Yosef, and he then spoke harshly, with a threatening undertone. Rav Shimon Schwab[1] asks what happened that can account for this rapid transition? He answers in the name of Rabbi Bloch from Telz: This teaches us the significance of taking responsibility, *ahrayut*. It's all about our state of mind, he explains. The second we accept responsibility, everything changes and HaKadosh Barukh Hu reveals our hidden *kohot* that we may not have been aware we had.

The moment Yehuda took responsibility for the situation, for Binyamin, he became a different person. He became reinvigorated with hidden strengths and abilities he didn't know he had. He knew what he had to do, and he obtained the will to do it.

We can generalize this message, says Rav Schwab. In any area of *avodat Hashem*, we can be lackadaisical, not so into it…but then, if we just make the decision that we *must* do something, we can tap into unbelievable reservoirs of strength within us. As soon as we accept the burden, Hashem helps us out. So much in life is just about the decision, the will to accomplish. Once we do that, everything else becomes secondary. It's all about the *ratzon*, the power to persevere.

I once heard from one of my *rebbeim* that he went to the Steipler for a *berakha* when he was newly married. First, he asked for a *berakha* for children, then for *shalom bayit*, and the Steipler blessed him. Then he asked for a *berakha* for success in learning, and to that, the Steipler said no. Learning doesn't need a *berakha*, he said. To achieve success, you just have to work hard. If you decide you want to work at it, you'll see success. A *berakha* won't help, because it's all about your decision. The Stepiler couldn't give my *rebbe* that type of *berakha*, because his success is all up to him.

Rav Chaim Shmuelevitz suggests that we find this is true of Yaakov Avinu as well.[2] Rashi says that the *pasuk* (*Bereshit* 28:10) mentions that Yaakov slept there because he hadn't slept in fourteen years. Rav Chaim doesn't think it means that he didn't sleep at all; rather, it means

---

1. Rav Shimon Schwab, *Maayan Beit Hashoeva* (New York: Mesorah Publications, 2001), 107.
2. Rav Chaim Shmuelevitz, *Sihot Musar* (Jerusalem, 2004), *maamar* 32, p. 138.

Yaakov didn't have a good night's sleep in fourteen years. He just dozed here and there because he was so driven. He was on fire for Torah, and if someone is driven, then they can accomplish unbelievable things. If we have the drive, we can get away with minimal sleep for fourteen years.

We're familiar with this idea when it comes to adrenaline. For example, in a dangerous situation, *has veshalom*, human beings are able to do extraordinary acts, because nothing stands in the way of *ratzon*. That's how Yaakov Avinu was able to remove the stone from the well single-handedly when he saw Rachel Imenu.

It's up to us to tap into our inner strength. It facilitated Yehuda gaining courage to face the viceroy, and it will reveal hidden strength and determination to take responsibility upon ourselves.

"How Can I Appear Before My Father If the Child Is Not with Me?"

כי איך אעלה אל אבי והנער איננו אתי פן אראה ברע אשר ימצא את
אבי. (בראשית מד:לד)

For how will I go up to my father if the boy is not with me? Let
me not see the misery that will befall my father!" (*Bereshit* 44:34)

When Yosef demanded that Binyamin remain with him, Yehuda
responded: How can I appear before my father if Binyamin is not with
me?

Rabbi Mordekhai Eliyahu quotes one of his *rebbeim* and offers a
deeper understanding on this *pasuk*.[1] He says this *pasuk* is a message to
each of us: How will we be able to stand before our Father in Heaven if
our children aren't with us? What does this mean?

When we stand before HaKadosh Barukh Hu after 120 years,
He's going to ask us not only about ourselves, but also about how we

---

1. Rav Mordekhai Eliyahu, *Darkhei Hora'ah* (Jerusalem, 2001), 363.

educated our children. We will be judged for whether we put a lot of effort and thought into our children's *hinukh*.

Children are given to us as a deposit to guard, cherish, and take care of, but they are not ours. Everything belongs to HaKadosh Barukh Hu. Why does Hashem give us the gift of children? So that we can help them serve Him.

In the future, we will be asked, "Did you pick the appropriate school for your children? How much were you involved in their development? How much time did you put into making them into *talmidei hakhamim*, God-fearing Jews? Or did you choose a school for convenience or a social reason?" Our highest value has to be to facilitate our children to become the best *ovdei Hashem* they can become.

That's the deeper meaning of this *pasuk*. How can I go up to HaKadosh Barukh Hu with nothing to show for my children?

A father has to train his child to go to *shul*, even if he can't sit for so long, even if he steps out in the middle to get some air and play a little. The main point is for the child to become accustomed to going to *shul* and experiencing davening. That will create an everlasting memory in the child's mind.

Rabbi Mordekhai Eliyahu says that when Moshe stood before Pharaoh and asked him to send out *Bnei Yisrael*, Pharaoh asked "With whom do you want to leave?" Moshe responded, "With everyone! The young, the old, *every last person*." Pharaoh said, "Why do you need the kids? If you're going for *ruhniyut*, to bring offerings, just send the men. Don't bring your kids, they'll just disturb you. Let the children stay here." Moshe responded, "No, that's not the way we do it. Our children come too." The root of the argument was about *hinukh yeladim*. Moshe said it's never too young to start education, and without the little ones, we won't go, because there's no purpose to *avodat Hashem* if there is no youth around to learn from the adults who are doing it.[2]

We also learn this idea from the mitzva of *hakhel*. The children were commanded to come too, and if parents had to sacrifice something

---

2. See *Keli Yakar* on *Shemot* 10:8.

from their own *avoda* because they were busy with strollers and lunches, etc., that's what Hashem wanted.[3]

Rabbi Mordekhai Eliyahu tells of a time he was in *Hutz LaAretz*, and on Friday night in *shul*, he saw that not one child was there. He got up to speak and said, "There's such darkness in this *shul*." The *gabbai* felt bad and wanted to get a *Shabbat goy* to make the *shul* brighter. Rabbi Eliyahu said, "*Has veshalom*! It's Shabbat. That's not what I was referring to!" Again, he repeated that it was so dark. An eye doctor stood up and offered to help. So, Rabbi Eliyahu repeated himself and explained, "There's such darkness here, because there are no children present." Then he spoke about the importance of *hinukh yeladim*, of bringing children to *shul*.[4]

The first words we teach our children should be *Torah tziva lanu Moshe*, not "Abba" or "Mommy."[5]

We have to remember: "How will we be able to stand before our Father in Heaven if our children aren't with us?" Our children are gifts provide to us so we can positively influence and educate them. May we do our utmost to fulfill our task.

3. See Hagiga 3a and Rashi on *Devarim* 31:12.
4. We also must be cognizant of any disturbance our children may cause and train them to respect the sanctity of the *shul*. See *Mishna Berura* 343:3.
5. Sukka 42a; Rambam, *Hilkhot Talmud Torah* 1:6.

Yosef's Rebuke to His Brothers

וַיֹּאמֶר יוֹסֵף אֶל אֶחָיו אֲנִי יוֹסֵף הַעוֹד אָבִי חָי וְלֹא יָכְלוּ אֶחָיו לַעֲנוֹת אֹתוֹ
כִּי נִבְהֲלוּ מִפָּנָיו. (בראשית מה:ג)

And Yosef said to his brothers, "I am Yosef. Is my father still alive?"
but his brothers could not answer him because they were startled
by his presence. (*Bereshit* 45:3)

At the beginning of this week's *parasha*, Yehuda stands up for Binyamin
to protect him, at which point, Yosef reveals himself. The brothers were
so shocked and scared, they couldn't answer.

The Beit HaLevi quotes Midrash Rabba on the above *pasuk*,[1]
which says:

אוי לנו מיום הדין אוי לנו מיום התוכחה...לכשיבא הקב״ה ויוכיח לכל
אחד לפי מה שהוא...על אחת כמה וכמה....

Woe to us from the day of judgment, and woe to us from the day
of rebuke...at which time, Hashem will come and rebuke each
person according to who he is...all the more so....

---

1. *Beit HaLevi on Bereshit and Shemot,* 46.

Yosef, the youngest of the twelve of Yaakov's sons (other than Binyamin), shocked his brothers into speechlessness. The midrash says that if Yosef had such an ability over them, *all the more so,* when Hashem rebukes us after 120 years, it will be impossible for us to respond. If the brothers couldn't answer Yosef, then surely we won't be able to answer Hashem.

There are a number of questions that can be raised on this midrash. First, what great rebuke did Yosef actually give the brothers here? In fact, there doesn't appear to be any rebuke in the *pasuk* at all! The only words Yosef said were, "I am Yosef. Is my father still alive?" There wasn't a negative word in his revelation to them, and a few *pesukim* later, he even attempts to appease them! What exactly was the rebuke here?

Second, why is the wording of the midrash so long-winded? The midrash says, "At which time, Hashem will come and rebuke each person *according to who he is*." What does this last phrase mean?

Finally, a third question: Why did Yosef ask if their father was still alive, if Yehuda had just told him that Yaakov was alive?

These questions lead the Beit HaLevi to an important conclusion: Yosef had no intention of appeasing his brothers at this point. In reality, says the Beit HaLevi, this *pasuk* is a biting rebuke to them. He wasn't asking if their father was still alive. He was asking something deeper.

Yosef's question was a rhetorical one: "Is it possible for my father to still be alive?" Yosef wanted to know. "How can it be that through all the pain you put our father through, he's still alive?" *Ha'od avi hai* is a rhetorical question that undermines their previous claims. Yehuda had just stood up to Yosef and said, "You can't take Binyamin, it'll kill our father. Have mercy on him." Yosef responded, "I'm Yosef. Remember what happened to me? What happened to your mercy for our father twenty-two years ago?"

The greatest rebuke a person can receive is when his lifelong beliefs are disproven, based on his own inner contradictions. "Oh, really? But *you* didn't act that way!" That was Yosef's rebuke: You're asking for mercy when you yourself didn't practice mercy? That's the ultimate rebuke, that's the "woe to us." Woe to us when, in the future, Hashem will rebuke us with rebuke that is specific to our lives and excuses. The ultimate and deepest rebuke will be proof from our own life. When we present Hashem with our defenses, He will show us how we contradict our own claims.

This applies to all areas of our life. Often, people exempt themselves from *emuna* or learning Torah, claiming they don't have the head for it, the abilities. Hashem will answer them, "Oh, but you had enough intelligence to become an engineer? You can't get to *minyan* on time, but for a vacation you can get to the airport on time?"

The Beit HaLevi ends with a midrash about Eliyahu HaNavi. Once, Eliyahu met an *am ha'aretz*. He asked the individual, "What are you going to say to Hashem after 120 years?" The person answered, "Don't worry, I have defenses: I wasn't given *bina* and *daat*. My IQ is not high enough to understand learning." So, Eliyahu asked him, "What do you do for a living?" The man answered, "I'm a trapper," to which Eliyahu replied, "Who taught you how to make nets, where to throw them, how to trap animals? For that you were given enough *daat*? You obviously have enough *daat*."

The man realized his faults and began to cry. Eliyahu comforted him and said, "Dont worry, you're not alone. Everyone uses this excuse, but their own actions disprove their claims."

We should internalize Yosef's rebuke of his brothers and make sure to be consistent, to avoid making invalid excuses for our actions or lack thereof.

Rabbi Asher Weiss[2] expands on the *Beit HaLevi*. Rabbi Weiss explains that Yosef's words were most definitely words of rebuke, though without being sharp. His message was scarier than any sharp words and scarier than images of punishment and *Gehinnom*. He used the scariest thing of all: the truth, and there's no escaping the truth.

We spend our life running away: from Hashem, from ourselves, from our inner voice. Our *neshama* constantly begs us to get up, to serve HaKadosh Barukh Hu, and all the while we think we're running toward something, we're really just running away from that inner call of our *neshama*.

But, ultimately, there will come a time when there will be no more running. That's the message of the midrash when it says, "Woe

---

2. Rav Asher Weiss, *Minhat Asher: Sihot Al HaTorah* (Jerusalem, 2008), 98.

to us from the day of judgment." In the future, on the day of judgment, our silence will be deafening. All we'll be able to say is, "Hashem, we are too ashamed to show our faces."

If it could happen to the sons of Yaakov, it could happen to anyone. For twenty-two years, they lived with a pit in their stomachs. Yosef was a sore topic, but they never did anything about it. They just kept running away from that voice of *emet*, pushing it away. Suddenly, they came face to face with the *emet* they'd been running away from for twenty-two years. Yosef said just two words, *ani Yosef*, "I am Yosef," but it was enough to shock them into silence – a silence that only *emet* can cause.

For twenty-two years, the sons of Yaakov defended their action. They came up with explanations: he's a persecutor, he tattles on us, he's not fit for leadership, he's a false prophet, etc. But none of it was the *emet*. Explains Rabbi Asher Weiss: We, too, defend our actions in the name of Torah or a positive mitzva, we come up with excuses. That trait can be traced back to the sons of Yaakov!

The brothers never retracted on their sale of Yosef until he said *ani Yosef*. Our whole life, the *emet* is trying to be heard. We just have to listen and be objective to the truth.

The *minhag* is to blow one hundred sounds of the shofer on Rosh Hashana. Why one hundred? The Talmud Yerushalmi tells us that Sisera's mother cried one hundred cries when she heard her son had been killed, and therefore, we blow one hundred sounds.[3]

Why do we base our *shofar*-blowing on the mother of an enemy general who tried to destroy Klal Yisrael? Sisera's mother waited at the window for her son to return from war. As the time stretched on and he still had not returned, everyone tried to calm her down, attempting to convince her that he was on his way and that the delay was due to him collecting spoils from the war, but slowly, as the sun set, all the excuses fell away. She realized that he was not going to return, and when she came face to face with this *emet*, she could not control her cries. That's what Rosh HaShana is about: coming face to face with the truth, when there are no more excuses with which we may defend ourselves.

---

3. Quoted in *Tosafot*, Rosh HaShana 33b.

That was *ani Yosef.* Face the truth: no matter how painful it may be. One cannot live a false life, trying to avoid the truth. Although it may hurt, facing the truth is the only way to repair a mistake and move onward and upward. Yosef taught this to his brothers and to the generations that follow.

God Made Me Viceroy of Egypt

מהרו ועלו אל אבי ואמרתם אליו כה אמר בנך יוסף שמני אלקים לאדון
לכל מצרים. (בראשית מה:ט)

Hasten and go up to my father, and say to him, "So said your son, Yosef: God has made me a lord over all the Egyptians." (*Bereshit* 45:9)

Yosef instructed his brothers to rush back to their father and tell him Yosef was the leader in Egypt. Why did Yosef emphasize that he was a ruler? Did he think it would matter so much to Yaakov that he was a ruler in Egypt? Wouldn't Yaakov's only care be that Yosef was alive?

The *Darkei Musar*[1] answers this in the name of the Ruzhiner Rebbe. We're missing the point of the *pasuk*, he claims. Yosef was emphasizing "Hashem made me viceroy…" His message was, "Tell our father that I know that everything I have is from HaKadosh Barukh Hu."

The *Darkei Musar* expounds on this. We always say, "X gave me a promotion" or "Y did this for me," but we're not being precise. Who was behind X and Y's actions? Yosef did not say that Pharaoh made

---

1. Rav Yaakov Neiman, *Darkhei Musar* (Tel Aviv: Or Yisrael Press, 1979), 90.

him a viceroy or that Pharaoh put him in charge. Instead, he attributed it all to Hashem.

That's the news he was sending to his father: that throughout this ordeal, Yosef kept his *emuna* in Hashem and recognized the hand of God in all that transpired.

The *Darkei Musar* adds that this message is so real and applicable at all times, but *kal vahomer* when Hashem does such open miracles in our days. In 1967 He puts the many into the hands of the few, and the Israeli army overcame its Arab enemies. We witness many modern-day miracles in the State of Israel on a daily basis. We have to be careful not to pat ourselves on the back and claim that this is the result of our own might, but must acknowledge that it is all *yad Hashem*.

The more we believe that, the more the world will believe it. If the Jews don't believe that it's all from HaKadosh Barukh Hu, then no one else will.

Significance of
Taamei HaMikra

ויגש אליו יהודה ויאמר בי אדני ידבר נא עבדך. (בראשית מד:יח)

Then Yehuda approached him and said, "Please, my lord, let now
your servant speak." (*Bereshit* 44:18)

The Gemara (Nedarim 37a) teaches us that our tradition is not only about
the letters of the Torah, but about the *te'amim*, the cantillation notes, as
well. These notes go all the way back to Ezra HaSofer.[1]

There is a tradition as to how precisely to write each letter in the
Torah. The Vilna Gaon, often saw ideas unseen by others, hinted to by
the *te'amim*. sometimes interprets them.

A classic example is the opening *pasuk* in our *parasha*.[2] The names
of its notes, in sequence, are *kadma ve'azla revi'i zarka munah segol*. This
sequence, explains the Gra, itself answers an obvious question on the

---

1. Rav Chaim Soloveitchik would make the *baal koreh* repeat a word if he read it with
   the wrong *te'amim*. See Rav Yosef Dov Soloveitchik, *Shiurim LeZekher Abba Mari*,
   vol. 2, 211–12. We don't follow this practice; see the Rema, *Orah Hayim* 142:1.
2. See *Peninim MiShulhan HaGra* (Jerusalem, Moreshet HaYeshivot, 1997), 85.

pasuk: Why did Yehuda step forward to address Yosef? Why didn't Reuven, the firstborn, step up?

The literal meaning of these *te'amim* is: "The fourth one got up and went, he threw away the treasure set aside." That is, Yehuda, the fourth son, was the one to step up, because he had staked his entire future on protecting Binyamin, even his reward in the next world.

This shows how even the cantillation notes are not haphazard, but often emphasize something significant.

The Message of *Egla Arufa*

ויְדַבְּרוּ אֵלָיו אֵת כָּל דִּבְרֵי יוֹסֵף אֲשֶׁר דִּבֶּר אֲלֵהֶם וַיַּרְא אֶת הָעֲגָלוֹת אֲשֶׁר
שָׁלַח יוֹסֵף לָשֵׂאת אֹתוֹ וַתְּחִי רוּחַ יַעֲקֹב אֲבִיהֶם. (בראשית מה:כז)

And they told him all of Yosef's words that he had said to them, and he saw the wagons that Yosef had sent to carry him, and the spirit of their father Yaakov was revived. (*Bereshit* 45:27)

Throughout the twenty-two years that Yosef was in Egypt, Yaakov never forgot about Yosef and never stopped mourning him. Yet, when the brothers told Yaakov that Yosef was alive, Yaakov was not put at ease until he saw the *agalot,* wagons, that Yosef sent. *Hazal* say that if you switch the vowels in the word *agala*, you can read it as *egla* (as in *egla arufa*), which was the last concept that Yosef and Yaakov had studied together before Yosef was sold. The wagons appeased Yaakov because he saw that Yosef still remembered his Torah and was still an *oved Hashem*.

The commentators wonder what was so special about the *sugya* of *egla arufa.*

HIZKUNI

The Hizkuni on *Parashat Vayeshev* offers a pragmatic explanation: The Torah tells us that when Yaakov asked Yosef to tend to his brothers, it says that he sent him from the *valley* of Hevron. This is a strange description, as Hevron is usually referred to as being on a mountain. The Hizkuni explains that Yaakov wanted to fulfill the mitzva of *levaya,* of escorting someone upon his departure. Yosef asked Yaakov why he was walking him to the outskirts of the city, and Yaakov then explained the mitzva of *levaya* and its significance, which led to a discussion of *egla arufa* as it likewise relates to how a guest is treated upon departure.

RAV SHLOMO ZEVIN

Rav Zevin explains the message in his classic creative style.[1] When an anonymous corpse is found between two cities, the city that is closest sends out its elders, who proclaim, "We did not cause this person's death." They are in essence asserting that they had not let the guest leave their city without accompanying him and sending him with food. What's the message of this ceremony?

Says Rav Zevin, a person is responsible for the effects of his actions, but not only for the effects that occur immediately. Rather, he is held accountable even for the ripple effects that occur in the future. In other words, a person can be a murderer even if he doesn't openly stab someone. Causing a death indirectly is also murder, as taught by *egla arufa.*

When Yaakov learned the *sugya* of *egla arufa* with Yosef, he was providing Yosef with spiritual fodder for all the years he would be alone. He taught Yosef the concept of the effects of his actions, and Yosef saw this very lesson in real time. His brothers sold him, and it led him to become the ruler of Egypt and be in a position to provide his family with food. When Yaakov saw the *agalot* and recalled the *sugya* of *egla arufa,* he was comforted, because he was reassured that Yosef had internalized the important lesson that all of our actions have consequences.

RABBI YOSEF NEHEMIA KORNITZER

Rabbi Yosef Nehemia Kornitzer[2] expresses a similar idea. Included in the recitation of the elders at the *egla arufa* ceremony is a snippet about

---

1. *LaTorah VeLaMo'adim,* 83.
2. Rav Yosef Nehemia Kornitzer, *Hidushei Rav Yosef Nechemia* (Jerusalem: Chemed, 1998), 114.

the exodus from Egypt: "Please, Hashem, grant an atonement for this nation that You redeemed from Egypt."

Rabbi Kornitzer explains that in Egypt, we didn't have much in the area of *zekhuyot*. We weren't too involved with mitzvot during our slavery. We definitely were not redeemed based on our merit at that time. Rather, Hashem redeemed us on credit, based on the potential He saw in us. He knew how great we would become, and He redeemed us because of that. In essence, the exodus from Egypt was an act of Hashem based on our potential, based on the future.

This idea of future potential plays a major role in *Yiddishkeit*. In *Parashat Bereshit*, Hashem said to Kayin after he killed his brother Hevel, "The voice of the *bloods* of your brother are crying out to me."[3] By using the plural of "blood," Hashem's message to Kayin was he hadn't just killed one person, but he had destroyed all the potential within Hevel, robbing Hevel of all the descendants that would have come from him. The blood of all those descendants who had lost their chance to live was crying out to Hashem.

When it comes to the anonymous corpse, the elders were not responsible only for the actual dead man that was lying before them, but they were also responsible for all the future generations, all the potential that was cut off with this man's death. Therefore, the elders had to ask for atonement for the loss of potential as well, hinted to in the words that reference the exodus from Egypt. Hashem focuses on potential, not just on the here and now.

Why did Yosef hint to this when sending *agalot* to his father? Yosef knew that his father may very well not believe that Yosef was still alive, or even if he did believe that fact, he wouldn't believe that Yosef was still God fearing. Who could possibly remain a *tzaddik* in such a corrupt land, or anywhere in the world, for that matter, when no one other than Yaakov's family believed in HaKadosh Barukh Hu? Therefore, Yosef referenced the *egla arufa*, the message to his father being, "Even if you think I am no longer pure and holy, come down to me in Egypt anyway in the merit of the potential within me – the potential of my descendants."

---

3. *Bereshit* 4:10, and see Rashi.

RABBI NISSAN ALPERT

Rabbi Nissan Alpert offers a different approach in *Limudei Nissan*.[4] If we analyze this mitzva, we can discover Yosef's intent behind sending this message. Why do specifically the leaders have to be involved and express that they did not spill this blood? Would we think that the leaders of the generation caused a person's death? Perhaps the message of this mitzva is that all of Israel is responsible for one another. If a Jew is in need, the greatest members of the generation have to bear the responsibility. The leaders specifically have to take care of all members of Klal Yisrael. They are the ones who have to take responsibility.

Yosef always felt responsible for his brothers, for his family, and for Klal Yisrael. We see examples throughout the *parshiyot*:

- Why did he report on his brothers? Because the sons of the *shefahot* (Bilha and Zilpa) were being made fun of, and he couldn't stand idly by while a fellow Jew was being ridiculed.
- When Yaakov sent Yosef to check on the brothers in Shekhem, Yosef could have protested, saying that he risked being killed by his brothers. Instead, he accepted the mission because he cared about his brothers. He felt responsibility for them.
- In the jail in Egypt, Yosef took care of everyone by interpreting their dreams.
- As viceroy of Egypt, he took care of the nation and his family by ensuring that they had food.

The subject of e*gla arufa* typified Yosef's very essence. Yosef is referred to as *Yosef HaTzaddik*. Not many people in our history are called a *tzaddik*. In the Torah, only Noach and Yosef are granted that appellation. What's the common denominator between Noach and Yosef? Both were the only two people who essentially sustained the world, and that is righteousness. Noach took care of the entire world in the Ark, and Yosef fed the world.

A hint to this idea of righteousness representing sustaining others is in *Ashrei*:

---

4. Rav Nissan Alpert, *Limudei Nissan* (New York: Otzar Hasefarim, 1991), 290.

פּוֹתֵחַ אֶת יָדֶךָ וּמַשְׂבִּיעַ לְכָל חַי רָצוֹן. צַדִּיק ה' בְּכָל דְּרָכָיו וְחָסִיד בְּכָל
מַעֲשָׂיו. (תהילים קמה:טז-יז)

Open your hands and satiate all living beings. Righteous is
Hashem in all His ways and a hasid in all His actions. (*Tehillim*
145:16–17)

The *pasuk* praises Hashem for sustaining all life, and then immediately
refers to Hashem as *Tzaddik*.

There was no greater way for Yosef to inform Yaakov that he was
alive in Egypt than by hinting to *egla arufa*, because it relayed to Yaakov
that Yosef was taking responsibility for the Jewish people. This message
made Yaakov finally believe that Yosef was alive.

Yaakov's *Keriat Shema*

ויאסר יוסף מרכבתו ויעל לקראת ישראל אביו גשנה וירא אליו ויפל
על צואריו ויבך על צואריו עוד. (בראשית מו:כט)

And Yosef harnessed his chariot, and he went up to meet Yisrael
his father, to Goshen, and he appeared to him, and he fell on his
neck, and he wept on his neck for a long time. (*Bereshit* 46:29)

When Yaakov was finally reunited with Yosef after twenty-two years of
separation, the *pasuk* describes only how Yosef cried on Yaakov's shoul-
ders. Rashi explains that Yaakov was reciting *Shema*. Why did Yaakov
have to recite *Shema* at precisely that moment? After not seeing his son
for over two decades, Yaakov could not wait another thirty seconds and
recite Shema later?

We will offer two explanations.

The first explanation ties into *Parashat Vayehi*, when Yaakov
bestows upon Yosef honor befitting a king (by rising for Yosef despite
being on his deathbed).

Why do we honor a king or ruler? Honoring a human dignitary
is a display of recognition of Hashem's greatness. It is as if we are proclaiming that we understand that Hashem has chosen this person to be
in a great position deserving of honor. Hashem chooses the rulers of
the world, and while it appears to us that people choose their leaders,

we must remember that it is really Hashem who is running the show. Ultimately, we have to recognize that all authority flows from HaKadosh Barukh Hu, and *that* is what we are respecting in a human ruler, the Godliness in him. If someone denies God's involvement in earthly rulership, that's actually minimizing the power of the human leader. The *berakha* we recite when we encounter a non-Jewish leader is a way of demonstrating our respect for him. We are indicating to him that he is so great that we bless God in his presence!

The *Ketav Sofer*[1] bases this on a *pasuk* in *Mishlei*:

ירא את ה' בני ומלך עם שונים אל תתערב. (משלי כד:כא)

Fear Hashem, my son, and the king, and with those who study, do not mix in. (*Mishlei* 24:21)

The *pasuk* teaches us that if we fear Hashem, it will afford us the proper perspective with respect to an earthly king to be able to appropriately revere him. If we realize that everything comes from Hashem, and we honor Him, then consequently we will demonstrate proper honor to a human leader.

The second half of the *pasuk* teaches a separate lesson: Anyone who thinks the king has laws that are separate from those of heavenly rulership and that he has nothing to do with HaKadosh Barukh Hu is mistaken. If one differentiates between heavenly rulership and earthly rulership, he is diminishing the honor of an earthly ruler.

If we put this all together, we can understand why Yaakov said *Shema* at the moment he met Yosef. The *Ketav Sofer* explains beautifully that Yaakov was giving Yosef the ultimate honor – it was as if he was saying the *berakha* of *shenatan mikhevodo lebasar vadam,* "That [Hashem] gave from His honor to flesh and blood" – the blessing that is recited upon seeing a king. Yaakov was acknowledging that all kingship, all rulership and authority, comes from the One Above. This may even be the source from which *Hazal* created this *berakha*.

---

1. *Ketav Sofer Al HaTorah, Bereshit* 41:28.

A second approach to this question is that of the *Shvilei Hayim*, who answers this question based on a Ramban. The Ramban explains the reason for Yosef not revealing himself earlier as being because he understood his dreams to be a form of prophecy, and he waited for them to be fulfilled. He believed it was not his place to intervene with the fulfillment of the prophecy but rather to do what he could to allow the dreams to come true.[2]

As Yosef was heading down to Egypt as a slave, he thought of all the Torah he had learned from Yaakov, Torah that included the knowledge of the *Berit bein HaBetarim*. He knew he was just a pawn in the hand of Hashem. He recognized that Hashem wanted him down in Egypt as part of the trajectory of Jewish history. Therefore, since he was a part of the divine plan, there was no place for him to reveal himself to his father earlier than Hashem planned. Yosef was calm throughout his sojourn in Egypt, because he understood that he was part of Hashem's plan.

Since he believed entirely in the fulfillment of the decree, he knew his father would live, since Yaakov would have to come down to Egypt as part of the prophecy. In order not to mess up Hashem's plan, he didn't reveal himself early.

We can compare this to a person who is in the middle of reciting *Shemoneh Esreh*. This person ignores anyone who attempts to talk to him, because he is in the middle of conversing with Hashem. It was as if Yosef was saying *Shemoneh Esreh* for twenty-two years. He was busy with his *avoda* and refused to interrupt it. He didn't want to and could not reveal himself to his father any earlier than he did, because he was busy with his *avoda*. Even though he knew his father was in tremendous pain, he conquered his own desire (to reveal himself) for the will of Hashem.

What does this have to do with Yaakov reciting *Shema*? There are two types of *Keriat Shema*, says the *Shvilei Hayim*.[3] The first is the *mitzva deoraita* to recite *Shema* twice a day. The second type may not be reciting the actual words of *Shema*, but rather recognizing that Hashem is in charge, and accepting that all is from Him (*kaballat ol Malkhut*

---

2. See earlier in the book – Parashat Miketz: *The Purpose of Yosef's Charade.*
3. Rabbi Chaim Elazary, *Shvilei Hayim* (Canton OH, 1947), 77.

Shamayim). This second type of obligation applies when we experience extreme moments in our life; at that moment, we must recognize that this is not "normal"; it is the hand of Hashem.

This second type of *Shema* is the equivalent of *shiviti Hashem lenegdi tamid* – the understanding and belief that all is part of the divine plan. Whether one is experiencing a tremendous *simha* or a tragedy, one must "say" *Shema* at that moment, which means internalizing and believing that the event came about through Hashem.

Maybe that is what Rabbi Akiva meant when he spoke of *Keriat Shema* during his torture and death – he recognized that Hashem is in charge in every moment of life, that all is from Him.

We learn from this that we must say *Shema* always, and that our love for Hashem has to be greater than any other feeling in our lives. Yosef, by not doing what he wanted to do – which was to reveal himself to his father – was in essence "reciting *Shema*" for those twenty-two years he was in Egypt. He was refusing to "mess up" the divine plan, instead believing that Hashem was in control of everything.

When the moment of truth finally came, Yosef was nervous that Yaakov would not understand that the past twenty-two years were all for a good cause, that Yosef had not forgotten about Yaakov, and he had not revealed himself to Yaakov only *because* of his love for him. Yosef showed this by hugging and kissing his father, and crying. That's what he had to do at that moment: show Yaakov that he loved him so much and that he, too, had been in pain all the years he was separated from him.

What did Yaakov do? As a show of recognition for what Yosef had done, he recited *Shema*. He was showing that he understood Yosef. He wanted to calm Yosef down, so he was giving him a hint through *Keriat Shema* – the mitzva that portrays our belief in the divine plan of Hashem.

Yosef and Yehuda: The First *Baalebatim*

וישב יוסף את אביו ואת אחיו ויתן להם אחֻזה בארץ מצרים במיטב
הארץ בארץ רעמסס כאשר צוה פרעה. (בראשית מז:יא)

Yosef settled his father and his brothers, and he gave them property in the land of Egypt, in the best of the land, in the land of
Ramesses, as Pharaoh had mandated. (*Bereshit* 47:11)

The *pasuk* describes how Yosef settled his brothers and father in Goshen and supported them there. Rav Yosef Soloveitchik comments that
this teaches that Yosef was the first *baalebos*, the first lay leader.[1] Until
this point in history, people toiled to support themselves. They planted,
harvested, and prepared food for their families. There was no division
of labor. Then came Yosef.

Rav Soloveitchik teaches that Yosef began the tradition of great
Torah lay leaders, whom we call *baalebatim*, who concern themselves
with the material conditions of the Torah and the Jewish people. Rav
Soloveitchik then describes the three characteristics of a great *baalebos*:

---

1. Rabbi Joseph B. Soloveitchik, *Humash Mesorat HaRav* (New York: OU Press,
   2013), 345.

First, the *ba'al habayit* feels a clear awareness of his responsibility not only for himself, but for the entire Jewish community. Second, the *ba'al habayit* has a pragmatic mind; he has an aptitude for decision-making and decision-executing. Finally, the *ba'al habayit* is a visionary. He is a dreamer. He looks to the stars.

A *baal habayit* feels that he has a responsibility for the community and acts on his feelings. He is a doer. Yosef was a dreamer, but he was also a pragmatist who cared for his family. That is the tradition that Yosef passed on through the generations.

Rav Chaim Kanievsky makes similar points about Yehuda.[2] Yaakov sent Yehuda to Goshen to set up a yeshiva. Why didn't Yaakov send Levi, the leading Torah scholar of the brothers? Or even Yissaskhar? Yehuda represented *malkhut*; what did he have to do with setting up a yeshiva? Yehuda, explains Rav Hayim, represented the *baal habayit*, the one who gets things done. We need those movers and shakers, the ones who can execute, in addition to the Torah learners. Yaakov was confident that Yehuda, his son who earlier stood up to Yosef and was a leader among his brothers, was the one who would be able to successfully prepare the proper environment for the rest of his children upon their arrival in Egypt.

In our tradition we have rabbinic leaders and lay leaders, and we learn about them through Yosef HaTzaddik. Yosef is referred to as a *tzaddik*, which highlights that the responsibility and the job of lay leaders is no less significant than that of the rabbinic leaders. It is this partnership that enables the tradition to be transferred to the next generation.

---

2. Rav Chaim Kanievsky, *Ta'ama DeKra* (Bnei Brak, 1996), 59.

Asara BeTevet and the Sale of Yosef

The Beit Yosef (*Orah Hayim* 550) quotes the Avudraham as declaring that *Asara BeTevet*, the Tenth of Tevet, is unlike any other fast day besides Yom Kippur, in that if it would fall on Shabbat, the fast would not be postponed, rather, we would fast on Shabbat.[1] While the Tenth of Tevet cannot actually fall on Shabbat because of how our calendar works, it *is* the only fast that can fall on a Friday, and we go into Shabbat fasting. The Beit Yosef asks: What is so unique about *Asara BeTevet* that it trumps Shabbat?

The Hatam Sofer[2] explains that there are two other fasts that trump Shabbat: a fast due to a bad dream, and of course Yom Kippur. What is the common theme between these two fasts? The Hatam Sofer explains that one may not fast on Shabbat for a past event, as a symbol of mourning. Yom Kippur, however, is about our future. It is about the divine decision for the year ahead. It is not a day of mourning the past, therefore, we are permitted to fast on Shabbat. Similarly, a fast due to

---

1. This opinion is discussed and rejected by many *Aharonim*. It is beyond the scope of this work to discuss the various approaches.
2. Hatam Sofer in his commentary on the siddur.

a bad dream can also be on Shabbat because it is a fast to prevent a future calamity.

With respect to the fast of the Tenth of Tevet, every single year on that day Hashem decrees whether there will be a Tisha BeAv that year! That's why we can fast on the Tenth of Tevet – because it's for the future. It's the day every year that will determine whether Tisha BeAv that year will be a Yom Tov or not.

Rabbi Barukh Simon, in *Imrei Barukh*,[3] adds in the name of Rabbi Shlomo Fischer that we know that specific sins caused *Shiva Asar BeTammuz* and Tisha BeAv, days of terrible tragedy. Tisha BeAv was a result of the sin of the spies, while *Shiva Asar BeTammuz* was decreed as a result of the sin of the Golden Calf. What triggered *Asara BeTevet*? Rabbi Fischer suggests that, while he doesn't know for sure because *Hazal* don't explicitly provide an answer, he would guess that it was the sale of Yosef. The *mazal* of Tevet is a goat, and it was goat's blood that covered up the sin of the sale of Yosef.

If *Asara BeTevet* is connected to the sale of Yosef, then it behooves us every year at this time to remember what the sin of the sale of Yosef was all about and work on our *ahavat hinam* and *ahavat ahim* so we can do our part in helping turn Tisha BeAv into a Yom Tov.

---

3. Rav Barukh Simon, *Imrei Barukh* (New York: MBH Publications, 2005), 215.

Parashat Vayehi

Yaakov's Request Not to Be Buried in Egypt

ויקרבו ימי ישראל למות ויקרא לבנו ליוסף ויאמר לו אם נא מצאתי חן
בעיניך שים נא ידך תחת ירכי ועשית עמדי חסד ואֱמת אל נא תקברני
במצרים. (בראשית מז:כט)

When the time drew near for Yisrael to die, he called his son
Yosef and said to him, "If I have now found favor in your eyes,
now place your hand beneath my thigh, and you shall deal with
me with lovingkindness and truth; do not bury me now in Egypt."
(*Bereshit* 47:39)

As Yaakov Avinu's end neared, he called to Yosef and expressed his
desire not to be buried in Egypt. Why did Yaakov specifically state the
"negative," that he did not want to be buried in Egypt, rather than the
positive – that he desired to be buried in Me'arat HaMakhpela with his
forefathers? Rashi on this *pasuk* offers three explanations:

1. Since the dirt of Egypt would turn to lice during the plague of
    lice, Yaakov did not want to be buried in that dirt.

2. Yaakov did not want to have to roll to Eretz Yisrael at the time of the resurrection of the dead.[1]

3. Yaakov did not want the Egyptians to worship him as a deity.

These answers serve to deepen the question: Why didn't Yaakov just ask to be buried in *Eretz Yisrael*?

Rabbi Eliyahu Schlesinger[2] suggests that at the end of *Parashat Vayigash*, the Torah states that *Bnei Yisrael* lived in Goshen and "they took hold of it" (*Bereshit* 47:27). This implies that *Bnei Yisrael* were getting a little too comfortable in Egypt. Yaakov already saw the writing on the wall. He saw what was happening to Am Yisrael and realized the tremendous danger his descendants would be in if they felt too comfortable in exile. He saw that his children stood the risk of forgetting about *Eretz Yisrael*. Therefore, says Rabbi Schlesinger, Yaakov emphasized the fact that he didn't want to remain in Egypt, even after his death. He was telling his children that they were getting too comfortable outside of *Eretz Yisrael*.[3]

On a very practical level, if Yaakov were to be buried in Egypt, it would make it all the more difficult for his children to leave, as they would never want to leave Yaakov's body behind. A cemetery usually symbolizes a people's eternal connection with a land, and Yaakov didn't want them to have that excuse. Yaakov was relaying to his sons his desire to be buried in Eretz Yisrael, but more importantly, he was in a sense instructing them that the land of Egypt was not the place to call home or the place in which to create a permanent abode.

---

1. See Rashi on Ketubot 111a (*"Al Yidei Gilgul"*).
2. Rabbi Eliyahu Schlesinger, *Eileh HaDevarim* (Jerusalem: Keter Vilna, 1999), 213.
3. The *Keli Yakar* at the end of *Parashat Vayigash* (*Bereshit* 27:27) expresses a similar thought. He notes that they initially came down to live temporarily (*lagur*), but they ended up settling there (*vayeshev*).

Yaakov's Illness

From this week's *parasha,* we learn why we bless someone when they sneeze. *Pirkei DeRabbi Eliezer* states:

מיום שנבראו שמים וארץ לא היה אדם עוטש וחיה מחליו אלא בכל מקום שהיה או בדרך או בשוק והיה עוטש היה נפשו יוצאה. עד שבא יעקב ובקש רחמים על זאת. (פרקי דרבי אליעזר פרק נ"א)

From the time of creation there was never a man who sneezed and lived, rather wherever he was, whether on the road or in the marketplace, once he would sneeze his soul would leave, until Yaakov asked for mercy. (*Pirkei DeRabbi Eliezer,* chap. 51)

Until Yaakov's era, whenever it was time for someone to die, no matter where they were, they would sneeze and die. There was no such thing as getting sick. There was no degenerative process. People slowed down, yes. As we know, the Torah describes Avraham as growing old. Aging happened, but not illness.

This was reality, until Yaakov turned to HaKadosh Barukh Hu and asked for a warning of his death. Yaakov said:

רבונו של עולם אל תקח נפשי ממני עד שאצוה אל ביתי את בני ואת בני בני.

Master of the world, don't take my life until I can inform my household, my children and grandchildren. [1]

He begged Hashem to give him a warning, to let him know that time was closing in on him, so he would have time to prepare for his death. Yaakov was the first one who experienced illness before death. Therefore, says *Pirkei DeRabbi Eliezer*:

חייב אדם בשעת עטושו להודות להקב"ה שנהפך ממות לחיים.

When a person sneezes, he must thank Hashem for turning death into life. [2]

Perhaps this is why, until today, after a sneeze people respond with wishes of good health and blessing.

Rabbi Yissocher Frand comments on this idea and says:[3]

I once heard a radio newscaster comment on an air disaster, "Thank Heaven, they never knew what hit them. When a bomb goes off on an aircraft at thirty thousand feet, there is no time to think. You're just dead in an instant. They never had a chance to think, 'Yikes, I'm about to die.' They were spared the pain and anguish of looking death in the face. Boom, and they were dead, just like that."

Well, I suppose that is one way of looking at it, but it is not the Jewish way. The *Pirkei DeRabbi Eliezer* describes the Jewish way. Terminal diseases may be painful, but at least they give a person a warning that he is about to depart from this world. He is forewarned that he must tie up the loose ends.

For a person to have time to say *Shema Yisrael* is worth everything. Yaakov Avinu davened that death should *not* happen in an instant.

---

1. *Pirkei DeRabbi Eliezer*, chap. 51; also quoted by Hizkuni on *Bereshit* 48:1.
2. Ibid.
3. *Rabbi Frand on the Parashah* (New York: Artscroll, 2001), 80.

We are not asking for pain; rather, we are appreciating that there is a warning before death so we can utilize our last bit of time to make a *heshbon hanefesh*, to be able to introspect. As Rav Frand states:

> A person leaving this world...must do teshuvah for his transgressions and shortcomings and prepare his soul for the next world.... A lifetime of activity calls for a lot of wrapping up. A person who is struck by a bus and never knows what hit him will never have the opportunity to bring his life to a fitting conclusion. He misses out on a very great blessing.... For those who believe that death is the end, blissful ignorance at the moment of death is perhaps preferable to a few moments of agony. But for those who believe in the immortality of the soul, in punishment and reward in the next world, in an eternal afterlife, a few precious moments of preparation are priceless indeed.

That's why Yaakov Avinu requested this warning. He didn't want death to come suddenly. He wanted the time that a warning would grant him so he could prepare himself for death.

The Gemara (Berakhot 5a) tells us that if someone has trouble focusing on *avodat Hashem*, he should learn Torah. If that doesn't work, he should say *Shema*. It continues to list a number of things one can do. The last option, if nothing else works, is to think about the day of death. The Hafetz Hayim asks: What does it mean when it says "the day of death"? Why doesn't it just say "death"? He explains that thinking about his last day on this earth will get a person to focus. If he thinks that he only has a few hours left, he will thus utilize every second, knowing that his remaining time on this earth is so limited. A mishna in *Pirkei Avot* warns us: *hazman katzar vehamelakha meruba* (time is short, yet there is lot to accomplish). May we be able to make the most of our time.

Yaakov or Yisrael?

In *Parashat Vayishlah*, Yaakov's name is changed to Yisrael, yet we see that he is still referred to by both names. At times, even within one *pasuk*, both names are used. For example, in the following *pasuk*:

ויגד ליעקב ויאמר הנה בנך יוסף בא אליך ויתחזק ישראל וישב על
המטה. (בראשית מח:ב)

And [someone] told Yaakov and said, "Behold, your son Yosef is coming to you." And Yisrael summoned his strength and sat up on the bed. (*Bereshit* 48:2)

In contrast, after Avram's name is changed to Avraham and Sarai's name is changed to Sarah, they are never referred to thereafter by their original names. Why are both Yaakov and Yisrael used? *Hazal* tell us (Berakhot 13b) that there is a special halakha about Avraham, but that simply begs the question: What is the underlying message?

Rabbenu Bahya here offers two explanations. The basic explanation is that there really is not a name change, but a name added. From the time Yaakov got his second name, the Torah switches off and calls him both. All other name switches in the Torah were exclusive, whereas with Yaakov it was *not*. Avram became Avraham, and we are not allowed to call him Avram. Sarai became Sarah, and Sarai no longer existed. Here, the name Yisrael did not replace the name Yaakov.

But there is a deeper explanation, says Rabbenu Bahya. There is a purpose to the use of each name – whenever the Torah refers to "Yaakov" it is in reference to physical aspects. Yaakov is going to die, Yaakov lived in Egypt, etc. After all, why was he called Yaakov? His name was based on a physical event: he was born holding on to Esav's ankle. Yaakov is his physical, worldly name. The name Yisrael, in contrast, always reflects the spiritual; he was called Yisrael because he fought with and overcame an angel.

We know the *ikar* is spirituality, but it is impossible to fully negate our physical body, because we wouldn't be able to live. Yet, we must remember that the body is just the holder of our *neshama*, and our body is secondary. That's the deeper meaning of his two names. The name Yaakov wasn't completely uprooted because we cannot completely destroy the physical. Just because Yaakov became Yisrael doesn't mean he could get rid of the physical. However, the physical became secondary to the spiritual.

My *rebbe*, Rabbi Michael Rosensweig,[1] once suggested another idea. Perhaps the name Yaakov is used whenever Yaakov did something that pertains to him personally, whereas the name Yisrael is used when he acted as part on the national destiny of Klal Yisrael, whenever he did something representative of being the third *av*. Yaakov was going to die, but Yisrael was going to pass on to his children the legacy of Am Yisrael. Reading the Torah with this theory in mind provides us with a glimpse at what relates to Yaakov on a personal level in contrast to what is being related on a national level.

---

1. *Rosh Yeshiva* at Rabbi Isaac Elchanan Theological Seminary of Yeshiva University, and *Rosh Kollel* of the Beren Kollel Elyon.

The *Berakha* to Efraim
and Menashe

It is now customary to bless one's children each Friday night with *Birkat Kohanim* (the blessing the *kohanim* are charged to convey to Am Yisrael), with an introductory phrase of ישמך אלוקים כאפרים וכמנשה – Hashem should place you like Efraim and Menashe. Why do we bless our children to be like Efraim and Menashe. Aren't there greater *tzaddikim* like Avraham, Yitzhak and Yaakov, or Moshe Rabbenu, whom we would prefer our children emulate? What is so unique about Efraim and Menashe that we want our children to emulate their character traits?

We will offer three explanations:

BNEI YISSASKHAR: NO SIBLING RIVALRY

The *Bnei Yissaskhar*, in *Igra DeKalla*, his commentary on the Torah, suggests that Efraim and Menashe were the first siblings in history that we know of who didn't have sibling rivalry. Until then we witness many sets of brothers that engaged in disputes. For example: Kayin and Hevel; Yitzhak and Yishmael; Yaakov and Esav; Yosef and his brothers. We bless our children to be like Efraim and Menashe with respect to the aspect of brotherly love. Yaakov was aware of their special relationship and so he did not fear any adverse repercussions by switching his hands and providing the younger of the brothers with the greater blessing. We bless our children that they should be able to establish the relationship that existed between Efraim and Menashe, so they can avoid sibling rivalry and live in peace and harmony together. Witnessing one's children respecting each other brings the greatest *nahat* and joy to a parent.

RABBI ZALMAN SOROTZKIN: FIRST
TO LIVE AS JEWS IN EXILE

Another approach as to why we bless our children to emulate Efraim and Menashe is provided by Rabbi Zalman Sorotzkin, the author of *Oznayim LaTorah*.

Just moments before the *berakha*, Yaakov asks, "Who are these children?" What did Yaakov mean? He saw in the future that their descendants wouldn't be perfect, so he asked, "Do they deserve *berakhot*?" Yosef answered, "Hashem gave them to me." Then Yaakov agreed to bless them.

What exactly transpired prior to the blessings? Why did Yaakov's attitude change? *Hazal* tell us that at that moment, Yaakov wanted to reveal when the redemption would come. He saw clearly before him the whole future of Klal Yisrael, the tragedies, the physical and the spiritual destruction. He saw every detail: pogroms, crusades, assimilation, and the freedom that has led to spiritual depravation.

When Yaakov saw all that, he said, "Who are these people I see in the future who will sometimes willingly throw off the yoke of Torah?" But then Yosef said, "These are the children that Hashem gave me," and Yaakov saw children who were able to withstand the pressures of Egypt. He saw grandchildren who learned Torah. Even though Yaakov foresaw the corruption of the future, he gave *berakhot* – that specifically blessed his descendants to be like these children who managed to withstand the corruption and depravity of the society around them.

Efraim and Menashe were in the slavery along with the rest of Klal Yisrael. They didn't exclude themselves by claiming to be Egyptian. They accepted upon themselves the yoke of exile, as part of all their Jewish brethren. Yaakov saw where they were coming from and that they had managed to succeed spiritually despite that. Therefore, he blessed his descendants to be like them, to be able to survive in an unfriendly environment, in an environment that was anti-everything they believed in.

We select to bless our children to emulate Menashe and Efraim who were able to remain strong and committed to Judaism irrespective of the adverse culture and environment in which they were surrounded. This is the *berakha* that every parent wants to convey – that their children should not be influenced by the adverse values of the society around them, no matter in which country they live.

Rabbi Sorotzkin also points out that the secret of Menashe and Efraim's success boils down to the education their father provided for them. The *pasuk* says:

ויברכם ביום ההוא לאמור בך יברך ישראל לאמר ישמך אלקים כאפרים וכמנשה. (בראשית מח:כ)

So he blessed them on that day, saying, "Through you, Israel will bless, saying, 'May God make you like Efraim and like Menashe.'" (*Bereshit* 48:20)

When Yaakov said *"bekha"* ("through you"), he was talking to Yosef. Says Rabbi Sorotzkin, the greatest measure of a person is what type of *hinukh* he provides to his children. Whether his education succeeds or not is beyond his control. We can only do our best, and the rest is *siyatta dishemaya*. Yet, we have to do the utmost we can to ensure that our children are being given the best education possible

YAM SIMHA: NO GENERATION GAP

The *Yam Simha*[1] suggests yet another explanation as to why we bless our children to emulate Efraim and Menashe. He infers an answer from a previous *pasuk*, where Yaakov says:

אפרים ומנשה כראובן ושמעון יהיו לי. (בראשית מח:ה)

Efraim and Menashe shall be mine like Reuven and Shimon. (*Bereshit* 48:5)

---

1. Rabbi Yisrael Moshe Fried, *Yam Simha* (Lakewood, 1997), 143.

We know the reality that every generation experiences a spiritual decline from the previous generation, what we call *yeridat hadorot*. Every generation that is further from the source, further from *Maamad Har Sinai*, drops a spiritual notch. Yet, Yaakov saw that Menashe and Efraim didn't fall spiritually; rather, they jumped in their spiritual level – they were just like his own sons.

The Gemara (Sanhedrin 105a) states:

מכל אדם מתקנא חוץ מבנו ותלמידו.

A person is jealous of everybody in the world other than his son and his *talmid*.

A father thinks, if only my son should outdo what I do! Therefore, every Friday night, when a father gives this *berakha* to his child, his hope is: "Outshine me. Don't contribute to *yeridat hadorot*. Be greater than me!" That is why we bless our sons to be like Menashe and Efraim specifically. They were two people who didn't experience *yeridat hadorot* and were on par with their father.[2]

A similar idea is expressed by Rav Yosef Soloveitchik.[3] He cites a gemara (Kiddushin 30a) that states:

אמר רבי יהושע בן לוי כל המלמד בן בנו תורה מעלה עליו הכתוב כאילו קיבלה מהר סיני.

Rabbi Yehoshua ben Levi says, "Anyone who teaches Torah to his grandson is treated by the Torah as having received it from Mount Sinai."

---

2. In a similar vein, Yaakov learned with Yosef's children, and in a way, Yaakov was stating that when one learns Torah, it transcends any generational gap. Imagine entering a time machine and landing in a different era. If a Jew were to meet Rashi or the Rambam, a most interesting discussion about Torah would ensue. When one shares Torah, there is no generation gap. To Yaakov, this is what Efraim and Menashe symbolized, and that is the blessing we wish to convey to our children.

3. Rav Michel Shurkin, *Harerei Kedem*, vol. 2 (Jerusalem, 2004), sec. 122, p. 356.

The Rambam adds that there is a special merit of learning Torah with a grandchild, and it is greater in some ways than learning with a child.[4]

The problem, though, says Rav Soloveitchik, is that the Rambam also says that if you have a choice between your son and grandson for *talmud Torah*, your son comes first. If you only have enough money to pay for a *melamed* for either your son or your grandson, your son's education is your primary obligation, which seems to mean the opposite of the previous words of the Rambam.

Which is it, then? We can find our answer based on a Ramban, says Rav Soloveitchik. The Ramban in *Sefer HaMitzvot* counts a separate negative mitzva that the Rambam doesn't count: the mitzva to never forget the experience of Mount Sinai.

There are two elements of Torah that we have to give over to the next generation. The first is *talmud Torah*, which is actual information in the form of halakha, Mishna, Gemara – the whole breadth of Torah. The second is the *Har Sinai* element, which is the *emunat haTorah*, the development of our tradition, the Jewish identity, and the passion.

When it comes to the first type, says Rav Soloveitchik, a son takes precedence over a grandson, whereas when it comes to passing the torch on to the next generation, the continuity of the Jewish people, it is considered a greater accomplishment to pass it on to someone two generations down.

Based on this idea, maybe this is why we bless our children to be like Efraim and Menashe. Yaakov was the first person to have such a relationship with his grandchildren, where a grandfather learned Torah with his grandsons. We're giving the *berakha* to our children that not only should they learn Torah from us, but they should carry the torch into the next generation, pass on the fire of Har Sinai. It's really a *tefilla* when we give this *berakha*, a *tefilla* of the father that he should be *zokhe* to pass on the torch of the tradition.[5]

---

4. Rambam, *Hilkhot Talmud Torah* 1:2.
5. See Rav Abraham Besdin, *Reflections of the Rav*, vol. 2 (Hoboken, NJ: Ktav, 1989), 17, where Rav Soloveitchik provides an emotional description of his experience of feeling the *Baalei Mesora* entering the room when he is studying Torah.

Through My Sword and Bow

ויאמר ישראל אל יוסף הנה אנכי מת והיה אלקים עמכם והשיב אתכם
אל ארץ אבתיכם. ואני נתתי לך שכם אחד על אחיך אשר לקחתי מיד
האמרי בחרבי ובקשתי. (בראשית מח:כא-כב)

And Yisrael said to Yosef, "Behold, I am going to die, and God
will be with you, and He will return you to the land of your forefathers. And I have given you one portion over your brothers,
which I took from the hand of the Amorite with my sword and
with my bow." (*Bereshit* 48:21–22)

Yaakov promises Yosef the city of Shekhem, which he took from the
Emorites "through [his] sword and [his] bow." According to Onkelos,
this does not refer to an actual war with weapons. He translates *harbi*
and *kashti* not as "my sword" and "my bow" but as "my prayer" (*tzaloti*) and "my petition" (*ba'uti*). We are familiar with these words, which
refer to two types of prayer from *Kaddish* – "*titkabel tzaloton uba'uton.*"

This leaves us with two questions: What is the difference between
these two words? And why is there imagery of weapons when it comes
to prayer? Let us present two approaches to this issue.

The *Meshekh Hokhma*[1] suggests that *tzaloti* refers to our fixed prayers, the structure of *shevah, bakasha,* and *hodaa* (praise, request, and thanks), which was written by Hazal themselves. *Ba'uti* refers to personal requests we make to Hashem.

The difference between these two types of prayers, according to the *Meshekh Hokhma*, is that when it comes to the structured prayer, the words were written by *Hazal* and thus have inherent power, so even if we lack perfect *kavana* while we're davening, our prayer is effective. Regarding the personal, additional prayers we compose on our own, there is nothing inherently powerful about those words, so our prayer needs *kavana* to be effective.

Tzaloti, says the *Meshekh Hokhma*, is therefore represented by a sword, which is inherently sharp and easily cuts and draws blood. The prayers formulated by *Hazal* are the same. *Ba'uti* is represented by a bow, whose power is dependent on the expertise and *kavana*, so to speak, of the archer and how far back he pulls. Our intentions and the depth to which we pull back determine the power of our prayer!

Rabbi Menahem Genack, in *Birkat Yitzhak*,[2] offers a different explanation. What is the difference between these two types of prayers? *Tzaloti* refers to private, personal requests – for sustenance, health, *shalom bayit*, etc. They are personal prayers that affect individuals. *Ba'uti* refers to national prayers – for world peace, rebuilding the *Beit HaMikdash*, restoring justice to the world, etc.

A sword is a weapon that is used when one is standing close to an enemy. It is used in hand-to-hand combat, like personal prayers, which are between the person praying and Hashem, up close, in desperation. For national prayers, one shoots the bow knowing that the target is a little further away and the answer might be a little longer in coming, all the while understanding that the salvation is a process.

We should seek to engage in both forms of prayer, both personal and national prayer. Even if we may feel as if our salvation is a bit far off, our prayer is heard and can have an impact – perhaps not as immediately as a sword, but as a bow.

---

1. *Meshekh Hokhma, Bereshit* 48:22.
2. Rabbi Menahem Genack, *Birkat Yitzhak* (New York: Mesorah Publiations, 2013), 70.

Birkhot Yaakov?

Many of Yaakov's *berakhot* to his sons don't actually appear to be *berakhot*. In fact, it seems Yaakov rebuked Shimon and Levi! What exactly were these statements of Yaakov?

Rav Shlomo Wolbe[1] answers with a powerful lesson: The greatest *berakha* anyone can receive is the realization and recognition of who they are and their strengths and weaknesses. Yaakov made sure to inform each of his children of their unique characteristics. Yaakov's message to them before his departure was that if you know who you are, you can improve yourself.

He told his children, "This is who you are. So far you haven't reached your potential, but if you know who you are, you can work on it." Look at who Levi became – the greatest of the *shevatim*! Yaakov told Levi who he was and Levi capitalized on it; he took to heart the constructive criticism.

Then Rav Wolbe quotes a *Hazal* that tells us that when we go up to *Shamayim* after 120 years, three angels greet us and ask us for our name. When we don't know what our name is, we are beaten by the angel. This is where the Shelah's custom to recite a *pasuk* at the end of *Shemoneh Esreh* that corresponds to one's name is sourced. What is it

---

1. Rav Shlomo Wolbe, *Shiurei Humash* (Jerusalem, 2009), 375.

about our name? What's the significance of remembering our name, and why if we forget it are we are beaten?

Rav Wolbe explains that it means we forget who we are, or we never even knew. A name reflects the essence of a person, our true nature. The angels are asking, "What is your essence? What was your focus in life?"[2]

We have to look within ourselves and discover the *middot* that define us. Rav Wolbe quotes Rav Yeruham Levovitz, who says we each possess core attributes that affect all our other *middot*. For example, if someone's *midda* is *emet*, that could have a ripple effect on how he davens, gives *tzedaka*, conducts himself in business, etc. Sometimes, a person's root can be a negative *midda*, like anger, and our role is to overcome and channel it so we can best fulfill our mission on this earth with the package we were given. Reuven's *midda* was to move too quickly. That can be used to act rashly, but he could channel that to something good, like *zerizut*.

A person may have a tendency to kill. Rather than become a murderer he can channel that desire into a positive action and become a *mohel, shohet,* or surgeon.[3]

The *berakhot* of Yaakov were his revelations to his children. He told them what their root *middot* were, which is the ultimate blessing – and that is why we call them all *Birkhot Yaakov* even if they don't appear to be blessings. Yaakov defined each tribe and transmitted to each son what his powers were, and through that, each tribe could accomplish and fulfill its potential.

May we be blessed with the ability to understand our strengths and weaknesses so that we will be able to achieve our full potential.

---

2. In Hebrew, a name is a *shem* – spelled שם – which also may be read as *sham*, "there." A name is where is person is at in life – he is *sham*, there.
3. See Shabbat 156a.

A Time for Criticism

ראובן בכרי אתה כחי וראשית אוני.... פחז כמים. (בראשית מט:ג)

Reuven, you are my firstborn, my might, and the beginning of my strength.... You are restless like water. (*Bereshit* 49:3)

Prior to Yaakov's death he gathered his children to bless them. What was Yaakov's message to Reuven? Rashi on *Devarim* (1:3) claims that what Yaakov said to Reuven was actually a rebuke – *musar* for an incident that transpired years earlier.[1] The question can be asked, though, why didn't Yaakov give Reuven *musar* earlier, when the actual transgression occurred? Why did he wait until the end of his life to scold Reuven for what he did?

Rashi answers that Yaakov specifically waited until the end of his life because he feared that it would be difficult for Reuven to accept his rebuke, and if Yaakov would alienate him, he might leave the fold.

This is a curious statement. Reuven fathered one of the twelve tribes. He was a holy son of Yaakov. What was the likelihood of Reuven leaving the fold of Torah? Many people in history received rebuke and didn't leave *Yiddishkeit*, and here we're talking about Reuven, not just anyone! What exactly is Rashi driving at?

---

1. See Rashi on *Bereshit* 35:22.

Rav Avigdor Nebenzahl[2] suggests an answer to this dilemma: What Reuven would actually have done had he been given *musar* right away is unknown to us, but there is a clear message to us here, and that is: There was the slightest notion in Yaakov's mind that Reuven would leave the path of Torah if his honor was trampled on, so he didn't take the risk.

We can learn from Yaakov's actions the severity of wounded pride. When we're slighted in any way, it can lead us to act irrationally. If Yaakov was worried about someone like Reuven, one of the sons of Yaakov, leaving the fold over wounded pride, then we need to take care not to offend others in a way that can lead them to act irrationally and may lead them astray.

We see this very point play itself out in our history. We all know the mishna that says that every Jew has a place in the world to come. But the ensuing *mishnayot* (in the tenth *perek* of the Gemara in Sanhedrin) lists the exceptions to the rule, those who forfeited their share in the next world. One of the exceptions is Yeravam ben Nevat, the first king of the ten tribes that broke away from the house of David. He set up his own temple in Northern Israel and caused *Bnei Yisrael* to worship *avoda zara* rather than go to the *Beit HaMikdash*. He was a *talmid hakham* who went bad.

The *pasuk* in I *Melakhim* (13:33) says that Yeravam never repented of his evil ways "after this event." The Gemara asks: After *which* event? What event is the prophet referring to? The Gemara explains:

אחר הדבר הזה לא שב ירבעם מדרכו הרעה מאי אחר? אמר ר' אבא
אחר שתפשו הקב"ה לירבעם בבגדו ואמר לו חזור בך ואני ואתה ובן
ישי נטייל בגן עדן אמר לו מי בראש? בן ישי בראש, אי הכי לא בעינא.
(סנהדרין קב.)

After this event Yeravam did not return from his evil ways. After which event? Says Rabbi Aba, after *HaKadosh Barukh Hu* grabbed Yeravam by his clothes and said to him: Repent, and you, and I, and Ben Yishai will walk together in Gan Eden. Yeravam then asked: Who will lead? Hashem responded: Ben Yishai will lead.

---

2. Rav Avigdor Nebenzahl, *Sihot Al Sefer Bereshit* (Jerusalem, 2004), 347.

Yeravam responded: In that case, I am not interested. (Sanhedrin 102a)

Hashem turned to Yeravam and appealed to him to do *teshuva*. "Come back to Me," said Hashem. "Do *teshuva!*" Imagine if Hashem would address us personally and directly – we would jump at the opportunity!

Hashem then promised Yeravam that if he did *teshuva*, Hashem, Yeravam, and David HaMelekh would walk in Gan Eden together. What a wonderful offer! Yet what was Yeravam's response? "Who is first in line on this stroll through Gan Eden? Who will lead the way?" David or Yeravam?

Hashem answered, "David HaMelekh will walk in the front." Yeravam then declared that if he wasn't first in the procession, he didn't want any part of it.

See what honor can do to a person! How low can it bring someone! That's what Yaakov was worried about, so he waited until the end of his life to provide Reuven with *rebuke*.

The Ramhal writes about honor in the eleventh chapter of *Mesillat Yesharim*. The desire for honor is the greatest desire in the world. If a person wouldn't have this great desire, he'd be satisfied with whatever he possesses. He would not care what type of food he consumes, what clothing he adorns, or the house in which he dwells. Honor is the strongest desire in the world, says the Ramhal. That is why Yaakov was so careful not to offend Reuven with *musar* until the end of his life.

Yaakov is teaching us that it is crucial to recognize that each individual has a certain degree of self-pride, and when that is shattered, there is no predicting the irrational ramifications. On the one hand, we need to keep this in mind when criticizing others. Additionally, we need to be careful when we are the recipient of criticism and accept it with an open mind and in stride. We cannot let it shatter our self-confidence but rather assist us in making ourselves better individuals.

Yosef's Request of His Brothers

ויאמר יוסף אל אחיו אנכי מת וא־להים פקד יפקד אתכם והעלה
אתכם מן הארץ הזאת אל הארץ אשר נשבע לאברהם ליצחק וליעקב.
(בראשית נ:כד)

Yosef said to his brothers, "I am going to die; God will surely
remember you and take you up out of this land to the land that
He swore to Avraham, to Yitzhak, and to Yaakov." (*Bereshit* 50:24)

At the end of *Parashat Vayehi*, Yosef spoke to his brothers and made
them swear that they would take his bones out of Egypt. Why did Yosef
ask his brothers to take care of this task, and not his own children? His
children were old enough to take charge and fulfill such a mission, and
usually a father directs his children to deal with his funeral arrangements
and not his siblings.

Several commentators address this question, and we will look
at several of them.

MESHEKH HOKHMA

The *Meshekh Hokhma*[1] suggests that Yosef was nervous about his sons.
Only half of Menashe's tribe made it into *Eretz Yisrael*, while the other

---

1. *Meshekh Hokhma, Bereshit* 50:24.

half settled on the other side of the Yarden River. Yosef didn't want to take chances with his burial spot, so he asked his brothers, the majority of whom made it to *Eretz Yisrael*, to take care of this task.

MOSHAV ZEKENIM

The *Moshav Zekenim* quotes a gemara (Sota 13b) that states that Yosef asked his brothers to take his bones to Egypt in order to give them the opportunity to do *teshuva* for selling him. They sold him out of Canaan, and this gave them the opportunity to return him to Canaan, bringing the events full circle.

RAV YOSEF KARO: MAGGID MEISHARIM

Rav Yosef Karo[2] suggests that Yosef saw through *ruah hakodesh* that some members of the tribe of Efraim left Egypt early and never made it to Canaan. So, again, since Yosef wanted to ensure that his bones would make it back to *Eretz Yisrael*, he requested that his brothers take care of his burial.

RAV YOSEF SOLOVEITCHIK

Rav Yosef Soloveitchik[3] suggests another approach. Yosef wanted to become one of the tribes again. He wanted his name on the High Priest's breastplate. His request was deeper than a simple burial. He was asking his brothers to take him back as their brother. To achieve this, Yosef had to be buried, and this had to be done by his brothers. In the Rav's words:

> To accomplish this realignment, Yosef had to repair the breach in the relationship with his brothers, a relationship that had been strained since childhood. He somehow had to inculcate love and respect where previously there had been distrust and fear.
>
> There is a subtle double meaning in Yosef's request: "The removal of my remains" from Egypt should "elevate" my standing from estrangement to an integral constituent of the tribes of Israel.

---

2. Rav Yosef Karo, *Maggid Meisharim, Parashat Beshallah.*
3. *Humash Masoret HaRav* (New York: OU Press, 2013), 373.

In this way, the antitheses of Yosef's dream came to pass. Yosef figuratively prostrated himself before his own brothers as he begged them to fulfill his dying request. He was now utterly dependent on his brothers to attain his own redemption.

Ultimately, Moshe is the one who went to get Yosef's bones when it was time to leave Egypt. Moshe was a descendent of Levi, one of the protagonists in the story of the sale of Yosef. This was therefore the ultimate rectification for the sin of the sale.

The brothers bowed down to Yosef, Yosef bowed down to his brothers, and now they were all back together. He asked them to take him in, make him part of the twelve tribes, and keep him for eternity. *Vayehi* ends with the unification of the brothers, and the stage is set for Am Yisrael to go from individuals to a nation, as we enter *Sefer Shemot*.

Shemot

Parashat Shemot

The Significance of Names

Why is this *parasha* called *Parashat Shemot*, which means "names"?

When we hear someone call our name, it makes us feel proud. We realize that someone is noting and acknowledging our presence. One's name is of special significance. It describes the essence of a person. On the other hand, a name can also be superficial and external; after all, numerous people can share the same name. How significant can a name be, therefore, if many people have the same name? A name is in effect a paradox. It is unique and specific to a person yet shared by many. The Lubavitcher Rebbe[1] explains that our *parasha* is known as *Parashat Shemot* because the *parasha* is also a paradox. *Shemot* is all about redemption, yet the parasha is filled with the challenging experiences of Am Yisrael in Egypt. As the redemption starts, things get worse, and the *parasha* ends on a low. Yet despite this low point, we know it is the first step of redemption, just as a seed has to first destroy itself before it can bear fruit.

---

1. *Chumash: The Gutnick Edition* (New York: Kol Menachem, 2008), *Shemot*, 1.

That is the message of *Parashat Shemot*. On the surface, it may appear as though nothing is happening (like a name tells you nothing about a person), yet we know that redemption is in fact sprouting in the background. *Parashat Shemot* (like its title, "names") is superficially a concealment of the Jewish spirit, but deep down, that spirit always remains intact and alive.

A NAME OR ANONYMITY?

In a similar vein, it is interesting to note that despite the name of the *parasha*, after the opening list of those who descended to Egypt, there is no mention of names until Moshe is born. The Torah refers to individuals without using their names.

We are introduced to a new king without being told his name. Later, the king's daughter is referred to as "Pharaoh's daughter" (*Bat Pharaoh*) and not by her given name. Moshe's parents, who we know are Amram and Yokheved, are introduced as "a man from the house of Levi" and "a daughter of Levi." The real names of Shifra and Pua are not revealed.[2] Why is no mention made of any of these people's names?

Perhaps the Torah wants to highlight that the protagonist here is indeed Moshe, and everyone else is less significant in the story. Hazal tell us that each individual has three names: (1) the name given by one's parents; (2) the name used by one's friends (nicknames, diminutives); and (3) the name, or reputation that one creates for himself.[3] May we follow Moshe's lead and do what we must to create a positive name for ourselves.

---

2. Rashi explains that these were titles given to the nurses due to care they provided to the infants.
3. *Midrash Kohelet.*

Feeling like a Stranger

ואלה שמות בני ישראל הבאים מצרימה את יעקב איש וביתו באו.
(שמות א:א)

These are the names of Bnei Yisrael who are coming to Egypt
with Yaakov; every man came with his household. (*Shemot* 1:1)

Why does the Torah use the word *haba'im* – "who are coming" – instead
of the past tense *sheba'u* – "who came"? The children of Yaakov had
arrived in Egypt years earlier, in *Parashat Vayigash*, so why imply that
they are coming now? Several commentators offer suggestions.

Yagdil Torah[1] suggests that the word *haba'im* indicates that Yaakov implanted in his children the feeling that they should never sense
as if they are *toshavim* – "residents, citizens" in whatever exile they find
themselves. They should not feel comfortable; rather, they should feel
as if they have just arrived.

Usually, the longer someone is present in a location, the stronger
his sense of belonging develops. He starts out feeling like a stranger in a
strange land, but with time, he starts to feel like he belongs there. However, if at every moment one feels as though he doesn't belong in that

---

1. Rav Moshe Menachem Ludmir, *Yagdil Torah* (Jerusalem: Genesis Press 1991/2008),
   Shemot, 9.

place, he will not attempt to fit in, and he will keep dreaming about his true home. That's the message of *haba'im*. Yaakov Avinu imparted this feeling to his children so that they would never feel like Egypt is home. Indeed, Am Yisrael didn't change their names, language, or mode of dress – among the first things that an immigrant changes when trying to fit into a new culture – while in the Egyptian exile.

The first words of the *haftara* of *Parashat Shemot* are *haba'im yashresh Yaakov* (*Yeshayahu* 27:6). This phrase literally means, "[in days] that are coming, Yaakov will take root." However, on a deeper level, this can mean that Yaakov implanted the message of *haba'im* in his children. We should never feel comfortable with the present state of affairs, never think that right now is the be-all and end-all, that it is our ultimate destiny. We should always feel like we are still coming, that we have not yet arrived. Not to be content with the present but to work towards a brighter future.

Yagdil Torah then tells a story in the name of the *Beit Yisrael*, the Gerrer Rebbe, that a certain *hasid* went to the Belzer Rebbe and told him of his economic misfortunes. The Rebbe sent the *hasid* to a distant town, promised that he would find financial success there, and requested that the *hasid* send a letter to the Rebbe soon after his arrival.

The *hasid* moved and immediately experienced financial success. He sent a letter informing his Rebbe that he was doing well. However, lamented the *hasid*, the spiritual state of affairs in the town was very sorry, indeed, and the *hasid* was not happy with it. The Rebbe replied that the *hasid* should remain in the town despite the spiritual challenges. The next letter from the *hasid* was similar, but the Rebbe assured him that all was okay; he should continue what he was doing.

In the third letter, the *hasid* finally sounded relieved. He told the Rebbe that he had acclimated to the new spiritual and material conditions and would be okay. This time, the Rebbe responded that the *hasid* should immediately return home. The moment the *hasid* got comfortable with the spiritual dangers, it was time for him to leave. As long as one is aware of spiritual danger, his guard is up, and he stands a chance. But the moment he considers the situation to not be that bad, when he stops feeling like *haba'im* – then it's time to move on.

Rav Yosef Soloveitchik[2] explains the term *haba'im* in a similar fashion but includes the perspectives of both the Egyptians and the children of Israel. In addition to Bnei Yisrael separating themselves and retaining their identity by not changing their names, language, or dress, Rav Soloveitchik asserts that the Egyptians also viewed us – unjustifiably – as strangers in the land. As the Rav states:

> The term *haba'im* suggests that the people of Egypt did not consider the Israelite nation as part of their state, society, and culture; they looked upon them as if they had just entered Egypt. How long must one remain in a country to be considered a citizen? The words of Pharaoh to his advisors suggest that he considered Bnei Yisrael as having just arrived.... This belief in the otherness of the Jew repeats itself throughout history. Jews lived in Germany even before the Dark Ages. During the Middle Ages, Bnei Yisrael supported Germany from within; they were an integral part of society, yet centuries later they were wiped out.

Bnei Yisrael had been in Egypt for generations. Yosef had saved the country from starvation, and Yaakov had stopped the famine! And yet, the Egyptians refused to look upon Bnei Yisrael as natives, as people who belonged and had a right to belong. They had short memories. We see a repeat of this same attitude throughout history in all the different exiles. The essence of anti-Semitic doctrine throughout history has always depicted the Jew as a stranger. They charge that we are strangers, *Ivrim*, others. We never assimilate ourselves into any community. We are outsiders.

The term *haba'im* describes how we should view ourselves and the boundaries we need to construct, but it also depicts how we were viewed by the Egyptians and, unfortunately, by many of our neighbors throughout Jewish history. If we don't recognize that we are separate, they will separate us from them against our will, as we have seen too often throughout history.

---

2. *Humash Masoret HaRav* (New York: OU Press, 2014), 3.

Hakarat HaTov

Rav Avigdor Nebenzahl[1] points out that an underlying theme of the first five *parshiyot* of the book of *Shemot* is *hakarat hatov* – "gratitude and acknowledgment of a benefactor." Sometimes it can be very hard to recognize and acknowledge all the good that has been bestowed upon us. We often have great excuses to justify why we don't owe any debt of gratitude to someone who has been kind to us. "They owed me." "I paid for it." "It was not big deal for them." "It wasn't even that helpful." "I didn't ask for help." "They had ulterior motives." These are just a few of the ways we justify our lack of gratitude.

Nevertheless, *hakarat hatov* is one of the cornerstones of our faith, and we witness it in several dimensions in the beginning of the book of *Shemot*.

First, we are introduced to the *midda* of *kefui tova* – "denial of goodness" of Pharaoh. The Torah says:

ויקם מלך חדש על מצרים אשר לא ידע את יוסף. (שמות א:ח)

A new king arose over Egypt who did not know Yosef. (*Shemot* 1:8)

---

1. Rav Avigdor Nebenzahl, *Sihot Al Sefer Shemot* (Jerusalem, 2004), 13.

Whether or not it was the same Pharaoh who had ruled during the time of Yosef, this denial was extraordinarily ungrateful to Yosef, who had saved the country in its time of distress.

This attribute of *kefui tova* from people ultimately leads to having the *midda* of *kefui tova* toward Hashem. Soon after he rejected the goodness of Yosef and his people, Pharaoh said:

מי ה' אשר אשמע בקלו לשלח את ישראל. (שמות ה:ב)

Who is Hashem that I should heed His voice to let Israel out? (*Shemot* 5:2)

In contrast, the *midda* of *hakarat hatov* is exemplified many times by Moshe Rabbenu. From the first plague, we learn of Moshe's strong *midda* of recognizing good done to him when he refrained from striking the sea or the land because the dirt and the water had previously saved him.[2]

The Torah rewards dogs because they did not bark when we left Egypt, commanding us to throw them dead animal carcasses.

ובשר בשדה טרפה לא תאכלו לכלב תשליכון אותו. (שמות כב:ל)

You shall not eat dead animals lying in the field; rather, you shall cast it to the dogs. (*Shemot* 22:30)

At first glance, these are strange examples. One can understand that it behooves us to show appreciation to a person who provided us with a benefit, but water and soil are inanimate objects. In fact, the water and soil that Moshe refrained from striking were not the same water and soil that rescued him. Water flows continually, and the earth that hid the body of the Egyptian killed by Moshe was not the same earth that he would have hit to begin the plague of lice. Similarly, the dogs that we feed with our nonkosher carcasses are not the same dogs that remained silent when we left Egypt. Why, then, must we show them *hakarat hatov*?

---

2. Moshe was saved by the water as a baby when he was placed in a basket on the Nile. He was saved by the earth when it covered the Egyptian guard he killed for striking a Jewish slave.

Rav Nebenzahl explains that we offer thanks not because the provider needs the appreciation; rather, the recipient ought to recognize his dependency on the assistance of another. The Hebrew word for thanks, *hodaa,* is also the word for "admission" of a debt. One who gives thanks is essentially admitting their dependency on others. Perhaps this is why it is difficult to say thank you.[3]

Sefer HaHinukh explains:[4]

וכשיקבע זאת המדה בנפשו יעלה ממנה להכיר טובת האל ברוך הוא...

When this trait becomes engrained in a person, it will lead one to recognize the good that Hashem has bestowed upon all.

Showing appreciation to others leads one to appreciate all that Hashem has provided to him. Rav Nebenzahl cites a story about Rabbi Yisrael Zev Gustman, the *rosh yeshiva* of Yeshivat Netzah Yisrael. Rabbi Gustman, at the age of eighteen, served on the *beit din* of Rabbi Hayim Ozer Grodzinski in Vilna. During the Holocaust, Rabbi Gustman hid in the bushes and forests to avoid the Nazis. Years later, he was seen watering the plants at his yeshiva in Jerusalem. When asked why he was doing this trivial task, he responded that it was his way of showing his appreciation to the bushes that saved his life in Vilna. Even though those were not the same bushes, he felt obligated to express his appreciation to the same species in a different geography, exemplifying the *midda* of *hakarat hatov.*

We have to realize that the *midda* of *hakarat hatov* is a fundamental principle in Judaism. We are known as "Yehudim," whose root is also *hodaa.* We must make it an integral part of who we are.

---

3. Rav Hutner in *Pahad Yitzhak,* Hanukka 2:2, notes that we have both of these meanings in the *Shemoneh Esreh.* We recite *modim anahnu lakh she'ata,* "admitting" God's omnipotence, as well as *nodeh lekha...al hayeinu,* "thanking" Hashem for our lives.
4. *Sefer HaHinukh, mitzva 33, kibud av va'eim.*

The Land Was Filled with Them

ובני ישראל פרו וישרצו וירבו ויעצמו במאד מאד ותמלא הארץ אתם.
(שמות א:ז)

And Bnei Yisrael were fruitful, and increased abundantly, and multiplied, and became exceedingly mighty; and the land was filled [with] them. (*Shemot* 1:7)

Why does this *pasuk*, which describes how Israel proliferated greatly in Egypt, use the word *otam*, "them" – instead of *mehem,* "from them"? It is awkward to say, "the land was filled them." The Netziv comments that *otam* is written *haser*, without a *vav*; therefore, it can be read as *itam* – "with them."

At the end of *Sefer Bereshit*, the tribes had settled in Goshen, established a yeshiva, and were living separately from the Egyptians. Suddenly, at the beginning of *Parashat Shemot*, we read that "the land was filled with them." What happened to Bnei Yaakov who originally settled in Goshen, apart from the Egyptians?

At this point, Bnei Yisrael no longer lived only in Goshen; rather, they lived *itam* – "with [the Egyptians]." They lived wherever they found housing, to the point where they mixed completely with the Egyptians.

This is why Hashem had to "pass over" houses of Bnei Yisrael during the plague of *makkat bekhorot,* the death of the firstborns.

With this wording, the Torah tells us why the Egyptians began to hate Bnei Yisrael and why the decrees started. Bnei Yisrael became disgusting in the Egyptians' eyes when they stopped following Yaakov's plan, which was to live separately from them, in Goshen. They no longer wanted that restriction. They wanted to mix into and be part of Egyptian society. As soon as Bnei Yisrael tried to become part of that society, the Egyptians turned on them.

Rabbi Chaim Volozhiner is quoted as stating: "If Bnei Yisrael don't make Kiddush, the gentiles make Havdala." If we do not separate ourselves, if we don't remain in Goshen voluntarily, we are going to be forced into Goshen.

The *Meshekh Hokhma* explains that this is why we hold a glass of wine at the Seder while reciting *vehi she'amda,* which describes how our enemies constantly tried and failed to destroy us.[1] The word *vehi* ("and this") attests to the fact that it is *this* very glass of wine that symbolizes what protected us from assimilating throughout the generations. The laws of *yayin nesekh* and *stam yeynam,* which proscribe gentile wine, establish a separation between Jews and non-Jews. The beginning of the end for Bnei Yisrael is when "the land becomes filled with them."

---

1. *Meshekh Hokhma, Parashat Va'era* 6:6.

Implanting Anti-Semitism

ויקם מלך חדש על מצרים אשר לא ידע את יוסף. (שמות א:ח)

A new king arose over Egypt who was unfamiliar with Yosef.
(*Shemot* 1:8)

The *Be'er Yosef*[1] asks two questions on this *pasuk*, based on Rashi and
Onkelos. Rashi explains that the "new king" was either a new king, literally, or the same old king, whose decrees were "renewed" (*nit'hadshu
gezerotav*). Onkelos translates the verse as follows:

A new king arose over Egypt who did not uphold Yosef's decree.
(*Shemot* 1:8)

What is Rashi referring to when he describes the decrees as being
"renewed"? The decrees were presumably *new*, not *renewed*! And
regarding Onkelos, what was "Yosef's decree" that the new king "did
not uphold"?

The *Be'er Yosef* explains that Pharaoh had one goal: to subjugate,
enslave, and torture the children of Israel. The problem with his plan,
though, was the positive feelings of his nation toward Yosef's family

---

1. Rav Yosef MiSalant, *Be'er Yosef* (Jerusalem, 1972), *Shemot*, 180.

and descendants; after all, Yosef had saved them from starvation. How could Pharaoh convince his people to hate Bnei Yisrael and agree that his plan was of national importance? Yosef undoubtedly went down in history as a great person, but now Pharaoh wanted to repay his goodness with evil.

Pharaoh's first step was to uproot the laws Yosef established. When Yosef ruled Egypt during the years of famine, he sold food to the Egyptians, and as they ran out of money and then all possessions that they could use to purchase food, Yosef compelled the Egyptians to sell themselves as slaves to Pharaoh. Additionally, he forced them to uproot themselves and move to different parts of the land to show that they did not own the land, but that all land was owned by Pharaoh. The only people this law did not apply to were Bnei Yisrael who lived in Goshen. Thus, the natives became strangers, and the strangers became natives. This was all part of Yosef's plan to allow his family to settle in Egypt undisturbed by the Egyptians.

Now, Pharaoh stood up and incited his nation against the children of Israel, telling them that Yosef's intentions were purely for his own benefit and that of his family. "We are the real Egyptians, and it's time for things to revert to what they were before Yosef came. You are an Egyptian if you were born here, and only you truly belong here! Anyone else is a stranger and has no rights here!"

This is how the *Be'er Yosef* understands the word *nit'hadshu*. In order to be able to carry out his wicked plan against Klal Yisrael and subjugate them, Pharaoh used flattery, telling his nation that none of them were really slaves. He "renewed" the law by making Bnei Yisrael the slaves instead of the Egyptians. The law was not new, but it was renewed and reversed: Egyptians became free and could own land, and Bnei Yisrael became slaves.

Based on this, says the *Be'er Yosef*, we can understand the next *pasuk* in a more profound way.

ויאמר אל עמו הנה עם בני ישראל רב ועצום ממנו. (שמות א:ט)

He told his nation that the people of Israel are more plentiful and mightier than us. (*Shemot* 1:9)

The word *rav* can mean "numerous" or "master." Pharaoh meant that Bnei Yisrael had been the masters over the Egyptians for long enough. It was time to turn the tables.

Now, we can also understand a curious passage in the Haggada. In the *tzei ulemad* section, each word of the four *pesukim* recited when bringing *bikkurim* (*Devarim* 26:5–8) is expounded. The Haggada, based on the *Sifrei*, explains the phrase *vayareiu otanu hamitzrim* – "the Egyptians were evil to us" by quoting our *pasuk* about Pharaoh strategizing to outsmart the children of Israel. How does this prove anything? This *pasuk* does not explain how the Egyptians were evil to us, rather it describes their fears of the evil that we might do to them.

Rabbi Immanuel Bernstein[2] says in the name of the Beit HaLevi on *Parashat Shemot* that the Haggada does not interpret *vayareiu otanu hamitzrim* to mean "the Egyptians were evil to us"; rather, he says that it means "the Egyptians made us out to be evil." They demonized us. The *pasuk* cited by the Haggada makes perfect sense, as it describes exactly how Pharaoh turned Egyptian opinion against the children of Israel.

This strategy has been emulated by anti-semitic leaders throughout history: first demonize and dehumanize the children of Israel; then, strip them of property and rights; and in the last stage, attack, enslave, and eradicate them.

---

2. *Darkness to Destiny: The Haggadah Experience* (Beit Shemesh: Mosaica Press, 2014), 82.

It's the Little Things That Make a Great Person

ויאמר מלך מצרים למילדת העברית אשר שם האחת שפרה ושם השנית
פועה. (שמות א:טו)

The king of Egypt told the Hebrew midwives, one named Shifra and the second named Pua. (*Shemot* 1:15)

Who were the two midwives, Shifra and Pua? *Hazal* inform us that they were really Yokheved and Miriam, Moshe's mother and sister, respectively. Rashi on this *pasuk* explains the reason for their pseudonyms:

שפרה: זו יוכבד על שם שמשפרת את הולד. פועה: זו מרים שפועה
ומדברת והוגה לולד כדרך הנשים המפייסות תינוק הבוכה. (רש"י
שמות א:טו)

Shifra…because she beautified (*meshaperet*) the infants; Pua… who poo-pooed, spoke to, and made noises at the infants, like mothers do to pacify a crying infant. (Rashi on *Shemot* 1:15)

What was so significant about beautifying and coddling the babies that the Torah named the midwives for these actions? These details seem so inconsequential compared to the big picture of what Yokheved and Miriam were accomplishing by saving the lives of the Jewish children.

Rav Yeruham Levovitz[1] suggests that these seemingly little actions were tremendous. Great people take little things and make them great. A great person views the smallest detail in context, seeing every tiny factor as an opportunity to get closer to HaKadosh Barukh Hu. Every small act is, in reality, great. Small people are the opposite. They take great things and trample them, minimizing truly tremendous opportunities.

All they were doing was coddling the babies, which seems like such a small act. But these small acts were, in actuality, saving Am Yisrael, by giving these children a chance to survive. Therefore, Yokheved and Miriam were defined by these seemingly small actions that were really great achievements.

There's no such thing as a big or small opportunity, says Rav Yeruham. Rather, it all depends on us.

A story in the Gemara is right on point. Turnus Rufus asked Rabbi Akiva, "If Hashem loves poor people so much, why doesn't He just provide them with enough money for them to sustain themselves?" Rabbi Akiva responded, "Because He's giving us opportunities to become great, to earn merits."[2]

Do we have this in mind when we drive carpool, when we pick up a grocery item from the store because our parent asked us to? We're fulfilling the mitzvot of be fruitful and multiply, educating children, and honoring parents! Every little act can be turned into something great! We need to look at the small things we do in life and realize the amazing impact that they have. It's the little things that make a great person.

---

1. Rav Yeruham Halevi Levovitz, *Daat Torah* (Jerusalem, 2001), *Shemot*, 6.
2. Bava Batra 10a.

Evidence of Moshe's Leadership Qualities

ויהי בימים ההם ויגדל משה ויצא אל אחיו. (שמות ב:יא)

And it came to pass in those days, when Moshe matured and went out unto his brethren. (*Shemot* 2:11)

What is so unique about Moshe Rabbenu that he was selected as the leader of Am Yisrael? The Torah does not explicitly specify anything about Moshe – just that Hashem appeared to him at the burning bush and ordered him to act as the leader of Am Yisrael.

Perhaps the text alludes to Moshe's unique qualities that made him the appropriate choice as a leader.

Nechama Leibowitz points out that the first three interactions that Moshe has with others that are described in the Torah portrays Moshe's true personality.[1] Moshe is present at three disputes, and rather than act as a passive bystander, he leaps into action to protect the underdog.

The first event occurred when Moshe left Pharaoh's palace and witnessed an Egyptian man beating an Israelite slave:

---

1. Nechama Leibowitz, *Studies in Shemot* (Jerusalem: WZO, 1978), 39.

ויהי בימים ההם ויגדל משה ויצא אל אחיו וירא בסבלתם וירא איש
מצרי מכה איש עברי מאחיו. ויפן כה וכה וירא כי אין איש ויך את
המצרי ויטמנהו בחול. (שמות ב:יא-יב)

And it came to pass in those days, when Moshe matured and
went out unto his brethren, and looked on their burdens; and
he saw an Egyptian smiting a Hebrew, one of his brethren. And
he looked this way and that way, and when he saw that there
was no man, he smote the Egyptian and buried him in the sand.
(*Shemot* 2:11–12)

Moshe immediately intervened to save the Israelite slave's life.

The second event Moshe witnessed was an argument between
two Israelites, Datan and Aviram:

ויצא ביום השני והנה שני אנשים עברים נצים ויאמר לרשע למה תכה
רעך. (שמות ב:יג)

He went out on the second day, and there were two Hebrew men
in a scuffle, and he said to the wicked one: Why are you hitting
your friend? (*Shemot* 2:13)

When Moshe witnessed that a dispute between Jews was turning physical, he intervened and asked, "Why are you hitting your friend?"

The third event occurred when Moshe arrived in Midian. He was
a fugitive, and we would have expected him to maintain a low profile.
However, he witnessed the local shepherds harassing Yitro's daughters,
and he immediately intervened to defend them.

ולכהן מדין שבע בנות ותבאנה ותדלנה ותמלאנה את הרהטים להשקות
צאן אביהן. ויבאו הרעים ויגרשום ויקם משה ויושען וישק את צאנם.
ותבאנה אל רעואל אביהן ויאמר מדוע מהרתן בא היום. ותאמרן איש
מצרי הצילנו מיד הרעים וגם דלה דלה לנו וישק את הצאן. (שמות
ב: טז-יט)

The priest of Midian had seven daughters; and they came and
drew water, and filled the troughs to water their father's flock. And

the shepherds came and drove them away; but Moshe stood up and helped them, and watered their flock. And when they came to Reuel their father, he said: "How is it that you have returned so soon today?" And they said: "An Egyptian delivered us out of the hand of the shepherds, and moreover he drew water for us, and watered the flock." (*Shemot* 2:16–19)

What do we learn about Moshe's personality from these scenarios? He could not stand idly by when injustice was being committed. Moshe showed compassion to the oppressed. He did not distinguish between a dispute among an Israelite and a non-Israelite, a dispute between Israelites, and a dispute between non-Israelites.

In Midrash Rabba, at the beginning of *Sefer Vayikra*, there are no less than ten names attributed to Moshe Rabbenu: Yered, Hever, Yekutiel, Avigdor, Avi Socho, Avi Zanoach, Tuvia, Shmaya ben Netanel HaSofer, Halevi (ben Evyatar), and Moshe. Yet the one name that stuck is Moshe. Why is that? It seems somewhat ironic, as the Torah tells us that the name Moshe was given to him by Batya, Pharaoh's daughter, as she said: "Since I raised him (*meshitihu*) from the water [the Nile River]."[2] Why is the name that derived from that event the one name that outlasted the others? How did the name Moshe personify his personality?

I heard in the name of Rav Yehuda Amital that water represents the ultimate in conformity. If you place water in a bottle, it takes the shape of the bottle. Moshe was the antithesis of the characteristic of water. Moshe did not just go with the flow – when he saw an injustice, he was not afraid to take a stand, even if it was unpopular. He was taken from the water (*ki min hamayim meshitihu*) – in a way symbolizing "anti-water." He was a non-conformist and did what Hashem wanted him to do.[3]

Moshe Rabbenu couldn't *not* get involved! This is what made him the leader he was. He saw an argument, and he had to break it up. A Jewish leader is someone who gets involved, who wants to make the

---

2. *Shemot* 2:10.
3. On a deeper level, the name "Moshe," from *min hamayim meshitihu*, may relate to Moshe's having led the Jewish people's exit not only from Egypt but literally out of the water, during *Kriat Yam Suf.*

world around him a better place, even if it is not the Jewish world specifically. He does the right thing even when it is not according to popular opinion. We can strive for the same: not to be just bystanders, but rather to take responsibility and action in order to achieve justice and make this world a better place.

The Burning Flame Within

וירא מלאך ה' אליו בלבת אש מתוך הסנה וירא והנה הסנה בער באש
והסנה איננו אכל. (שמות ג:ב)

And the angel of Hashem appeared unto him in a flame of fire
out of the midst of a bush; and he looked, and behold, the bush
burned with fire, and the bush was not consumed. (*Shemot* 3:2)

In the Haggada, we recite the famous words: a*vadim hayinu lePharo
beMitzrayim* – "we were slaves to Pharaoh in Egypt." Why does it matter *where* we were slaves, though? Why couldn't we just say a*vdei Paro
hayinu* – "we were Pharaoh's slaves." Wouldn't that be simpler and parallel the beginning of *Hallel*: *Hallelu, avdei Hashem* – "Give praise, O
servants of Hashem" (*Tehillim* 113:1)?

Rav Yosef Soloveitchik[1] explains as follows: Why did Hashem
choose a bush, a shrub, to reveal himself to Moshe for the first time?

Throughout the *parshiyot*, we find Moshe wondering several times
why Bnei Yisrael merited to be redeemed. He saw members of Am Yisrael
who were willing to hand him over to Pharaoh, who did not get along

---

1. Rav Hershel Schacter, *MiPeninei HaRav* (Jerusalem: Flatbush Beit Hamidrash,
2001), 281.

with each other, who worshipped idols, and who were on the 49th level of impurity! Moshe wondered why they even merited to be redeemed.

How did Hashem respond to Moshe's curiosity? In a burning bush, whose inside was not consumed, as if to tell Moshe: Am Yisrael might seem cold on the outside, but deep down inside everyone is a fire that never gets extinguished. The bush was aflame and was not being consumed. Moshe only saw the cold on the outside, but inside, each member of Klal Yisrael has a burning flame.

Now we can understand the wording of the Haggada. Being called *avdei Paro* means that we fully and completely identified with Pharaoh. But we were never *avdei Paro* – that was only on the outside. It was superficial. We may have been servants to Pharaoh physically, socially, and politically – *avadim hayinu leParo* – but we were never *avdei Paro*. We became *avdei Hashem*, not *avadim leHashem*. We have to realize that every Jew has this flame inside, and in every Jew has a deep love for Hashem – a fire.

Based on this, says the Rambam, we can understand Hashem's promise to us that we *will* ultimately do *teshuva*, however unlikely it may seem. We are like an *ayal*, a hind yearning for a water source, sometimes without even knowing where it is. And just as an *ayal* is instinctively drawn to water, so man is instinctively drawn to Hashem, as it says in *Tehillim* (42:2): "Like a hind crying for water, my soul cries for You, Hashem." Sometimes we find our way to the *beit midrash* without even knowing how we got there. That's the deep love every Jew has inside for HaKadosh Barukh Hu.

What is symbolized by the bush? The burning bush is the lowest of vegetation, yet there was still a fire there. No matter how low a Jew may fall, that spark still burns inside of him.

It is interesting to note, that the Yiddish word for grandchild is *einekl*. On a deeper level, we can suggest that this comes from *einenu ukal* – "was not consumed," like the burning bush. If we pass along our tradition to our children and grandchildren, that flame will never be extinguished!

Removing Shoes, Removing Barriers

ויאמר אל תקרב הלם של נעליך מעל רגליך כי המקום אשר אתה עומד
עליו אדמת קדש הוא. (שמות ג:ה)

And He said: "Do not come closer; remove your shoes from your feet, for the place whereupon you stand is holy ground." (*Shemot* 3:5)

At the burning bush, Hashem instructed Moshe to remove his shoes because, as the *pasuk* explains, Moshe was standing on holy ground.

A mishna in *Pirkei Avot* (2:4) teaches us not to procrastinate: "Do not say, 'When I have time I will study,' for perhaps you will not have time." Life is always busy, and if you don't find time now, you will likely never find the time.

The Hafetz Hayim[1] postulates that we always think we're going to be less busy at a different time. Therefore, we push things off. This is what this *pasuk* is alluding to: The place you are standing *right now* is holy, ripe for action. The *here and now* has so much potential. If right

---

1. *Hafetz Hayim, Al HaTorah* (Bnei Brak, 1972), 95.

now is a specifically challenging time for you, that may be Hashem's exact purpose in sending you the challenge *right now*.

Right where you are is holy ground. What does the rest of the *pasuk* mean when it tells Moshe to take off his shoes?

The Hafetz Hayim explains that a person can always serve HaKadosh Barukh Hu and get closer to Him, but he must break the barriers that separate him from Hashem. Take off your shoes; place your feet directly on the ground, with no barrier or separation – that is what taking off one's shoes symbolizes. The *kohanim* did not wear shoes in the *Beit HaMikdash* for this exact reason: There could not be any barrier while they were performing their duty. So, too, must we remove the barriers that break our connection with Hashem.

The *Be'er Yosef*[2] offers another explanation for the symbolism of removing one's shoes. Yehoshua bin Nun was also told to remove his shoes when he met the angel outside Yericho. Similarly, the *kohanim* don't wear shoes in the *Beit HaMikdash*, the ultimate holy place. Today, *kohanim* do not wear shoes while performing *Birkat Kohanim*. On Yom Kippur, we don't wear shoes. Another halakha applying to shoes is that in the morning blessings one recites the *berakha* of *she'asa li kol tzarki* to thank Hashem for shoes.[3]

What exactly is the message here? The *Be'er Yosef* quotes the Maharshal, who cites a *pasuk* from *Tehillim* (8:6): "You have made [man] little less than divine and adorned him with glory and majesty."

The *Kuzari* explains that there are four levels of being in this world: *domem* (inanimate), *tzome'ah* (plants), *hai* (animals), and *medaber* (people, humans).[4] Humans are at the top of this pyramid, which signifies that everything under us was created for our use, to help us serve HaKadosh Barukh Hu. We are the chosen ones of the creations.

What action symbolizes our rulership over animals? Wearing leather shoes, and trampling on animal hide with each step we take. That act is a symbol of our dominion and authority over everything in the world. When we recite this *berakha* in the morning, we are thanking

---

2. Rav Yosef MiSalant, *Be'er Yosef* (Jerusalem, 1972), *Shemot*, 198.
3. *Shulhan Arukh, Orah Hayim* 46:1.
4. *Sefer HaKuzari*, first essay, 31–43.

Hashem for shoes, because when we put on our shoes in the morning, we realize that everything in the world exists for us to serve HaKadosh Barukh Hu. That is what the words "everything is at his feet" (*Tehillim* 8:7) symbolize. When we take leather to make our shoes, we are showing clearly that we are using the animal kingdom and everything else to serve HaKadosh Barukh Hu. Therefore, when we enter a holy place, where we *don't* have dominion, we take off our shoes. We do not have authority in a holy place. There, we acknowledge that we are not on top.

The Gemara states that if someone doesn't bow at the *berakha* of *modim* in *Shemoneh Esreh*, his spine will turn into a snake.[5] What's the connection between a snake, the spine, and bowing in *modim*? The Maharal explains that the snake was the king of the animals, but it did not know how to bow, how to lower itself. Man, however, the king over the earth, bows in *modim* to acknowledge that he is not always in control. But if he does not bow, he is no better than a snake, so his spine turns into a snake.

On Yom Kippur, we do not wear shoes, because it is a day when we are in the presence of HaKadosh Barukh Hu. On this great day, it is as if we are all in the *Beit HaMikdash*. Interestingly, there is no mitzva to physically travel to the *Beit HaMikdash* on Yom Kippur, because on Yom Kippur, every place in the world is a *Beit HaMikdash*. HaKadosh Barukh Hu is everywhere. We don't have to go anywhere to find Him. On Yom Kippur, the whole world becomes holy ground. That is why we must remove our leather shoes on Yom Kippur as well.

---

5. Bava Kama 16a.

The Significance of *Brit Mila*

ויהי בדרך במלון ויפגשהו ה׳ ויבקש המיתו. (שמות ד:כד)

And it came to pass on the way to the lodging-place, that Hashem met him, and sought to kill him. (*Shemot* 4:24)

At this point in the *parasha*, the *pesukim* have already been describing the beginning of the process of the redemption for some time. Hashem told Moshe to head back to Egypt and demand that Pharaoh release Am Yisrael. Moshe packed up his family and set out. Suddenly, there are three *pesukim* that seem to be an interruption of the story, describing how Hashem nearly kills Moshe for neglecting to perform *brit mila* for his son. After Moshe's wife performs the *brit mila*, the *pesukim* return to the story of the redemption.

What are these *pesukim* doing here? What connection do they have with the events surrounding them?

Rabbi Avraham Rivlin[1] explains a connection between *brit mila* and redemption. *Brit mila*, says Rabbi Rivlin, is a mitzva meant to counteract local negative influences. It's a mitzva that reminds a Jew that, in

---

1. Rabbi Avraham Rivlin, *Iyunei Parasha* (Kerem B'Yavneh, 2008), 27.

all areas of his life, he is different from a gentile and must control himself, but specifically in the area of desire, as the Rambam says in *Moreh Nevuhim*: *Brit mila* is about a person reducing physical pleasure so that it does not control them. That is the opposite of what Egypt stood for and celebrated. Therefore, the message of *brit mila* was inserted specifically here, right before Moshe went down to Egypt, the land that negated what a *brit mila* represents.

In a more general way, says Rabbi Rivlin, *brit mila* is not just a reminder about desire and *erva*. It also serves as a general reminder to a Jew that he is different – he has a different purpose in life than all the other nations of the world. He quotes the *Sefer HaHinukh*, who writes that Hashem commanded the mitzva of *brit mila* to establish a permanent sign on the physical body of a Jew – to show that we are different to the other nations on every level, physical, and spiritual.

This was noted precisely here in the *pesukim* because Bnei Yisrael were about to become a nation, about to become this *am hanivhar*, the chosen and different nation. *Brit mila* symbolizes this point and teaches us this message; therefore, we focus on *brit mila* right before Moshe headed down to Egypt.

Rabbi Shimshon Refael Hirsch[2] offers an alternative explanation as to why these *pesukim* appear now. In the *pesukim* immediately preceding the *brit mila*, says Rabbi Hirsch, we read about HaKadosh Barukh Hu "bargaining" with Moshe Rabbenu, convincing him that he is the right person to lead children of Israel. At this point, it is important for us to know that no matter how great Moshe Rabbenu was, no human being is indispensable to Hashem if he is not fulfilling Hashem's commands and being the proper servant he is supposed to be.

> This is how it seems "vayevakesh hamito" ("sought to kill") must be understood, a word which is doubly difficult if applied to God. God does not wish the death of any man, and he whom God wishes to kill is dead. But taken this way, this word tells us the most important fact that God's plans are dependent on no man ... no man, not even a Moshe Rabbenu, is indispensable to God. It

---

2. *The Pentateuch*, Shemot (Gateshead: Judaica Press, 1989), 50.

disposes of the erroneous idea into which we might have been led by the previous verses, by the insistence with which God pressed Moshe to undertake the mission. We also see here how God does not overlook any fault in His messenger, not even in Moshe.[3]

Right after Hashem pressed Moshe to accept this position of leading Am Yisrael out of exile, Hashem almost kills Moshe for not fulfilling His command of *brit mila.*

There is so much in this *parasha* that describes the humanness of Moshe Rabbenu, probably in part to dispel the beliefs of any nation that believes in the divinity of human beings. This point is emphasized at the beginning of the *parasha,* where it describes how the greatest human being who ever lived came from human parents (*Shemot* 2:1).

Here, too, says Rabbi Hirsch, we see this point realized. If Moshe couldn't be perfect in this area, Hashem would have chosen a different leader. We have to realize that there is only one thing in this universe that is perfect and eternal, and that is HaKadosh Barukh Hu. Many religions turn their leaders into gods. Moshe Rabbenu was a great man, but he, too, was human.

---

3. Ibid.

Enhancing Appreciation of Freedom

A fundamental question asked by many is: Why did things have to be this way? Why did we need to become slaves before and experience pain and agony prior to becoming a free nation? Why did the development of Am Yisrael have to start this way?

This same question can be asked often when reviewing our history. Avraham and Sarah davened for a hundred years to be blessed with a child, and when they finally had Yitzhak, Hashem asked for Avraham to sacrifice him. Only once Avraham nearly killed his son did Hashem grant him his life back. Why the taking and then the giving? Why do we need to lose before we can keep? Rabbi Jonathan Sacks, in *A Letter in the Scroll*, suggests the following:

> The answer is this: What we have, we eventually take for granted. Only what we lose and are given back again do we not take for granted but consciously cherish and constantly protect.[1]

---

1. Rabbi Jonathan Sacks, *A Letter in the Scroll* (New York: The Free Press, 2000), 109.

HaKadosh Barukh Hu had to plant in our biological makeup that we need to appreciate what we have. We, personally, didn't live through the exodus from Egypt, but we have an obligation to remember and relive it every year, because freedom is only appreciated when we don't have it. Only once Klal Yisrael had been slaves were they able to appreciate being free people. Before we could appreciate freedom, we had to lose it.[2]

---

2. We may add that there are many mitzvot connected to remembering Egypt, reminding us that we were slaves there. Perhaps these mitzvot are intended to reinforce our appreciation of freedom. In addition, we are also commanded to recall that we were once slaves in Egypt so that we remember the feeling of being second-class citizens and that we treat those less fortunate than us with proper respect and dignity.

Parashat Va'era

Harsh Messages, Spoken Softly

וידבר אלקים אל משה ויאמר אליו אני ה'. (שמות ו:ב)

And God spoke unto Moshe, and said unto him: "I am Hashem."
(*Shemot* 6:2)

This *pasuk* describes a conversation between Hashem and Moshe,
and one can wonder at the use of two verbs *vayedaber* and *vayomer* to
describe the same utterance. Rav Yitzhak Zilberstein raises this question and develops it a little further.[1] We know that the term *vayedaber*
is usually reserved for harsh speech, whereas *vayomer* implies a softer
mode of speech.[2] Why, then, does the *pasuk* use both terms? If Hashem
was giving Moshe a little *musar*, why does the *pasuk* also use the softer
form of speech?

Rav Zilberstein explains that by using both of these words, the
Torah teaches us the correct way to give *musar*. One may have to give
over a sharp message – biting, serious words – but while the content

---

1. Rav Yitzhak Zilberstein, *Aleinu Leshabe'ah*, vol. 2, 122.
2. See, for example, *Keli Yakar* on *Devarim* 32:1.

might be sharp, the way the message is expressed should be soft and loving. That's how we can have both phrases in the same *pasuk*.

This message is specifically applicable in our generation, when so many people are far from Torah and mitzvot. Those non-observant Jews look to practicing Jews to see how we act and behave – specifically in our speech and our conduct. Our *middot* are the first impression we make. They form the basis on which others judge us.

Rav Yeruham Levovitz[3] comments on Yaakov's interactions with the shepherds back in *Sefer Bereshit*. He points out that Yaakov prefaced his words of *musar* to the shepherds with the word *ahai* – "my brothers." He started off that way because *musar* has to be given gently, softly. *Musar* is never supposed to put another person down.[4]

The first message that the Ramban includes in his famous letter to his son is that he should not get angry or raise his voice, for when one does so, he loses control and his message will not be accepted. It's so easy for us to lose it – with a neighbor, student, child, or fellow drivers on the road – so we have to work on this trait of remaining in control.

We carry the torch of Torah and *mitzvot*, so we must be super sensitive to how we are perceived. We should look at how many people are not Torah observant and then check ourselves to see if maybe we are not doing things right. If we would act in the way we should, it would be easy for others to draw inspiration.

Rav Zilberstein shares a personal story.[5] Once, he caught a cab and was very surprised at the driver's appearance – braided hair, many piercings – to the point where Rav Zilberstein did not feel comfortable sitting next to him. Seeing Rav Zilberstein's discomfort, the driver rushed to defend himself. "Don't judge me from my looks," he said, opening his shirt to reveal his *mehudar tzitzit*. Rav Zilberstein was very surprised, to say the least, to see *tzitzit* on a person who looked so far from any form of Torah observance. The driver related his story:

---

3. Rav Yeruham Halevi Levovitz, *Daat Torah, Parashat Vayetzeh*.
4. See also in this volume *Parashat Vayetzeh*, "My Dear Brothers," in the name of the Ponovezher Rav.
5. *Aleinu Leshabe'ah*, vol. 2, 122.

I'm in the process of doing *teshuva*. For now, I'm not ready to get rid of my hairstyle and jewelry, but I'll get there one day. But I've already decided to wear *tzitizit*, and let me tell you why.

One time, I picked up a passenger who appeared to be a very important rabbi. I brought him from Holon to Bnei Brak. When we arrived at his house in Bnei Brak, the Rebbe turned to me and said, "You must be hungry and thirsty. Come upstairs with me and have something to eat. But keep the meter running – I don't want you to lose money because of this."

Of course, I wanted to turn off the meter, but I couldn't argue with him. So I went upstairs to his house and had something to eat and drink with him. When I finished, he said, "You probably didn't put on *tefillin* today. Would you like to put on *tefillin* with me? It's all on me, don't worry; just keep the meter running."

I have driven many passengers, yet I had never met one like this *rebbe*. He touched my heart so deeply, to the point that I thought: If there are Jews like this in the world, I want to be among them.

The driver continued his story and described how the Rebbe walked him to his car to check the meter, paid him in full, and even gave him a tip because he had made the driver walk up the stairs to his house.

This is how we're going to get more Jews to keep Shabbat and keep kosher! If we're noble in our *middot* and interpersonal behavior, we can inspire others to come close to Hashem.

How much did it cost the Rebbe? Maybe 25 shekels? Twenty-five shekels to bring someone back to HaKadosh Barukh Hu? For such a petty sum, he was able to inspire another Jew to return to his roots.

Rav Zilberstein ends his with an interpretation of a *pasuk* in *Mishlei* (9:8): "Don't reprove a scoffer lest he hate you; rebuke a wise person, and he will love you." The plain meaning of this *pasuk* is that if you know that someone won't listen to your criticism, don't rebuke them. Rav Zilberstein suggests a deeper idea: The goal of rebuke is not to make someone feel like he is a scoffer, that he is low. That will cause him to hate you. Rather, tell him he's wise, that his actions are unbecoming of who he is. Prove to him that he's great, and in this way, you will manage to inspire him.

To Influence Others, One Must Himself Believe

וידבר משה לפני ה' לאמר: הן בני ישראל לא שמעו אלי ואיך ישמעני
פרעה ואני ערל שפתים. (שמות ו:יב)

And Moshe spoke before Hashem, saying: "Behold, Bnei Yisrael have not hearkened unto me; how then shall Pharaoh hear me, as I am of uncircumcised lips?" (*Shemot* 6:12)

Hashem commanded Moshe to go to Pharaoh and demand that he release the Jews from slavery. Moshe argued that if Bnei Yisrael hadn't listened to him, why would Pharaoh?

What, though, is the connection between Bnei Yisrael not listening and Pharaoh not listening? Rashi claims that this is one of the ten unanswerable *kal vahomer*s in the Torah: If Bnei Yisrael didn't listen to Moshe, then all the more so, Pharaoh wouldn't!

Rabbi Eliyahu Schlesinger[1] asks: What exactly is the *kal vahomer* here? Bnei Yisrael had a good reason not to listen; as the *pasuk* tells us, they were exhausted from their work. They didn't listen to Moshe

---

1.   Rabbi Eliyahu Schlesinger, *Eileh HaDevarim* (Jerusalem: Keter Vilna, 1999), 266.

because they were suffering. Pharaoh was in a very different situation, so how can we infer from them to him?

Additionally, in last week's *parasha*, when Hashem commanded Moshe to go to Pharaoh, Moshe asked what he was supposed to tell the children of Israel. Why did Moshe ask about speaking to the children of Israel? That's not what Hashem commanded him to do! Why did Moshe assume he would have to speak to Bnei Yisrael before he went to Pharaoh?

Rabbi Schlesinger poses yet a third question, which can perhaps also be the beginning of an answer: There's a midrash at the end of last week's *parasha* that says Pharaoh didn't want Bnei Yisrael to even think or speak about redemption. Was Pharaoh so concerned that his lowly slaves would manage to pull off a rebellion? Something truly worried him about such talk; what was it?

Rabbi Schlesinger teaches us a fundamental rule of *hinukh* from here: "It is impossible to convince anyone of anything if the speaker himself or his messenger is not convinced of the merits."

If a teacher, parent, friend, or speaker is not on fire, there is no way they can light up someone else. Only if someone believes in something with all his heart does he stand a chance of impacting anyone else.

Moshe here was acting on behalf of Klal Yisrael. He was their *shaliah*; Hashem sent him to redeem the children of Israel. If Bnei Yisrael didn't believe that redemption could happen, there's no way that Moshe, as their *shaliah*, would be able to influence Pharaoh. All influence starts with the influencer.

Rabbi Schlesinger cites Rabbi Yaakov Kamenetsky who suggests that the word *mashpia*, "influence," is derived from the word *meshupa*, "slanted," because that's how influence works. That's how one makes an impact. If someone is passionate about something, it can flow down onto others. You can't give something if you don't have it. This is true for everything, says Rabbi Schlesinger. A *rav*, a teacher, a parent, a speaker, a friend – none will succeed unless they believe in what they are saying and in the truthfulness of their endeavor.

Moshe was told that he was to go to Pharaoh on behalf of the children of Israel. He realized that for him to represent them, they first had to be convinced, and so, he assumed automatically that he had to go speak with them. This, therefore, was why Pharaoh didn't want them talking among themselves. He knew that the roots of redemption are when the people start thinking about the idea and becoming convinced that it could happen. That's why he could not let them even discuss it.

We can now understand Rashi's *kal vahomer*: If the children of Israel, whom Moshe was representing, didn't believe in redemption, then of course Pharaoh, who Moshe had to convince to release the children of Israel, wouldn't believe him.

The Rav and the Rebbe

הוא אהרן ומשה אשר אמר ה' להם הוציאו את בני ישראל מארץ מצרים
על צבאתם. הם המדברים אל פרעה מלך מצרים להוציא את בני ישראל
ממצרים הוא משה ואהרן. (שמות ו:כו-כז)

These are Aharon and Moshe, to whom the Lord said, "Bring
out Bnei Yisrael from the land of Egypt according to their hosts."
These are they that spoke to Pharaoh, king of Egypt, to bring out
Bnei Yisrael from Egypt. These are Moshe and Aharon. (*Shemot*
6:26–27)

The *parasha* starts with a conversation between Hashem and Moshe,
and then it interrupts the narrative in order to explain the lineage of
Moshe and Aharon. After this interruption, the Torah returns to the
story at hand. The wording of the *pasuk* seems to serve as a reminder
of where we left off.

Pasuk 26 states: *Hu Aharon uMoshe*. The next *pasuk* repeats this
phrase, but lists them in the opposite order: *Hu Moshe veAharon*. *Hazal*
tell us that their names are listed in interchangeable order throughout
the Torah to teach us that they were equals.

Rav Yosef Soloveitchik has a different interpretation.[1] Moshe and Aharon represented two types of leaders, and Jewish leadership needs both aspects – the Moshe aspect and the Aharon aspect. Sometimes this duality comes in the form of two different personalities, as with Moshe and Aharon, and at other times, it's in the same person, which is a level to which great Jewish leaders should and do aspire. Moshe represented the *malkhut,* kingship, form of teaching, and Aharon represented the *kohen gadol* form of teaching. In Rav Soloveitchik's own words:

> Both Moshe and Aharon were teachers, but their methods and temperaments differed. The two major traditions of Torah teaching may be called that of the *malkhut* (king)-teacher and that of the *kedusha* (saint)-teacher. Moshe was the prototype of the king-teacher and Aharon represented the saint-teacher. Both of them were enlightened minds, molded characters, and propagated the word of God.... Nevertheless, their methods, their approaches, and the media they employed were different. In terms of ultimate objectives, they were very close to each other, but their emphases varied.
>
> The king-teacher addresses himself to the mind. He engages the intellect, analyzing, classifying, clarifying, and transmitting the details of halakha with precision... Moshe, the Rambam, the Vilna Gaon, Rav Chaim Soloveitchik reflect the king-teacher par excellence.
>
> The saint-teacher, in contrast, even as he deals with the text, focuses his attention upon the invisible, intangible soul of the Torah.

Rav Soloveitchik suggests that the Moshe type of leader represents the mind, teaching on an intellectual level, while the Aharon type of leader leads with the heart, on an emotional level. The king-teacher inspires us through our minds, our intellects. But that's not enough. Aharon, of course, follows and teaches halakha, but he also reaches the people on an emotional level. Rav Soloveitchik continues:

---

1. *Humash Masoret HaRav* (New York: OU Press, 2014), 54.

The saint-teacher is a leader of the masses, for all Jews have hearts which can be set aflame. All Jews possess sensitive souls and seek God.... Moshe was a model of the *Rav*; Aharon of the *Rebbe*. Moshe was a *kevad peh*, a non-verbal person, not given to small talk, easy socializing, and extensive negotiations. He was *Rabbenu*, a scholar... [The Torah] emphasizes Aharon's lips, his persuasive style and closeness to the people. His title was not *Rabbenu*, but *Hakohen*, which signifies a minister of God.

Nowadays, the *Rav*, the contemporary king-teacher, has absorbed many of the qualities of the *Rebbe*, not only teaching but coming close to his people. The *Rebbe*, representing the modern saint-teacher, now also emphasizes the scholarship and the teaching role.

Rav Soloveitchik notes that these days the leadership role is a mix of the two. The line marking the classic differences between the *rav* and the *rebbe* are somewhat blurred, because it is the job of every leader today – *rabbanim* and parents – to lead in the most effective manner, which is a combination of the mind and heart.

The *pasuk* exclaims both *hu Moshe veAharon* and *hu Aharon uMoshe* because both are needed in the role of leadership in all generations.

The Purpose of the Plagues

ואני אקשה את לב פרעה והרביתי את אתתי ואת מופתי בארץ מצרים.
(שמות ז:ג)

And I will harden Pharaoh's heart, and multiply My signs and My
wonders in the land of Egypt. (*Shemot* 7:3)

Many commentators have different understandings of the purpose of
the plagues. The Rambam maintains that all of the plagues formed a
single punishment.[1] He explains that a person can sin so gravely that
his *teshuva* is withheld and is not accepted by Hashem. Pharaoh reached
this low level, and so Hashem hardened his heart, preventing him from
doing *teshuva* and ensuring that all of the plagues would come to pass.[2]

Sforno, however, has a different insight, stating that Pharaoh had
the free will to do *teshuva* all the way up until the plague of the death
of the firstborn.[3]

---

1. Several commentators explain how each plague was a punishment for a specific crime
   of the Egyptians. See, for example, Rabbi Shimshon Refael Hirsch's *midda-keneged-
   midda*-based approach.
2. Rambam, *Hakdama LeMesekhet Avot – Shemona Perakim, perek* 8; Rambam, *Hilkhot
   Teshuva* 6:3.
3. Sforno on *Shemot* 7:3.

Hashem wants humans to do *teshuva*, as it says: "'By My life,' says Hashem, 'I do not want the wicked to die, but for the wicked to repent from his ways and live!'" (*Yehezkel* 33:11). Hashem therefore increased his miracles and wonders in Egypt so the Egyptians would return to him. Accordingly, the plagues were not only for the children of Israel, but also for the Egyptians – to bring them to *teshuva*.

According to Sforno's approach, how can we explain the hardening of Pharaoh's heart? How was he expected to do *teshuva* if his heart had been hardened by Hashem against just that?

Sforno explains that *teshuva* can take on one of two forms: *teshuva* out of fear and *teshuva* out of recognition of Hashem. There is no doubt, he says, that if Hashem wouldn't have hardened Pharaoh's heart, leveled the playing field a little bit, Pharaoh would have sent Bnei Yisrael out earlier – not because of any feelings of humility or repentance, but only to alleviate his suffering. But this would have gone against the purpose of the plagues, so Hashem hardened Pharaoh's heart. Nevertheless, the possibility of doing real *teshuva* out of true recognition of Hashem remained opened to Pharaoh until the end. If Pharaoh would have wanted to humble himself and do *teshuva*, nothing would have stood in his way.

Thus, the hardening of Pharaoh's heart, according to Sforno, did not remove his ability to do *teshuva*. It only removed the fear that would have motivated repentance from fear, but left open the option of doing real *teshuva*.

The Teaching Staff

The staff wielded by Moshe and Aharon features prominently in many stories throughout the Humash, and there are several lessons that can be learned from it. One is mentioned by *VeKarata LaShabbat Oneg*:

The Torah describes Hashem's command to Moshe to turn his staff into a snake.

כי ידבר אלכם פרעה לאמר תנו לכם מופת ואמרת אל אהרן קח את מטך והשלך לפני פרעה יהי לתנין. (שמות ז:ט)

לך אל פרעה בבקר הנה יצא המימה ונצבת לקראתו על שפת היאר והמטה אשר נהפך לנחש תקח בידך. (שמות ז:טו)

When Pharaoh shall speak unto you, saying: "Show a wonder for you," then you shall say unto Aharon, "Take the staff, and cast it down before Pharaoh, that it become a *snake*." (*Shemot* 7:9)

Go to Pharaoh in the morning, when he comes out of the water; and you shall stand by the river's brink to meet him; and the staff which was turned to a *serpent* you shall take in your hand. (*Shemot* 7:15)

Hashem told Moshe and Aharon that Pharaoh would ask for a magical sign to prove that their message from God was true. In *pasuk 9*, the

Torah describes Hashem's command: that Aharon should throw his staff to the floor, where it would become a *tanin*, which Rashi defines as a snake. A few *pesukim* later, in *pasuk* 15, the Torah refers to the same staff and says that it had turned into a *nahash*, a different term for "snake" than the one used in *pasuk* 9.

The *Siftei Hakhamim*[1] explains that the difference between the two terms is that a *tanin* is a water snake, whereas a *nahash* is a terrestrial snake. When Hashem told Moshe and Aharon to show Pharaoh a sign, Hashem said the staff would become a *tanin*. This would showcase a double miracle: (1) their staff turned into a snake, and (2) not just any snake, but a *water snake*, which generally can only live in water. However, when Hashem commanded Moshe to meet Pharaoh at the water, He referred to the snake as a *nahash*, because at the water, a greater miracle would be for the staff to become a terrestrial snake. Hashem was very precise, making the miracles even greater to prove the truth to everyone.

WHY A STAFF?

The Midrash tells us that magic was so rampant in Egypt that any Egyptian child could turn a stick into a snake.[2] In that case, why did Hashem command Moshe and Aharon to perform something that even a five-year-old Egyptian could do?

The *Be'er Yosef*[3] quotes this question from the Midrash, with an additional famous question from the Rambam:[4] Why were the Egyptians punished for enslaving Bnei Yisrael if it was preordained that they would be in a land that was not theirs and be subjugated by the nation there? Hashem told Avraham about this at the *Brit bein HaBetarim*. Why was Egypt punished if they were just following Hashem's orders?

The Raavad[5] and Ramban[6] answer that while Hashem allowed the Egyptians to subjugate Bnei Yisrael, He hadn't given permission, so to speak, for the Egyptians to torture and kill them. The Egyptians

---

1. *Siftei Hakhamim, Shemot* 7:10.
2. Menahot 85b.
3. Rav Yosef MiSalant, *Be'er Yosef* (Jerusalem, 1972), *Shemot*, 208.
4. Rambam, *Hilkhot Teshuva* 6:5.
5. Ibid.
6. *Bereshit* 15:14.

went far beyond what God had decreed, and that's why they were held responsible for their actions. In addition, the Ramban adds, the decree was that the Egyptians as a nation will subjugate Bnei Yisrael but each individual Egyptian had his free will to select to what degree to be involved and to what extent to enslave the Jews.

Since the Egyptians knew about this decree and felt justified in torturing the children of Israel, it was very possible that they didn't believe that Hashem was going to punish them. Therefore, Hashem told Moshe and Aharon to take their staff and turn it into a snake. A staff is something with no inherent power. Its power is completely dependent on the power of its wielder. It is merely a means used to achieve a result, a tool. Hashem, therefore, wanted to hint to the Egyptians that while they were supposed to be Hashem's "tool" and just follow His commands, they acted independently, like a snake. Their actions had nothing to do with what Hashem wanted them to do.

The *Be'er Yosef* adds that if the Egyptians hadn't gone beyond the decree and added to the torture, they would not have been punished for enslaving the children of Israel. That's what the staff was meant to teach them: that they were only supposed to be the staff of Hashem and not do more than they had been intended to do. Like a *nahash*, they did what they wanted to do, going beyond Hashem's decree.[7]

DOUBLE MIRACLE

וישליכו איש מטהו ויהיו לתנינם ויבלע מטה אהרן את מטתם. (שמות ז:יב)

For they cast down every man his staff and they became serpents; but Aharon's staff swallowed up their staffs. (*Shemot* 7:12)

Aharon threw down his staff, which turned into a snake, and then the Egyptians threw down their staffs, which also became snakes. Aharon's

---

7. See Arakhin 15b: In the future, all the other animals gathered and questioned the snake. A lion kills and then eats its prey, as does the wolf and others. The snake, however, just poisons...but what pleasure does it derive from that? This behavior is symbolic of the type of slavery that was imposed by the Egyptians on the Jews: hard labor for the sake of it, without any benefit to the Egyptians.

staff then proceeded to swallow the sticks of the Egyptians. The *Siftei Hakhamim*[8] says that this display was a double miracle: Aharon's staff swallowed up the others, and it did so while it was in the form of a staff, as opposed to a snake.

Asks Rabbi Benzion Firer in his *Panim Hadashot BaTorah*,[9] why was this double miracle necessary? Wouldn't it have been enough of a miracle for Aharon's snake to swallow all the other snakes? Why did it specifically have to be his staff swallowing the other staffs?

Rabbi Firer suggests a powerful idea: This staff of Aharon and Moshe would be used many times over the next few months to punish and rebuke the Egyptians and prove to them who the real God is. If their staffs were swallowed up inside Aharon's, then every time they would be punished by Aharon's staff, it would hurt them so much more. The lesson would really hit home!

We see throughout history how Hashem uses the tool that the gentiles wished to use against us as their punishment – like Haman was hanged on the very gallows he had erected for Mordekhai.[10]

---

8. *Siftei Hakhamim, Shemot* 7:12.

9. Rabbi Benzion Firer, *Panim Hadashot BaTorah* (Tel Aviv: Sinai, 1990), *Shemot.*

10. A priest once asked Rav Hayim Volzhiner why the *pasuk* in *Tehillim* says: "Praise Hashem, all you nations; extol Him, all you peoples, for great is His kindness toward us; the faithfulness of Hashem endures forever. Halleluka" (117:1–2). Why would non-Jews praise Hashem for having done kindness to the children of Israel? Rav Hayim explained: There are times when gentiles wish to carry out attacks and cause severe damage to Jews, and Hashem blocks their plans. Only the gentiles are aware of those situations and recognize how generous Hashem is and all the protection He affords to the Jewish people. That is why the gentiles praise Hashem – for all that they wanted to do and were unable to accomplish, of which we were unaware.

The Source of
Hakarat HaTov

ויאמר ה' אל משה אמר אל אהרן קח מטך ונטה ידך על מימי מצרים
על נהרתם על יאריהם ועל אגמיהם ועל כל מקוה מימיהם ויהיו דם
והיה דם בכל ארץ מצרים ובעצים ובאבנים. (שמות ז:יט)

And Hashem said unto Moshe: "Say unto Aharon: Take your staff
and stretch out your hand over the waters of Egypt, over their
rivers, over their streams, and over their pools, and over all their
ponds of water, that they may become blood; and there shall be
blood throughout all the land of Egypt, both in vessels of wood
and in vessels of stone." (*Shemot* 7:19)

Hashem commanded Moshe to tell Aharon to initiate the plague of
blood. Rashi quotes that the reason Moshe didn't bring the first three
plagues is because of the *hakarat hatov* he had to show to the water and
earth that had protected him. The water had protected Moshe when his
mother left him in a basket in the Nile, and the earth covered up the
corpse of the Egyptian he had killed. Hitting the water or earth to bring
about a plague wouldn't have been an appropriate display of *hakarat
hatov* on Moshe's part.

The *Shemen HaTov*[1] asks a simple question based on a Gemara in Bava Kama (92b), which cites the source for *hakarat hatov* as being a *pasuk* in *Parashat Ki Tetzeh*: "Do not despise the Egyptian, for you were a stranger in his land" (*Devarim* 23:8). In other words, we owe them *hakarat hatov* because they hosted us in their land.

The *Shemen HaTov* cites the Hatam Sofer who asks why the Gemara uses the *pasuk* in *Parashat Ki Tetzeh* as the source for *hakarat hatov* and not these *pesukim* right here in *Shemot*, much earlier in the Torah, where Moshe displayed *hakarat hatov* to the water and earth. The Hatam Sofer answers that *Hazal* chose this *pasuk* because the Egyptians seem the least likely to have deserved any *hakarat hatov*. They enslaved us! They threw our babies into the Nile! But despite all that, we still owe them *hakarat hatov* because they *did* do something about which we could be minutely positive.

A Jew finds something positive even in a situation that seems completely terrible. Even though the Egyptians were mostly wicked, we can't disregard the tiny amount of good they gave us. We have to find the *tov* within the *ra*. Most things in life are multifaceted; therefore, we can't define any one event by just one aspect of it. Even in Egypt, we can find a tiny bit of positivity.

The Egyptian experience was hard, but we have to search for the *tov* within it. In a situation in which we fail to find the good, we have to fall back on our belief that all is from HaKadosh Barukh Hu. We believe that Hashem has a divine plan; therefore, all that happens is for our best.

Rav Yosef Soloveitchik offers a *mashal* of a beautiful tapestry.[2] The work is breathtaking. Every detail is a treat to the eyes. But if you turn the tapestry over and look at the back, you see a mess of strings and knots and mixed colors. It's a disaster!

The back of the tapestry, says Rav Soloveitchik, is this world, where things seem disastrous and appear out of place. We live in a world of darkness, with finite understanding. But nothing is truly bad – we just don't see the front of the tapestry.

---

1. Rabbi Bernard Weinberger, *Shemen HaTov – Al HaMo'adim* (Brooklyn, 1988), 268.
2. Rabbi Yosef B. Soloveitchik, *"Kol Dodi Dofek,"* in *Divrei Hagut VeHaarakha* (Jerusalem 1982), 11.

That's why *hakarat hatov* is learned from the *pasuk* in *Devarim* and not from here. We are taught about this *midda* specifically in a place where there doesn't seem to be anything good or deserving of *hakarat hatov*. It's easy to feel *hakarat hatov* in a situation where the *tov* is so obvious; it's a much greater level to feel the appreciation even in the darkest times.

The *Shemen HaTov* adds that perhaps the words of *Hazal, lehazhir gedolim al ketanim* – "to admonish the older about the minors" mean to make sure that we don't just look at the big picture, but that we also look at the small details and see all the different levels of every experience.

Anger Mismanagement

ויאמר ה' אל משה אמר אל אהרן נטה את ידך במטך על הנהרת על
היארים ועל האגמים והעל את הצפרדעים על ארץ מצרים. ב ויט
אהרן את ידו על מימי מצרים ותעל הצפרדע ותכס את ארץ מצרים.
(שמות ח:א)

And Hashem said unto Moshe: "Say unto Aharon: Stretch forth
your hand with your staff over the rivers, over the canals, and over
the pools, and cause *frogs* to come up upon the land of Egypt."
And Aharon stretched out his hand over the waters of Egypt; and
the *frog* came up, and covered the land of Egypt. (*Shemot* 8:1)

Rashi points out that this *pasuk* switches from the plural *hatzefarde'im*,
the frogs, to the singular *hatzefarde'a*, the frog, and he quotes *Hazal*, who
explain this discrepancy:

צפרדע אחת היתה והיו מכין אותה והיא מתזת נחילים נחילים.

There was one big frog, and every time the Egyptians hit it, it
split and multiplied.

317

Rabbi Yaakov Yisrael Kanievsky, also known as the Steipler,[1] asks a seemingly obvious question: If the frog multiplied each time the Egyptians beat the frog, why did they continue to do so? It completely defies logic! They saw the consequences of their actions, so why didn't they just *stop*?

The Steipler explains that we see from here the power of anger. A person can become so angry that he begins to act irrationally. Then, despite the reality that stares him in the face, he can't control his reaction. The Egyptians saw that it wasn't helping to hit the frog, but their anger made them unable to think straight and control themselves. And so, they kept on hitting!

Rav Shimshon Pincus[2] takes this one step further and says that when we react out of anger, we're ultimately hurting ourselves. Every time we react in anger, hoping it will affect someone else, it really boomerangs, and we just hurt ourselves. This is the reality of every situation of anger. The Egyptians were angry and reacted in anger, which only made the situation worse.

If we stop and don't retaliate when we're angry, the situation will usually calm down. Reacting and responding to a situation tends to escalate and worsen it. Every time we feel ourselves getting angry, we should remember the Egyptians hitting the frogs and realize that it is only logical to stop before we get out of control.

Rav Pincus suggests that this reality applied to all the plagues: If the Egyptians would have just let us go, they could have stopped getting hit by plagues and spared themselves a lot of pain. Each time they hit us, they were, in actuality, hitting themselves. They brought the plagues upon themselves through their stubbornness and bad *middot*.

This is true for all of us. We have to realize that everything is sent our way for a purpose, and that if we react in anger, we're just hurting ourselves.

A story is told of a rabbi who kept what he referred to as his "anger jacket." Whenever he would get angry, he would put on this anger jacket. He kept this anger jacket on the third floor of his house. By the time he climbed three flights and reached his anger jacket, a few minutes had

---

1. Rabbi Yaakov Yisrael Kanievsky, *Birkhat Peretz* (Bnei Brak, 1990), 28.
2. Rav Shimshon Pincus, *Tiferet Shimshon* (Jerusalem: Yefe Nof, 2009), 61.

passed, and he realized he was no longer as angry as he had initially been. We need to take a deep breath and calm down rather than immediately react when we are angry to ensure that we don't overreact or say or do something that we may regret later.

In a correspondence between the Rambam and Rav Ovadia the *ger*, the Rambam addresses a debate that Rav Ovadia had with his rabbi about the status of Muslims.[3] The Rambam writes that Muslims are not idolaters, because even if they believe in a false prophet, they do not believe in the wrong God. Moreover, said the Rambam, Rav Ovadia should know that anyone who got angry at him over his past was in fact an idolater, as *Hazal* tell us, "view anyone who gets angry as an idolater." They will have to do *teshuva* for idolatry, says the Rambam, something Rav Ovadia himself would not have to do!

From this letter, we see clearly that when a person is angry, they are considered an idolater – for worshipping themselves.

The Rambam in *Hilkhot De'ot*[4] notes that though Hashem desires that we follow the middle path, there are two exceptions to this principle, where we must go to the opposite extreme: anger and arrogance. Let us learn from the words of the Rambam and the Steipler and refrain from exhibiting anger.

---

3. *Igrot HaRambam; Igeret LeRav Ovadia Hager.*
4. Rambam, *Hilkhot De'ot* 2:3.

Only One

ויעש ה׳ את הדבר הזה ממחרת וימת כל מקנה מצרים וממקנה בני
ישראל לא מת אחד. וישלח פרעה והנה לא מת ממקנה ישראל עד אחד
ויכבד לב פרעה ולא שלח את העם. (שמות ט:ו-ז)

And Hashem did that thing on the morrow, and all the cattle of
Egypt died; but of the cattle of the children of Israel, not one
died. And Pharaoh sent, and behold, there was not so much as
one of the cattle of the Israelites dead. But the heart of Pharaoh
was stubborn, and he did not let the people go. (*Shemot* 9:6–7)

The Malbim[1] comments on the wording of these *pesukim* and points
out a change in the words used to say that none of the flocks of Bnei
Yisrael died: The first *pasuk* says *lo meit ehad*, "not one died" – and the
second says, *lo meit… ad ehad*. What does *ad ehad* mean? What does
this odd extra word signify?

The Malbim cites two other *pesukim* where *ad ehad* appears. The
first is at the Splitting of the Sea:

וישבו המים ויכסו את הרכב ואת הפרשים לכל חיל פרעה הבאים
אחריהם בים לא נשאר בהם עד אחד. (שמות יד:כח)

---

1. *Malbim Al HaTorah, Shemot* 9:6.

And the waters returned, and covered the chariots, and the horsemen, even all the host of Pharaoh that went in after them into the sea; there remained not so much as one of them. (*Shemot* 14:28)

The other is at the war of Bnei Yisrael against Sisera, at the beginning of *Sefer Shoftim*:

ובָרק רדף אחרי הרכב ואחרי המחנה עד חרשת הגוים ויפל כל מחנה
סיסרא לפי חרב לא נשאר עד אחד. (שופטים ד:טז)

And Barak chased after the chariots and after the camp, until the location of the nation, and all of Sisera's camp fell by the sword, there remained not so much as one of them. (*Shoftim* 4:16)

In these two places, *Hazal* explain that *ad ehad* means that nothing was left *except for one*. Regarding the Splitting of the Sea, this would mean that only one survivor remained from the Egyptians, and that was Pharaoh. With regards to the war against Sisera, everyone died except for one person: Sisera.

Here, too, says the Malbim, it must be that the *pasuk* intends that not a single animal died *except for one*. The Malbim suggests that the one animal that died belonged to a blasphemer, the son of an Israelite woman and an Egyptian man.

ויצא בן אשה ישראלית והוא בן איש מצרי בתוך בני ישראל וינצו
במחנה בן הישראלית ואיש הישראלי. ויקב בן האשה הישראלית את
השם ויקלל ויביאו אתו אל משה ושם אמו שלמית בת דברי למטה דן.
(ויקרא כד:י-יא)

And the son of an Israelite woman, whose father was an Egyptian, went out among the children of Israel; and the son of the Israelite woman and a man of Israel strove together in the camp. And the son of the Israelite woman blasphemed the Name, and cursed; and they brought him unto Moshe. And his mother's name was Shelomit, the daughter of Dibri, of the tribe of Dan. (*Vayikra* 24:10–11)

Pharaoh saw that every single animal belonging to the Egyptians died, which was a clear sign of the hand of Hashem. Yet, when he realized that the animals of one Israelite died,[2] he chose to focus on that as proof that it was all a coincidence and not the hand of God.

When a person has an attitude of disinterest and doesn't want to believe, then the greatest act of God can stare him in the face, and he'll choose not to see it. Similarly, when Hashem told Moshe that the plague of the death of the firstborn would occur at midnight, Hashem used the term *bahatzot*, at midnight, while when Moshe transmits the message, he says *kahatzot*, approximately at midnight.[3] Why the change? For a similar reason. People who want to disbelieve will say, "Hey, on my watch, it happened at 12:01 – so God was wrong. It did not occur at midnight."

The Ramban brings an example of this attitude from *Parashat Beshallah*. The *pasuk* says: "Moshe stretched out his hand over the Reed Sea, and Hashem brought eastern winds, and He made the sea into dry land and the waters split" (*Shemot* 14:21). The Splitting of the Sea was the greatest revelation of Hashem that Am Yisrael ever experienced, yet what did the Egyptians say? "Wow, what a huge tide, that's incredible. I've never seen such a thing before."

The Ramban[4] says that Hashem made the eastern winds blow to give the Egyptians (and the world) the opportunity to attribute the Splitting of the Sea to a natural phenomenon. Hashem gave them the option to believe that it was the wind that had split the sea. If someone has such an attitude – that he refuses to attribute anything to the hand of God – then he can experience the Splitting of the Sea, and it won't make any impression on him.

---

2. Pharaoh did not recognize that it was not so simple that this animal's owner was really Jewish, based on Jewish law.
3. See *Berakhot* 3a.
4. Ramban on *Shemot* 14:21.

Lessons from the Name of a Plague

The Torah assigns names to most plagues that describe the nature of the plague. The plague of *dam* was blood, *tzefarde'a* was frogs, etc. But then we get to the plague of wild animals, and the Torah names the plague *arov*, which means "mixture." Why didn't the Torah call it *hayot ra'ot*? Instead, the Torah describes just an element of the plague: that it was a mixture of animals. What is significant about that detail that the Torah refers to the plague by that name?

The *Be'er Yosef*[1] explains that the mixture itself highlights the miraculous nature of this plague. As we know, all animals require a specific climate to survive. A polar bear, a camel and a crocodile all need completely different climates. So how did all these animals get to Egypt and survive? It was actually a major part of the miracle: Hashem created the specific climates around each animal so that they could all exist in Egypt. That was the greatness of the plague of *arov* – the mixture itself.

Perhaps that it what is being alluded to in the *pasuk*:

ומלאו בתי מצרים את הערב וגם האדמה אשר הם עליה. (שמות ח:יז)

---

1. Rav Yosef MiSalant, *Be'er Yosef* (Jerusalem, 1972), *Shemot*, 214.

The houses of the Egyptians shall be full of swarms of animals, as well as the land upon which they appear. (*Shemot* 8:17)

The *pasuk* states that the homes of the Egyptians will be full of the animals, but it then adds, "as well as the land upon which they appear." In other words, animals that came from different geographies required their specific habitat to survive, and they came along with a "piece" of their natural surroundings.

Another example that highlights the supernatural aspect of a plague is expressed in the *pasuk*:

הנני ממטיר כעת מחר ברד כבד מאד אשר לא היה כמהו במצרים למן היום הוסדה ועד עתה. (שמות ט:יח)

Behold, tomorrow, about this time, I will cause it to rain a very grievous hail, such as that which has not been in Egypt, from the day it was founded even until now. (*Shemot* 9:18)

In connection with the plague of hail, Rashi explains that the words "tomorrow, about this time" teach us that Moshe made a scratch on the wall and said that when the sun would reach that line on the wall, the plague of hail would begin. Why did he only draw this scratch on the wall for this plague?

The *Be'er Yosef* explains, within the answer to this question lies the miracle: Since when is the sun out during a hailstorm? It was sunny and balmy in Egypt while the hail came down! During the storm, the sundial Moshe referenced previously was being utilized. This wasn't a typical hailstorm, but rather a miraculous plague from God.

These two examples highlight the supernatural aspects of the plague, clearly depicting the hand of Hashem and His miraculous ways.

Parashat Bo

Who Goes to Worship Hashem?

ויושב את משה ואת אהרן אל פרעה ויאמר אלהם לכו עבדו את ה'
א־להיכם מי ומי ההלכים. ויאמר משה בנערינו ובזקנינו נלך בבנינו
ובבנותנו בצאננו ובבקרנו נלך כי חג ה' לנו. (שמות י:ח ט)

And Moshe and Aharon were brought again unto Pharaoh; and
he said unto them: "Go, serve Hashem your God; but who and
who shall go?" And Moshe said: "We will go with our young and
with our old, with our sons and with our daughters, with our
flocks and with our herds we will go; for we must hold a feast
unto Hashem." (Shemot 10:8–9)

Moshe and Aharon went to warn Pharaoh of the impending plague of
locusts, and Pharaoh's servants pleaded with him to allow Bnei Yisrael
to go to the desert to worship their God. Pharaoh then summoned
Moshe and Aharon to return, at which point he asked them who would
be required to leave Egypt to participate in the offering of sacrifices.

The *Keli Yakar* raises a number of questions on these *pesukim*, the
first being why Pharaoh used the double term *mi vami haholkhim* – "who

and who shall go" instead of simply "who." Secondly, Pharaoh used the present perfect tense *haholkhim* – "those who are going" or "the goers" instead of the future tense *yelekhu* – "those who will go." Moreover, says the *Keli Yakar*, Moshe replied to Pharaoh: "*We will go* with our young and with our old, with our sons and with our daughters, with our flocks and with our herds *we will go*." Why the repetition of *nelekh* – "we will go"? Finally, what did Moshe mean by *ki hag Hashem lanu* – "for we must hold a feast unto Hashem"? Who else would it be for?

The *Keli Yakar* answers all of these questions with one common principle: Pharaoh wasn't really asking who would be going. He basically assumed and decreed that only the men would be able to participate. He was, in essence, telling Moshe: "*Mi vami haholkhim*" – using the double language to indicate: "Look around to the right and then to the left; look around at the rest of the world – who generally goes to offer sacrifices? Only men!" Pharaoh spoke in the present tense using the term "*haholkhim*" because he wasn't asking Moshe who would go to *this* festival; rather, he is rhetorically asking who *generally goes* to bring sacrifices. Pharaoh knew Moshe would ask for everyone to participate, so Pharaoh was negotiating: "Come on, Moshe, be honest with me. You're going to sacrifice? Take the men; they're the only ones who sacrifice."

Moshe's response was: We will go with our young and old. Don't compare our worship of Hashem with the customs of other nations. We *all* go, our whole families, because "*we* must hold a feast unto Hashem" – all of us, collectively, *lanu*. The sacrifices are at the center of a bigger festival. All other nations bring sacrifices, and that's where the worship starts and ends. We sacrifice as part of a festival in which we all participate. The *Keli Yakar* states: "It is known that man's celebration is only complete when his wife and children can partake in the celebration."

If the family is unable to celebrate together, then something is lacking, because *hag* should bring families together. Moshe repeated *nelekh* to explain to Pharaoh that we need youths and elders so they could worship, and young sons and daughters to enhance the holiday joy. "You're right," said Moshe, "only the older boys and men are necessary for the sacrifices, but everyone else has to be involved for the *simha* element."

On a similar note, in connection with the mitzva of *hak'hel*, we are commanded to bring "men, women, and small children." Imagine taking a journey to the *Beit HaMikdash* together with the entire nation, an opportunity for an incredibly spiritually uplifting experience, with a two-year-old who is crying and constantly requires our attention. Having your children there will obviously sacrifice some of the spiritual experience. Yet, the Torah stresses the importance of educating one's children. Worshipping Hashem is not just for adults. The entire religious experience must be imbued in us from childhood. That is why Moshe demanded that even the children and elderly had to participate in the offering of sacrifices in the desert.

BAAL HATURIM

Another interpretation of *mi vami haholkhim* is offered by the Baal HaTurim. Pharaoh "saw" what would happen to Am Yisrael after they left Egypt, whether through prophecy or some other way. He was asking: Why do you so badly want to leave Egypt? You're so desperate to leave, but do you even realize that you're not going to enter *Eretz Yisrael* right away anyway? "Do you know *mi vami haholkhim*, who will be entering *Eretz Yisrael*?" Pharaoh asked. "Only two of your men (Yehoshua and Kalev, represented by the words *mi vami*) will make it in; the rest are going to die in the desert."

The Baal HaTurim adds that the *gematria* of *mi vami haholkhim* actually equals *Kalev uBin Nun*.

Moshe's answer to Pharaoh was, "actually, a lot more than two of us are going to enter *Eretz Yisrael*. The young under twenty and the old over sixty are going in, too, because they will not be condemned to die in the desert." That is the reference to "we will go with our young and with our old."

That, says the Baal HaTurim, is the deeper meaning of this conversation.

Lessons of the
Korban Pesah

There are many lessons to be learned from the laws of the *Korban Pesah*. We will explore several.

SEFER HAHINUKH: ROYALTY

The Torah commands that the *Korban Pesah* be eaten in the house and cannot be taken outside.

בבית אחד יאכל לא תוציא מן הבית מן הבשר חוצה ועצם לא תשברו
בו. (שמות יב:מו)

> In one house shall it be eaten; you shalt not remove any of the meat out of the house; nor shall you break a bone thereof. (*Shemot* 12:41)

What is the reason behind this prohibition? The *Sefer HaHinukh*[1] suggests that because we eat the *Korban Pesah* as a symbol of our freedom, we must eat it in the way that royalty would eat it – inside the house. Royals don't eat outside on the run; kings eat at home, sitting, and in

---

1. *Sefer HaHinukh*, mitzva 20.

a relaxed manner. Their time is theirs. They don't leave in the middle of their meal. Since we are like royalty on the night of Pesah, we must act like it.

MESHEKH HOKHMA: DISCIPLINE

With respect to the preparation of the original *Korban Pesah* in Egypt, the Torah dictates:

דברו אל כל עדת ישראל לאמר בעשר לחדש הזה ויקחו להם איש שה לבית אבת שה לבית. (שמות יב:ג)

> Speak unto all the congregation of Israel, saying: On the tenth day of this month they shall take to them every man a lamb, according to their fathers' houses, a lamb for a household. (*Shemot* 12:3)

Hashem commanded Bnei Yisrael to bring a sheep into their homes on the tenth of Nisan, four days before they would be redeemed. Why was a four-day waiting period necessary?

The *Meshekh Hokhma*[2] explains that Hashem wanted to take us out of Egypt in an orderly and disciplined way. He didn't want us to escape like a wild mob. Obviously, after 210 years of forced labor, all of Klal Yisrael just wanted to get out. Additionally, the entire Egyptian nation was probably on the verge of civil war, desperate for Pharaoh to release Bnei Yisrael so as not to lose all their firstborns. Would anyone have said anything if Bnei Yisrael had left? The Egyptians would probably all have been thrilled, and nobody would have stopped Bnei Yisrael from leaving.

For *this* reason Hashem commanded the four-day waiting period. The sheep would be tied to a bed for four nights, bleating the whole time, and the Egyptians would have to suffer the pain of witnessing their gods tied up to the Bnei Yisrael's bedposts and then watching as they were roasted whole.

That was the purpose of the four days: HaKadosh Barukh Hu wanted to show the world that Bnei Yisrael could leave at that very moment, but didn't do so because they were waiting to be told to do so

---

2. *Meshekh Hokhma, Shemot* 12:3.

by Hashem. They were disciplined and orderly rather than spontaneous and disorganized. *Yiddishkeit* is not only about following the dictates of the Torah, but it is also about being organized and disciplined.

Perhaps this is also why Bnei Yisrael were commanded to eat the *Korban Pesah* whole, without any broken bones, so that it was done in a neat and orderly fashion, not in an animalistic way. Additionally, on several occasions, the Gemara[3] dictates that a *talmid hakham* has to act properly and dress immaculately so as not to appear disheveled. It is essential that all we do is viewed by others in a positive light, so we create a *kiddush Hashem*.

RAV AHRON SOLOVEICHIK

Rav Ahron Soloveichik[4] expands on this idea of orderliness, linking it to the moment of liberation. Most often, when there's a change of leadership in a country, anarchy results, and utter chaos reigns. There are several reasons why this is so: There is confusion, fear of the unknown; moral laws fall by the wayside as people thrill at their newfound freedom; the pent-up emotions of the people come to the fore; and often, in their anger over their hurt, they hurt others.

At the exodus from Egypt, although there was a change in rulership, says Rav Soloveitchik, the usual chaos that follows the collapse of a regime was blatantly missing. When we left Egypt, there was perfect order. We did not leave a second earlier than we were told to leave. We left as a nation, in calm quiet, because while we may had been liberated, we were not free; when a Jew experiences physical freedom, it does not mean that he no longer has moral and ethical standards to uphold.

Hazal tell us that the only truly free person is one who engages in Torah. The more we subjugate ourselves to HaKadosh Barukh Hu, the more we appreciate life. It's only when we don't have the proper appreciation of halakha that we feel chained down to the Torah. Judaism, however, through its restrictions and laws, guides us to a meaningful and truly free life.

---

3. Shabbat 114a.
4. Rav Ahron Soloveichik, *Logic of the Heart, Logic of the Mind* (Jerusalem: Genesis Press, 1991), 138.

The halakhot of the *Korban Pesah* were a message to Bnei Yisrael regarding their newfound freedom. Chaos had no part in their redemption; they were told exactly where to be on that night. They were instructed to stay put in their homes, not to run around, not to go out to street corners. Everyone was to remain in their house and be accounted for, eating exactly what Hashem told them to eat. Only when Hashem would tell them to go would they get up and leave.

Many of the halakhot of the *Korban Pesah* are all about showing that our freedom is not like other freedoms. The exodus from Egypt wasn't about overthrowing a regime and becoming free; rather, it was precisely at our moment of liberation that our subjection to Hashem began.

OZNAYIM LATORAH: UNIFICATION

Rabbi Zalman Sorotzkin[5] offers yet another lesson to be learned from the laws of the *Korban Pesah*.

It took a long time for Bnei Yisrael to become a nation. There was a lot of divisiveness before we finally unified. Every single sibling relationship in the Torah, from Kayin and Hevel through the tribes, was rife with discord, which is why we ended up in Egypt. Egypt served to purify us and heal us from this issue that was so ingrained in us. We had to go through the pain of Egyptian servitude *together* in order to feel unity, a unity that was a necessary achievement in our becoming a nation.

The *Korban Pesah* was the first national *korban*. The defining *korban* of the Jewish nation, the *korban* that binds Bnei Yisrael together. It is the *only korban* of which every single Jew must partake, serving as a lesson that we are all in it together. The *Korban Pesah* was all about unity. Even if a person could eat an entire lamb himself, he was not allowed to do so with the *Korban Pesah*; it had to be shared. The commandment was to eat it in groups, and no one was allowed to leave his group.

This command was meant to accustom Bnei Yisrael to a life of unity and love. At least once a year, they would have to sit together, and if any conflict occurred, they were forced to resolve it. No one could leave. The main message of the *Korban Pesah* is a message of unity.

---

5. Rabbi Zalman Sorotzkin, *Oznayim LaTorah* (Jerusalem, 1990).

Appreciating the Significance of a Moment

וימהר פרעה לקרא למשה ולאהרן ויאמר חטאתי לה' א-להיכם ולכם.
ועתה שא נא חטאתי אך הפעם והעתירו לה' א-להיכם ויסר מעלי רק
את המות הזה. (שמות י:טז-יז)

Then Pharaoh called for Moshe and Aharon in haste, and he
said, "I have sinned against Hashem, your God, and against you.
Now, therefore, forgive my sin only this once and entreat the
Lord your God that He may take away from me only this death."
(*Shemot* 10:16–17)

When the plague of locusts began, Pharaoh panicked and hurried to call
for Moshe and Aharon, begging for "this death" to be removed from
Egypt. For some reason, this plague upset Pharaoh very much, to the
extent that he called it *mavet* – "death."

First, asks Rabbi Zalman Sorotzkin in *Oznayim LaTorah*,[1] why
did Pharaoh panic more from this plague than any other? This is the
only one, until this point, that he referred to as *mavet*. Further, why was
Pharaoh in such a hurry? He didn't hurry in any other plague, only here.

---

1. Rabbi Zalman Sorotzkin, *Oznayim LaTorah* (Jerusalem, 1990).

The *Oznayim LaTorah* explains that Pharaoh knew the nature of locusts. He knew that if they stick around too long, they start laying eggs. If it is hard to get rid of locusts, it is impossible to get rid of their eggs. After a while, the situation becomes hopeless. A whole new generation of locusts is born, worse than the first round. He realized what a *mavet* the locusts were and that if he left the locusts enough to lay eggs, this plague would be a long-term disaster.

In a way, we can view this reaction of Pharaoh in a positive light. Pharaoh realized the power of a second. If you're not alacritous, if you don't act right now, then for generations to come, there will be destruction.

The *Ketav Sofer*[2] highlights a similar point based on a *pasuk* that appears later in the *parasha*:

ושמרתם את המצות כי בעצם היום הזה הוצאתי את צבאותיכם מארץ מצרים ושמרתם את היום הזה לדרתיכם חקת עולם. (שמות יב:יז)

And you shall observe the feast of unleavened bread, for in this selfsame day have I brought your hosts out of the land of Egypt; therefore, shall you observe this day throughout your generations by an ordinance forever. (*Shemot* 12:17)

Rashi quotes *Hazal* on the above *pasuk*, who say:

רבי יאשיה אומר אל תהי קורא את המצות אלא את המצוות כדרך שאין מחמיצין את המצה כך אין מחמיצין את המצווה אלא אם באה לידך עשה אותה מיד. (רש״י שמות יב:יז)

Rabbi Yoshia said: Don't read [the word as it is written in the *pasuk*] *matzot*, but rather [as] *mitzvot*; just as one should not let the dough rise, one should not allow mitzvot to pass – rather, if [a mitzva opportunity] comes your way, fulfill it immediately. (Rashi on *Shemot* 12:17)

Just as we don't allow *matzot* to become *hametz*, don't let mitzvot become *hametz*. Don't delay the fulfillment of mitzvot so as not to lose

---

2. *Ketav Sofer Al HaTorah*, 98.

the opportunities. Those who are vigilant do mitzvot at the earliest opportunity: "*Zerizin makdimin lemitzvot.*"

The *Ketav Sofer* questions what this Rashi, however beautiful the idea is, has to do with the rest of the *pasuk*. If we understand the first three words of *pasuk* 17 as, "observe the mitzvot so that we don't lose the opportunity to fulfill them," how does that connect with the rest of the *pasuk*, that Hashem took us out of Egypt? What is the connection between the first and second parts of the *pasuk*?

The *Ketav Sofer* answers this question with an exact parallel to the idea from the *Oznayim LaTorah* about Pharaoh's hurry to address the issue of the locusts: Just like *matza* needs constant vigilance to prevent it from becoming *hametz*, and even one second can turn it into *hametz*, so too, with ourselves. If we don't control the *hametz* within us – the *yetzer hara* – and guard ourselves every second, then we can lose valuable mitzvot in just a single moment.

The *pasuk* stresses that we must guard the mitzvot zealously, because if we don't act *right now*, there will never be future generations. There never will be a Klal Yisrael. Hashem took us out right away so that we would have a future.

We see how substantial even one second is, how important every moment is for the continuity of the individual and the nation.

Borrowing Money from the Enemy

דבר נא באזני העם וישאלו איש מאת רעהו ואשה מאת רעותה כלי
כסף וכלי זהב. (שמות יא:ב)

Speak now in the ears of the people and let them ask every man
of his friend and every woman of her friend jewels of silver and
jewels of gold. (*Shemot* 11:2)

Why did Hashem request from Moshe, using the word *na*, "please," to
instruct Bnei Yisrael to borrow gold and silver vessels from the Egyptians before leaving Egypt?
Rashi explains:

אין נא אלא לשון בקשה, בבקשה ממך הזהירם על כך שלא יאמר אותו
צדיק אברהם (בראשית טו יג) ועבדום וענו אותם קיים בהם (שם יד)
ואחרי כן יצאו ברכוש גדול לא קיים בהם.

The term *na* connotes a request. He phrased it as a request so
that Avraham would not claim: Hashem fulfilled His promise
to enslave them, but His promise that they leave with riches, He
did not fulfill.

The word *na* always connotes a request. Hashem was requesting that Bnei Yisrael not forget to leave Egypt with these valuable items so that Avraham wouldn't have a complaint against Hashem that He kept the part of the *Brit bein HaBetarim* that promised the slavery of the children of Israel, but not the part about Bnei Yisrael leaving with wealth.

Now, this begs a basic question: Wouldn't Hashem keep His word anyway? Would Hashem really not have fulfilled the promise in its entirety if not for Avraham's complaint?

Additionally, the word *na* seems to suggest that Bnei Yisrael did not want to take the valuables, that Hashem had to convince them to take the wealth. Why is that?

Rabbi Zalman Sorotzkin[1] answers that only now in the twenty-first century do we understand this *pasuk* and *Hazal*. We couldn't understand it for thousands of years, and only now, after the Holocaust, is it clear to us.

There have been major controversies over the past decades about German reparations. One side abhors the idea of taking money from the Germans, as the Germans do not deserve to feel like money can cleanse themselves of their sins. Money cannot forgive the evil committed, and we won't allow them to feel absolved from the atrocities they committed. We cannot possibly put a monetary value on our fellow brethren who were murdered in cold blood.

The other camp believes that the Germans did enough injustice by murdering millions of Jews; they don't deserve to profit off of us as well. "Absolutely not," they say. "But at least give us our money back!"

The issue is a very murky one, yet this debate is not a new one. This is exactly what Bnei Yisrael felt when they were leaving Egypt. After 210 years of subjugation, some Jews felt that the least they deserved was the Egyptians' valuables, while the other side wanted nothing from the Egyptians. The issue was very unclear.

Hashem, therefore, requested of Bnei Yisrael to take the Egyptians' valuables. He didn't use an objective, flat-out command. Instead, He asked for a favor, as it were, because there were many who wanted

---

1. Zalman Sorotzkin, *Oznayim LaTorah* (Jerusalem, 1990).

nothing from these murderers of their families. Hashem saw that it would be hard for many of Bnei Yisrael to take anything from the Egyptians, as if taking Egyptian money was putting a price on their murdered babies, so He couldn't force them to do it. Instead, He just requested it, in the name of Avraham Avinu.

NETZIV: WERE THE EGYPTIANS OUR FRIENDS?

The Netziv[2] questions the wording of the *pasuk*. Why does the Torah say, *me'et re'ehu* – "from his friend"? Were Bnei Yisrael and the Egyptians *friends*? "From his master," "from his persecutor," maybe…but *"friend"*?

The Netziv points out that, earlier, the Torah uses a different description for the Egyptians, referring to "each woman will ask of her *neighbor*" (*Shemot* 3:22). The Torah does not use the term "friend" at that point.

The Netziv explains that initially the Egyptians were definitely not friends with the Jews. Far from it! However, during the twelve months that the plagues took place, the Egyptians developed somewhat of a relationship with the Jewish people. They didn't exactly become friends, but through the miraculous display of the plagues, they slowly started coming around. During the plague of wild animals, some Egyptians actually sought refuge in Goshen. They saw the writing on the wall. So, over the course of the plagues, the unpleasant relationship between the Egyptians and Bnei Yisrael started to wane.

Additionally, an element that furthered this positive change occurred during the plague of darkness. One might wonder how the Egyptians didn't starve during the three days of darkness that froze them in their places. And the only reason they did not is because Bnei Yisrael came and fed them. Unbelievable!

Pharaoh's whole plan had been to dehumanize Bnei Yisrael, to convince everyone that the blood of Israel was cheap, but Hashem showed the Egyptians what kind of people we really are – the most refined nation, the only nation that would feed its own captors. So,

---

2. Netziv, *Haamek Davar*, *Shemot* 11:2.

ultimately, at the time of the exodus from Egypt, Bnei Yisrael had won favor in the eyes of the Egyptians. From their perspective, Bnei Yisrael were indeed "friends."

In truth, the whole purpose of the plagues was to bring the Egyptians to recognize Hashem and that Am Yisrael is His chosen nation. This mellowing of feelings was a fulfillment of that purpose.

Redemption Begins at Midnight

ויאמר משה כה אמר ה': כחצת הלילה אני יוצא בתוך מצרים. (שמות יא:ד)

And Moshe said: "This is what Hashem said: 'About midnight will I go out into the midst of Egypt.'" (*Shemot* 11:4)

Hashem told Moshe that He would take Bnei Yisrael out of Egypt at *hatzot*, "midnight." Why was this timing so important? The *Netivot Shalom* answers with a fundamental principle about cycles of life.

Everything in this world, all creation, begins with darkness that is followed by light. The *Netivot Shalom* quotes the *Zohar*, who says that the only true light is one that comes after darkness. This has been reality since Creation, as the Torah says, "it was evening, and it was morning." Darkness must come before light, because light is appreciated more after darkness. Morning is so much more special because it follows a dark night.

The same idea holds true with people, including with Am Yisrael. At the *Brit bein HaBetarim*, Hashem promised Avraham that his descendants would be slaves and then be redeemed. Why did we need the slave experience? Couldn't we go straight into redemption without having experienced exile?

The answer is "no," because Hashem ordained that light and redemption can only come after darkness and exile. The ultimate light must contrast with darkness. This concept can be called growth; just as Hashem could have created the world to be permanently light but didn't, He could have made us to be born as mature adults instead of babies. Instead, we are born as babies, "in the dark," without knowledge, so we can spend our lives growing and bring light into our lives.

This, according to the *Netivot Shalom*, is why the redemption had to take place exactly at *hatzot*. *Hatzot* is the epitome of darkness. The first half of the night is still spiritually and metaphysically affected by the light of the previous day. A minute after *hatzot*, the night is already affected by the light of the next day. At precisely *hatzot*, the midpoint of the night, there is pure and utter darkness, deriving no light from the previous day or the next day. That is exactly when the plague of the first-born occurred, because the redemption comes from the darkest moment.

The pinnacle of darkness means it is time for the ultimate redemption. That is how we view our lives, how we view Am Yisrael, and how we must view every challenge that we experience in life. Whenever there is utter darkness, the time is ripe for the ultimate redemption. Even if we do not see the ultimate light in our lifetime, we believe that the redemption will come after the darkness, because that is how Hashem created the world. First, darkness. Then, light.

The First Mitzva: The Blessing on a New Month

החדש הזה לכם ראש חדשים: ראשון הוא לכם לחדשי השנה. (שמות יב:ב)

This month shall be unto you the beginning of months; it shall be the first month of the year to you. (Shemot 12:2)

The mitzva of blessing the new month was the first mitzva commanded of Bnei Yisrael, and immediately following it are the mitzvot relating to the *Korban Pesah*. The *Be'er Yosef*[1] asks: Is there a specific connection between the mitzva of blessing the new month and the mitzva of *Korban Pesah*? Why do these mitzvot immediately precede the exodus from Egypt? Additionally, if one were to look through the *pesukim* that discuss the mitzvot of *Korban Pesah*, the word *bayit* is repeated very often. It would seem that the home, the family unit, somehow played a major role in the mitzva of *Korban Pesah*. But what role?

The *Be'er Yosef* cites a midrash to answer these questions. In *Devarim*, the exodus from Egypt is described as God "taking a nation from within a nation" (*Devarim* 4:34). The midrash explains this term

---

1. Rav Yosef MiSalant, *Be'er Yosef* (Jerusalem 2009), *Shemot*, 227.

by comparing the exodus from Egypt to a birth: Like a baby disconnects from its mother's womb and exits, Bnei Yisrael exited Egypt.

The message of the midrash is that just as a baby inside its mother is physically connected, we, too, were connected to Egypt. After 210 years of living in the womb of Egypt, we were entirely entrenched in their culture. A baby cannot be forced out of the womb, as it can harm the baby. Only once labor has begun is the baby ready to emerge. Similarly, while Bnei Yisrael were so entrenched in Egypt, the exodus from there was not yet possible. As long as we were being nourished by Egyptian culture, Hashem wasn't going to forcibly wrench us out. Hashem first "induced labor," and only once we were ready to leave did He take us out.

Thus, all the mitzvot we received in the period leading up to the exodus from Egypt were part of the separation process. They were the start of labor. The very first commandments regarding the *Korban Pesaḥ* were to take Egyptian gods, tie them up next to their beds, and then kill them. The beginning of the labor process required Bnei Yisrael to recognize that the lamb was not a god, that only Hashem should be worshipped. Another commandment that Bnei Yisrael received was to perform *brit mila* – which symbolizes controlling desires – while Egypt was known as the world's capital of promiscuity. We needed the mitzva of *brit mila* to separate us from the depravity of Egypt. The fact that the *Korban Pesaḥ* could only be eaten by Bnei Yisrael in their homes – which had the blood of the *Korban Pesaḥ* on the doorposts – further reinforced the idea of separation from the surrounding Egyptian environment. Thus, every detail of the mitzvot that Bnei Yisrael received prior to the exodus from Egypt symbolized this separation.

With regard to blessing the new month, the mitzva isn't just about the calendar – it is specifically about the *lunar* calendar. The sun and the Nile played major roles in Egyptian culture, and the focus on the moon, through the mitzva of blessing the new month, emphasized our dissimilarity to the Egyptian culture. As we know, the moon doesn't generate its own light. Rather, it reflects the light of the sun. Furthermore, the amount of light the moon reflects depends on its proximity and angle toward the sun. The further it is from the sun, the more light it can reflect.

So, too, with our liberation from Egypt. Only once we were far enough from the Egyptians could we begin to reflect the light of Hashem and the Torah. We must keep our distance from the world of falsehood in order to fully reflect the light of Torah. Our calendar thus distinguishes us from the cultures surrounding us.[2]

---

2. Several other explanations have been provided as to why the first mitzva given to *Bnei Yisrael* is blessing the new month. One suggestion is that now that as a nation we were "free," it does not mean that we are to waste time. The first thing we need to do is to sanctify time in order to ensure that we are productive and that we perform mitzvot as *avdei Hashem* and not as *avadim leParo*. See Sforno (*Shemot* 12:2): Now that time is in our hands, we have to use it productively.

The Connection between the Two *Tefillin*

At the end of the *parasha,* we are introduced to the mitzva of *tefillin*:

והיה לך לאות על ידך ולזכרון בין עיניך למען תהיה תורת ה' בפיך
כי ביד חזקה הוצאך ה' ממצרים. (שמות יג:טז)

And it shall be for a sign upon your thy hand and for frontlets
between your eyes; for by strength of hand of Hashem brought
us forth out of Egypt. (*Shemot* 13:16)

Rabbi Aharon Lewin, in *HaDerash VeHaIyun,*[1] quotes the Gemara in
Hullin (9a) that defines a *talmid hakham* as someone who knows how
to tie the knot of the *tefillin.*

There is a midrash that tells us that when Moshe Rabbenu wanted
to understand HaKadosh Barukh Hu, so to speak, Hashem said, "You
can only see My back; you can't see My front."[2] *Hazal* say that when
Hashem showed Moshe His back, Moshe saw the knot of Hashem's

---

1. Rav Aharon Lewin, *HaDerash VeHaIyun* (Jerusalem: Chorev, 1969), *Shemot,* 113.
2. *Shemot* 33:23.

tefillin. Here, again, we see this emphasis on the knot of *tefillin*. What are we to learn from the emphasis on the knot of *tefillin*?

Rabbi Levin explains that there are two parts of the *tefillin*: the *shel rosh* and the *shel yad*. The *shel rosh*, which is placed on the head, represents the mind; the *shel yad*, which is wrapped around the arm and faces the body, represents the heart. They can also represent the areas of *bein adam laMakom* and *bein adam lahaveiro*, respectively. The heart symbolizes our connection to other Jews, and the mind represents our connection to Hashem.

We can't have one without the other! The two *tefillin* are linked to one another. For example, one may not steal (a *mitzva bein adam lahaveiro*) in order to eat *matza* (a *mitzva bein adam laMakom*). One must not trample one area of *avodat Hashem* in the name of another. The knot does not only refer to the knot of one of the *tefillin*, but the tie that binds the two *tefillin* together!

Hashem displayed the knot of *tefillin* to show Moshe that the two parts of the *tefillin* are connected to each other. Hashem essentially disclosed to Moshe that we need both of these elements to be a complete Jew. That is why a *talmid hakham* has to be an expert in the knot of *tefillin* – it means being an expert in the balance between *bein adam laMakom* and *bein adam lahaveiro*.

We all have to be experts in this connection between the mind and the heart, between the intellect and the heart, and in that way, we will merit a true exodus every day of our life.

Parashat Beshallah

One-Fifth Exited Egypt

ויסב א־להים את העם דרך המדבר ים סוף וחמשים עלו בני ישראל
מארץ מצרים. (שמות יג:יח)

God led the people around by way of the desert to the Reed Sea,
and Bnei Yisrael were armed when they went up out of Egypt.
(*Shemot* 13:18)

The *pasuk* tells us that Bnei Yisrael left Egypt *hamushim*. Onkelos interprets this obscure word to mean "armed." Rashi, after citing this interpretation, offers another interpretation:

דבר אחר חמושים אחד מחמשה יצאו וארבעה חלקים מתו בשלשת ימי
אפילה. (רש"י שמות יג:יח)

An alternative interpretation: one-fifth left, and four-fifths died
during the three days of darkness. (Rashi on *Shemot* 13:8)

According to this second explanation, only one-fifth of Klal Yisrael left
Egypt. The other four-fifths died during the plague of darkness because
they felt it was better to remain in Egypt.

The *Be'er Yosef*[1] quotes two other translations of the *pasuk*. Rabbi Yonatan ben Uziel explains: "Every family went out of Egypt with five children." And the *Targum Yerushalmi* says, "Bnei Yisrael left Egypt armed with good deeds."

Rabbi Yonatan ben Uziel's idea is pretty amazing: Every family had the same number of children! And the *Targum Yerushalmi* seems pretty vague. What good deeds were they "armed" with as they left Egypt? After all, *Hazal* tell us they were lacking the merit of mitzvot,[2] which is why Hashem commanded them to fulfill the commandment of *brit mila* and *Korban Pesah*.

The *Be'er Yosef* beautifully unifies these two interpretations in his explanation of *hamushim*. Four-fifths of Bnei Yisrael may have died during the plague of darkness because they weren't believers and did not deserve to participate in the exodus from Egypt. However, what about their children? They didn't deserve to die! Thus, at the time of the exodus from Egypt, four-fifths of the children of Klal Yisrael didn't have parents.

Explains the *Be'er Yosef*, the one-fifth of Klal Yisrael who survived took care of the other four-fifths! Doing the math, besides each family taking their own children, they took another four families' children as well. Each family took their own kids plus four other sets of children, and that's what Rabbi Yonatan ben Uziel means – each family left with five (sets of) children.

Usually, when a family goes on a trip, they would not be too willing to take along more children. Certainly, if it meant taking these children permanently, there would be few offers. But when Klal Yisrael left Egypt and took these other children with them, there were no parents who would claim these kids at a later date. Each family took in four additional sets of children *without* complaining, and *that* was the good deed they were involved in as they left Egypt – adopting children who didn't have parents. Accordingly, all three explanations of the word *hamushim* can be understood cohesively.

Perhaps this is the deeper meaning of the *pasuk*:

---

1. Rav Yosef Salant, *Be'er Yosef* (Jerusalem 2009), *Shemot*, 227.
2. *Arumim min hamitzvot* (naked from mitzvot); see the *Mekhilta* on *Parashat Bo*.

כה אמר ה׳ זכרתי לך חסד נעוריך אהבת כלולתיך לכתך אחרי במדבר
בארץ לא זרועה. (ירמיהו ב:ב)

'So said Hashem: I remember to you the lovingkindness of your
youth, the love of your nuptials, your following Me in the desert,
in a land not sown. (Yirmeyahu 2:2)

This *pasuk* is usually translated to mean that Hashem remembers when
we were a young nation, redeemed from Egypt, and we had complete
emuna in Him. The *Be'er Yosef*, however, explains these words according
to their straightforward meaning: the *reference to the hesed* of Klal Yisrael's youth is with regard to these young orphaned children that were
adopted by those who merited to leave Egypt.

Recognizing Man's Vulnerability

ופרעה הקריב וישאו בני ישראל את עיניהם והנה מצרים נסע אחריהם
וייראו מאד ויצעקו בני ישראל אל ה'. (שמות יד:י)

Pharaoh drew near, and Bnei Yisrael lifted up their eyes, and behold! The Egyptians were advancing after them. They were very frightened, and Bnei Yisrael cried out to Hashem. (*Shemot* 14:10)

The Torah tells us that as Bnei Yisrael found themselves trapped between the Egyptians who were chasing them from behind, and the Reed Sea which was in front of them, they called out to Hashem. Rashi explains that they latched onto the art of prayer of their forefathers – they prayed like Avraham, Yitzhak, and Yaakov.

Rav Yeruham Levovitz in *Daat Torah* says: Why was this so significant? Did they not pray earlier? We are told while Bnei Yisrael were in Egypt that Hashem heard their cries. Why does Rashi highlight only here that their prayer was on such a high level?

The Gemara[1] cites an incident where Raba Bar Bar Hana was once traveling on a boat when he and his colleagues saw an island and decided to disembark. They made themselves comfortable and started setting up their dwelling. To their surprise, when they lit a fire and started cooking, the "island" began to shake. They quickly jumped off the island and swam back to their boat, only then realizing that what they thought was an island was really a large aquatic creature.

What is the message of this mysterious story? Often in life, we think we are on *terra firma*. Everything is stable; everything is on a natural course of behavior. And yet we fail to realize that at any moment, as sometimes happens in life, our "island" turns into a "whale," and we are thrown by one of life's surprises. We often fail to recognize that every single moment of our lives is dependent on the One Above. Viewed in this way, we might suggest that each moment of life is a potential *et tzara* (a moment of danger or despair).[2] Each moment is an opportunity to daven to Hashem for divine protection and intervention.

A similar idea can be gleaned from the gemara at the end of *Masekhet Sota*.[3] The Mishna lists various *middot* (traits) that left this world, once the tanna that excelled in that *midda* passed on. The Mishna states that when Rebbi left this world, so did true humility. The Gemara says that Rav Yosef declares: "Don't list humility in the Mishna. Humility did not leave the world with Rebbi. After all, I'm still here!" This obviously does not seem to reflect true humility. Maybe there is a deeper idea here. In numerous places in *Hazal*,[4] Rav Yosef needed to be reminded

---

1. Bava Batra 73b. This story is part of the lengthy discussion there of tales of Raba Bar Bar Hana.
2. There is a well-known *makhloket* between the Rambam and the Ramban as to whether *tefilla* is a biblical or rabbinic commandment. The Rambam (positive mitzva 5) believes it is a biblical commandment, while the Ramban (*shorashim*) believes that *tefilla* is required only when one is in an *et tzara*, a dangerous situation or state of despair. Rav Yosef Soloveitchik explains that there is really no disagreement between the Rambam and the Ramban as to whether *tefilla* is a biblical commandment. The Rambam agrees with the Ramban that one is only obligated to daven at an *et tzara*, but the Rambam believes that every second is a potential *et tzara* – our fate is in God's hands and at any second our world can be turned upside down.
3. Sota 49b.
4. For example, see Ketubot 2a and Rashi there.

of his teachings by his students, since he was ill and forgot much of his learning. Rav Yosef, then, is teaching us, "Do you think it's hard to be humble, to recognize that God is in charge? Just look at my life! Look at the capricious nature of where life takes you, and the vulnerability to external forces! My life, *d'ika ana*, is a lesson for all in humility, to realize that we are not fully in charge of our destinies."

Now we can return to Bnei Yisrael at the Reed Sea. True *tefilla* can only come out of a sense of dependence and need for divine assistance. Recognition that I can't do it myself is a *sina qua non* for classic prayer. That is exactly what Bnei Yisrael experienced as they approached the Reed Sea. Water in front, Egypt in back, there was only one way to turn – and that was up! That's the secret behind Rashi's comment that *davka* here, they acted in a way that mimicked their forefathers concept of true prayer.

This is what we hope to experience when we stand before Hashem in our daily *tefillot*: to understand our vulnerability and to turn to Hashem to seek His guidance, assistance and protection.

Entering or Crossing the Reed Sea

ויסר את אפן מרכבתיו וינהגהו בכבדת ויאמר מצרים אנוסה מפני ישראל
כי ה' נלחם להם במצרים. (שמות יד:כה)

Hashem removed the wheels of their chariots, and they rode slowly. So Egypt said, "We must flee from Israel, for Hashem is fighting against Egypt for them." (*Shemot* 14:28)

Why did Hashem remove the chariot wheels? Couldn't Hashem just have drowned the Egyptians? What difference do the wheels make? Furthermore, it sounds like this miracle is what caused the Egyptians to despair. What was so amazing about this specific miracle that the Egyptians gave up?

The Tosafists ask another question: According to the *pesukim*, Bnei Yisrael were in a place called Eitam before and after they passed through the Reed Sea. How is this possible? They explain that Bnei Yisrael never actually crossed the Reed Sea! They made a semicircle, going in and coming out on the same side.[1] So why did they go into the sea if not to pass through?

---

1. See *Tosafot* Arakhin 15a for a diagram of the path of Am Yisrael's journey through the Reed Sea.

The Hizkuni[2] explains that the purpose of going into the Reed Sea was only to lead the Egyptians into it so that they would then drown. Bnei Yisrael went in only to lead the Egyptians in.

Says the *Mekhilta*,[3] ten miracles occurred at the Reed Sea, and one of them was that the sea split into twelve paths – one for each tribe. If there were twelve paths, and the Egyptians followed Bnei Yisrael down every path, then the Egyptians who were on the innermost part of the semicircle would reach the other side before Bnei Yisrael on the outermost circle. To prevent that, the wheels came off of the Egyptians' chariots. The lack of wheels slowed down the Egyptians on the innermost circle so they wouldn't reach the other side first.

It is interesting to note that the Torah refers to a wheel (in the singular), *ofan*. If both front wheels were removed, the Egyptians may have been able to continue riding forward by having their front axel's drag. However, removing only one wheel caused the vehicles to spin out of control, so they would be unsuccessful in their pursuit of Am Yisrael.

---

2. Hizkuni *Shemot* 14:25.
3. *Mekhilta Shemot* 14.

Past, Present, and Future

אז ישיר משה ובני ישראל את השירה הזאת לה' ויאמרו לאמר אשירה
לה' כי גאה גאה סוס ורכבו רמה בים. (שמות טו:א)

Then, Moshe and Bnei Yisrael sang this song to Hashem, and
they spoke, saying, "I will sing to Hashem, for very exalted is He;
horse and its rider He cast into the sea." (Shemot 15:1)

A midrash states that Moshe was always involved in activities described
by the word *az*, "then."

כל פרקמטיא של משה לא היתה אלא ב"אז" - "אז יבדיל מה שלש
ערים" "אז ישיר משה".

Moshe's dealings were connected with "then" – "then, Moshe
established three cities of refuge," "then, Moshe sang."

A parallel is drawn between the first *pasuk* in *Az Yashir* and a *pasuk*
in *Parashat Va'ethanan* describing how Moshe designated three cities
of refuge: *az yavdil Moshe*. What exactly links these two actions of
Moshe? How does the song parallel the designation of cities of refuge?

Rav Shlomo Zevin[1] explains that a person's actions must always be focused not just on the present but also on the future. We can't live in a vacuum of the here and now. We must focus on the present, but we also must contemplate how our actions may impact the future.[2]

The word *az* describes the true essence of living in the present and for the future. In the above midrash, *Hazal* focus on the *az* of the cities of refuge because this specific example drives the point home. Moshe established three of the six cities in Transjordan during his lifetime, notwithstanding that they did not officially have the protective status of cities of refuge until Yehoshua established the other three cities of refuge in *Eretz Yisrael*. Why did Moshe bother with the mitzva at all and not just leave it to Yehoshua to do at the right time? Moshe's actions had no halakhic effect at the time anyway![3] Rabbi Zevin explains that Moshe specifically did it to teach us that one must plan for the future. We must perform actions now that will serve the next generations.

Moshe was a man of *az*. He lived in the present but thought about the future. We have to use the past as a springboard for future growth, internalizing all we have learned up until now. Without a past and present, there can be no future. A Jew lives in all three. The Torah connects these three aspects of time, and Moshe taught us this concept with *az*.

A story is told in Hagiga of Honi Hame'agel, who met a man who planted carob trees that take seventy years to bear fruit.[4] Honi asked him, "Why bother, if you won't enjoy the fruits of your labor?" He replied, "Just as I found grown carob trees, planted by my grandparents, I am planting for my grandchildren." He was acting today to achieve results for the future.

On Sukkot, we shake the four species, which, according to a midrash, correspond to different parts of our bodies. The *lulav* represents the spine; the *hadasim*, the eyes; the *aravot*, the lips; and the *etrog*,

---

1. *LaTorah VeLaMo'adim*, 116.
2. *Hazal* tell us: "Who is wise? One who anticipates the future" (Tamid 32a).
3. See Makot 9a; Rambam, *Perush HaMishnayot, Pirkei Avot* 4:2, where he refers to this as a "half a mitzva" and explains that Moshe still desired to execute it.
4. Hagiga 23a.

the heart. The *Shemen HaTov*[5] wonders about a discrepancy in this comparison: Three out of the four species match up numerically with the specified parts of our body. We have one heart and one spine, like one *etrog* and one *lulav*. There are two *aravot*, like our two lips, but there are three *hadasim*, while we have only two eyes.

The *Shemen HaTov* explains that a Jew really has three eyes: the past, present, and future. He connects this to a mishna in *Pirkei Avot* (3:1): "Know from where you came, where you are going, and before Whom you will ultimately give an accounting." We must know our past, present, and future. May we all become cognizant of every act we do so it can positively impact our future and the future of our children.

---

5. Rabbi Bernard Weinberger, *Shemen HaTov – Al HaMo'adim* (Brooklyn, 1988), 148.

Why *Shira* Now?

What was it about the Splitting of the Sea that prompted Bnei Yisrael to sing *shira*? Why did they not sing at any earlier point, specifically after any of the awe-inspiring plagues? We sing this *shira* every single morning, immediately following the words, *vayaaminu baHashem uveMoshe avdo* – "they had faith in Hashem and His servant Moshe." This intensifies the question: Did Bnei Yisrael only begin to have faith in in Hashem after the Splitting of the Sea?

Rabbi Zalman Melamed,[1] founder of the Beit El yeshiva, answers this question with a concept that is relevant to this day. There is a corrupt mentality that existed then and, unfortunately, still exists today. Some of Bnei Yisrael felt that Hashem was dealing too harshly with the Egyptians. They were worried that the Egyptians would worsen things for them after each plague Hashem dealt them. Somehow, they forgot about their infants who had been tossed into the sea. They chose to forget about the baths Pharaoh took in Israelite blood. They erroneously viewed the Egyptians as victims and themselves as aggressors, despite the very obvious falsehood of that belief. These members of Bnei Yisrael worried that the whole world would think negatively of them for treating their oppressors so harshly.

---

1.   Rabbi Zalman Melamed, *LaZeman HaZeh* (Bet El: MeAvnei Hamakom, 2014), 60.

When a member of Bnei Yisrael chooses to side with their oppressors, to defend them, no miracle is great enough. This point is relevant even today, unfortunately. Throughout history, we have been made to feel like the aggressor, and our enemy the victim.

What can be done to drive out this mentality? Hashem had to push the reset button on us. Hashem performed a miracle that was like an electric shock – it froze the entire world for a few seconds, and then, we rebooted. The Splitting of the Sea left no doubts for anyone. No one had any choice but to believe.

A midrash describes this concept very well with a *mashal*. A dove was being chased by a predatory bird. It finally found a crevice in a rock to hide in, but then, it saw a snake lying in wait there. On one side, the dove was being chased by a predatory bird, and on the other side, it was trapped by a snake. Bnei Yisrael was that dove at the Splitting of the Sea. The Egyptians' cruelty was undeniable at that moment when Hashem performed the Splitting of the Sea, the greatest divine revelation that had ever occurred. At that moment, everyone was shocked into belief.

The *Sefer HaHinukh* explains that the idea of a *mikve* is that when we emerge from the water, it is as if we're recreated, a totally new person.[2] He compares it to a baby emerging from the amniotic fluid of its mother's womb. The baby is created when it leaves that water and exits the womb.

That is what happened at the Splitting of the Sea. Bnei Yisrael were reborn as they emerged from the waters. At that point, they no longer pitied their killers, and they recognized their misplaced pity. As the Gemara[3] tells us: One who has mercy on the cruel will end up being cruel to those who deserve mercy. We learn this from Shaul, who had mercy on Amalek and later massacred the entire city of Nov.

We are a merciful nation, but we must realize who our enemy is and not have misplaced mercy on them. This was the *shira* by the sea. It was the moment when every single member of Bnei Yisrael recognized the extent of Hashem's greatness, and they couldn't hold themselves back from singing His praises.

---

2. *Sefer HaHinukh*, mitzva 173.
3. See Yoma 22b.

Bittersweet

ויבאו מרתה ולא יכלו לשתת מים ממרה כי מרים הם על כן קרא שמה
מרה... ויצעק אל ה' ויורהו ה' עץ וישלך אל המים וימתקו המים שם
שם לו חק ומשפט ושם נסהו. (שמות טו:כג, כה)

They came to Mara, but they could not drink water from Mara,
for it was bitter; therefore, it was named Mara.... So, he cried out
to Hashem, and Hashem instructed him concerning a piece of
wood, which he cast into the water, and the water became sweet.
There, He gave them a statute and an ordinance, and there He
tested them. (*Shemot* 15:23, 25)

Bnei Yisrael traveled for three days after leaving the Reed Sea, and they
found no water. When Bnei Yisrael arrived in Mara, they couldn't drink
the water, because it was bitter. Hashem's response was to teach them
a way to sweeten the water. Why did He provide for them in this way
instead of simply giving them fresh water in the first place?

The Kotzker Rebbe comments that the phrase *ki marim hem* – "for
it was bitter" – is *not* intended to describe the water, as a simple reading of the *pasuk* implies; rather, it refers to Bnei Yisrael themselves. The
water wasn't bitter – the people were.

After witnessing all the miracles in Egypt and the Splitting of the
Sea, the people felt so close to Hashem. *Hazal* say that a maidservant

witnessed at the Reed Sea what even our greatest prophets did not witness! But then, three days passed without any communication from Hashem, and suddenly, they felt lost. They began to fear that perhaps God's mission was to take them out of Egypt, and now, that mission was complete. We were on our own. How could we survive by ourselves through this desert? This was what caused the "bitterness" and depression among the people. When someone is upset, everything is bitter. If one is to offer a child an ice cream while they are in the midst of a tantrum, they will reject it and say that at that bitter moment, everything is bitter.

Rabbi Zelig Pliskin[1] expounds on the Kotzker Rebbe's words:

> If a person feels bitter, nothing in life appears positive. Anyone looking for faults and defects will always be able to find them. A bitter person makes himself miserable, and those in his environment suffer with him... By sweetening one's own outlook, one will live in a much sweeter world.

So much of life depends on our attitude. If we have a positive attitude and the ability to see beyond current difficulties, then everything is great and wonderful. But if we have a bitter attitude, then even the sweetest things are bitter.

Perhaps that is why Hashem has Moshe insert a tree into the water. The tree represents Torah, our "tree of life." Bnei Yisrael needed to understand that they don't need to witness miracles on a daily basis to feel close to Hashem. Through the Torah, one can achieve this intimacy. It was at Mara that Hashem first taught us *hok umishpat*, the first mitzvot. This was a transformative moment when we began to experience closeness to Hashem through the study and observance of the Torah.

This event is also referenced as the source for reading the Torah every Monday and Thursday, lest we go three days in a row without "water" – another symbol for Torah.[2]

---

1. Rabbi Zelig Pliskin, *Growth Through Torah* (Jerusalem: Bnei Yaakov Publishers, 1998), 175.
2. Bava Kama 82a.

Rabbi Pliskin quotes Rabbi Yehezkel Abramsky, who comments on a gemara in Yevamot that says, "*talmidei hakhamim* increase peace in the world."[3] Rabbi Yehezkel explains that *talmidei hakhamim*, through the Torah they study, develop a pleasant outlook on everything in their life. They pass on this energy of *shalom* and tranquility, thereby increasing the peace and happiness in the world.

May we merit to overcome bitterness by coming close to Hashem through His Torah.

---

3. Yevamot 122b.

The Taste of the Manna

ויאמר משה זה הדבר אשר צוה ה' מלא העמר ממנו למשמרת לדרתיכם
למען יראו את הלחם אשר האכלתי אתכם במדבר בהוציאי אתכם מארץ
מצרים. (שמות טז:לב)

Hashem commanded Moshe to preserve an omer of manna so
that future generations could see the miracle Hashem performed
for Bnei Yisrael in the desert. (*Shemot* 16:32)

Rabbi Shlomo Zevin[1] explains that the manna, as we know it, is the
symbol of livelihood. There are three messages in the manna, he says,
that Hashem wants us to remember for all generations. These messages
are: "Equality, refinement, and taste."

The aspect of equality means that every single person received
exactly what he needed, no more and no less. If one took extra, the sur-
plus would rot. If one didn't gather the right amount, he would still have
exactly the amount he needed. The lesson to us is that a person has to
do *hishtadlut*, but at the end of the day, we all get exactly what we need.

The aspect of refinement means that manna was absorbed into
their bodies in its entirety. Bnei Yisrael never excreted bodily waste from
the manna. It was perfect nutrition. Similarly, our livelihood must be

---

1. *LaTorah VeLaMo'adim*, 119.

clean and pure, with no excess or waste attached. There can be no lying, stealing, or any other unsavory behavior involved in earning a living. Our efforts and results have to be completely pure.

With respect to the third aspect, taste, the manna, as we know it, tasted however the eater wanted it to taste. This teaches us that whatever package Hashem gives us, we can make it taste however we choose. The magic of the manna is realizing that we can make a good package taste bad and a bitter package taste delicious. It's all in our attitude. It's our decision.

The manna laid the foundation upon which we are to view our personal wealth. We need to make the best with what we are allotted, earn an honest living, and appreciate what we have. Only then will we recognize the blessing that is bestowed upon us.

Remembering Amalek

וַיֹּאמֶר כִּי יָד עַל כֵּס קָהּ מִלְחָמָה לַה' בַּעֲמָלֵק מִדֹּר דֹּר. (שמות יז:טז)

And he said, "For there is a hand on the throne of the Eternal, that there shall be a war for Hashem against Amalek from generation to generation." (*Shemot* 17:16)

The Abarbanel asks why Amalek is so unique that there is a special positive mitzva to remember what they did to us. We don't have a similar mitzva regarding any other nation. Is it only because they were the first to attack us? Why are they considered our mortal enemies?

Rabbi Aharon Lewin explains the Abarbanel in his *sefer HaDerash VeHaIyun*.[1] Amalek was unique in that almost every other nation that attacked us was out for Jewish blood. Amalek, however, were anti-Hashem – their anti-Jewish sentiments were secondary to their antagonism toward Hashem. They attacked us only in order to undermine the *emuna* that was flowing through the world immediately following the Splitting of the Sea. The *gematria* of Amalek is *safek* – doubt and uncertainty. Amalek's mission was to instill doubt into the world. Rashi explains that *asher karkha baderekh* means "they chanced upon you on the way." They maintained that everything was chance and happenstance;

---

1. Rav Aharon Lewin, *HaDerash VeHaIyun, Shemot, Parashat Beshallah.*

that even the events in Egypt and at the Reed Sea were natural phenomena and not miracles.

That is why we stand up as we read the *pesukim* of *Parashat Zakhor*. We attest to the fact that we will never forget how they trampled on Hashem's honor. That is the meaning of the words of the *pasuk*: *ki yad al kes Ka* – Hashem's throne (*kes*) and name (*Ka*) will not be complete (*kisei* and YKVK, respectively) until Amalek is totally wiped out and the entire world recognizes Hashem's providence. This will occur when the *Mashiah* arrives and the final battle against Amalek is won.[2]

---

2. See also in this book *Parashat Tetzaveh*, "*Parashat Zakhor* and Remembering Amalek."

Who Fights for Us?

ה׳ ילחם לכם ואתם תחרישון. (שמות יד:יד)

Hashem will fight for you, but you shall remain silent. (*Shemot* 14:14)

Rabbi Bernard Weinberger asks, in *Haggadat Shemen HaTov*,[1] why, at the Splitting of the Sea, Hashem instructed us to remain quiet and told us that He would fight for us, but when it came to the battle against Amalek only a few days later, Bnei Yisrael had to fight and stand up for themselves? What's the difference between these two situations, both of which involved Bnei Yisrael being attacked by another nation? This exact question is part of what bothered Yitro – he couldn't understand this point. This contradiction is what motivated him to go to Bnei Yisrael and search for the truth.

The *Shemen HaTov* answers by differentiating between physical and spiritual dangers. Egypt was a physical danger. The Egyptians wanted to kill us off. When the danger to us is physical, we have to do our *hishtadlut* to protect ourselves, but we also have to realize that ultimately, Hashem is doing the work. That's what happened at the Reed

---

1. Rabbi Bernard Weinberger, *Haggadat Shemen HaTov* (New York, 2014), 252.

Sea. Nahshon went into the sea up to his nose. That was his *hishtadlut* – but then, Hashem did the rest.

When it comes to our fear of Heaven and our spiritual state, we have to fight tooth and nail to protect ourselves. It's *all* in our hands. Hashem is in the background in these situations. It's up to us to fight for our spiritual survival. Amalek wanted to destroy our religion. It was a direct attack on the essence of Hashem. Since Amalek was a spiritual danger to us and a personal attack on Hashem, we had to be at the forefront of the battle to defend ourselves and our creator.

Parashat Yitro

An Appropriate Name
for the *Parasha*

Why is this *parasha* named after Yitro, a Midianite priest? True, he was Moshe's father-in-law, but many other very worthy individuals did not merit having a *parasha* named after them. Moreover, the Torah is given in this *parasha*. Is *Parashat Yitro* the most appropriate and befitting title for the *parasha*?

We offer two explanations: The first focuses on why Yitro deserved to have a *parasha* named after him, and the second explains why it is appropriate for *Parashat Yitro* to be the name of the *parasha* that contains the giving of the Torah.

Rashi, in his explanation of the first *pasuk* in the *parasha*, lists seven names by which Yitro was known. When describing one of the names, Yeter, Rashi explains (*Shemot* 18:1) that it was:

על שם שיתר פרשה אחת בתורה: "ואתה תחזה."

Due to him adding a chapter to the Torah – beginning with *ve'ata tehezeh*.

368

It is a bit strange that Rashi specifically states that the chapter that Yitro added to the Torah begins with *pasuk* 19, *ve'ata tehezeh*. If one looks closely at the text, it becomes apparent that in *pasuk* 14, after Yitro witnesses the process by which Moshe judges the people, he begins a dialog with Moshe, first criticizing the existing process and then offering an alternative solution. So why doesn't Rashi say that the extra section contributed by Yitro starts at *pasuk* 14?

Perhaps we can suggest that Rashi is trying to teach us an important lesson. It is easy to criticize. So often do we witness or experience a situation where we disagree with the way people act or deal with the situation. There is always that person in the back of the *shul* or on the *shul* board that complains and criticizes. Yitro's greatness was that he did not mean to simply critique Moshe in a negative way; he truly wanted to help move things along more efficiently. Yitro not only criticized, but he offered a solution! Rashi highlights this point by crediting Yitro not with his critique (*pasuk* 14) but with his solution (*pasuk* 19).

The *Ohr HaHayim*[1] suggests that the reason this *parasha* was named after Yitro is to highlight to that generation and to the generations that follow that we Jews have much to learn from other nations. There is genius among the nations, and there are some great ideas among those who aren't Jewish. We did not necessarily merit receiving the Torah because we were the smartest nation – an important lesson to learn right before receiving the Torah. As *Hazal* tell us:

אם יאמר לך אדם: יש חכמה בגוים – תאמן... (ואם יאמר לך אדם)
יש תורה בגוים – אל תאמן, דכתיב: "מלכה ושריה בגוים אין תורה".
(מדרש איכה רבה פרשה ב סימן יג)

If a man shall tell you: There is knowledge with gentiles, believe him.... [if he should tell you] there is Torah with gentiles, don't believe him. As it states: Royalty and officers of the gentiles have no Torah. (*Midrash Eikha Rabba* 2:13)

---

1. *Ohr HaHayim Al HaTorah, Shemot* 18:1.

We can believe in the knowledge we obtain from other nations, so long as it does not conflict with the precepts of the Torah. Similarly, in *Pirkei Avot* (4:1), we are taught, "Who is wise? One who learns from all people." Not all Jews, but all *people.*

Yitro taught us to offer solutions, not just criticism, and that we have much to learn from others.

What Did Yitro Hear?

וישמע יתרו כהן מדין חתן משה את כל אשר עשה א-להים למשה
ולישראל עמו כי הוציא ה' את ישראל ממצרים. (שמות יח:א)

Now Moshe's father-in-law, Yitro, the priest of Midian, heard all that God had done for Moshe and for Israel, His people, that Hashem had taken Israel out of Egypt. (*Shemot* 18:1)

Hazal in Zevahim (116a) note a peculiarity in this *pasuk*. It first says that Yitro heard everything that Hashem did for Moshe and the children of Israel, and it then states that he heard that Hashem took Bnei Yisrael out of Egypt. When reading the *pasuk*, it seems as though something is missing, as if Yitro heard something else in addition to the news about the exodus from Egypt. Therefore, Rashi lists two other events that he heard about:

מה שמועה שמע ובא? קריעת ים סוף ומלחמת עמלק.

What did [Yitro] hear about and come [on account of]? The Splitting of the Sea and the battle with Amalek.

The *Ketav Sofer*[1] raises a question on this Rashi: If one were to add these two events into the *pasuk* right after the words "all that God had done …,"

---

1. *Ketav Sofer Al HaTorah*, 112.

the events would be out of chronological order. The exodus from Egypt should come first, followed by the Splitting of the Sea and the war with Amalek. Why, then, is the *pasuk* out of order? Moreover, why did Rashi say, "What did Yitro hear about and come on account of?" That seems slightly verbose. Couldn't he have just written "What did Yitro hear?" What is Rashi trying to emphasize with his choice of words?

The *Ketav Sofer* suggests that many of that generation believed that the ultimate purpose of the plagues was to punish Pharaoh for subjugating Bnei Yisrael. No one assumed that their purpose was to take Bnei Yisrael out of Egypt. While the plagues were happening, they couldn't have proven that their purpose was to get Bnei Yisrael out of Egypt, because they hadn't been let out yet! Thus, the plagues seemed to have been done purely to punish the Egyptians.

This was exactly what Yitro originally thought. He didn't see the plagues as a proof of any special relationship between HaKadosh Barukh Hu and Am Yisrael. However, once he heard about the Splitting of the Sea and the victory against Amalek, when he realized that Hashem had changed nature for the children of Israel, he understood that there is a special relationship between Hashem and Klal Yisrael. He then realized that the plagues, too, were not just about punishing the Egyptians; here, he saw the continuation, that the exodus from Egypt really served an ultimate purpose, a purpose that was all about Klal Yisrael and not about the Egyptians. These two miracles, the Splitting of the Sea and the victory against Amalek, made everyone, including Yitro, realize retroactively that everything from Hashem had been purely for Am Yisrael.

Therefore, the words of Rashi, *ma shemua shama*, specify that Yitro heard about all the events and internalized the true nature of them. He heard about the Splitting of the Sea and the war with Amalek and finally understood that the actions had all been to redeem Bnei Yisrael from Egypt, not just to punish the Egyptians. In truth, we find often in life that we don't fully understand an event in real time, only retrospectively.

We see another example of this at the Seder, in the order in which we say *pesah*, *matza*, and *maror*. If *maror* symbolizes the bitterness of slavery, it should come first, not last! The *Korban Pesah*, symbolizing how Hashem skipped over the houses of Bnei Yisrael during the plague of the death of the firstborn, came later.

The point, though, is that only once we have the *pesah* and the *matza* do we realize the purpose of the *maror* – that the bitter exile was also part of the divine plan. Yitro realized this only after he saw the unique events of the Splitting of the Sea and the war with Amalek. Only then did he appreciate what the exodus from Egypt was really about.

With this understanding, says the *Ketav Sofer*, we can also grasp the intent of a *pasuk* later in the *parasha*.

ויספר משה לחתנו את כל אשר עשה ה׳ לפרעה ולמצרים על אודת
ישראל את כל התלאה אשר מצאתם בדרך ויצלם ה׳. (שמות יח:ח)

Moshe told his father-in-law [about] all that Hashem had done to Pharaoh and to the Egyptians on account of Israel, [and about] all the hardships that had befallen them on the way, and [that] Hashem had saved them. (*Shemot* 18:8)

The *pasuk* tells us that Moshe told Yitro everything that Hashem had done *al odot Yisrael* – "on behalf of Israel." That's the emphasis that Yitro only realized now. Anyone could have heard the events, but Yitro realized what they were all about. Moshe proved that they were all for the benefit of Am Yisrael.

The Meaning of the Names of Moshe's Children

ואת שני בניה אשר שם האחד גרשם כי אמר גר הייתי בארץ נכריה. ושם
האחד אליעזר כי אלקי אבי בעזרי ויצלני מחרב פרעה. (שמות יח:ג ד)

And her two sons, one of whom was named Gershom, because
he [Moshe] said, "I was a stranger in a foreign land." And one
who was named Eliezer, because [Moshe said,] "The God of my
father came to my aid and rescued me from Pharaoh's sword."
(*Shemot* 18:3–4)

Several commentators are puzzled as to why Moshe named his sons outside of the chronological order of the events referenced by the names.
The event for which he named Eliezer (that he was saved from Pharaoh's
sword after he killed an Egyptian) happened before that of Gershom
(he subsequently became a stranger in a foreign land, Midian). As Rav
Moshe Feinstein[1] points out, he should have named his first son Eliezer
and his second son Gershom.

Even stranger is why Moshe would want to memorialize the event
that led to the naming of Gershom at all. Living in a strange land, away

---

1. Rabbi Moshe Feinstein, *Darash Moshe* (New York: Mesorah Publications, 1994), 120.

from Klal Yisrael, and surrounded by temptation ... wouldn't he want to forget that time? Instead, he named his son for it!

In his *Darash Moshe*, Rav Moshe answers with an important principle that applied when Rav Moshe said it decades ago, and it still resonates today.

Moshe, in naming his son Gershom, was thanking Hashem for helping him hold onto his identity in Midian, where he was surrounded by pagans. He was thanking Hashem for helping him retain his feeling of being a *ger*, for not assimilating into those impure surroundings.

Moshe easily could have been elected an official in Midian. He was charismatic, powerful, and smart. But he chose not to assimilate; rather, he stayed separate, an outsider, so he could stay loyal to Hashem and not succumb to the temptations around him.

Therefore, says Rav Moshe, he named his *first* son Gershom. It was only because Moshe maintained his identity and loyalty to Hashem through his sojourn in Midian that he could retroactively thank Hashem for saving him from Pharaoh. Had he been saved from Pharaoh's hand only to succumb to the impurities of Midian, his salvation would have been for naught. Only because he remained apart from everyone in Midian was he able to look back and see that it had been worthwhile to save him; thus, he named his second son Eliezer.

The message is evident to our generation, the generation immediately following the greatest tragedy in the history of the children of Israel, the Holocaust. We have to ask ourselves: Was the salvation of Bnei Yisrael from the Nazis worthwhile? If we are strong in our observance of mitzvot throughout this exile, then the salvation was worthwhile. The test is the generation *after* the tragedy. If we are still loyal to our heritage, then retroactively, we can say the salvation was worthwhile.

Every Day Is the Day
After Yom Kippur

ויהי ממחרת וישב משה לשפט את־העם ויעמד העם על משה מן הבקר
עד הערב. (שמות יח:יג)

It came about on the next day that Moshe sat down to judge the
people, and the people stood before Moshe from the morning
until the evening. (*Shemot* 18:13)

The *pasuk* states that *mimaharat* – "on the next day" – Moshe sat and
judged the nation. Rashi quotes a midrash to explain this word:

מוצאי יום הכיפורים היה כך שנינו בספרי ומהו ממחרת למחרת רדתו
מן ההר.

It was the day after Yom Kippur, that is what was taught in Sifri,
and what is the next day? The day after Moshe descended from
the mountain.

It was the day after Yom Kippur, the day after Moshe descended from
the mountain. Rashi then demonstrates a calculation to prove that

the day that Moshe sat to judge the nation was indeed the day after Yom Kippur.

The Ramban argues with Rashi, saying it could not be the day after Yom Kippur, because the *pasuk* makes no mention of Yom Kippur. Moreover, the Ramban says, the word does not literally mean the next day, but some time later:

> ואין דעתם לומר שיהיה ממחרת רמז ליום הכפורים כי יום הכפורים לא נזכר בכתוב שיאמר עליו ממחרת. וגם כן אין הכונה שיהיה ממחרתו ממש. (רמבן שמות יח:יג)

The intention is not that "the next day" is a hint to Yom Kippur, because Yom Kippur is not referred to in the text as "the next day." In addition, the intention is not literally the next day. (Ramban on *Shemot* 18:13)

If so, how do we understand the midrash that explicitly states that it was the day after Yom Kippur?

Rav Yosef Soloveitchik[1] says that the word *mahar* always serves to connect today with yesterday, either by comparing it or contrasting it, depending on the context.

For example, when the Torah describes what happened with the Spies, it uses the term *mimaharat* the morning after Bnei Yisrael got the decree that they wouldn't be entering *Eretz Yisrael*. When they woke up in the morning, they had a new attitude, a positive one, one of: "No, we will go up." They were wrong, but the word *mahar* in the *pasuk* shows a contrast between their feelings of despair of the previous night and their positive feelings the following morning.

However, *mahar* can also build on yesterday. Yesterday is all but an experience not yet extinguished with the passage of time. Today is a reflection of yesterday.

An example of this parallel would be *mimaharat haShabbat*. The day following Pesah is no ordinary day; rather, it is a continuation of the beauty of the holiday.

---

1. *Humash Masoret HaRav* (New York: OU Press, 2014), 150.

What about the *mimaharat* in our *pasuk*? Explains the Ramban: Moshe lived his life as if every day was the day after Yom Kippur, specifically in judgment, as in the case of our *pasuk*.

What is it about Yom Kippur that could help us understand proper judgment? What kind of attitude and *hashkafa* does a judge need, which we can learn from Yom Kippur and from Moshe Rabbenu? Rav Soloveitchik explains:

> Whenever Moshe sat in judgment, it was the day after Yom Kippur for him. Why? Most *dinei Torah* result not in strict halakhic decisions, but rather in *p'shara*, compromise. Compromise is the ideal legal solution, not strict adherence to legality. After the parties agree to compromise, the judge still exerts authority, as if it were a strict *p'sak*.... The judge is not an arbitrator. He is a *shofet*, judge.... Compromise in Judaism is unique. In other legal systems, the judge may recommend compromise or arbitration. But by doing so, he relinquishes the right to settle the case. In Judaism compromise and strict legality are treated equally.... A double goal is pursued, which strict legality cannot accomplish. In secular courts, one of the parties involved must get hurt...Judaism does not acknowledge the principle of contradiction. Both parties may be right. "Two verses contradict each other till a third one comes and decides between them." The third verse does not say that one of the *pesukim* is wrong. Both are accepted. Judaism may recognize both the thesis and the antithesis as true.... Both participants give up something. This is judgment that is righteous.[2]

Why do most *batei din* try to come to a *peshara*, "compromise," in judgment? *Peshara* is a combination of justice and *tzedaka* – that's the only way to understand how you can have *mishpat* together with *tzedaka*, when *mishpat* means strict judgment. In other legal systems, compromise is not the ultimate; it is considered extra-legal. But when it comes to Judaism, we try to compromise so that there is not one winner and one loser. There isn't one party against the other party. The *shofet*, "judge,"

---

2. Ibid.

is a teacher. He tries to bring opposite elements together, tries to get a little flexibility from both sides in order to come up with a solution that's acceptable to everyone involved. That's what *peshara* does. Neither party comes out thinking they are 100 percent in the right and the other is 100 percent in the wrong. Rather, it serves to bring them together with a just and fair solution.

Similarly, Yom Kippur is about compromise. No one is perfect on Yom Kippur, but we have some good excuses. Life is difficult, and we're human. We have a *yetzer hara* and desires, so we beg HaKadosh Barukh Hu to meet us halfway, to make a *peshara*. "We're doing our best, please make a *peshara*," we beseech. "Compromise with us, help us out."

That is the message of Yom Kippur. Each side gives a little. HaKadosh Barukh Hu doesn't use His attribute of strict judgment in full on Yom Kippur, but He doesn't just let us do what we want, either. Both sides compromise and that's the message of Yom Kippur.

The lesson of *mimaharat* – Moshe took the message of Yom Kippur with him whenever he sat in judgment.

Unknown Intentions

ויאמר יתרו ברוך ה' אשר הציל אתכם מיד מצרים ומיד פרעה אשר
הציל את העם מתחת יד מצרים. עתה ידעתי כי גדול ה' מכל הא-להים
כי בדבר אשר זדו עליהם. (שמות יח:י-יא)

Yitro said, "Blessed is Hashem, Who has rescued you from the
hands of the Egyptians and from the hand of Pharaoh, Who
has rescued the people from beneath the hand of the Egyptians. Now I know that Hashem is greater than all the deities,
for with the thing that they plotted, [He came] upon them."
(*Shemot* 18:10–11)

Yitro came to join Moshe and Bnei Yisrael in the desert, acknowledging and praising Hashem for the tremendous acts He had performed
for them.

What do the last words of pasuk 11 mean: *badavar asher zadu
aleihem*? Rashi explains, based on Onkelos:

במים דמו לאבדם והם נאבדו במים. (רש"י שמות יח:י)

They plotted to destroy Bnei Yisrael through water, and they were
punished through water. (Rashi on *Shemot* 18:10)

Yitro recognized the *midda-keneged-midda* aspect in the way in which the Egyptians were punished. He understood that through the very means with which the Egyptians had attempted to destroy the children of Israel, they themselves were killed. The Egyptians had intended to drown the savior of the children of Israel, to destroy them through water, and the Egyptians were ultimately punished by being drowned in water.

Taking Rashi's definition a little further, Onkelos adds that Hashem paid the Egyptians back for every *thought* they had to harm the children of Israel, even if the plan wasn't carried out. Yitro was amazed when he saw that Hashem paid back the Egyptians not only for what they did but also for what they *wanted* to do to the children of Israel.

The Brisker Rav[1] asks: How could Yitro know the Egyptians' *thoughts?* How did he know they had certain plans if they never came to fruition? Only someone who had been part of the planning process and advisory board would know what the Egyptians had thought of and planned, answers the Brisker Rav. And as we know from *Hazal* (Sota 11a):

שלשה היו באותה עצה בלעם איוב ויתרו.

Three were present when that advice was offered: Bilaam, Iyov, and Yitro.

Yitro was on the inside. He was one of Pharaoh's advisors at the meeting for the Final Solution. Yitro knew exactly what had been planned, and so he was able to say this praise of HaKadosh Barukh Hu.

---

1. Rav Yitzhak Zeev Soloveitchik, *Griz Al HaTorah* (Jerusalem, 1981), 17.

Parallels within the Ten Commandments

There is a tradition mentioned by the *Me'iri* that parallels the two halves of the *luhot*, i.e., pairing the commandments written on the right side of the *luhot* with those on the left side – one with six, two with seven, three with eight, etc.

The first set is commandments one and six: "I am the Lord" is congruent with "Don't kill."

Belief in HaKadosh Barukh Hu is the opposite of murder. Someone who denies God and pushes God out of the picture is, as it were, killing Him. *Hazal* actually describe the builders of the Tower of Bavel as murderers because they denied Hashem's existence. One can also suggest that the act of murder is equivalent to not recognizing the image of God in the victim.

The second parallel is between the second and seventh commandments: "Don't have another God" is congruent with "Don't commit adultery."

Idolatry may be equated with adultery. Throughout *Tanakh*, whenever Klal Yisrael strayed from Hashem, their act was described by the Torah as promiscuity and adultery, acts of straying from one's designated partner.

The fourth and ninth commandments are paired: "Remembering the Shabbat" is congruent with "Don't be a false witness."

Keeping Shabbat corresponds to not providing false testimony, because that is precisely what Shabbat is all about – a testimony that Hashem created the world. We recite Kiddush on Shabbat to attest that Hashem created the world.

The last set, the fifth and tenth commandments, are: "Honor your parents" is congruent with "Don't covet."

Honoring one's parents parallels coveting because coveting is a focus on oneself, it is self-centeredness, while honoring parents is a recognition that one is not the center of everything. It is the acknowledgment that there is someone to whom I owe appreciation for my very existence.

The most challenging one to explain is the parallel between the third and eighth commandments: "Don't use God's name in vain" is congruent with "Don't steal."

What exactly is the connection between not using Hashem's name in vain and stealing?

The *Me'iri*[1] suggests two ideas. The simple *peshat* is that stealing could easily lead to denying the act and swearing falsely in court about it. A deeper explanation, suggested by the *Me'iri* is to define the word *tisa* as "bear" or "carry." *Lo tisa*, he explains, can be interpreted as "Don't wear/bear/carry God's name in vain," i.e., don't dress and act on the outside like a righteous person, but then act in a manner that isn't appropriate for such a person.

As the *Me'iri* states:

שלא מתעטף בטליתך והולך וגונב שלא תהא מניח תפילין והולך ומרמה את הבריות שזהו נשיאת שמו של הקב"ה לשוא.

Don't wrap yourself in a *tallit* and go and steal; don't wrap yourself in *tefillin* and go and trick the masses, for that is carrying God's name in vain.[2]

---

1. *Me'iri* in his introduction to the Talmud.
2. Ibid.

If I look like a *frum* person on the outside, but I behave in a manner that does not befit a righteous individual, I am transgressing the prohibition of stealing people's knowledge. I am misleading people, "stealing" a positive opinion. This is the connection between not utilizing Hashem's name in vain and stealing.

The Abarbanel[3] raises a fascinating question about the structure of the Ten Commandments. It is known that the first five are considered *bein adam laMakom*, while the last five are commandments *bein adam lahaveiro*. Why is it necessary to list five commandments *bein adam lahaveiro*? Why did the Torah not just command us right here to love our neighbor as we love ourselves? Wouldn't this include all five prohibitions – not to murder, commit adultery, steal, lie, or covet?

The Abarbanel offers an insightful answer that portrays the depth of the Torah. The last five commandments are to teach us in the most comprehensive and all-encompassing way how to act toward one another.

Do not murder. The greatest harm one can cause to another is to end their life. In fact, Rav Saadia Gaon explains that all 613 commandments can be found within the Ten Commandments. Viewing this commandment as a broader category, it would encompass any harm caused to another person.

Do not commit adultery. *Hazal* teach us that the relationship between husband and wife is the closest human relationship. In fact, they go so far as to state *baal ke'ishto* and *ishto kegufo* – husband and wife share an identity. They are like one person. If the greatest harm you can cause to another is by causing them physical harm, the second greatest harm you can cause is taking someone's spouse.

Do not steal. *Hazal* interpret this commandment to refer to kidnapping. After one's spouse, a child is one's most cherished possession. From a broader perspective, it would also include taking another's physical possessions.

Do not lie. After causing physical harm, taking one's closest companion, taking one's children or physical possessions, the next level of harm is caused verbally. By falsely accusing someone, or, in a broader

---

3. Abarbanel, *Shemot* 20:12.

sense, speaking evil about another can cause them great pain and suffering.

Do not covet. Even just thinking negatively about another, by being jealous of them, will lead one to act differently to that individual.

We see that the Torah specifically selected these five commandments in descending order to highlight the five major categories whereby one can harm another and to ensure that we refrain from inflicting such harm on others. Once we understand the Abarbanel's interpretation, we see the depth of the Torah. Only Hashem could have considered this when selecting the five commandments *bein adam lahaveiro* so they would be all encompassing.

How to Overcome Jealousy

לא תחמד בית רעך לא תחמד אשת רעך ועבדו ואמתו ושורו וחמרו
וכל אשר לרעך. (שמות כ:יד)

You shall not covet your neighbor's house. You shall not covet
your neighbor's wife, his manservant, his maidservant, his ox, his
donkey, or whatever belongs to your neighbor. (*Shemot* 20:14)

How could God command us not to covet, a feeling in our heart that
seems impossible to prevent? To a certain extent, I can control carrying out my feelings and refrain from stealing or lying. But to prevent
myself from feeling jealous? How can one control thoughts of jealousy
that enter one's mind? It's so easy and natural to see something and
desire it.

Ibn Ezra[1] offers a *mashal* of a princess who is passing through
the countryside while on a journey. Would a simple villager ever think,
"I wish I could marry the princess"? Such a thought would never occur
to him, because it is so unrealistic. Similarly, a human would never be
jealous of a bird's wings and dream of having a set of his own.

That's how we have to view our lives. We are like the villager and
the other person is like the princess. They are untouchable. We each

---

1. *Ibn Ezra* 20:14.

have exactly what we are meant to have, and it's not realistic to think something belonging to someone else should be mine.

Rav Eliyahu Dessler[2] comments that one would never look at a friend and wish he had the other's eye prescription. It's understood that those are his eyes, and these are mine, and it's not realistic to think any other way. That is how we need to view our lives and everything we have. We have to focus on reality and internalize that Hashem has given us what is best for us.

An alternative explanation is provided by Rabbi Yaakov Greenboim in his book *Lehitaneg BeTaanugim*.[3] The *pasuk* does not just tell us not to covet in general; rather, it lists specific items with respect to which we should not covet: We should not covet a neighbor's house, wife, housekeeper, animals, etc. It then concludes with an all-encompassing phrase: "and all of your friend's possessions." Why, then, did the Torah need to specify particular items? The all-encompassing phrase of "all of his possessions" would suffice to include the prohibition of coveting in its totality.

Rabbi Galinsky answers this question and explains that when we desire something that belongs to someone else, we focus only on the item we want. However, the Torah here is teaching us that when we look at someone else, we can't just pay attention to the one item we want. We have to realize that that item is part of a package deal.

My friend in *shul* may have a luxury home, but he has a draining job, difficult kids, and a very sticky family situation. If you covet what your neighbor has, you want to be like him – you cannot cherry pick, you have to look at the entire picture. Maybe he has challenges that you would not want. When Hashem created us, He tailor-made our package to fit us as individuals, and our friend's package won't suit us.

How do we conquer our coveting? By focusing on every single thing that a person has and realizing that we wouldn't do very well with the entire package. We must internalize that Hashem has a whole package and plan for each of us. Once we're happy with all the details of our package, we'll be able to conquer any feelings of jealousy toward others.

---

2. *Mikhtav Me'Eliyahu*, vol. 1 (Jerusalem, 1991), 136.
3. Rabbi Yaakov Greenboim, *Lehitaneg BeTaanugim* (Jerusalem, 2013), 230.

The Method of Transmission Is of Utmost Importance

ומשה עלה אל האלקים ויקרא אליו ה' מן ההר לאמר כה תאמר לבית
יעקב ותגיד לבני ישראל. (שמות יט:ג)

Moshe ascended to God, and Hashem called to him from the mountain, saying, "So shall you say to the house of Yaakov and tell the sons of Israel." (*Shemot* 19:3)

Rashi points out the double wording of the *pasuk* used to describe a statement being made – *tomar* and *tageid*:

לבית יעקב: אלו הנשים תאמר להן בלשון רכה. ותגיד לבני ישראל:
עונשין ודקדוקין פרש לזכרים, דברים הקשין כגידין.

"To the house of Yaakov" (*Beit Yaakov*): these are the women – to them, speak softly. "And tell the sons of Israel": explain to the men the details of punishment, the harsh items.

Rashi explains that there are two ways of speaking here – gently and harshly.

Rav Shlomo Wolbe[1] expounds on this idea and delivers the message of Rashi: It's not about what you know, but how you transmit it. In other words, one must know how to present Torah, how to express it to others, in order to deliver a message properly.

Having the ideas and the knowledge is the first step. But the most important part is knowing how to express them. Sometimes we have to give over a message in a gentle manner and at other times, in a harsher manner. It depends on the venue, the audience, and the time. Imparting a message is itself a skill that may even be greater than the knowledge itself.

Rabbi Mordechai Gifter notes that the Gemara talks about Hillel's eighty students (Sukka 28a). It divides them into thirty great ones who could have been like Moshe Rabbenu, thirty like Yehoshua bin Nun, and the final twenty as *beinonim* – "those who are in between." The greatest of the *beinonim* was Yonatan ben Uziel, who was so great that any bird that flew over his head became scorched.[2] The "smallest" of the *beinonim* was Yohanan ben Zakkai, whom the Gemara describes as knowing just about everything!

Who led Klal Yisrael? Who was the *gadol hador*? Rabbi Yohanan ben Zakkai, the "smallest" of them all. He was the one who saved Klal Yisrael during the Hurban, who instituted nine enactments commemorating the *Beit HaMikdash*. Why was he the leader if he was the "smallest"? Rabbi Gifter[3] explains that it is for this exact reason: It is not about what we know. If one does not know how to give over a message in the right manner, if one does not know how to give over Torah like it is sweet as honey and delicious, then one can't be a *gadol*. As much as one must know, he must have the skill to package it in a beautiful delivery. Rabbi Yohanan ben Zakkai was the greatest transmitter of Torah in that generation.

---

1. Rav Shlomo Wolbe, *Shiurei Humash* (Jerusalem, 2009), 150.
2. See Rashi and *Tosafot* on Sukka 28a for a fascinating argument with respect to this fire.
3. *Pirkei Torah* (Wickliffe, OH, 1992).

Rav Wolbe adds a thought from Rabbi Daniel of Kelm, who comments on a cryptic phrase penned by the Rosh. The Rosh says that one should talk Torah at the table. Rabbi Daniel wonders what the innovation is here; one must talk in Torah wherever one is, always! He answers that the innovation is knowing *how* to tell a *vort* in such a way that it will inspire the listeners. If that is not the goal, the *devar Torah* is pointless. The speaker must understand the audience and be on the same wavelength as him in order for his message to hit home.

Similarly, the Me'iri on the first mishna in *Pirkei Avot* explains the phrase "make a fence around the Torah" to refer not to setting boundaries or *gezerot* – a "safer" Torah, as many interpret the phrase – but to knowing and being careful to address the crowd to whom one is delivering a *devar Torah*. One must set boundaries when speaking Torah – do not speak too long, and do not speak above the people or beneath them. One must be careful to address the crowd properly so as to achieve the greatest impact. "Make a fence around the Torah" means making sure that the Torah is within the grasp of the people. It is not enough to gather the knowledge. The mode of transmission of the material is crucial in order to inspire others.

Tu BiShevat: Man Is Compared to a Tree

כי האדם עץ השדה. (דברים כ:יט)

Man is like the tree in the field. (*Devarim* 20:19)

The Torah compares man to a tree. In what way? How are they analogous?

First, halakhically speaking, what is the difference between a tree and vegetable? The difference is that a tree lives throughout the year even though it produces fruit only during one season, whereas when a vegetable it is not in season and producing, it dies. An apple tree is always alive, even though it only produces apples in its season. A potato patch, by contrast, is dead when it is not in season, and a banana plant is completely dried out when it's out of season. The number-one attribute of a tree is that it is always alive, even though it only sometimes bears fruit.

Second, a tree functions against gravity. A tree grows upward, and nutrients flow upward from the roots into the branches.

What is the message of these two concepts?

Rabbi Eliyahu Schlesinger[1] explains that a Jew is compared to a tree because he is always alive. He always has the strength of growth – to

---

1. Rabbi Eliyahu Shlesinger, *Eileh Hem Mo'adai* (Jerusalem, 1999), 307.

produce, to bear fruit. Even when it is winter, when it feels like we aren't producing anything, we are still alive and performing. The potential is always alive within us. Sometimes we have to go against the grain and defy gravity. We may have to push against the entire world, which is trying to force us to conform. A Jew has to stand on the other side, all alone, like *Avraham HaIvri*. Defying gravity, we have to push up and use the power Hashem gave us to stand up for our principles.

Tu BiShevat always falls out in the winter months, when it's hard for us to imagine the spring. It falls out during the cold and dreary winter months because that is its message: to remember that the *ko'ah* is inside of us even when we can't see it or feel it. It is always present, and we must capitalize on it.

Rabbi Schlesinger cites the Hida who suggests additional comparisons between trees and people. First, a tree bears fruit according to the level of work and care put into it. The more you water the tree and care for it, the greater your yields will be. So too a person – the more we focus on ourselves and our spiritual pursuits, the more we invest in ourselves and our quest for growth, the greater fruit we will bear. Our success will be evident in our yields.

Also, a tree bears fruit every single year and never takes a break. Similarly, as Jews we can never take a break from the Torah and mitzvot.

Another comparison is the common need for water. A tree needs water in order to survive and thrive. Without water, it would die. And, as we know, Torah is compared to water. A person can't survive without water or Torah.

Additionally, says the Hida, just like a tree needs the right amount of water to survive, and all other environmental elements have to be appropriate for it to thrive, man must ensure that his whole environment is proper and appropriate for his growth and spiritual well-being.

Another similarity is that a tree is always looking toward the sun, which helps it grow. So, too, man needs a *rav* who shines light on the correct path, so he knows the correct way to go.

Finally, says the Hida, a tree needs air to grow, and a person needs the correct atmosphere to grow. One needs a *beit midrash* in which to learn, a proper environment for his Torah study to thrive.

When we think of Tu BiShevat, Rosh HaShana for the trees, we should also contemplate and internalize its meaning for us and our personal growth.

Parashat Mishpatim

Ethics Derived from the Torah

ואלה המשפטים אשר תשים לפניהם. (שמות כא:א)

And these are the ordinances that you shall set before them.
(*Shemot* 21:1)

Rashi comments on the first word of this *parasha*, noting that the letter
vav usually signifies a connection to the preceding topic. In this case,
however, what could possibly be the connection between receiving the
Torah at Sinai (the ending of the previous *parasha*, *Parashat Yitro*) and
the intricate laws of interpersonal relationships (*Parashat Mishpatim*)?
Rashi suggests that just as the Ten Commandments in the previous *parasha* were transmitted at Mount Sinai, so too, the laws of interpersonal
relationships and damages were transmitted at Mount Sinai.

Rabbi Shlomo Zevin[1] explains that this one letter, which symbolizes a connection between the two topics, emphasizes the completely
different outlook on interpersonal relationships that we as Jews have
versus that of the rest of the nations. Every nation has laws regarding

---

1. *LaTorah VeLaMo'adim*, 130.

interpersonal behavior. The difference between their laws and ours is one tiny letter, the *vav*. This *vav* at the beginning of the *parasha* is the secret to it all.

Our interpersonal laws are not man-made and are not just for the betterment of society. Rather, our laws regarding how we treat other people are dictated directly from HaKadosh Barukh Hu, just like the rest of our Torah that was transmitted at Mount Sinai. The laws of all the other nations are based on humanly decided morals and ethics, focused on keeping society intact. Without any such laws, society wouldn't be able to survive. Without a government, there is pandemonium.

Our laws, however, source from Mount Sinai and were not created based on human logic. A man-made law does not withstand a change of attitude among the people. When man makes the law, man can amend and revise the law. If one so desires, he can conjure any excuse to defend a heinous crime. This is exactly what occurred throughout our history of suffering through pogroms, Crusades, and the Holocaust, which all circumvented the basic ethics of not murdering. When a person decides to engage in inhumane acts, he begins to rationalize and then justify such immoral activity.

Our laws, however, don't stem from our logic. Rather, they come directly from Hashem and thus can't be compromised.

That's the message of the one little letter that starts off our *parasha*. The nitty-gritty details of every law mentioned in *Parashat Mishpatim* are as God-given as the Ten Commandments.[2]

The *Bnei Yissaskhar*, in his *sefer* on Humash, *Igra DeKallah*, offers another explanation as to why the *parasha* begins with a *vav*. A person might view the laws of *Parashat Mishpatim* as irrelevant to him, because he has no desire to be a judge. This attitude is wrong. The *Bnei Yissaskhar* explains that when *Hazal* stipulate in *Pirkei Avot* that one should avoid being a judge, they refer only to someone who *could* be a judge, someone who knows every nitty-gritty detail of halakha (4:9). If in that situation,

---

2. See earlier in this book, *Parashat Vayera*, "Ethics from Sinai," for the explanation of Rav Ovadia of Bartenura as to the location of the introduction to *Pirkei Avot* listing the chain of the tradition from Moshe to the Men of the Great Assembly, highlighting that ethics were transmitted from Mount Sinai.

he is not strict on his honor and allows someone else to be the judge, it is praiseworthy.

But for us laypeople, who will probably never function as a *dayan*, we are just as obligated to know every single detail of *kol haTorah kula*. The point of Torah isn't just to know what to do in a specific case, but even what to do in a hypothetical case, because that's what brings us closer to HaKadosh Barukh Hu. The more we understand the inner workings of the Torah, the closer we get to Him.

This brings us back to our question. The connection of *Parashat Mishpatim* to *Parashat Yitro* is that just like everyone understands the greatness of the Ten Commandments and studies them, so too should we be studying every detail of the laws listed in *Parashat Mishpatim*. Just like it would be unfathomable for people not to study the Ten Commandments, it should be the same regarding *Parashat Mishpatim*. We are all obligated to learn it in depth even if we will never serve as judges.[3]

---

3. This is even a step further than the Hafetz Hayim's recommendation to study *Kodashim* and *Teharot*. He strongly supported learning these tractates because they will *become* practical when *Mashiah* arrives.

The Secret to Becoming a *Hasid*

The Slonimer Rebbe[1] cites a gemara in Bava Kama that discusses the attributes of a *hasid*, "pious man":

> Rav Yehuda tells us, "He who wants to be a *hasid* should focus on the laws and details of *nezikin* (damages)." Rava disagrees; he says one should focus on *Pirkei Avot*. The third opinion is that one should study *berakhot*.[2]

The Slonimer Rebbe questions the hypothesis of this gemara: Why does studying the laws of damages make someone a *hasid*? I can understand the opinions of studying *Pirkei Avot*, which focuses on *middot*, or *berakhot*. That obviously reflects *hasidut*. But what does *nezikin* have to do with *hasidut*?

The Slonimer Rebbe explains that there are four root categories of *avot nezikin* under which an act of damage can fall, and these are

---

1. Rav Shalom Noach Berezovsky, *Netivot Shalom, Shemot*, 176.
2. Bava Kama 30a.

symbolic of the four roots of all sin in the world. These four categories are: *shor* (ox), *bor* (pit), *maveh* (tooth), and *hever* (fire).

The first type, damage caused by an ox, symbolizes problematic behavior, outright sins. The next, a pit, symbolizes the act of falling into despair. When one views himself as a nobody, he can easily fall into a pit of despair, which leads to transgression. The third category is the tooth, which symbolizes the transgression of consuming forbidden foods and sins in the area of *berakhot*. The final root, fire, symbolizes physical desires that are like the *yetzer hara* burning within us. Every sin falls into one of these categories. Therefore, when Rav Yehuda states that one who wants to become a *hasid* has to study the area of damages, he refers to these four roots of sin.

The Gemara uses the term *hasid*. It doesn't state "Who wants to *do a hesed?*" Rather, it says, "Who wants to *be a hasid?*" A *hasid* is one who is defined by his *hesed*. Anyone can perform an act of *hesed*, but it takes a special person to *be* a *hasid*.

Ultimately, the goal is to have the *hesed* turn us into a *hasid*. Avraham was pained when he didn't have guests because he didn't just perform *hesed*; rather, he was a *hasid*. He was in more pain from not having guests than he was from the *brit mila*. That is someone who is a *hasid*, not just someone who performs *hesed*. Avraham is personified by his *hesed* and that is what transforms him into a *hasid*.

Therefore, explains the Slonimer Rebbe, these three *Amora'im* are teaching us the secret to becoming a *hasid*: one cannot just perform acts. Rather, his root has to be good. They are telling us the strategy to follow to become pious.

The Maharsha (Bava Kama 30a) teaches us that there are three areas in *avodat Hashem*, which correspond to the three different opinions in the above gemara: *bein adam laMakom* (Berakhot), *bein adam lahaveiro* (nezikin), and *bein adam le'atzmo* (Pirkei Avot). When one has perfected himself in these three areas, he will be the ultimate halakhic personality and the pious person he was aiming to be.

Perfecting one's *bein adam lahaveiro* in a manner of *middat hasidut* wouldn't mean repaying a friend for harm he caused – that would be the very least demanded of him. Rather, a *hasid* is careful to prevent such harm from occurring in the first place. *Middat hasidut* comes from a strong recognition of other people's property that ensures that one is never even indirectly involved in a way that will negatively affect his neighbor. *Hasidut* means thinking about consequences and then avoiding behavior that would lead to such results. For example, people used to hide their dangerous items deep in the ground so that others wouldn't be damaged by them. They could easily have said, "Hey, it's your problem you got hurt; what were you doing in my field?" However, their *middat hasidut* dictated that they prevent such harm from occurring, however wrong the culprit would be.

When it comes to *bein adam le'atzmo*, *Pirkei Avot* is the guide for how to work on our *middot* and personality. From *Pirkei Avot*, we learn to perform mitzvot for the right reason not to gain honor or respect. *Pirkei Avot* is a manual for how to work on ourselves. If one doesn't focus on this area of self-perfection, he will be sorely lacking.

The third opinion, to study *berakhot*, is obviously the area of *bein adam laMakom*. When one internalizes what *berakhot* is all about, he will bring himself to great heights. We need to understand that it's not just about saying a *berakha*, but it's about recognizing that everything we have is from Hashem. We say *berakhot* throughout our day in order to remind ourselves of this point. The *Hakhamim* established so many *berakhot* of praise (after using the bathroom; upon hearing thunder and seeing lightning; after eating, etc.), so we are constantly reminded about Hashem throughout the course of our day.[3]

We can now understand that contained within *Parashat Mishpatim* are the keys to perfecting ourselves in these three areas of *avodat Hashem*.

---

3. See Rambam at the beginning of *Hilkhot Berakhot* where he suggests that reciting blessings is a way in which we can constantly show our recognition of and appreciation to Hashem.

Modern Applications of Torah Concepts

In this week's *parasha*, we have the halakha regarding a pit that is dug and then results in harm to another person. The *pasuk* states:

וכי יפתח איש בור או כי־יכרה איש בר ולא יכסנו ונפל שמה שור או
חמור... (שמות כא:לג)

> And if a person opens a pit or if a person digs a pit and does not cover it, and a bull or a donkey falls into it… (*Shemot* 21:33)

When we read this halakha, we wonder at its relevance to us; after all, most of us don't dig pits! Rav Shlomo Zalman Auerbach, how-ever, applies this concept to a more frequent and relevant scenario. He teaches us that all halakha is alive and that we just need to understand how to apply it properly. Rav Avigdor Nebenzahl[1] writes that he once heard Rav Shlomo Zalman base a halakhic ruling on the *pasuk* cited above. In the not-so-distant past, many dry goods were bought from big, open sacks. Things didn't come individually wrapped in labeled bags. There were giant sacks of goods; you dug your spoon in, weighed

---

1. *Sihot LeYom HaKippurim* (Jerusalem, 2004), 208.

your pick, and paid for it. Once, a storekeeper made a mistake and gave a customer salt instead of sugar. She cooked everything with this salt and realized afterward that all her food was ruined from the salt. The woman demanded the merchant pay for all the damaged food due to his mistake. The merchant was willing to return the cost of the salt and provide her with the sugar she requested, but did not believe he should be liable for all the indirect damages that had occurred due to his inadvertent error.

The question was brought before Rav Shlomo Zalman, who ruled that the storekeeper was responsible for all the damage caused, based on a gemara about a *bor hamitgalgel*. The Gemara teaches that if one leaves a dangerous item in the street and it gets kicked around and then someone gets hurt by it in a different spot than where the item was originally left, the person who initially placed the object in the public arena is responsible. Rav Shlomo Zalman learned from this that the situation with the storekeeper was a *bor hamitgalgel*: he performed an act of damage that caused harm in a different location.

Rav Nebenzahl comments that if you look only at the surface story, you can wonder what each of these scenarios has to do with the other or with reality. The storekeeper didn't sell a *bor*! But Rav Shlomo Zalman was able to read these foundations in the Torah and then apply them to real life. Many of the laws of *Parashat Mishpatim* may at first seem irrelevant, as we don't often deal with oxen, fires, and pits, yet they may be applied in a modern context and are very relevant even in our modern society.

Another example of an application of the halakhot of a *bor* that may not seem obvious comes from Rav Yitzhak Zilberstein:[2] An individual parked in an illegal spot, and when a bus tried to pass by, it damaged the car and the bus. The question arose as to who was responsible to pay for the damages.

The Gemara in Bava Kama 27b discusses this scenario. If a person leaves something in a public place, and then someone trips on it, who is responsible? One of the opinions holds that the one who damaged the object that was in the public property is exempt from paying for the damage he caused. The person is not held responsible, because it is

---

2. *Hashukei Hemed*, Bava Kama 27b.

not expected of anyone to look around everywhere while he's walking to make sure nothing is in his way.

Rav Zilberstein applied that concept to our case. The car was left in a way that disturbs other drivers, so the bus driver was exempt from liability. We can't expect the driver to be so careful if the car was in the way and the space was very tight.

We have to realize that every action we take in a public place has a domino effect, and we have to be very careful not to harm other people. Any time we even slightly disturb other people, our little action could have great ramifications. For example, blocking a street doesn't just annoy drivers, it can rack up an expensive bill for someone sitting in a cab waiting for the traffic to clear; it can cause financial damage to someone who will be late to their destination. We have to keep in mind that even in instances where ultimately the one who caused damage is exempt, that person still performed an act that is forbidden, and we must be careful to avoid such circumstances. We should act like a *hasid* and consider the potential impact our actions may have on others before we engage in a seemingly minor violation.

Appreciation, Even
After Wrongdoing

ואנשי קדש תהיון לי ובשר בשדה טרפה לא תאכלו לכלב תשלכון
אתו. (שמות כב:ל)

And you shall be holy people to Me, and flesh torn in the field
you shall not eat; you shall throw it to the dog[s]. (*Shemot* 22:30)

Rashi explains that *anshei kodesh*, "holy people," are people who don't
eat *neveilot* – "carcasses of kosher animals that did not have appropriate
shehita" and *treifot* – "animals that were slaughtered properly but were
discovered to have a mortal condition." The Torah commands us to
throw the meat of *neveilot* and *treifot* to the dogs. Rashi notes that this
is the reward of the dogs for not barking as we left Mitzrayim.

The *Daat Zekeinim*[1] also asks why the Torah specifies dogs, and
not other animal recepients. The scenario the *Daat Zekeinim* suggests is
that of a shepherd's guard dog, which failed to save a sheep from attack.
In this *pasuk*, the Torah commands us to provide this *neveila* to the guard
dog. Why, in this situation, should the shepherd reward the guard dog
for failing at its job? The Torah here is teaching us the *midda* of *hakarat*

---

1. *Shemot* 22:30.

hatov. Just because the dog messed up one time, this shouldn't mean that we ignore all the times that it served its master loyally. Hashem specifically wants the shepherd to reward the dog at that point so that he is not a denier of the goodness done to him. Keep everything in perspective, says the Torah.

We might skim over this *pasuk*, regarding it as hardly relevant. However, we have to focus on it and apply the lesson to our lives. If someone commits a wrongdoing to us one day, we shouldn't suddenly forget all the good that they did for us until that point or what they will continue to do for us in the future. If this idea applies to animals, *kal vahomer*, it applies to people.

The Gemara at the end of the first *perek* in Sota says that the Torah begins and ends with *hesed*.[2] It ends with HaKadosh Barukh Hu burying Moshe Rabbenu. We would think that the first act of *hesed* was the creation of the world itself, the ultimate act of *hesed*. And yet, that is not the example given by the Gemara: "And Hashem made for Adam and for his wife shirts of skin, and He dressed them" (*Bereshit* 3:21).

Hashem clothed Adam and Chava. Why is this the example used, and not creation? To answer this question, we have to look at the context of this *pasuk*. First, Adam and Chava sinned, then they were punished, and then Adam named his wife Chava. Right after that, Hashem clothed them. What is the deeper meaning of these *pesukim*?

The commentaries explain that since Adam's reaction *could have been* "Look what you caused – you brought death into the world!" However, instead, he forgave his wife. Adam was able to keep things in perspective, to see beyond the moment and acknowledge that Chava was the mother of mankind, despite her sin. Right after Adam acted in that compassionate and forgiving manner, Hashem did the same by providing them with clothes. Hashem could have said that their embarrassment at their nakedness was their just deserts for sinning. He instead was forgiving to Adam, just as Adam had been to Chava. This is not just *hesed*; it's *hesed* after being wronged. That's why the Gemara emphasized this example; it magnified a *hesed* that seems insignificant.

---

2. Sota 14a.

The Torah commands the shepherd to give the *treifot* to the dog because the dog did so much for him and will continue to do so. The Torah teaches us to ignore one misdeed and instead focus on the good. This lesson applies to all of our relationships, especially within our homes and offices.

Controlling Desires: A Step toward Holiness

ואנשי קדש תהיון לי ובשר בשדה טרפה לא תאכלו לכלב תשלכון
אתו. (שמות כב:ל)

And you shall be holy people to Me, and flesh torn in the field
you shall not eat; you shall throw it to the dog[s]. (*Shemot* 22:30)

What does being holy have to do with not eating *treifot* and *neveilot*?
Rabbi Mordekhai Eliyahu, in *Divrei Mordekhai*,[1] quotes Rashi to explain
the connection between the first and second parts of the *pasuk*. Rashi
says: "If you are holy and abstain from *neveilot* and *treifot*, you are Mine."

Rabbi Eliyahu asks what was so amazing about what the dogs
did at the exodus from Egypt that forevermore we reward them with
our nonkosher meat? The dogs would have barked if Hashem hadn't
stopped them. Why do they deserve reward? Also, why is the litmus
test for deciding if something is considered *hametz* on Pesah based on
whether it is fit for a dog's consumption? Why specifically a dog?

Rabbi Eliyahu explains that we can learn a few things from the
dogs. First, the dog teaches us that we can control our natural inclinations

---

1.   Rabbi Mordekhai Eliyahu, *Divrei Mordekhai* (Jerusalem: Dorot), 175.

and desires. Hashem told them not to bark, so they didn't. That is what Bnei Yisrael saw as they were becoming a nation. As they were about to become a free people, they needed the message that they could control their natural tendencies. To be holy people, they had to learn this *midda*, which the dogs taught them. The lesson is that not everything that comes naturally is appropriate or divinely blessed. There are many types of desires we may experience, but we must control ourselves.

We learn this same idea from a midrash on the *pasuk* in *Tehillim*: "The sea saw and it fled." What did the sea see? It saw the coffin of Yosef and went against its natural tendency and ran backward. Where did it get that power from? The sea saw Yosef, who was able to overcome the natural desire of a human being and control himself, and thus the sea was able to overcome its nature. Being a holy nation means knowing how to control ourselves and knowing what is appropriate or not for us.

Perhaps that is why dogs are the yardstick for *kashrut* on Pesah: A dog is the symbol for us of being able to suppress inappropriate behavior.

The Proper Time for Sukkot

וחג הקציר בכורי מעשיך אשר תזרע בשדה וחג האסף בצאת השנה
באספך את מעשיך מן השדה. (שמות כג:טז)

And the festival of the harvest, the first fruits of your labors, which you will sow in the field, and the festival of the ingathering at the departure of the year, when you gather in [the products of] your labors from the field. (*Shemot* 23:16)

The *Meshekh Hokhma* asks why Sukkot is not referenced by name in this *pasuk* and is instead referred to as *hag ha'asif* – "a festival of gathering."[1]

He suggests an idea based on the Vilna Gaon, who notes the opinion of the *Tur*. The *Tur* writes that the reason we have Sukkot in Tishrei instead of Nisan is because we want it to be clearly recognizable that we're sitting in the sukka because we were commanded to do so, and not for pleasure. If we celebrated Sukkot in the spring, people would think that we keep the *yom tov* because it's beautiful outside. In the fall, however, it's cold out, and yet we move outside for a week. This way, people recognize that it's *leshem mitzva* and not for our personal pleasure.

---

1. In *Parashat Emor,* the holiday is referred to as *hag hasukkot.*

The Vilna Gaon offers a different explanation. He explains in his commentary on *Shir HaShirim* that if you do the math, Moshe remained on Mount Sinai for 120 days – three sets of forty days. The first time he went up was the seventh day of Sivan, and he came down on the seventeenth of Tammuz, at which point he broke the *luhot*. Then, he went back up on the eighteenth of Tammuz and returned on *Erev Rosh Hodesh Elul*, when he told Bnei Yisrael that they had been forgiven. The final time he went up was on *Rosh Hodesh Elul*, and he returned on Yom Kippur with the second set of *luhot*.

At that point, on the following day, Moshe announced the building of the *Mishkan* and requested that people bring in donations. On the twelfth and thirteenth of the month, they collected donations from the people. On the fourteenth day of Tishrei, they began to build the *Mishkan*, and on the fifteenth day, the Clouds of Glory returned. The clouds that had disappeared at the time of the sin of the Golden Calf returned with the building of the *Mishkan*, and *that* is why we celebrate Sukkot on the fifteenth of Tishrei. It is not that we moved Sukkot from the spring to the fall. The actual Clouds of Glory surrounded us in the desert beginning on the fifteenth of Tishrei – which is why we celebrate Sukkot specifically on that day!

The *Meshekh Hokhma*[2] adds an unbelievable suggestion to this argument: Maybe the *yom tov* of Sukkot didn't even exist before the sin of the Golden Calf. There was a *hag ha'asif*, but there may not have had the mitzva of sukka, and that is why the Torah only refers to the *hag ha'asif* in *Parashat Mishpatim*, before the sin!

---

2. *Shemot* 23:16.

Experience the Moment

ויאמר ה' אל משה עלה אלי ההרה והיה שם ואתנה לך את לחת האבן
והתורה והמצוה אשר כתבתי להורתם. (שמות כד:יב)

And Hashem said to Moshe, "Ascend to Me on the mountain
and *remain there*, and I will give you the stone tablets, the law
and the commandments, which I have written to instruct them."
(*Shemot* 24:12)

Hashem commanded Moshe to ascend the mountain and receive the
luhot. I heard a beautiful idea in the name of the Kotzker Rebbe. Why
did Hashem first request that Moshe "ascend the mountain" and then
demand *heyeh sham* – "be there." Isn't that redundant? Obviously if
Moshe went up the mountain, he'd be there. Where else would he be?

The Kotzker Rebbe, Rav Mendel MiKotzk, sharply answers that
often we can "ascend a mountain," but not really be there. For example,
we might attend a *shiur* and be physically present, but not truly *there*. We
may be at a wedding or other *simha*, but we feel somewhat spaced out.
We may be physically located somewhere but our mind is elsewhere. The
Kotzker Rebbe teaches: Don't just go up the mountain. Rather, experience the situation you're in, whatever it is. *Be there!*

Our generation suffers from multitasking overload. We are often
involved in so many activities that we aren't focusing on any of them. The

Torah is teaching us an important lesson. Don't go somewhere physically but leave your head or heart out of it. It is our job to maximize our experience at all times, to keep our head in the game and get the most out of every experience.

Parashat Teruma

Value Is Created

אבני שהם ואבני מלאים לאפד ולחשן. (שמות כה:ז)

Onyx stones and filling stones for the *efod* and for the breastplate.
(*Shemot* 25:7)

At the beginning of the *parasha*, the Torah lists all the materials that
Bnei Yisrael donated to the *Mishkan*. The *pesukim* seem to list the items
in descending order, starting from gold and silver and continuing down
to materials, hides, and oil. Then the final *pasuk* lists the precious stones
that were donated for the *hoshen* and the *efod*.

The *Ohr HaHayim*[1] asks: Why were the precious stones listed last?
Precious stones are even more valuable than gold and silver; shouldn't
they have been listed at least prior to the hides and oils?

The *Ohr HaHayim* suggests several answers. His first is that
perhaps they are listed last because they were brought last. The
nesi'im, "tribal leaders," donated the precious stones for the *hoshen*
and *efod* because that was all that was left to donate by the time they

---

1. *Shemot* 25:7.

came forward. Another answer he suggests is that as it says in the Gemara in Yoma (75a), the precious stones were brought in on clouds (the word *nesi'im* means "clouds" in other contexts). Nobody had to work hard or give up much to donate them – no effort or loss of money was involved. Accordingly, Hashem listed them last, because Hashem isn't interested only in *what we do*, but also in *how we do it*.

Rav Chaim Shmuelevitz[2] notes an interesting fact in one of his *sihot*. He says that "there is only one *mitzva mideoraita* that involves bowing down." That is the mitzva of *bikkurim*. What makes it special in this regard? Rav Chaim Shmuelevitz explains that it is because of the unbelievable self-sacrifice that this mitzva involves. A farmer works so hard, putting great effort into the planting process. Yet, for the first three years, he can't touch the produce; it is called *orla* and is off limits. Finally, in the fourth year, he's still restricted from benefiting from his plants until he has separated the first fruits (the *bikkurim*) for Hashem.

Channeling such hard work toward Hashem brings a person to a level of total nullification before Hashem, which is symbolized by bowing down. All a farmer does is worry about his fields, and then he gifts it to HaKadosh Barukh Hu.

When we complete a *masekhet* in *Gemara*, we recite a certain *tefilla* that includes in it the phrase: "We toil and are rewarded for our hard efforts, and they toil and are not rewarded for their efforts." What exactly does that mean? Isn't all hard work rewarded?

The *Hafetz Hayim Al HaTorah* famously explains this phrase as follows: When a person brings his shoes to a shoemaker for repair, if the shoemaker spends two hours and is unable to repair the shoes, he receives no compensation for the time he spent trying to repair the shoes. However, if one spends two hours struggling with a *Tosafot*, or a complicated Gemara, although he does not fully comprehend the content of what he read, he receives a reward for his efforts.

There is tremendous value in working hard to achieve a goal. When things come easy, they are not always appreciated. We should invest in the means and not just in seeking to achieve a goal. That is why the precious stones, which were brought without the efforts of Bnei

---

2. *Sihot Musar* (Jerusalem, 2004), 211.

Yisrael, are listed last in the sequence of valuables that were contributed to the *Mishkan*. Not only are the goods valued, but the means by which the goods were obtained are also valued.

Learning *Middot* from Measurements

The Torah provides specific measurements for each vessel in the *Mishkan*. It is interesting to note that with respect to the *Aron*, it states:

ועשו ארון עצי שטים אמתים וחצי ארכו ואמה וחצי רחבו ואמה וחצי קמתו. (שמות כה:י)

They shall make an of acacia wood, two and a *half* cubits its length, a cubit and a *half* its width, and a cubit and a *half* its height. (*Shemot* 25:10)

The measurements of the *Aron*'s length, width, and height are each listed with measurements of a half.

With respect to the measurements of the *Mizbe'ah* (Altar), the Torah states:

ועשית את המזבח עצי שטים חמש אמות ארך וחמש אמות רחב רבוע יהיה המזבח ושלש אמות קמתו. (שמות כח:א)

> And you shall make the Altar of acacia wood, five cubits long and five cubits wide; the Altar shall be square, and its height [shall be] three cubits. (*Shemot* 28:1)

The measurements of the Altar are all in whole numbers. None of the length, width, or height values include any half measurement.

With respect to the measurements of the *Shulhan*, the Torah states:

> ועשית שלחן עצי שטים אמתים ארכו ואמה רחבו ואמה וחצי קמתו.
> (שמות כה:כג)

> And you shall make a table of acacia wood, two cubits its length, one cubit its width, and a cubit and a *half* its height. (*Shemot* 25:23)

The measurement of the *Shulhan* is mixed. Its length and width are in whole numbers, while its height is in a half measurement.

The *Keli Yakar* is puzzled by the distinctive measurements of these three vessels. Why are the measurements of the length, width, and height of the *Aron* all in half measurements, while the measurements of the *Mizbe'ah* are all in whole numbers, and the measurements of the *Shulhan* are mixed? Perhaps there is a lesson to be learned with respect to the significance of each of these vessels from their measurements.

The Aron: The *Keli Yakar* explains that the dimensions of the *Aron* teach us a powerful lesson about spirituality. The half measurements teach us that we, too, are incomplete. When it comes to holy matters, we should always be looking up at people who are higher than we are and recognize that we can strive to further improve ourselves. This is the idea of *kinat sofrim tarbeh hokhma* – "jealousy among scholars will increase wisdom by motivating everyone to achieve even greater knowledge."

The *Keli Yakar quotes* a beautiful idea: The ultimate goal of knowledge is to realize that we can't know Hashem. The *Baal HaMa'or*[1] once

---

1. Rabbenu Yonah, *Pirkei Avot* 6:6.

said that he didn't realize that he knew something until he realized that he didn't know anything. Realizing that we know so little and there is so much more to know, is in itself is a virtue. However, if one thinks he knows everything, he truly knows nothing.

That is the symbolism in the broken measurements of the *Aron* – which houses the *luhot*. When it comes to Torah, there is always more to learn; we should never feel complete, as if we know it all.

Rabbi Zalman Sorotzkin, in *Oznayim LaTorah*, offers a different suggestion as to why the *Aron* is measured in half measurements. The *Aron* held the broken and complete *luhot*, as well as a *sefer Torah* – all physical representations of the written Torah. However, the written Torah is only half the Torah, the other half being the oral Torah. The measurements of the *Aron* serve to teach us that what lies within it is only half. Without the oral Torah, one has only half the Torah.

As we know, throughout our history there have been attempts to deny the veracity or relevance of the oral Torah. However, each of these sects has disappeared – the Karaites, the Samaritans, the Sadducees, and others. If you reject the oral Torah, you won't survive.

The Shulhan is where the daily bread (*lehem hapanim*) was placed. It had a combination of whole and half measurements. Perhaps this is to teach us that when it comes to material wealth, we have to feel like Yaakov Avinu did when he said *yesh li kol* – "I have everything." The full measurements symbolize completion, having everything. However, we can't only feel that way after we've filled every one of our desires. Rather, as the half measurements represent, our desires for materiality should be incomplete; we shouldn't want so much. We should have few desires and feel like we have everything. As it states in *Pirkei Avot* (4:1), "Who is wealthy? One who is satisfied with his lot." We should feel complete with a partial amount, hence the combination of whole and half measurements. Our half portion should completely satisfy us.

The Mizbe'ah symbolizes peace between HaKadosh Barukh Hu and Am Yisrael. Therefore, the complete dimensions of it represent our perfect and complete connection with Him. We bring sacrifices to be forgiven. When one repents, it must be done wholeheartedly. True *teshuva* cannot be completed with a partial feeling of regret. In the *Avinu Malkenu* prayer recited on the *Yamim Nora'im* and fast days, we ask

Hashem to help us achieve *teshuva sheleima* – "complete *teshuva*." This is symbolized by the complete measurements of the *Mizbe'ah*.

From the variance in measurements of each vessel, we gain a deeper understanding of how we ought to develop our *middot*.

Inward and Outward

In *Aleinu LeShabe'ah*,[1] Rav Yitzhak Zilberstein quotes a comment of his father-in-law, Rav Elyashiv, about the *Aron*: There are two vessels described in this *parasha* that are compared to a *talmid hakham*: the *Aron* and the Menora, which both symbolize Torah. Why do we need two vessels to represent Torah?

Each vessel represents a different element of a *talmid hakham*'s nature. Like the *Aron*, which is secluded, never seen by anyone other than the *kohen gadol*, a *talmid hakham* has to have a very private side – a private connection with Hashem. Just as no one may enter the Holy of Holies, the *talmid hakham* should have an inner world that no one knows.

On the other hand, he must also be like the Menora. He cannot keep only to himself. Rather, he has to shine forth and illuminate his surroundings.

This might also be the idea behind a king's obligation to have two *sifrei Torah*. The Gemara in Sanhedrin (21b) teaches that a king must always have one *sefer Torah* with him constantly, which he brings along when he attends meetings and public functions, and when he goes to war. The king is also obligated to have a second *sefer Torah* that he keeps in his treasure house (safe). Why the need for two Torahs? Why does

---

1. Vol. 2, 442.

one – the one that is constantly with him – not suffice? Perhaps the answer is based on what Rav Elyashiv suggests above. The king is a public figure whose task is to serve the people. He has to have a "public" display of the Torah. However, the king cannot forget his own personal connection and commitment to Torah, and therefore is required to possess an additional more "personal" Torah that is concealed from the public.

Having too much of one aspect could hinder a leader's greatness. A great person has to have a balance of both: the introspective side that's privately connected to Hashem, and the public side whereby he is able to positively influence others.

Our Personal *Mishkan*

Rav Yosef Soloveitchik[1] draws a parallel between the *Mishkan* and our personal homes by focusing on the vessels that are described in this week's *parasha*. We can learn a valuable lesson for our own marriages by exploring the symbolic meaning of each of the physical vessels contained within the *Mishkan*.

The purpose of the *Mishkan* could not have been just to have a location at which to bring sacrifices. If it was only about sacrifices, we wouldn't need anything more than a *Mizbe'ah*, an altar. What would be the need for the rest of the *Mishkan*? Why a fancy structure? Why so many vessels? Bnei Yisrael could have continued serving Hashem the way their ancestors had – by building a *Mizbe'ah* when needed.

The main purpose of the *Mishkan*, explains the Rav, was to build a home for Hashem. Hashem commanded us to build a place where He could be *metzamtzem*, "minimize," His Infinite Self so that we would have a tangible, physical place to go to visit Hashem, so to speak, and be inspired.

Rav Soloveitchik explains that the vessels in the *Mishkan* symbolize the basic ingredients a home requires. A table (*shulhan*), a lamp (*menora*), and a chair (the *Aron* was a throne for Hashem, Who is called

---

1. *Divrei HaRav* (Jerusalem: OU Press, 2010), 139.

Yoshev keruvim) help create a home. The golden *Mizbe'ah*, however, is what we do in the house once it is built; therefore, it wasn't included in this *parasha*. Offerings are what we *do* in the house, but they are not part of what makes it a home.

What do these three vessels symbolize? Rav Soloveitchik quotes a *pasuk* from *II Melakhim*: "Now let us make a small walled upper chamber, and place there for him a bed, a table, a chair, and a lamp; and it will be that when he comes to us, he will turn into there" (4:10).

This *pasuk* describes a conversation between the woman of Shunam and her husband, when she broached the idea of building an apartment attached to their house as a guesthouse for Elisha the Prophet. She described a room with a bed, a chair, a table, and a lamp. Rav Soloveitchik explains that the *Mishkan* was an apartment for HaKadosh Barukh Hu, so to speak. Therefore, the very same pieces of furniture were included in His home. The *Aron* represents the chair and bed – the place for *hashraat haShekhina* – where Hashem's glory resides. Then there were the *Shulhan* and the Menora. The same vessels that are needed for a human guest were placed in Hashem's home to give us the opportunity to visit Hashem, so to speak.

Rav Soloveitchik explains further that we cannot compare only in one direction. If the *Mishkan* was a "home," then our homes have to become a *Mishkan*. We can bring Hashem into our own homes with these very same vessels – beds, tables, and lamps.

The bed symbolizes *taharat hamishpaha*; the table represents *kashrut* and *hakhnasat orhim*, hosting guests; and the lamp represents the learning and observing Torah in the home. These are the three tenets upon which a home must be built.[2]

---

2. This idea can be expanded upon with a slightly different perspective. The *Aron* may symbolize the Torah, which should be the foundation of a couple, as it was the foundation for the *keruvim*, the two angelic figures that stood upon the *Aron*. The *Menora* may symbolize *shalom bayit*, "peace in the home," as is represented by the Shabbat candles. The *Shulhan* symbolizes hosting guests and sharing songs and Torah during meals. The *Kiyor* (vessel used for washing) symbolizes purity. The *Mizbe'ah* may symbolize the *korbanot*, the sacrifices that a couple has to make for each other, which eventually draw them closer (from the root *kuf-reish-beit* – which means "to bring close").

Is Hashem Our Shepherd, Guard, or Father?

ועשו לי מקדש ושכנתי בתוכם. ככל אשר אני מראה אותך את תבנית
המשכן ואת תבנית כל כליו וכן תעשו. ועשו ארון עצי שטים: אמתים
וחצי ארכו ואמה וחצי רחבו ואמה וחצי קמתו. (שמות כה: ח-י)

And they shall make Me a sanctuary and I will dwell in their midst.
According to all that I show you, the pattern of the *Mishkan* and
the pattern of all its vessels, and so shall you do. They shall make
an *Aron* of acacia wood, two and a half cubits its length, a cubit
and a half its width, and a cubit and a half its height. (*Shemot*
25:8–10)

The *Be'er Yosef*[1] cites a midrash that asks why the command to build
the vessels of the *Mishkan* is formulated in the singular, *ve'asita*, with
the exception of the *Aron*, where the Torah uses the plural, *ve'asu*. The
Midrash answers that the *Aron* symbolizes Torah, and since everyone
has a portion in Torah, the command was stated in the plural. The crown
of Torah is the only crown that is open to all, unlike the crown of the
kehuna and the crown of *malkhut*.

---

1. *Shemot*, 298.

The Midrash then brings three metaphors to describe the relationship between Hashem and Am Yisrael. The first comparison is to a shepherd and his sheep.

אמר הקב"ה לישראל אתם צאני ואני רועה שנאמר (יחזקאל לד) "ואתן צאני צאן מרעיתי אדם אתם."

HaKadosh Barukh Hu said to Israel: You are My sheep and I am the Shepherd, as it says in *Yehezkel* (34:31), "And you are my sheep, the sheep of My pasture; you are man."

The second *mashal* is to a guard over a vineyard.

אתם כרם שנאמר (ישעיה ה) "כי כרם ה' צ-באות בית ישראל" ואני שומר.

You are likened to a vineyard, as is stated in *Yeshayahu* (5:7), "For the vineyard of the Lord of hosts is the house of Israel," and I am the Guard [of the vineyard].

The final comparison brought by the Midrash is to that of a father and son.

אתם בנים ואני אביכם שנאמר (דברים י"ד) "בנים אתם לה' אלקיכם."

You are children, and I am your Father, as it is stated in *Devarim* (14:1), "You are the sons of Hashem your God."

Hashem calls Himself our Father and asks that we build an apartment for Him so He can come visit us. The Midrash thus describes Hashem as a Shepherd, a Guard over a vineyard, and a Father.

The *Be'er Yosef* asks two questions concerning this midrash. First, he asks, what is the message of these three comparisons? Why is Hashem specifically compared to these three roles? Second, what is the connection between the first half of the midrash, which proclaims that everyone has a portion in Torah, and the second half?

The *Be'er Yosef* answers that the first part of the midrash informs us that Torah applies to every Jew. In every generation, Bnei Yisrael need a connection to Torah and mitzvot. A person's lifeline is his connection to the Torah. Although we don't have an *Aron* or *Mishkan* today, our *shuls*, schools, yeshivot, and *batei midrash* are the modern-day equivalents. Our Torah radiates from those places. Everyone, no matter who he is, needs and can have a connection to Torah.

The continuation of the midrash lets us know that this applies to every situation in which a Jew finds himself. The midrash provides three metaphors to represent the different circumstances a Jew may encounter.

Sometimes, we find ourselves in a land where everywhere we turn, we are treated like strangers, foreigners, outcasts. We feel the pains of being in exile, and we can be compared to sheep that are abandoned, forsaken. In these instances, Hashem says, "I'm your Shepherd, you are not forsaken."

There are other times when, despite living in exile, we are welcomed by the nations, and we dwell in peace, with full rights as citizens. In this kind of situation, it might be even easier to believe that we are safe even without any special connection to Torah. So, Hashem says, "You are a vineyard. You think you have delicious grapes and that everything is fine, but you need a Guard in order to survive." No comfort in exile ever lasts forever, so we need to sustain our connection to Hashem – through Torah. Hashem is the Guard of the vineyard, and if He removes His guidance and protection, we will fall.

But the ultimate relationship with Hashem that we strive to achieve is represented by the third metaphor. We don't want to be committed to Torah only when we're the sheep or the vineyard, desperate for Hashem's protection. Rather, Hashem wants us to feel like we are His children and that He is our Father. Unconditional love. That is the ideal relationship between Hashem and Am Yisrael.

The *Keruvim*: Wings Upward While Facing Each Other

והיו הכרבים פרשי כנפים למעלה סככים בכנפיהם על הכפרת ופניהם
איש אל אחיו אל הכפרת יהיו פני הכרבים. (שמות כה:כ)

The *keruvim* shall have their wings spread upwards, shielding the Aron cover with their wings, with their faces toward one another; [turned] toward the Aron cover shall be the faces of the *keruvim*. (*Shemot* 25:20)

The *pasuk* specifies that the wings of the *keruvim* were spread upward, while the base of the *keruvim* formed a single unit with the cover of the *Aron*. The *Shemen HaTov*[1] discusses the symbolism of this formation, which stood at the center of the *Mikdash*, at the place from which holiness flowed.

These spread wings symbolize that the goal of a Jew is to strive upward toward greatness. The base signifies that our spiritual yearnings

---

1. Rabbi Bernard Weinberger, *Shemen HaTov*, vol. 5 (New York: Talpiot Press, 2007), 106.

are grounded in the Torah, which lies inside the *Aron* from which the *keruvim* "grow."

Likewise, the Torah specifies that three of the vessels of the *Mishkan* have golden rims or "crowns": the *Aron*, the *Shulhan*, and the golden *Mizbe'ah*. However, there is a slight difference in the descriptions. With respect to the *Shulhan* and *Mizbe'ah*, the *pasuk* says, *ve'asita lo* – "[the crowns should be] fashioned *for* it." However, when it comes to the *Aron*, it says, *ve'asita alav* – "[the crown should be] fashioned *upon* it." The Torah is crowned by a constant upward striving, an infinite yearning.

But there's another message in the *pasuk* that qualifies this first message: the *keruvim* must face one another. The Torah is teaching us that spiritual accomplishments must never come at the expense of others. We must never step on someone else in order to improve our relationship with Hashem. We must bring others up with us, not step on them to raise ourselves. Sometimes in life, we find people who want to gain stature, even spiritual stature, by pushing others down. That's exactly what the *pasuk* is telling us not to do. Yes, our wings spread above, but still we face our fellow human beings.

How do we achieve this? *Hazal* tell us the faces of the *keruvim* were like children's faces. A baby understands that he is completely dependent on his parent. If we realize that we are entirely dependent on HaKadosh Barukh Hu, then we'll understand that there's no place for stepping on anybody else. That is the message of the *keruvim*. The way to achieve upward growth without harming our fellow man is by having the attitude of a child, who realizes that he is totally dependent on his parent. May we inspire and uplift our fellow children of Israel as we strive to enhance our spirituality.

Parashat Tetzaveh

Moshe's Presence in the *Parasha*

This is the only *parasha*, from *Shemot* until the end of *Sefer Bemidbar*, that doesn't mention Moshe.[1] It is considered to be the fulfillment of Moshe's request to Hashem to erase him from the Torah rather than destroy the Jewish people. Accordingly, Hashem erased him from one *parasha*.

The Vilna Gaon points out that even though Moshe's name is not explicitly mentioned in the text, there is a hint to him in the tally of the *pesukim* of the *parasha*. There are 101 *pesukim* in the *parasha*, and the *gematria* of the "hidden" letters of Moshe's name add up to 101. Meaning, if you spell out the letters of Moshe's name – הא-שׁין-מם – the additional letters add up to 101. Says the Vilna Gaon, Moshe is only absent on the surface level. His presence, however, is clearly felt.

Likewise, in most years, Moshe's yahrzeit falls out during the week of *Parashat Tetzaveh*. This, too, indicates that Moshe's absence, paradoxically, only intensifies his constant presence.

The Gemara in Eruvin (100b) teaches that had the Torah not been transmitted, we would have been able to learn certain morals and

---

1. Although in *Sefer Devarim* Moshe's name may not appear as often, it is because in *Sefer Devarim*, Moshe is speaking.

ethics from the world around us. We would learn not to steal from an ant and fidelity from a dove, among other lessons from the animal kingdom. Observing a tree would teach us that we do not always see the real basis for the stability of an item. The tree is standing firmly due to its deep roots that are not visible to the naked eye. Our own spiritual strength is derived from our ancestors, our parents and grandparents who may no longer be visible, but are surely felt as those who served as the spiritual foundation upon which we sprouted. This mirrors Moshe Rabbenu's invisible presence in our *parasha*.

Am Yisrael Is
Compared to Olives

ואתה תצוה את בני ישראל ויקחו אליך שמן זית זך כתית למאור להעלת
נר תמיד. (שמות כז:כ)

And you shall command the children of Israel, and they shall take
to you pure olive oil, crushed for lighting, to kindle the lamps
continually. (*Shemot* 27:20)

The midrash in Shemot Rabba comments on this *pasuk* and points
out that Bnei Yisrael are compared to many kinds of trees throughout
Tanakh: to grape vines, date palms, cedars, and more. Yet the prophet
Yirmeyahu specifically compares us to olive trees: "Hashem has called
you a thriving olive tree, beautiful in form" (*Yirmeyahu* 11:16). The
midrash lists three ways in which Bnei Yisrael are like olive trees.

First, when olives are all the way up in a tree, you have to shake
the branches to get the olives down. At that point, they get crushed at
the olive press, and then they are crushed even further, and the crush-
ing keeps happening until the olives yield oil. So, too, have the Jewish
people been crushed throughout history, but with what results? Proof
of our loyalty to Hashem. The Jew holds onto HaKadosh Barukh Hu

tenaciously, and the oil, our connection to Hashem, is revealed. Our being crushed brings us closer to HaKadosh Barukh Hu.

The second comparison is in our chemistry. Just as oil is the only liquid that never mixes with other liquids, Am Yisrael, too, cannot mix with the nations.

Finally, not only does oil not mix with other liquids, but no matter what you combine it with, the oil rises to the top; not only does it remain separate, it remains above. So, too, with Am Yisrael – when we do the will of Hashem, we rise to the top.

The *Shemen HaTov*[1] takes these three comparisons one step further and explains how they symbolize three types of Jew.

The first type is disconnected from the Torah and wants no connection to the Torah or Hashem. The only way he is identified as a Jew is when others identify him. He cannot hide his identity from our enemies. If a Jew fails to distinguish himself through sanctity, our enemies will isolate him. It is only under duress, when he is crushed and pressed, that he is revealed to be a Jew.

The second type is not the best in mitzva fulfillment but has the basic idea. They identify themselves as proud Jews and don't want to assimilate. It is this fear, this resistance to mixing, that keeps them separate.

The third type is what we all aspire to be. It's not enough for us to just stay separate; rather, we strive to live a sanctified and elevated life, as a light unto the nations. We aim for spiritual heights, and go beyond the letter of the law. That is why, as a people, we are compared to olives.

---

1. Rabbi Bernard Weinberger, *Shemen HaTov*, vol. 3 (New York: Talpiot Press, 2007), 108.

The Details of the *Mishkan*

The first half of *Parashat Tetzaveh* discusses the *bigdei kehuna*, the eight articles of clothing worn by the *kohen gadol*, and the four worn by the common *kohen*. This is followed by a discussion of the *milu'im*, the days when the *avoda* was practiced for the first time. This *parasha* is full of highly specific details, covered in exhaustive depth. Why is it so necessary for us to know every detail of the *Mishkan*, down to every screw and bolt and board?

In general, this *parasha* is not viewed as one of the most exciting ones. Therefore, Rabbi Adin Steinsaltz[1] puts it into perspective for us, providing us with a new appreciation for it.

There are two aspects of *Parashat Tetzaveh*. One aspect focuses on what the *Mishkan* signifies, and the second describes what the *Mishkan* is supposed to accomplish. These are two separate issues, but step one is a prerequisite for step two.

To help us understand this idea, Rabbi Steinsaltz compares the building of the *Mishkan* to the building a spaceship. It takes decades to build a spaceship. It is a complex system that is comprised of thousands of tiny pieces and details. A team of professionals, who have spent their lives studying and researching this area, work together to form a perfect

---

1. *Hayei Olam* (Jerusalem: Maggid Books, 2011), 171.

machine. Only after years of work are they finally ready to send it soaring into space. How will they know if the spaceship will be able to reach its destination? At long last, they flip the switch and watch with bated breath as the rocket shoots into the sky. Will it reach the heavens?

The goal of the *Mishkan* was to forge a connection between Am Yisrael and HaKadosh Barukh Hu, to create an abode in which Hashem's presence could dwell. In order to achieve such a lofty goal, step one had to be perfect, down to the last bolt. There could not be even a single imperfect detail. Then, the only way to ever know whether the *Mishkan* was perfect was to "turn on the engine." During the days of *milu'im*, the days when they finally actualized the purpose of the *Mishkan*, they were able to see whether they had done it right.

Rabbi Steinsaltz tells a story about satellites that were sent up to space. Every single day, a team of people checked every detail, repeatedly, to keep the satellite on its path. One day, one number was off, and it was missed somehow. This occurred right before the weekend, so it wasn't detected until Monday morning. But when they finally discovered the error, it was too late. The satellite was lost.

The *Mishkan*, too, *lehavdil*, needed this kind of attention to detail. So much work was put into creating it, and not until the *avoda* was done would they know if had achieved its goal. So they "flipped the switch." They did the *avoda*. And they waited.

Two million people stood and watched and waited...and no fire came down. After a week of trying, Aharon and Moshe davened to Hashem, and the fire finally descended upon the *Mizbe'ah*.

The details may seem boring, but if we were the engineers and the technicians, we wouldn't be bored because we'd understand the ultimate goal of all the nitty-gritty details.

We have to understand that all these *parshiyot* are the buildup for the pinnacle, which takes place in *Sefer Vayikra*.

Perhaps this is not even just a *mashal*; it's the reality. Just like an astronaut's suit cannot have even a tiny detail wrong or it will cost the astronaut his life, the *bigdei kehuna*, *lehavdil*, had to be utterly perfect. If a *kohen gadol* entered the "atmosphere" at the wrong moment, he would die! Perfection and attention to detail is necessary to achieve the result.

Now we understand that step two, the actual purpose of the *Mishkan,* could only be achieved if the structure was perfect down to the last detail.

A Torah View with
a Wide Lens

ועשית בגדי קדש לאהרן אחיך לכבוד ולתפארת. ואתה תדבר אל כל
חכמי לב אשר מלאתיו רוח חכמה ועשו את בגדי אהרן לקדשו לכהנו
לי. (שמות כח:ב-ג)

You shall make holy garments for your brother Aharon, for honor
and glory. And you shall speak to all the wise-hearted, whom I
have filled with the spirit of wisdom, and they shall make Aharon's garments to sanctify him, [so] that he serve Me [as a *kohen*].
(*Shemot* 28:2–3)

The Gemara in Zevahim[1] teaches us that each of the *bigdei kehuna* atoned
for a different transgression. For example, the *mikhnasayim* (pants) were
meant to atone for *gilui arayot* (illicit relations); the *mitznefet* (turban)
for *gasut haru'ah* (arrogance); the *ketonet* (frock) for *shefikhat damim*
(bloodshed); and the *efod* (apron) for *avoda zara* (idolatry).

The *Netivot Shalom*[2] asks, if the *bigdei kehuna* were supposed to
sanctify the *kohanim*, what does it mean that they atoned for these sins?

---

1. Zevahim 88b.
2. Rav Shalom Noach Berezovsky, *Netivot Shalom, Shemot*, 226.

Sanctification seems to imply something extra special! Serving as an atonement for bloodshed doesn't seem like sanctification. Not shedding blood is basic human decency! So how do we align this gemara with the simple reading of the *pasuk*?

Perhaps the solution may be found based on a *Tosafot* in Arakhin.[3] The Tosafists explain that the Gemara doesn't refer to the basic definition of these sins. We don't think the *kohanim* or most of Klal Yisrael were murderers. Rather, the clothes of the *kohen gadol* atoned for lesser forms of these sins, not the actual transgressions as we define them. Bloodshed, for example, refers to embarrassing people in public. As Jews, we have to live a sanctified existence. That means refining ourselves in areas that we as Jews define as sins. We have a broader definition of each of the *aveirot* than the rest of the world. For us, *gilui arayot* is more than what it means to the other nations. Even safeguards are included in this restriction. The same applies to murder. The world defines murder as physically killing someone, while we define it in a broader sense.[4]

The *Netivot Shalom* adds one final thought: The *parasha* starts out with a discussion of the Menora. Where does the Menora fit in? He suggests one answer, but maybe we can say that in order for us to understand the definition of these sins, we need to have the radiance of the Menora, the prism of Torah through which we can have greater insight. If we view the world through the lens of Torah, we will be able to define these precepts in the broader Torah sense.

---

3. Arakhin 16a.
4. *Hazal* explain that embarrassing someone may be considered as if one has inflicted physical damage on another.

Wisdom of the Heart

ועשית בגדי קדש לאהרן אחיך לכבוד ולתפארת. ואתה תדבר אל כל
חכמי לב אשר מלאתיו רוח חכמה ועשו את בגדי אהרן לקדשו לכהנו
לי. (שמות כח:ב-ג)

You shall make holy garments for your brother Aharon, for honor
and glory. And you shall speak to all the wise-hearted, whom I
have filled with the spirit of wisdom, and they shall make Aharon's garments to sanctify him, [so] that he serve Me [as a kohen].
(*Shemot* 28:2–3)

Moshe is tasked with assembling people of a specific type to prepare the
garments for Aharon HaKohen: *hakhmei lev* – "the wise-hearted." What
does the phrase *hakhmei lev* mean? Wouldn't it be prudent to seek tailors
or craftsmen over people with this vague attribute?

The *Peninei Torah*[1] explains that a *hakham lev* is someone who
seeks or desires wisdom, not just someone who has attained wisdom. If
we desire *hokhma*, Hashem will grant it to us. Shlomo HaMelekh was
granted one request, and he asked for wisdom. He hit the nail on the
head, and he received many other blessings along with wisdom.

---

1. Rav David Hadad, *Peninei HaTorah* (Beer Sheva, 1992), 148.

The *Peninei Torah* quotes a beautiful story. One time, Rabbi Yehoshua Isaac Shapira, also known as Rabbi Aizel Harif or Rabbi Aizel Slonimer, went to Yeshivat Volozhin to look for a boy worthy enough to marry his daughter. Since he obviously couldn't test all the boys, he went to the *bima* and asked a difficult question. He announced that whoever could answer the question would be selected to marry his daughter. The yeshiva came to life, with every student contemplating a solution to the riddle. The boys lined up with answers, but none were correct. When he saw that no answer was forthcoming, the *rav* got ready to leave the city.

As he began to pull away in his buggy, a boy, Yosef Shluper, came running after him. "Did you figure out the answer?" he asked the boy. "No, I did not. But please, don't leave before telling me, what is the answer to the riddle? I want to know!"

"You, I want for a son-in-law!" exclaimed Rabbi Aizel. To him, the desire to know the truth was as good to him as knowing. The boy didn't care about the honor; he just wanted to know the truth. The love for Torah meant more to him than knowing the answer, and it reflected his *hokhmat lev*. These are the people Moshe was required to select to prepare the garments of the *kohen gadol*. Those who desire wisdom, who seek the truth, are held in high regard.

It is interesting to note that usually wisdom is related to the head, where the brain is housed, while emotions are associated with the heart. Why here is wisdom attributed to the heart? Perhaps the message is that we cannot bifurcate our brain from our heart. We cannot just act intellectually; we must perform mitzvot wholeheartedly as well. When our heart seeks the truth, we can attain it.

The Symbolism of the Stones in the *Hoshen*

ואלה הבגדים אשר יעשו חשן ואפוד ומעיל וכתנת תשבץ מצנפת ואבנט
ועשו בגדי קדש לאהרן אחיך ולבניו לכהנו לי. (שמות כח:ד)

And these are the garments that they shall make: a *hoshen*, an *efod*, a robe, a tunic of checker-work, a cap, and a sash. They shall make holy garments for your brother Aharon and for his sons to serve Me [as *kohanim*]. (*Shemot* 28:4)

The first of the *bigdei kehuna* to be described is the *efod*, a kind of apron with shoulder straps, but no front. The straps connected to the *hoshen*, with an onyx stone atop each shoulder. On each of these stones, six of the tribes were listed.

Later, when the *pesukim* list the twelve stones of the *hoshen*, each of which corresponds to one of the tribes, we learn that Yosef's stone was the *shoham*. How could the same stone represent all of Klal Yisrael as well as Yosef in particular? The *Meshekh Hokhma* suggests that Yosef HaTzaddik represents all of Klal Yisrael. The *pasuk* in *Yirmeyahu*, "*Haben yakir li Efraim*" (My son Efraim, who is very dear to Me), uses Yosef's son, Efraim, to mean the entire Am Yisrael.

Moreover, the *Meshekh Hokhma* continues, each of the *bigdei kehuna* atoned for a different sin. The *efod* atoned for idolatry, the *hoshen* for violation of monetary law. Therefore, the *shoham*, which is the stone of the *efod*, symbolizes atonement for transgressions that stem from the intellect, from sins *bein adam laMakom*; idolatry is misguided, incorrect intellectual decisions. The *yashfe*, the final stone on the *hoshen*, the stone of Binyamin, atones for our interpersonal transgressions, our sins *bein adam lahaveiro*.[1]

Based on this idea, we can gain new insight into a gemara in Bava Batra.[2] The Gemara quotes a *pasuk* in *Yeshayahu*: "I will make your towers of *kadkod*, your gates from jewels, and all of your border walls of precious stones" (54:12). This *pasuk* describes the gates of Yerushalayim, whose towers will be made with *kadkod*, a type of stone. What stone, exactly? The Gemara states two opinions: the *shoham* or the *yashfe*. One opinion says it will be the *shoham* because it will atone in areas of *bein adam laMakom*. The second opinion says it's going to be the *yashfe*, to atone for sins *bein adam lahaveiro*.

The *Meshekh Hokhma* adds that the next *pasuk* in *Yeshayahu* says: "All your children will be taught by Hashem, and great will be the peace of your children." The first part of the *pasuk* refers to our relationship with Hashem, *bein adam laMakom*. The second half refers to peace among people, *bein adam lahaveiro*.

---

1. Binyamin was the only one of the twelve tribes who was not involved in the sale of Yosef. Even Yosef was held accountable for not making contact with his father for twenty-two years. It is also no coincidence that it was Binyamin's stone, the *yashfeh*, that is the subject of the Gemara's story about Dama ben Netina (Kiddushin 31a). Just like Dama was perfect in the mitzva of honoring his father, so too was Binyamin.
2. Bava Batra 75a.

Parashat Zakhor and Remembering Amalek

אשר קרך בדרך ויזנב בך כל הנחשלים אחריך ואתה עיף ויגע ולא ירא
אלקים. (דברים כה:יח)

How he happened upon you on the way and cut off all the strag-
glers at your rear, when you were faint and weary, and he did not
fear God. (*Devarim* 25:18)

Rabbi Moshe Sternbuch[1] comments that we are very *mahmir* with
respect to hearing *Parashat Zakhor*, being that it is the only biblically
obligatory Torah reading of the year, but he notes that the most important *humra* of *Parashat Zakhor* is to know the actual meaning of the
words as they are read. The word *karkha*, however, presents a problem.
What exactly does it mean? Rashi offers three explanations:

Rashi's first definition is that it refers to a coincidence – that
Amalek was in the desert as Bnei Yisrael left Egypt, and they bumped
into each other by chance. Or, says Rashi, it is an expression of impurity, because Amalek made Bnei Yisrael impure. His final *peshat* is that
it means "cold," that Amalek jumped in and cooled off Bnei Yisrael from

---

1. *Mo'adim UZmanim*, 132.

their state of belief in Hashem. Rashi compares Amalek's act to an individual who jumps into a boiling hot bath. That individual may get scalded, but he cools off the water and makes it easier for others to enter the tub.

Rabbi Sternbuch offers an explanation that merges these three interpretations. Amalek's goal is to persuade everyone that everything is coincidence, that there is no *hashgaha* in the world. This heretical idea is impure, and Amalek sullied the world with it, thus cooling off the *emuna* of the world and making everyone cold and distant from HaKadosh Barukh Hu. For the rest of time, any occurrence of less-than-full *emuna* in Hashem is a result of this *tuma* that Amalek brought into the world. This is what we are supposed to contemplate when remembering Amalek: that we should strengthen our *emuna* that nothing is coincidental in this world; rather, we must recognize the hand of God in all that transpires.

I once heard Rabbi Ephraim Wachsman suggest that one can learn the essence of Amalek from its name in Hebrew: עמלק. The first two letters spell *am*, a nation. The next two letters are the tallest (*lamed*) and the lowest (*kuf*) in the *alef-beit*. Amalek is a nation that drags the highest, most exciting events down to the lowest depths. They push Hashem out of the world.

This explanation can provide us with a deeper insight into Purim. This day is named after Haman's lottery because Haman's entire mentality, as a direct descendant of Amalek, was that everything is coincidental. He believed in the luck of the draw, but our victory on Purim was that we overcame this lottery, this belief in happenstance. Purim is all about overcoming Amalek, and *Parashat Zakhor* is about focusing on the fact that HaKadosh Barukh Hu is everywhere and watches over Klal Yisrael at all times, even when we don't see Him clearly.

Parashat Ki Tisa

The Hidden Lesson
of Giving Charity

כי תשא את ראש בני ישראל לפקדיהם ונתנו איש כפר נפשו לה׳ בפקד
אתם ולא יהיה בהם נגף בפקד אתם. זה יתנו כל העבר על הפקדים
מחצית השקל בשקל הקדש עשרים גרה השקל מחצית השקל תרומה
לה׳. (שמות ל:יב-יג)

When you take the sum of Bnei Yisrael according to their numbers, let each one *give* to Hashem an atonement for his soul when
they are counted; then there will be no plague among them when
they are counted. This they shall give, everyone who goes through
the counting: half a shekel according to the holy shekel. Twenty
gerahs equal one shekel; half of [such] a shekel shall be an offering to Hashem. (*Shemot* 30:12–13)

The Vilna Gaon[1] points out that the *trop* (cantillation notes) on the word
venatenu (give) is the *kadma ve'azla*, which teaches us a valuable lesson.
The Gemara[2] records that Rav Hiya used to instruct his wife, "When a

---

1. *Peninim MiShulhan HaGra*, 133.
2. Shabbat 151b.

poor person comes collecting, make sure to give him food quickly, even before he asks, so that he will treat our children in kind." Rav Hiya's wife was troubled by his comment. "Why are you cursing me?" she asked. "Our children don't need handouts!" Rav Hiya responded that a person's financial status is never certain and is always subject to change. In one generation, a family may be wealthy or poor, but in the next generation, or a few later, they may be in the opposite state.

Financial status is a *galgal hozer*, a wheel of fortune. That, says the Vilna Gaon, is what this word *venatenu* alludes to. The *kadma ve'azla* tells us to preemptively give *tzedaka*. Interestingly, the word *venatenu* is also a palindrome, reading the same way backwards and forwards – financial status goes around and around, like a wheel of fortune.

Later, the Vilna Gaon, like many other commentaries, asks why Bnei Yisrael were commanded to contribute only a half a shekel per person instead of a whole shekel. Many point out that it symbolizes the unity that must exist within Klal Yisrael – that we need to complete each other.

The Vilna Gaon, though, has a different explanation.[3] The Gemara tells us that giving *tzedaka* merits one to be spared from a decree of death. It is interesting to note that this idea is contained within the structure of the Hebrew word for "half" – *mahatzit*.

מ ח צ י ת

The middle letter of this word is *tzaddi*, צ, which stands for *tzedaka*. The letters closest to the middle are ח and י, which spell *hai* – life. The outermost letters are מ and ת, which spell *meit* – death. Thus, *tzedaka* gives life and keeps away death.

---

3. *Peninim MiShulhan HaGra*, 133.

Preparing to Perform Mitzvot

ועשית כיור נחשת וכנו נחשת לרחצה ונתת אתו בין אהל מועד ובין
המזבח ונתת שמה מים. (שמות ל:יח)

You shall make a washstand of copper and its base of copper for
washing, and you shall place it between the Tent of Meeting and
the Altar, and you shall put water therein. (*Shemot* 30:18)

Moshe was instructed to construct the *Kiyor*, the laver in which the
kohanim washed their hands and feet prior to serving in the *Mishkan*.

Interestingly, the placement of the *Kiyor* is not where we would
expect. It was placed out of the way of the *kohanim*, far from where
they entered the *Mishkan*.[1] Additionally, the Torah prescribes the death
penalty for failing to wash before engaging in the *avoda*. What is the
importance of their washing their hands and feet even if they knew
they were clean?

Rabbi Eliezer Kashtiel[2] of Eli explains that this washing was not
about becoming pure, because even *kohanim* who were completely pure

---

1. Its location is between the *Mizbe'ah* and the *Ulam*.
2. Rabbi Eliezer Kashtiel, *BeNefesh HaShabbat* (Eli, 2013).

had to wash. There is a deeper message. Often, although we are involved in mitzvot and good activities all the time, we forget that the purpose is not just about getting things done, acting out of routine. Rather, we need to focus on and realize what we're about to do, and that is what sanctifying oneself is about. If we would just do an act of preparation, so many of the activities would be more meaningful. If we take a moment to, so to speak, wash our hands and feet first, to sanctify ourselves before performing a mitzva, our mitzvot would have so much more depth. We have to make sure our external actions and our internal thoughts are aligned.[3]

This is also why the *Kiyor* was placed where it was. It served as a message to them not to think that they were casually washing their hands as they passed the *Kiyor* on their way to the *avoda*. Rather, the washing was an integral part of the *avoda*, important in and of itself.

David HaMelekh describes a person who is worthy of ascending *Har Hashem* as one with clean hands and a stout heart. It is not enough to turn away from evil. Rather, there must also be a tremendous focus on doing good, to ensure he is ready to go do the *avoda*.

Perhaps this is also why the *Kiyor* was built from mirrors. Every time the *kohanim* went to wash themselves, they saw their reflection, a reminder to look inside themselves to make sure they were focused on the *avoda* they were about to perform.

---

3. The Ritva (Pesahim 7b) describes the purpose of reciting a *berakha* prior to the performance of a mitzva: so that the person pronouncing the blessing is clearly articulating that he is about to perform a mitzva, as the fulfillment of a commandment of Hashem.

The Dual Aspect of Shabbat

The commentators tell us that the reason the first two *aliyot* of *Parashat Ki Tisa* are so long, while the remaining five are relatively short, is because we don't want a *Yisrael* to be called for the *aliya* in which we read about the sin of the Golden Calf. Therefore, the entire episode is covered in the two first *aliyot*, for the *kohen* and Levi, who didn't partake in the sin.

Immediately prior to the second *aliya*, the Torah repeats the laws relating to Shabbat:

ואתה דבר אל בני ישראל לאמר אך את שבתתי תשמרו כי אות הוא ביני וביניכם לדרתיכם לדעת כי אני ה' מקדשכם. (שמות לא:יג)

And you, speak to Bnei Yisrael and say: "Only keep My Shabbatot! For it is *a sign* between Me and you for your generations, to know that I, Hashem, make you holy." (*Shemot* 31:13)

Rabbi Yaakov Zvi Mecklenburg, in *HaKetav VeHaKabbala*, highlights a discrepancy in this *pasuk*. The *pasuk* first uses the plural, *Shabtotai*, and a few words later, references Shabbat as an *ot* – "a sign," in the singular. Rabbi Mecklenburg suggests that there are two aspects of rest on Shabbat: first, resting from physical activity, and second, resting our minds from mundane matters and instead reflecting on spiritualty. Therefore, every Shabbat contains a double resting, one physical and the other mental. The first aspect, the physical resting, is not the ultimate goal. That's only the first step, which is meant to lead to part two, which is the ultimate goal: focusing on spiritual matters. The physical rest is just a means of achieving the end of resting mentally. Still, these two aspects are two sides of one coin and form a single unit. That is why *ot* is in the singular.

Perhaps this is what *Hazal* meant[1] when they said if Bnei Yisrael would keep two Shabbatot, they would be redeemed immediately. The reason *Hazal* state we need to observe two Shabbatot and not one is because they are referring to these two *aspects* of Shabbat (physical and mental), which is essentially the ultimate fulfillment of Shabbat observance.

These two aspects can also reflect the two mitzvot of Shabbat: *zakhor* and *shamor*. *Shamor* refers to the prohibitions of Shabbat, while *zakhor* refers to the positive commandments we must do. *Shamor* would therefore include our rest from physical activities, which prepares the way for *zakhor*, the positive aspects on which we can now focus.[2]

---

1. Shabbat 118b.
2. To add an additional thought on Shabbat, the Slonimer Rebbe in *Netivot Shalom* points out that the three *Shemoneh Esrehs* of Shabbat share a phrase, with one differing word. On Friday night, we say "וינוחו בה," on Shabbat day, we say "וינוחו בו," and at Minha we say "וינוחו בם."

   The Slonimer Rebbe explains that Shabbat is likened to a wedding between Hakadosh Barukh Hu and Am Yisrael. Every Shabbat we get remarried to Hakadosh Barukh Hu. Friday night is the *kiddushin*, as we say, "אתה קדשת," Shabbat day is the *huppa*, and we say, "ישמח משה במתנת חלקו," and Minha is the *yihud*, as we say, "אתה אחד ושמך אחד..."

   The *Netivot Shalom* connects this idea to the בה, בו, and בם. The woman is the focus of *kiddushin*, as her status is changed through it. Therefore, we say בה on Friday night, alluding to the woman. During the *huppa*, the man is the active player, as he is welcoming the bride into his domain. Therefore, on Shabbat morning, we use the masculine form בו. *Yihud* is when they both come together, so the *lashon* is plural – בם. When we recite these three prayers on Shabbat, may we internalize our relationship with our Creator.

Shabbat and the Age
of the World

In one of his essays on the *parasha*, Rav Avigdor Nebenzahl[1] addresses two points, one regarding the concept of resting on Shabbat and one concerning the age of the world.

Hazal[2] say the world was created with ten utterances. Why didn't Hashem create it with just one? He could have just said *yehi olam*, and the world would have appeared in an instant. *Hazal* explain that Hashem created the world in ten utterances so that those that follow the commands of Hashem will have that much more reward for bettering a world that was created in ten utterances versus one. Conversely, those that transgress will be held accountable for destroying a world built on ten utterances versus a world built on one.

Rav Nebenzahl takes this question of *Hazal* one step further. He asks why, instead of uttering all ten utterances in one day, Hashem spread it out over seven days.

Rabbi Nebenzahl explains that if the whole world had been created in one day and then Hashem rested following completion of

---

1. Rav Avigdor Nebenzahl, *Yerushalayim BeMo'adeha – Shabbat* (Jerusalem, 2010), 31.
2. Avot 5:1.

the world, Shabbat would be the second day. Then, for the history of the world, every day would be either Erev Shabbat or Shabbat. But we wouldn't be able to exist like that. Shabbat needs a buildup, like all exciting things need a buildup. Therefore, although Hashem could have created the world in a day, He stretched it out for our benefit.

This explains why Hashem stretched creation out for several days. What of scientific views that the world is millions and billions of years old?

Rav Nebenzahl provides a *mashal* to a person who carves a statue of an old man. His statue is very realistic, with white hair, wrinkles, and a hunched back; the figure clearly resembles an octogenarian. When his work was complete, he showed it around and asked people, "How old do you think this guy is?" Some people answered, "Eighty years old," while others answered, "Why, he's just one day old – you made him today!"

Who is right? asks Rav Nebenzahl. Both of them, because it depends on the perspective of the viewer. The statue was fashioned to have all the properties of an eighty-year-old, but in reality, it was completed that very same day.

Hazal explain that everything was created fully grown. Items weren't created as babies or seeds, but as mature creations. Adam was created as an adult, and animals were created in their mature form. Similarly, says Rav Nebenzahl, the world was created mature. That's how it's possible that the world appears older than it is in actuality.[3]

Our rest on Shabbat is part of our testimony that Hashem created the world in seven days, thousands of years ago.

---

3. This is one of many approaches to the question of the age of the world. See also Rabbi Chaim Jachter, *Reason to Believe: Rational Explanations of Orthodox Jewish Faith* (Jerusalem: Menorah Books, 2017).

How Could Am Yisrael Have Committed the Sin of the Golden Calf?

וירא העם כי בשש משה לרדת מן ההר ויקהל העם על אהרן ויאמרו
אליו: קום עשה לנו אלהים אשר ילכו לפנינו כי זה משה האיש אשר
העלנו מארץ מצרים לא ידענו מה היה לו. (שמות לב:א)

When the people saw that Moshe was late in coming down from the mountain, the people gathered against Aharon, and they said to him: "Come on! Make us gods that will go before us, because this man Moshe, who brought us up from the land of Egypt, we don't know what has become of him." (*Shemot* 32:1)

How could the nation that witnessed all the miracles in Egypt and the Splitting of the Sea even contemplate serving another god? The *pesukim* describe how Bnei Yisrael thought that Moshe tarried too long in his return from Mount Sinai and thus believed that he was no longer alive. They then approached Aharon and requested that he make for them a god, because they didn't know if Moshe would ever return. Aharon responded to them by ordering them to bring their jewelry. Why did Aharon do that? Why did he not outright reject their request? Then, they made a calf and said, "This is your god, O Israel, that took you out of Egypt." Let's explore a number of opinions that address this issue.

RASHI: EREV RAV

Rashi, the great defender of Klal Yisrael, blames the sin of the Golden Calf on the *erev rav* – "the mixed multitude" that left Egypt with them.

Rashi explains that this thesis is grounded in the Torah. After the Golden Calf was built, the people pointed to it and stated, "This is *your* god" instead of "our god."

Rashi proves this idea further with the words in *pasuk* 7, when Hashem told Moshe to go down: "*your* people has acted basely." Why does Hashem say "your people" as if they are Moshe's but not His? Rashi explains that Hashem was referring to the *erev rav*, who joined Am Yisrael at Moshe's discretion. Moshe reasoned that it would be beneficial for the Egyptians that desired to convert to join Am Yisrael on its journey, without consulting Hashem as to whether to accept these Egyptian converts.

Throughout his commentary on the Torah, Rashi blames the *erev rav* for many of Klal Yisrael's problems.

The difficulty with Rashi's opinion is that it leaves us with a very fundamental question. If the sins of Klal Yisrael were really the fault of the *erev rav*, why are we still paying for these sins to this day? If we were misled, why were we held accountable? Remember, receipt of the *luhot* was delayed due to the sin of the Golden Calf.

RINAT YITZHAK: A LACK OF INTERNALIZING

The *Rinat Yitzhak*[1] suggests that from this blemish in our history, we learn that inspiration based on witnessing a miraculous event, if not internalized, will not last. One can argue whether or not the *erev rav* were *leshem Shamayim* when they joined Klal Yisrael. However, even if they were, their inspiration was a result of witnessing the plagues, which drove them to convert. From this, we see what happens when inspiration is based on external miracles and not based on substance. Inspiration

---

1. Rav Avraham Yitzhak Sorotskin, *Rinat Yitzhak al HaTorah* (Wickliffe, OH, 2001), 338.

based on Hashem's constant miracles that sustain the world and keep it going would be more lasting.

The Gemara in Yevamot (24b) states that in the days of Kings David and Shlomo, the *batei din* didn't accept converts. Many people want to convert when the Jews have it good. In a sense, this is what happened in the desert, too. But once the miracles stopped occurring, they lost their excitement.

RAMBAN: INTERMEDIARY OR LACK OF FAITH

The Ramban defends Bnei Yisrael and claims that they weren't looking to serve idolatry. Rather, they were seeking an intermediary between themselves and Hashem to replace Moshe, whom they believed was gone forever. They were panic stricken!

Rabbi Yaakov Kamenetzky[2] adds a similar idea. He tells us to put ourselves in their shoes: They were standing in middle of a desert. Their leader was gone, their food was gone, and there were no other options. It was a terrifying moment for them! Their sin, according to Rav Yaakov, was a lack of *faith* that Hashem was taking care of them. After experiencing all the miracles in Egypt, where was their faith? It is understandable, yet not excusable.

BEIT HALEVI: THE WRONG MEANS

According to the Beit HaLevi,[3] Bnei Yisrael had great intentions. They desired only a connection with Hashem. Their motives were pure. However, they made one fatal error: They attempted to do a "mitzva" without receiving a command from HaKadosh Barukh Hu. Someone can have the greatest of intentions, but if they don't go through the means that Hashem commanded, their action can actually be a sin instead. We are not allowed to make up our own means to get close to HaKadosh Barukh Hu. It doesn't matter what will make us "feel" spiritual; we must perform mitzvot the way Hashem commands. Doing what you "feel" is

---

2. *Emet LeYaakov* (New York: 1996), 340.
3. *Beit HaLevi, Ki Tisa*, 53.

about yourself. If you truly want to be close to Hashem, you have to follow what He commands in the Torah.[4]

The Beit HaLevi suggests that the *Mishkan* atoned for the sin of
the Golden Calf. The *Mishkan* represented a tangible means for Klal Yisrael to connect with Hashem. There is an interesting emphasis in *Parashat
Pekudei*, says the Beit HaLevi, on the words "as Hashem commanded
Moshe." Over and over, the *pesukim* reiterate that every single aspect of
the *Mishkan* – the boards, the sockets, the measurements – were made
precisely according to Hashem's instructions. In this way, the *Mishkan*
was an atonement for the *egel* – because every last detail of the *Mishkan*
was directly commanded by Hashem and was followed precisely. The
way to get close to Hashem is through the commandments He gave us.

---

4. According to the Netziv, in *Haamek Davar*, this was the transgression of Nadav and
   Avihu – attempting to get close to Hashem in a way that He did not command or
   sanction.

Why a Calf?

כי תשא את ראש בני ישראל לפקדיהם ונתנו איש כפר נפשו לה' בפקד
אתם ולא יהיה בהם נגף בפקד אתם. (שמות ל:יב)

When you take the sum of Bnei Yisrael according to their numbers, let each one give to Hashem an atonement for his soul when
they are counted; then there will be no plague among them when
they are counted. (*Shemot* 30:12)

An interesting question concerning the sin of the Golden Calf is why an
animal came out of the fire. The gold could have taken on any form – a
celestial body, a shape – so why did it specifically become an ox?

Rav Shlomo Zevin[1] connects the Golden Calf with the name
and first *pasuk* of *Parashat Ki Tisa*. The literal translation of *tisa* is to "lift
up" or "elevate." Rabbi Zevin draws a parallel between the "lifting up"
of Bnei Yisrael through the half-shekel and the sin of the Golden Calf.

What is the most obvious external difference between humans
and animals? A person walks upright, with his head up high, while an
animal walks on all fours, its head facing down. This external difference
symbolically reflects an inner distinction as well: People are governed
by their brains, so the brain sits atop the rest of the body. The mind is

---

1. *LaTorah VeLaMo'adim*, 150.

supposed to rule over the heart. If someone has a forbidden desire, he must overcome it with his intellect. An animal, on the other hand, has no control over its instinct. Its head is right next to its stomach and lower organs, because that is what governs the animal.

Consequently, if a person does not use his brain to control his body and desires, if he just focuses on the physical pleasures that lie before him, then he's no greater than an animal. His brain is not in charge.

Therefore, the ultimate, ideal state of a person is symbolized by standing upright, with the head in charge. But when desire and inappropriate thoughts take over, we're no better than animals.

Accordingly, the ox of the sin of the Golden Calf symbolized that Bnei Yisrael were acting like animals, following their desires instead of using their brains. We need to keep our heads up high and use our intellect before acting. Literally, *ki tisa* – to raise our heads.

How Could Moshe Have Broken the God-Given *Luhot*?

ויהי כאשר קרב אל המחנה וירא את העגל ומחלת ויחר אף משה וישלך
מידו את הלחת וישבר אתם תחת ההר. (שמות לב:יט)

Now it came to pass when he drew closer to the camp and saw
the calf and the dances, that Moshe's anger was kindled, and he
flung the tablets from his hands, shattering them at the foot of
the mountain. (*Shemot* 32:19)

The *Meshekh Hokhma* offers an interesting interpretation of the sin of
the Golden Calf and Moshe's subsequent destruction of the *luhot*. He
first explains that the Torah and *emuna* are the foundations of our nation.
There is nothing that is inherently holy that is separate from Torah.
All holiness flows from Torah, which is ultimately from HaKadosh
Barukh Hu.

The problem with the Golden Calf, explains the *Meshekh Hokhma*,
was that Bnei Yisrael attributed inherent power to Moshe Rabbenu.
They felt that he was godly and had special powers that had caused all
the miracles to take place. They believed in Hashem, but they thought

Hashem gave Moshe godly powers. When they thought he was gone forever, they felt a need to replace him with something else that would carry these same powers.

When Moshe came down the mountain with the *luhot*, he recognized their mistake. He realized that if he would preserve the *luhot* while he tried to educate the children of Israel, and then retrieve the *luhot* and present them, Bnei Yisrael would then ascribe special power to the *luhot*. They would turn the *luhot* into objects of worship, just like the Golden Calf.

Moshe took the most prized treasure he had ever received and smashed it in front of Klal Yisrael to show them that *nothing* has inherent holiness other than the Torah, which is from Hashem.[1]

The *Meshekh Hokhma*[2] suggests that this was also Calev's claim when he stood up against the *meraglim*, the spies: "And Calev silenced the people toward Moshe" – he silenced them by saying that it's not about Moshe's power. It's about a Jew's connection to Hashem. That itself will make the trip successful.

The *Meshekh Hokhma* adds another proof that nothing has inherent holiness: Moshe was one of four people in *Tanakh* whose name is repeated twice.[3] What was the "Moshe, Moshe"? It symbolized that Moshe was the same person before and after he spoke to HaKadosh Barukh Hu. He didn't change. Hashem is the One Who sanctifies us, and no one has inherent holiness.

---

1. Commenting on the last *pasuk* of the Torah, Rashi says that Moshe is praised for having destroyed the *luhot*: *asher shibarta – yeishar kohakha sheshibarta* ("that you broke – congratulations for having broken them"). In addition to the reason provided above by the *Meshekh Hokhma*, one must take into account that after spending forty days and nights on Mount Sinai with no food or sleep, learning the Torah directly from Hashem, it was not an easy task for him to destroy everything in one second. That itself took courage and humility.
2. *Bemidbar* 13:30.
3. Avraham, Yaakov, Moshe, and Shmuel.

Absence Makes the
Heart Grow Fonder

ויפן וירד משה מן ההר ושני לחת העדת בידו: לחת כתבים משני
עבריהם מזה ומזה הם כתבים. והלחת מעשה א־להים המה והמכתב
מכתב א־להים הוא חרות על הלחת. (שמות לב:טו-טז)

Now Moshe turned and went down from the mountain [bear-
ing] the two tablets of the testimony in his hand, tablets inscribed
from both their sides; on one side and on the other side they were
inscribed. Now the tablets were God's work, and the inscription
was God's inscription, engraved on the tablets. (*Shemot* 32:15–16)

The *Shemen HaTov*[1] asks a sharp question regarding these *pesukim*. The
luhot are mentioned earlier in this *parasha*, so why is this beautiful
description of the *luhot* being written by Hashem Himself reserved for
the end of the *parasha*, when they are about to be destroyed? Why is
the description delayed?

The *Shemen HaTov* offers two explanations. First, he explains, the
emphasis here may be to highlight Moshe's righteousness. As soon as

---

1. Rabbi Bernard Weinberger, *Shemen HaTov*, vol. 2 (New York: Talpiot Press,
   2007), 293.

Moshe realized what had to be done, he didn't hesitate, even though he was holding a gorgeous and valuable treasure. He had no idea whether or not a second set of *luhot* would be provided to Am Yisrael, but his commitment to truth allowed him to act in the manner that the situation called for.

An alternative explanation, says the *Shemen HaTov*, is that this points out a flaw in human nature. Often, we only appreciate things as we're about to lose them. It's human nature not to capitalize on what we have, and only to appreciate it once it's gone. The Torah therefore describes the beauty of the *luhot* just as they were about to be broken, thus reflecting this aspect of human nature.

Rabbi Frand speaks about this topic and points out the many ways in which we miss out on appreciating the blessings in our life when we focus on the challenges. How often do we not appreciate a loved one until it gets to the end of their life? What about our children, while they're young? Says Rabbi Frand:[2]

> The same applies to raising children. When our children are young and living with us, we have a hard time paying attention to the transience of their existence in our homes. Little children are difficult to handle. They wake us up in the middle of the night. They destroy the order and peace in our home. Teenagers can also be a major cause of sleeplessness and stormy times, not to mention issues like drivers' licenses, and others of equal emotional proportion. We are so caught up in the difficulty of raising our children that we often fail to realize how lucky we are to be spending time with them. Years later, when our nests empty out, we suddenly look back and wish we could hear the laughter of a two-year-old, the sound of little bare feet tapping on the floor, and yes, even the sound of toys being poured out in a room that we just cleaned. Believe it or not, we might even miss the cacophonous sound of (what they consider) music, and the clothes strewn everywhere.

---

2. *Rabbi Frand on the Parashah*, vol. 2, 160–61.

In life, we need to stop, take stock, and appreciate all we have. Never take anything for granted. There are so many relationships we have with family and friends that, unfortunately, we sometimes only truly appreciate them when they are gone.

Parashat Vayak'hel

It's Not Always the
Thought That Counts

ויקהל משה את כל עדת בני ישראל ויאמר אלהם: אלה הדברים אשר
צוה ה' לעשת אתם. (שמות לה:א)

Moshe assembled the whole community of Bnei Yisrael, and he
said to them: "These are the things that Hashem commanded to
make." (*Shemot* 35:1)

Many people incorrectly believe that the most important element in
Judaism is emotion and feeling, not action and the performance of
mitzvot. They further believe that one's thoughts and intentions are
what count, because Hashem knows what we mean and how we feel
inside. But while it's obligatory and wonderful to feel spiritual, experience being close to Hashem, and delve into the depths of halakha and
hashkafa, if that's where it ends, then we're missing the boat. That won't
get a person anywhere, and that's not what is desired of us by Hashem.

Mahshava, "intention," is considered like action only when there is
no option to do the action. If a person is stranded in Siberia and wishes
to buy an *etrog* but can't, Hashem accepts his thought in place of action.
But if someone has the opportunity to perform a mitzva and instead

focuses on his thoughts and feelings and doesn't carry it out, then he is not fulfilling his obligation.

We say in the Haggada, *yakhol meRosh Hodesh* – in reference to when we can start fulfilling the mitzva of telling the story of the exodus from Egypt from Rosh Hodesh Nisan. However, in fact, the Haggada clarifies, the mitzva is relevant only when we have the *matza* and *maror* before us. The mitzva is not just about talking and having the right intentions; rather, we have to actually engage in the mitzva on Pesah. Any other time is not a fulfillment of this mitzva.

Consider: If the world really ran according to the mentality that what matters is intention, very few people would do the right thing. Not many people have a philosophical mind great enough to perfect all of their thoughts and feelings. But everyone *can* perform the mitzvot. Appreciating the nuances and understanding behind every mitzva is not for everyone; if that was the ultimate goal, only some Jews would be able to perform mitzvot. However, fulfilling mitzvot is open to all, and then everyone on their own level can appreciate the philosophy behind the mitzvot based on their own level of understanding.

HaDerash VeHaIyun[1] quotes the last *pasuk* in *Kohelet*, which says that fearing Hashem and keeping His mitzvot are *kol ha'adam*, the entirety of man. Ultimately, that's what Hashem wants from every single person. We can perfect *doing* all of the mitzvot, no matter who we are.

The first *pasuk* in *Parashat Vayak'hel* says that Moshe gathered the *entire* nation and explained that the Torah is relevant to every single person because it's all about action – *laasot otam* (35:1). Every single Jew has that connection and can do the mitzvot. Sure, we must try to appreciate the mitzvot and their depth, but we can't forget the ultimate goal, which is the performance of mitzvot, actualizing everything into *avodat Hashem*.

Perhaps this is the meaning of a very difficult passage in the Talmud Yerushalmi.[2] A *pasuk* in *Devarim* says, "Hashem will remove all illness from us" (7:15).

---

1. Rav Aharon Lewin, *HaDerash VeHaIyun* (Jerusalem, Chorev, 1969), *Shemot*, 386.
2. Y. Shabbat 14:3.

What illness is the *pasuk* referring to? Rabbi Yaakov says *sereifa*, something burning hot, maybe fever. Rabbi Huna says it's *raayon*, which means "thought." The *Penei Moshe*, a commentary on the Yerushalmi, interprets this to mean anxiety and worries.

HaDerash VeHaIyun offers a different explanation: Perhaps it means the illness of believing that Hashem is only interested in *mahshava*, our intentions. The root of so many of our problems is that we don't take performance and action as seriously as we should. May we be able to always implement our positive intentions.

The First Shabbat Afternoon *Shiur*

ויקהל משה את כל עדת בני ישראל ויאמר אלהם: אלה הדברים אשר
צוה ה' לעשת אתם.... ויאמר משה אל כל עדת בני ישראל לאמר...
(שמות לה:א-ה)

Moshe assembled the whole community of Bnei Yisrael, and he
said to them: "These are the things that Hashem commanded to
make..." And Moshe spoke to the entire community of the children of Israel, saying: "This is the word that Hashem has commanded to say." (*Shemot* 35:1–8)

It is clear from the *pesukim* that Moshe taught the mitzvot of Shabbat
and the *Mishkan* to all of Klal Yisrael. The *Be'er Yosef*[1] comments that
this situation was very unusual; this was not the normal way that the
Torah was transmitted. The Gemara in Eiruvin (54b) tells us that when
Moshe transmitted the Torah, he gave everyone a chance to learn it
four times, because *Hazal* say it takes four times to start understanding something. The sequence was as follows: After Moshe learned the
Torah from Hashem, he would teach it to Aharon. Then Aharon's sons

---

1. Rav Yosef MiSalant, *Be'er Yosef* (Jerusalem, 1972), *Shemot*, 334.

would join them, and Moshe would address Aharon's sons. Follow-ing them, the elders entered, and Moshe addressed them in his les-son, with Aharon and his sons listening all the while. Finally, Moshe taught it to the rest of Klal Yisrael, with everyone else still listening in the background.

Then, Moshe would leave, Aharon would teach it to everyone, and then Aharon would leave, as he had heard the content four times at that point. Aharon's sons would do the same, then leave as well, and so forth with the elders. This provided everyone the opportunity to hear the commandments four times.

The *Be'er Yosef* wonders why it wasn't done this way in this week's *parasha*. Why did Moshe teach the mitzvot directly to Klal Yisrael?

The *Be'er Yosef* quotes a midrash (*Yalkut*):

רבותינו בעלי אגדה אומרים, מתחילת התורה עד סופה אין בה פרשה
שנאמרה בראשה "ויקהל" אלא זאת בלבד, אמר הקב"ה עשה לך קהילות
גדולות ודרוש לפניהם ברבים בהלכות שבת, כדי שילמדו ממך דורות
הבאים להקהיל קהילות בכל שבת ושבת ולכנוס בבתי מדרשות ללמד
ולהורות לישראל דברי תורה איסור והיתר כו'.

Our Rabbis say: From the beginning of the Torah until the end, there is no *parasha* that begins with the term *vayak'hel* (assemble) except for this occurrence. Hashem told [Moshe]: Assemble the people and teach them the laws of the Shabbat, so that the future generations can learn from you that on Shabbat, people should assemble in shuls and places of learning to spread Torah and explain what is permitted and what is forbidden.

The reason Moshe gathered Klal Yisrael and spoke to them directly about Shabbat was to teach them what we're supposed to do on Shabbat. This is the source for a rabbi's *shiur* on Shabbat afternoon. Moshe was laying the groundwork for what we're supposed to continue for generations in all Jewish communities, to partake in studying the laws pertaining to Shabbat on that very day.

Learning on Shabbat must play a central role in our Shabbat experience. There is a fascinating *makhloket* regarding the content of our learning on Shabbat. The *Shulhan Arukh*[2] states that a teacher should not teach new material to his students on Shabbat, since the children will not enjoy or connect to it. *Pithei Teshuva*[3] suggests that perhaps the opposite is true: one should teach new material on Shabbat, as review is often more tedious, less exciting, and less stimulating than learning something new. The underlying message for us from this discussion is that we should set aside time to learn on Shabbat and we should make sure that we choose an enjoyable, stimulating, and fulfilling topic to study on Shabbat to enhance our *oneg Shabbat.*

---

2. *Yoreh Deah* 245:14 (based in Nedarim 37a).
3. Ibid., 6.

Internalizing the
Impact One Person
Can Have on Us

ויצאו כל עדת בני ישראל מלפני משה. (שמות לה:כ)

The entire community departed from Moshe's presence.
(*Shemot* 35:20)

Why are the last two words of this *pasuk* necessary? If Klal Yisrael had
just stood before Moshe to receive a command, then obviously they left
milifnei Moshe – "Moshe's presence." What does the *pasuk* add by telling
us that all of Bnei Yisrael left Moshe's presence?

The *Darkhei Musar*[1] quotes the *Ohr HaHayim*, whose first explanation is that this teaches us that the proper way to leave a great person
or holy place is to walk backward. So maybe *milifnei* Moshe means that
they left him while facing him, walking backward.

A second answer from the *Ohr HaHayim* is that they were worried
that Moshe, who was so rich, would quickly make all the contributions

---

1.   Rabbi Yaakov Neiman, *Darkhei Musar* (Tel Aviv: Ohr Yisrael Press, 1979), 137.

himself. So, they walked out keeping their eye on Moshe Rabbenu, to make sure he didn't take the opportunity for himself.

But Rabbi Neiman, in his *Darkhei Musar*, quotes a third answer from the Alter of Kelm. When Bnei Yisrael left Moshe, it says, they left *with* him, meaning, you could tell they had just been in Moshe's presence. It was clear from their faces and behavior that they had just been with him.

We see a similar idea in Yoma (86a), which says that people should look at us and our actions and say, "He has great teachers, parents, *rebbeim.*" Our actions should speak in praise of how we were raised and taught.

Rabbi Neiman then adds yet another explanation, this one from the Dubno Maggid on *Parashat Masei*. The *pesukim* tell us that Moshe wrote down all of the children of Israel's travels; yet, the first *pasuk* says that Moshe wrote *motza'eihem lemaaseihem*[2] (their origins to their destination), but then the Torah later says *maaseihem lemotza'eihem* (their destinations from their origins). Why the switch in order?

To explain the change in order of the text, the Dubno Maggid provides a *mashal* of a man with an only child. The father becomes a widower and then eventually remarries a woman who is not interested in the son from her husband's first marriage. The father is very pained by the situation and can't wait to marry off his son. The day arrived when the son was to get married. As the father and son headed off to the wedding, the father asked the wagon driver, "How much time do we have left?" The son asked, "How long have we been driving?" They had similar-sounding questions, but each had a different focus. One was focused on the destination, the goal to marry off his son, and one was focused on where he came from, how far he was from the person who had made his life miserable.

Says the Dubno Maggid, Moshe recognized the value of *Eretz Yisrael*, so his focus was the direction of their travel, from their origins – *motza'eihem* – to their destinations – *maaseihem*. Klal Yisrael wasn't yet on that level, so their focus was retrospective, on how far from Egypt they had come.

---

2. *Bemidbar* 33:2.

Our *pasuk* says *milifnei Moshe* to show that Klal Yisrael always took where they came from with them. They didn't want to forget it and only focus on where they were going.

The goal in life is to take our wonderful experiences with us, to internalize them and not let them evaporate before they have a chance to shape us into who we are.

Prohibitions Elevate Holiness

לא תבערו אש בכל מושבותיכם ביום השבת. (שמות לה:ג)

You shall not kindle fire in any of your dwellings on Shabbat. (*Shemot* 35:3)

The Gemara in Shabbat (70a) discusses why this halakha about the prohibition of kindling a fire on Shabbat is singled out to be explicitly written, from all the other halakhot of Shabbat. One opinion maintains that the reason this *melakha* is distinguished from the other 39 *melakhot* is because its violation is punishable by lashes rather than by capital punishment. The second opinion offered, which is the accepted opinion, suggests that this prohibition is singled out to teach us that the *melakhot* are distinct acts, and to emphasize that a separate punishment is applied for the violation of each prohibition. In other words, if one's lapse of awareness caused him to accidently violate all of the 39 *melakhot*, he would be required to offer 39 distinct *korbanot hatat,* or sin offerings.

If one was not aware of the concept of Shabbat and violates several of the 39 *melakhot*, he is required to bring only one *hatat* offering. However, if one was aware of the concept of Shabbat, yet was unaware that the 39 *melakhot* are prohibited, then he has to offer 39 sacrifices (one for each violation of a prohibited act). The Gemara then asks, if one was aware of the *kedusha* (holiness) of Shabbat but was not aware that there are 39 prohibited *melakhot* on Shabbat, then what about Shabbat was one aware of? The Gemara answers that the individual was aware of the laws of *tehumim* (the boundary within which one may carry on Shabbat).

Why did the Gemara not just respond that he was aware of the concept of Shabbat? He knew that God created the world and rested on Shabbat but was not familiar with the intricate details of the 39 *melakhot*. Why did the Gemara have to come up with the reason that such an individual's minimal knowledge of Shabbat was with respect to the *melakha* of *tehumim*?

Explains Rav Hershel Schachter,[1] *kedusha* is not something that comes out of thin air. There is no abstract holiness. It has to be grounded. In order to be considered as someone who is aware of the *kedusha* of Shabbat, he has to be familiar with a *halakha* of Shabbat. The halakha reflects its holiness. Furthermore, this is not just any halakha. The Gemara did not cite *kiddush* or *lehem mishna* as an example of a halakha which he is familiar with. Why not? Because *kedusha* is reflected by limitations and prohibitions. A *kohen* has a certain level of *kedusha*, and he is prohibited from marrying certain women. The holiest place – the *Kodesh Kodashim* – is restricted to all but the *kohen gadol*, once a year. *Kedusha* is dependent on limitations and prohibitions. To understand the concept of *kedushat Shabbat*, one has to understand a practical application like *tehumim*, because the very definition of *kedusha* entails an obligation to observe additional prohibitions.

Rav Schachter adds, in the name of Rav Yosef Soloveitchik, that when a woman voluntarily fulfills a mitzva that is time-bound, *Baalei Tosafot* and Ashkenazic custom is to allow her to recite a *berakha*. Why? She is not obligated in this particular act; how can she state *"asher kidishanu"*? The answer is that in terms of *kedusha*, men and women are equal. Regarding the prohibitions, there is no difference, thus the *berakha* reflecting *kedusha* can be recited.

At times, one may feel that for a Torah-observing Jew there are so many restrictions and limitations. But it is precisely these limitations

---

1. *Rav Schachter on the Parsha* (Passaic, 2017).

that not only separate us, but elevate us. May we appreciate and fulfill not only the positive commandments but take great care in understanding and refraining from engaging in prohibited activities not appropriate for an *Am Kadosh*.

All Talk, No Action

ויבאו כל איש אשר נשאו לבו וכל אשר נדבה רוחו אתו הביאו את תרומת
ה׳ למלאכת אהל מועד ולכל עבדתו ולבגדי הקדש. (שמות לה:כא)

Every man whose heart uplifted him came, and everyone whose
spirit inspired him to generosity brought the offering of Hashem
for the work of the Tent of Meeting, for all its service, and for the
holy garments. (*Shemot* 35:21)

Why does the Torah use such a wordy description to tell us that Am
Yisrael donated to the *Mishkan*? It could easily have been written in a
shorter manner, something like, "They did exactly what Hashem commanded them."

Rabbi Yisrael Bronstein, in his *sefer VeKarata LeShabbat Oneg*,[1]
cites the Hida, who teaches us that it is very natural for someone who
has been inspired to feel uplifted and to get excited about translating
inspiration into deed. Often, when we hear of a need, an opportunity to
take action, or something spiritually exciting, we tell ourselves that we
will do it, but how often do we actually carry out our big plans and see
them to fruition? We usually procrastinate, cool off, and lose the initial
excitement. We start to second-guess ourselves and to think of lots of

---

1. Vol. 1 (Jerusalem, 1990), 121.

excuses why not to carry out our original plan. The inspiration wears off, and our thoughts are not translated into action.

This *pasuk* teaches us that every individual who was originally inspired to donate to the *Mishkan* carried through with his inspiration and took action. Every single person made good on his pledge.

This, explains Rav Pam,[2] is why the content of the *Parshiyot Teruma* and *Tetzaveh* is repeated in *Parshiyot Vayak'hel* and *Pekudei*. The Torah wants to emphasize that after all the times that the Torah says *ve'asita* – "any you shall make" – in *Parashat Teruma* and *Parashat Tetzaveh*, Bnei Yisrael carried through; *Parshiyot Vayak'hel* and *Pekudei* are full of *ve'asu* – "and they made."

Let us internalize this message and do all we can to take those moments of inspiration and turn them into prompt action.

---

2. Rabbi Shalom Smith, *The Pleasant Way: Adapted from the Teachings of Horav Avrohom Pam* (Lakewood, NJ: Israel Book Shop, 2002).

Proper Intent Enhances Our Actions

וכל הנשים אשר נשא לבן אתנה בחכמה טוו את העזים. (שמות לה:כו)

And all the women whose hearts uplifted them with wisdom, spun the goat hair. (*Shemot* 35:26)

Rabbi Yisachar Teichtal[1] explains that we learn a valuable lesson from the wording of this *pasuk* about the women *asher nasa liban* – "whose hearts moved them" to take part in the crafting of the *Mishkan*. Every single mitzva we do, and many actions we take in life, can be elevated to *lishma* through proper intent. Doing a mitzva or action for Hashem's sake adds tremendous significance to the act itself and makes it completely different qualitatively when we perform it with the proper motivation and intent.

Rabbi Teichtal writes about the settlement in *Eretz Yisrael* that anyone who was going to donate money to the settlement should say, "I hereby give this donation for the needs of building up our land" as he sends off the money. We can create worlds by having proper intention,

---

1. Rabbi Yisachar Teichtal, *Eim HaBanim Semeiha* (Jerusalem: Urim Publishers, 2000), 279.

and the value of a mitzva increases significantly with *lishma* intent. When a person performs a mitzva with the proper intentions, no harmful spiritual forces will be able to affect the mitzva.

From where does he learn this concept?

He quotes the *Maggid Meisharim*, a *sefer* by Rabbi Yosef Karo that records ideas he learned from an angel while he slept. Rabbi Karo points out in *Parashat Teruma* that the Torah uses the word *li* – "for Me" – repeatedly in Hashem's words. Each separate command contains a reminder that we are building the *Mishkan* to fulfill Hashem's will. Indeed, any time we are about to perform an action that involves sanctity, we should focus on, and even verbalize, that we are doing it *leshem Shamayim*. We say *likhvod Shabbat kodesh* as we shop or cook for Shabbat, and even when we eat on Shabbat. All of our actions can be uplifted by adding this little bit of concentration.

Returning to our *pasuk*, these women whose hearts were moved to action were all in the context of a mitzva. They did every act with proper intent. If we put our actions into the proper perspective, we can elevate everything we do. This ultimately brings Hashem's presence – the *Shekhina* – into our lives.[2]

---

2. A story is told of the Hafetz Hayim who was traveling with a student. After the student paid the wagon driver, the Rebbe looked disturbed. The student inquired as to why the Rebbe was disturbed. The Rebbe asked him, "When you paid the driver, did you have in mind that you are fulfilling several mitzvot, including: paying a worker on time, not paying interest, and several others?" In Israel, there is a sign in my barber shop listing seven mitzvot that one fulfills when paying the barber after a haircut. We can elevate our spirituality if we take a moment to consider our actions within a halakhic framework.

Where There's a Will, There's a Way

ויקרא משה אל בצלאל ואל אהליאב ואל כל איש חכם לב אשר נתן
ה' חכמה בלבו כל אשר נשאו לבו לקרבה אל המלאכה לעשת אתה.
(שמות לו:ב)

And Moshe called Betzalel and Ohaliav and every wise-hearted
person in whose heart Hashem placed wisdom, everyone whose
heart moved him to approach the work to do it. (*Shemot* 36:2)

The *Otzrot HaTorah*[1] quotes the Hafetz Hayim, who points out that this
pasuk is not a list of the people who Moshe summoned to take part in
building the *Mishkan*, but a description of those people who took part
in it. Accordingly, the *pasuk* should be understood and punctuated as
follows:

Moshe called Betzalel and Ohaliav and every wise-hearted person,
in whose heart Hashem placed wisdom – everyone whose heart
moved him to come forward to work and to do it.

---

1. Rabbi Eliyahu Chaim Cohen, *Otzrot HaTorah* (Bnei Brak, 2006), 308.

It seems strange, though, that *everyone* who was inspired had the skill to do the work, or that *every* wise person was also inspired to do the work. It is very unlikely that there was such a perfect correlation between those with the skill and those with the desire!

The process of building the *Mishkan* was extremely difficult and intricate. It demanded an unprecedented level of perfection. This *pasuk* explains that nobody just happened to have the necessary skills. Anyone who possessed the skills did so because Hashem placed the necessary wisdom in his heart. And why did they merit this gift from Hashem? Because their hearts moved them to take part in building the *Mishkan*. If someone had the skills, it was because Hashem gave them to him, because they so desired to be part of this process.

We learn from here that if you have the will to accomplish something, Hashem will meet you halfway. When someone has the will, Hashem provides him with the requisite knowledge.

A blind *talmid hakham* once came to Rabbi Isser Zalman Meltzer with two *sefarim*. He wanted a *haskama* from the *rav*, and he said, "These are the last *sefarim* I'm going to write." Rabbi Isser Zalman said, "What do you mean, these are going to be your last? *Halevai*, there should be many more!"

The man explained that very recently he had lost his vision. When the doctor checked his eyes, he was amazed that the man had any vision at all for the last number of years. Based on what he saw, he believed this *talmid hakham* should have lost his vision many years earlier. The *talmid hakham* explained to the doctor that the reason he had been able to see was because of his strong desire to produce these two *sefarim*. That was his goal, and he didn't think beyond it. When he finally finished the *sefarim*, he felt satisfied and decided he could relax – and that's when he lost his vision. While he still had his vision, his desire to do something for HaKadosh Barukh Hu kept it going. Once he felt he had accomplished his goal, Hashem wasn't going to make another miracle to restore his vision.

Rabbi Isser Zalman said he learned from this story that when someone is so moved, so driven, to accomplish something, Hashem helps him along. We must therefore always have goals, responsibilities, projects we are working on, because as long as we are working hard and focusing, Hashem blesses us with the strength and skill to succeed.

The *Otzrot HaTorah* then quotes Rabbi Yeruham Levovitz, who points to a midrash that teaches us to always push ourselves, even if the future is unknown. When we push ourselves, there is a chance that Hashem will give us more assistance, more *siyatta dishemaya*.

There is a *pasuk*[2] that tells us that a lazy person should go and watch an ant to become wise. The midrash explains that an ant prepares food all summer so that it will have enough to eat in the winter. But an ant only lives for six months! And all it needs to eat during its lifetime is one and a half grains of wheat! Why is it so busy collecting food? Why did Hashem create the ant with this nature?

There is something for us to learn from here. The ant seems to say, "Maybe Hashem will allow me to live a longer life. I will collect food just in case that happens." We can learn from an ant to do our *hishtadlut*, to move our hearts with a burning desire, and Hashem will do the rest.

---

2. *Mishlei* 6:6.

The Credit Is All Yours

ויעש את הכיור נחשת ואת כנו נחשת במראת הצבאת אשר צבאו פתח
אהל מועד. (שמות לח:ח)

And he made the washstand of copper and its base of copper
from the mirrors of the women who set up the legions, who con-
gregated at the entrance of the Tent of Meeting. (*Shemot* 38:8)

The *Kiyor* was made from mirrors donated by women. Rashi says that
Moshe was initially revolted by the idea of using these mirrors in the
Mishkan, as they had been used by the women for the "vain" purpose
of beautifying themselves. But Hashem told him to accept them, that
these mirrors are very beloved to Him. Why?

Rashi explains that the term *marot hatzovot* – "the mirrors of the
women who set up the legions" – refers to the the children of Israel who
were born because of these mirrors. In Egypt, the men of Bnei Yisrael
were forced to perform backbreaking labor. When they'd come home
after a long day, they just wanted to collapse. But the women would bring
them food and drink and make themselves attractive to their husbands.
Through this, many children were born.

There's a phrase in this Rashi, though, that is somewhat unclear.
He writes that the wife would look into the mirror with her husband –
an ancient selfie – and say, *ani na'eh mimkha* – "I'm more beautiful than

you." Why were they bragging about their beauty? Isn't it insulting to the husbands?

Rabbi Menachem Genack[1] quotes Rabbi Shmuel Kamenetzky, who explains that the phrase should be punctuated differently: *ani naah, mimkha* – "I am beautiful, *because* of you." They were attributing their beauty to their husbands, as if to say the man was like the sun and the woman the moon, reflecting his beauty. By making this statement, the depressed men were uplifted by the praise of their wives, who attributed their beauty to the love of their husbands. May we internalize this message and always appreciate our spouses and strengthen our relationships.

---

1. Rabbi Menahem Genack, *Birkat Yitzhak* (New York: Mesorah Publications, 2013), 147.

Parashat Pekudei

Foreshadowing the Destruction of the *Beit HaMikdash*

אלה פקודי המשכן משכן העדת אשר פקד על פי משה עבדת הלוים
ביד איתמר בן אהרן הכהן. (שמות לח:כא)

These are the numbers of the *Mishkan*, the Mishkan of the Testimony, which were counted at Moshe's command; [this was]
the work of the Levites under the direction of Itamar, the son of
Aharon HaKohen. (*Shemot* 38:21)

Rashi points out the repetition of the word *Mishkan* in the first words
of this *pasuk* and explains that it alludes to destruction of the two *Batei
HaMikdash*. The *Batei HaMikdash* served as collateral – a *mashkon* – for
the sins of Klal Yisrael. Hashem collected our debt to Him, so to speak,
by unleashing His fury on the Temples, buildings of sticks and stones,
instead of on us.

The Gemara in *Sanhedrin* (102a) quotes a *pasuk*:

483

וביום פקדי ופקדתי עליהם חטאתם. (שמות לב:לד)

On the day that I settle accounts, I will hold them accountable for their sin. (*Shemot* 32:34)

The Gemara explains that every tragedy that happened to Klal Yisrael throughout history is, in part, a punishment for the sin of the Golden Calf. The *Peninei HaTorah*[2] illustrates this idea with two *meshalim*:

> There was a king who got so angry at his son that he vowed to throw a boulder at him. Later, when his anger abated, he regretted his decision, but he was unsure what to do since he already swore. One of the king's good friends suggested that he break the stone into tiny pieces and throw those tiny pebbles at his son. In this way, the king would keep his word but not cause any physical damage to his son.
>
> In the same way, Hashem wanted to destroy Klal Yisrael after the sin of the Golden Calf. Instead, He took a *mashkon*, and we pay out our debt over time, through challenges and troubles, instead of having to pay it all at once, which would result in our destruction.

The second *mashal* is taken from the Dubno Maggid: An old man takes mercy on a prisoner, selling his own house and possessions to bail him out. The plan succeeds, and the newly released inmate runs to freedom. But what should he really have done upon his release from jail? Everything he could to get the old man's property back! The least this criminal could do is repay the generous old man!

Likewise, Hashem destroyed His own house, the *Batei HaMikdash*, to spare our lives from the prosecution of His attribute of strict judgment. Now that we have been spared, the least we can do is try to get the *mashkon* back, to do what we can to get the *Beit HaMikdash* rebuilt.[3]

---

2. Rav David Hadad, *Peninei HaTorah* (Beer Sheva, 1992), 35.
3. Rabbi Joseph B. Soloveitchik, *The Lord is Righteous in All His Ways,* explains that this is why our mourning is not as intense on the afternoon of Tisha BeAv. Exactly when the fire got more intense, our mourning gets less intense. The Rav explains this

Stones of Remembrance

ויעשו את אבני השהם מסבת משבצת זהב מפתחת פתוחי חותם על
שמות בני ישראל. וישם אתם על כתפת האפד אבני זכרון לבני ישראל
כאשר צוה ה׳ את משה. (שמות לט:ו-ז)

And they prepared the *shoham* stones, enclosed in gold settings,
engraved [similar to] the engravings of a seal, with the names of
the tribes of Israel. And he put them upon the shoulder straps of
the *efod* [as] stones of remembrance for the children of Israel, as
Hashem had commanded Moshe. (*Shemot* 39:6–7)

The stones of the *shoham* are placed on the *hoshen*, which is attached
to the *efod*, which is worn by the *kohen gadol*. In addition to informing
us of the requirement to place the stones on the *hoshen*, the reason for
such placement is included in the verse: so they can serve as "stones of
remembrance for the children of Israel."

Stones of remembrance: Who is supposed to remember, and
what are we supposed to remember? The tribes are inscribed next to
the stones. One can infer that Hashem remembers Am Yisrael and that

---

irony. Our mourning continues, but we take some comfort in the fact that Hashem
expressed His anger by destroying the *Batei HaMikdash* rather than Klal Yisrael. They
served as collateral for our lives. This is a bit of relief in a tragic time.

the *kohen gadol,* who is a representative of the Jewish people and performing the service in the Temple on their behalf, is acting so Hashem can remember them favorably.

The *Meshekh Hokhma*[1] offers an alternative suggestion, based on a famous midrash that perhaps the stones are there to trigger the children of Israel's memory. Bnei Yisrael should be reminded of having the name of their tribe engraved on the *kohen gadol's hoshen* as he enters the Holy of Holies as a means of deterring them from engaging in any form of transgression.

When Yosef HaTzaddik was about to be seduced by the wife of Potifar, the midrash tells us that his father's face appeared to him in the window and warned him not to succumb to her persuasion. The language used by the midrash is as follows: In the future, your children's names will be engraved on the *efod,* and your name shall be included among them; do you prefer that your name be erased from there and that you shall be known as one who visits harlots?

It is interesting that Yaakov, who could have said so many things to encourage Yosef to refrain from giving in to his desires at that moment, refers to the fact that his name will be engraved on the *efod* and that should convince Yosef to make the right choice, to overcome his urges and protect his reputation, so that he would be worthy of having his name sit alongside those of his brothers on the *efod* of the *kohen gadol.*

These stones, upon which the names of each tribe were engraved, are there to serve as a reminder for all of us to conduct our lives in a moral and ethical manner, in accordance with halakha, so that we merit to be listed adjacent to our brethren. Yosef was saved because he remembered what his destiny would be: that he would be on the *efod.* We also need to remember who we are: our potential, our future, and the future of our children.

We have to realize who we are and what we symbolize, and we have to live up to our potential. That's what Yosef realized. Hopefully, that will motivate us to live the lives we want to live.

---

1. *Meshekh Hokhma, Shemot* 39:6.

The Importance of Positive Reinforcement

וירא משה את כל המלאכה והנה עשו אתה כאשר צוה ה׳ כן עשו ויברך
אתם משה. (שמות לט:מג)

Moshe saw the entire work, and they had conducted it as Hashem
had commanded, so had they done, so Moshe blessed them.
(*Shemot* 39:43)

After Bnei Yisrael fulfilled all their tasks and completed the *Mishkan*,
how did Moshe react? He offered them a *berakha*. What's the message
of Moshe Rabbenu's reaction being a *berakha*?

Rabbi Jonathan Sacks[1] says, if you look at the language that's
used by the construction of the *Mishkan*, there are many parallels to the
creation of the world:

Three keywords appear in both passages: "work," "completed,"
and "blessed." These verbal echoes are not accidental. They are how the
Torah signals intertextuality, hinting that one law or story is to be read
in the context of another. In this case, the Torah is emphasizing that
Exodus ends as Genesis began, with the work of creation.

---

1. Rabbi Jonathan Sacks, *Lessons in Leadership* (Jerusalem: Maggid Books 2015), 115.

There's the creation of the world, and there's the building of the *Mishkan*. The difference is that the creation of the world was a divine creation, and the building of the *Mishkan* was an act of human creation. Yet, there are parallels that equate both scenarios. The creation of the world is tightly organized in series of sevens: There are seven days of creation; the word *tov* appears seven times; the word "God" appears thirty-five times; the word "earth" appears twenty-one times. The opening *pasuk* of *Sefer Bereshit* contains seven words. The complete text of the creation of the world is 469 (7 x 67) words long.

It's pretty amazing. It's all about "seven." Seven symbolizes the world, specifically Shabbat.

What about the *Mishkan*? *Parashat Vayak'hel-Pekudei* is similarly built around the number seven. The word *lev* is written seven times with regard to the *Mishkan*. The word *teruma* appears seven times in *perek* 40. The number seven also symbolizes the *Mishkan*, as the *Mishkan* is the microcosm of the world.

What is the message of Moshe's reaction to the building of the *Mishkan*? Moshe celebrated their achievement. Moshe congratulates them. "You did great! I'm really proud of you. You're amazing." He lifted them up.

By blessing them and celebrating their achievement, Moshe showed them what they could be. That is potentially a life-changing experience.

Rabbi Sacks cites an incident that is relevant. There was once a principal in a school who came to him and said, "Our school is failing. Students are leaving, there's no morale, I don't know what to do." Rabbi Sacks gave the principal one simple message.

"I want you to live by one word – *celebrate.*"

She turned to me with a sigh. "You don't understand – we have *nothing* to celebrate. Everything in the school is going wrong."

I said, "*Find* something to celebrate. If a single student has done better this week than last week, celebrate. If someone has a birthday, celebrate. If it's Tuesday, celebrate."

She seemed unconvinced, but promised to give the idea a try.

Eight years later, she came back and said, it's a changed experience. Because every little thing was celebrated.

We, as human beings, need positive reinforcement. We need to celebrate every little achievement, of ourselves, and of our children. That's today's generation. Today, we are Slobodka and not Novardok, to use those terms.[2] We're not about humbling people; we're about building people up. That's what Moshe Rabbenu did – he blessed them. Moshe gave them positive reinforcement. He did not just take for granted that they followed each and every commandment and built the *Mishkan* as directed. Moshe offered positive reinforcement and commended the people for having achieved such a tremendous accomplishment!

Celebration is an essential part of motivation. It turned a school around. In an earlier age and in a more sacred context, it turned the Israelites around. When we celebrate the achievements of others, we change lives.

---

2. These are known in the yeshiva world as symbolizing two different worldviews. Man is referred to as Adam, which according to Slobodka, is because Adam derived from *adame lo* – "I am like Him [God]," so I should hold myself up high and seek to achieve great things. Novardok stresses that the word Adam is derived from *adama,* "earth." One should be humble and always remember that he was created from the dust of the earth and is like dust before his Creator.

Hashem Helps Those
Who Help Themselves

ותכל כל עבדת משכן אהל מועד ויעשו בני ישראל ככל אשר צוה ה'
את משה כן עשו. (שמות לט:לב)

The work on the *Mishkan*, the Tent of Meeting, was *finished*, and
Bnei Yisrael *did* according to all that Hashem commanded Moshe;
so they did. (*Shemot* 39:32)

The Rama comments that the phrases of this *pasuk* seems out of order.
Shouldn't they "do" before they "finish"? He answers with a powerful
lesson. Although we cannot make a move in life without Hashem's
help, Hashem gives us credit as if we accomplished it on our own. We
get credit for every single mitzva we perform, even though Hashem
enabled us to perform it.

The Midrash says that Bnei Yisrael had difficulty building the
Mishkan, so they did what they could, and yet Hashem gave them full
credit anyway. This *pasuk* reflects this idea. All the work was finished
– the pasuk does not say that "they finished" the work, but that "it was
finished." Yet, how does the Torah describe it? As though (*kekhol*) Bnei

Yisrael did it all on their own. Hashem gave them the credit *as if* they had done it all.[1]

Hashem helps us every step of the way in life, but He gives us all the credit. We just have to do our part, our *hishtadlut*. We can't sit and wait for things to happen. Although all we do is credited to Hashem, we need to give it our all, and only then will Hashem do His part. As the saying goes, "God helps those who help themselves."

---

1. Similarly, when the midrash states that Pharaoh's daughter extended her arm many meters, at first she stretched out her arm and only thereafter did Hashem extend it further so that she could reach Moshe's basket. See this book, *Parashat Noach*, "Taking the First Step."

Patience Is a Virtue

ביום החדש הראשון באחד לחדש תקים את משכן אהל מועד.
(שמות מ:ב)

On the day of the first month, on the first of the month, you shall set up the *Mishkan* of the Tent of Meeting. (*Shemot* 40:2)

The *Mishkan* was erected in the month of Nisan, but the Midrash says it could have been ready earlier. According to *Hazal*, Moshe asked for donations for the *Mishkan* on the day after Yom Kippur, in Tishrei, and all the necessary funds were collected within a few days. Rabbi Yohanan says it took three months to build the *Mishkan*, which means it was ready in Tevet. Why, then, did the *Mishkan* sit in disuse for another three months? Why did Hashem want it to be inaugurated specifically in Nisan?

The *Be'er Yosef*[1] explains that, as we know, the *Mishkan* was an atonement for the sin of the Golden Calf. How so? The root of the sin of the Golden Calf was the *rush* to find spiritual avenues to connect with Hashem. They felt pressured to reach HaKadosh Barukh Hu as soon as they thought Moshe had died, so they created their own avenues in order to reach Him quickly.

---

1. Rav Yosef MiSalant, *Be'er Yosef* (Jerusalem, 1972), *Shemot*, 347.

Consequently, the atonement for their rush was to have the *Mishkan*, a direct connection to Hashem, in front of them and to have to wait to use it until Hashem commanded. At the time of sin of the Golden Calf, they jumped the gun, so the atonement was to *wait*. Everything must always be done at the time that Hashem says is appropriate.[2]

In addition, the *Mishkan* was a place for bringing offerings – and many commentaries say that when one brings an offering one is supposed to feel as if he himself is being offered on the Altar. Nisan is therefore an apropos time to begin bringing offerings, as Nisan is the month in which Yitzhak Avinu was born, and no one represents this *midda* like he does.

On the one hand, we need to run to perform mitzvot – but at the same time, while engaged in a mitzva, we need to act patiently and deliberately, performing it to perfection.[3]

---

2. Many of the great transgressions in history were due to a lack of patience. Shaul didn't wait for Shmuel to return. Adam and Chava could not refrain from eating from the Tree of Knowledge of Good and Evil (some commentators suggest that it would have been permissible to eat that fruit on Shabbat).

3. It is interesting to note that the well-known phrase is זריזין מקדימין למצוות, *zerizin makdimin lemitzvot* ("to mitzvot") – and not במצוות, *bemitzvot* ("in mitzvot"). This distinction highlights that one should act swiftly to *engage in the performance of* a mitzva, but once *involved* in a mitzva, one should perform the mitzva carefully and wholeheartedly.

The Significance
of the *Kiyor*

ונחשת התנופה שבעים ככר ואלפים וארבע מאות שקל. ויעש בה את
אדני פתח אהל מועד ואת מזבח הנחשת ואת מכבר הנחשת אשר לו
ואת כל כלי המזבח. ואת אדני החצר סביב ואת אדני שער החצר ואת
כל יתדת המשכן ואת כל יתדת החצר סביב. (שמות לח:כט-ל)

The copper of the waving was seventy talents and two thousand
four hundred shekels. From that, he made the sockets of the
entrance to the Tent of Meeting, the copper altar, the copper grat-
ing upon it, and all the implements of the Altar. (*Shemot* 38:29–30)

In the above *pesukim*, the Torah lists the amount of copper that was
donated to the *Mishkan* and what it was used for: the sockets that held
the *kerashim (planks)*, the outer *Mizbe'ah*, and the pegs.

The Abarbanel[1] raises a question: Wasn't the *Kiyor* also made of
copper? Yet, it isn't listed until later. Why aren't the *Kiyor* and its base
listed here? He answers that the other items were made from copper
donated by the men, whereas the copper used in the *Kiyor* was donated
by the women, in the form of their mirrors.

---

1. Abarbanel, *Shemot* 38:30.

Rabbi Shimshon Refael Hirsch[2] comments that it's noteworthy that the item that was used every single day specifically to sanctify and purify the *kohanim* for their *avoda* was made from such a physical and seemingly superficial object that women used to make themselves physically attractive:

> It is deeply significant that the vessel of the Sanctuary which was to represent "the moral 'keeping holy' of one's acts and efforts" was made out of the women's mirrors. Mirrors are articles which lay stress on the physical bodily appearance of people being an object of special consideration. So that it was shown that the physical sensual side of human beings is not merely not excluded from the sphere which is to be sanctified by the *Mikdosh*, but that it is the first and most essential object of this sanctification. After all, at rock bottom, as man has complete free will in moral matters, it is just this side of human nature which is necessary to come under the influence of the *Mikdosh*, if the sanctification of life which is aimed at is to be achieved.

We are required to elevate the physical and make it holy. Judaism doesn't reject anything; rather, as Hashem says, He wants us to be *anshei kodesh* – "holy *people*," not "holy angels." Hashem, therefore, wanted the most physical item to be used for this holy task in order to elevate it.[3]

---

2. *The Pentateuch, Shemot* (Gateshead: Judaica Press, 1989), 692.
3. One may suggest that specifically the *Kiyor* is made of mirrors for the following reason: Prior to engaging in their *avoda* in the *Mishkan*, the *kohanim* had to wash their hands in the *Kiyor*. Someone who transgressed inadvertently brings an offering as a form of repentance. If the same individual repeatedly brings such an offering, a *kohen* may question his sincerity. Perhaps he is violating the mitzvot purposely, not inadvertently. Therefore, when preparing to bring an offering, the *kohen* has to wash his hands in the *Kiyor*, where he will see his reflection, reminding him that before judging others, one must look into the mirror and judge himself.

Separate to Elevate

ויכס הענן את אהל מועד וכבוד ה' מלא את המשכן. (שמות מ:לד)

And the cloud covered the Tent of Meeting, and the glory of Hashem filled the *Mishkan*. (*Shemot* 40:34)

The Ramban, in his introduction to *Sefer Shemot* and in our *parasha*, mentions the idea that the *Mishkan* is a perpetuation of the experience of Mount Sinai. Rabbi Avishai David explains a deeper parallel between the *Mishkan* and Mount Sinai by highlighting a common denominator between them.[1]

Both Mount Sinai and the *Mishkan* were separated, cordoned off. No one but Moshe was able to ascend Mount Sinai. Everyone else was required to maintain a specified distance from the mountain. Similarly, there are areas within the *Mishkan* that are off limits to everyone but the *kohen gadol*.

The Ramban brings numerous examples of how holiness is reflected and created by *mehitzot* – "boundaries" or "barriers." When something is open and accessible to all, it has less inherent holiness. Similarly, in *Parashat Kedoshim*, the Ramban explains that we make

---

1. Rabbi Avishai David, *Shai LeAvi* (Jerusalem: Mishkan Publishers, 2017), 388.

ourselves holier by abstaining; by limiting and restricting ourselves, we create greater holiness.

There are numerous examples of this in Judaism. On Shabbat, there are limitations, and it is our holiest day. Marriage is an act of making a man and woman exclusive to one another, and it is called *kiddushin*.

In today's society, people feel the need to share everything on social media. We need to remember that we elevate ourselves by keeping things private. Just as the *Mishkan* and Mount Sinai were made holy by the barriers that cordoned them off, so too must we set boundaries to elevate ourselves.

Biographies of Sources

Compiled by
Yehoshua Paltiel

Abarbanel, Don Yitzhak – A Portuguese statesman, financier, and philosopher, the Abarbanel (1437–1508) is most famous for his commentary on the *Tanakh*. He served as treasurer to King Alfonso V and later was unsuccessful in bribing King Ferdinand to rescind the decree of the 1492 Spanish Expulsion. He left Spain with his co-religionists and eventually settled in Venice.

Aleinu Leshabe'ah – see Zilberstein, Rav Yitzhak

Alpert, Rav Nissan – Rav Alpert (1927–1986) was born in Poland but came with his family to America in 1939, first to San Francisco and then to the Lower East Side of Manhattan. He graduated valedictorian of the Washington Irving High School, and then learned at Mesivtha Tifereth Jerusalem, becoming one of the preeminent students of Rav Moshe Feinstein. He later taught at the R. Isaac Elchanan Theological Seminary of YU and eventually headed its *kollel* for *horaah* (*yadin-yadin*). His insights on the

Meiri and the Raavad on *Bava Metzia* have been published, as well as *Limudei Nissan* on the Torah.

Alshikh, R. Moshe – A student of Rav Yosef Karo and teacher of R. Chaim Vital, the Alshikh (1508–1593) was a prominent rabbi in Tzfat whose lessons on the *parasha* gained wide notoriety. They were published as *Torat Moshe*. *Marot Hatzove'ot* was later published on the Prophets.

Alter, Rav Yisrael – Commonly referred to as the Beit Yisrael after his work on the *parasha* and Hassidic thought, Rav Alter (1895–1977) escaped the Nazis and became the fifth Gerrer Rebbe. He re-established the Ger Hassidic sect in Israel and was also politically active, directing the Agudat Israel party in the Kenesset.

Amital, Rav Yehuda – Rav Amital (1924–2010) was born as Yehuda Klein in Romania and lost his family to the Nazis at Auschwitz. He was liberated by the Soviet Army and immigrated to Israel. He learned at Hebron Yeshiva and later the Kletzk Yeshiva in Pardes Hanna. He also studied under Rav Yaakov Moshe Charlop, and received his ordination from Rav Isser Zalman Meltzer. He joined the Haganah and fought in the War of Independence in 1948. He was instrumental in formulating the *hesder yeshiva* concept, and after the Six-Day War he founded Yeshivat Har Etzion and served as its *rosh yeshiva*. In 1988 he created the Meimad religious-Zionist party, and later served as minister-without-portfolio in the government of Shimon Peres. Some of his teachings have been published, including in English, such as *Jewish Values in a Changing World* and *Commitment and Complexity: Jewish Wisdom in an Age of Upheaval*.

Arukh HaShulhan – see Epstein, Rav Yechiel Michel Halevi

Attar, Rav Chaim ibn – Commonly known as the *Ohr HaHayim* after his commentary on the Torah, Rav Chaim was born in Morocco (1696) and died in Jerusalem (1743). His *Ohr HaHayim* combines the approaches of both the *midrashim* and the *pashtanim*, and gained such popularity that is now printed in almost all editions of the Torah with their classical commentaries. R. Chaim raised many prominent students, including the Hida (R. Haim David Azulai).

Auerbach, Rav Shlomo Zalman – Rav Shlomo Zalman (1910–1995) was born in Jerusalem and studied at the Etz Chaim Yeshiva. He later studied under Rav Tzvi Pesach Frank at his Kollel Kerem Tzion. He maintained a close relationship with Rav Chaim Ozer Grodzinski and the Chazon Ish. He authored his first book in 1935, *Me'orei Aish*, on the halakhic issues surrounding the use of electricity on Shabbat. He later wrote a two-volume work on agricultural laws. He served as *rosh yeshiva* of the Kol Torah Yeshiva in Jerusalem and became one of the foremost *poskim* of his time. *Hiko Mamtakim* is a collection of stories about and lessons learned from Rav Shlomo Zalman from over two hundred of his students.

Aviner, Rav Shlomo – Rav Aviner was born in 1943 in Lyon, occupied France, and evaded capture by being given a false identity. After the war, he became very active in Bnei Akiva, eventually becoming the national director in France. He studied physics and electrical engineering before making *aliya* at the age of twenty-three. He lived and worked at a religious kibbutz in the lower Galilee, Sde Eliyahu, and then went on to learn under Rav Tzvi Yehuda Kook at the Mercaz HaRav Yeshiva in Jerusalem. He served as the rabbi of Kibbutz Lavi, Moshav Keshet, and then Beis El. He is *rosh yeshiva* of Ateret Jerusalem (formerly Ateret Cohanim) and a prolific author. His works include *Tal Chermon* on the *parasha* and the holidays, and a collection of responsa, *She'elat Shlomo*. He also writes numerous short halakhic and hashkafic answers every week to questions posed through cell-phone texting.

Avraham ibn Ezra – Ibn Ezra (1089–ca. 1167) was a grammarian, poet, philosopher, and Bible commentator whose commentary to the Torah became one of the two touchstones for nearly all subsequent commentaries (along with that of Rashi). Leaving his native Spain to escape the persecution of the Almohods, he wandered extensively, through North Africa, Egypt, Israel, Italy France, England, and then finally back to Spain. He became a friend (and possibly son-in-law) of Yehudah Halevi, and it was during this time of his travels that he authored his commentary and two works on Hebrew grammar and philology.

Avramsky, R. Yehezkel – After being imprisoned in Siberia for fostering Jewish life in the communist Soviet Union, Rav Avramsky (1886–1976) moved to London where he lead the *beit din* for seventeen years. He later moved to Israel and served as *rosh yeshiva* of Slabodka in Bnei Brak. He is the author of *Hazon Yehezkel*, a 24-volume analysis of the Tosefta.

Baal HaTurim – R. Yaakov ben Asher (ca. 1269–ca. 1343) is often referred to as the Baal HaTurim after his most famous work, the halakhic compendium *Arba Turim*, upon which the *Shulhan Arukh* was modeled. His decisions were influenced by his famous father, R. Asher ben Yechiel (the Rosh), whom he followed from Cologne, Germany to Toledo, Spain. He also authored a commentary on the Torah.

Bahag – The *Halakhot Gedolot* is an influential halakhic compendium of the Talmud and is probably the first attempt at codifying all halakha by topic. Its author, believed by many to be Rav Shimon Kayyara of the ninth century, based his work on the *Halakhot Pesukot* of Rav Yehudai Gaon and the *She'iltot* of Rav Ahai Gaon. It is quoted frequently by the *Baalei HaTosafot* and was valued by Sephardic *Rishonim* as well.

Bahya ben Asher, Rabbenu – A student of the Rashba, Rabbenu Bahya (1255–1340) was a *darshan*, or preacher, in his native Zaragoza, Spain. He is most famous for his commentary on the Torah, whose style was patterned after the commentary of the Ramban.

Bartenura, Rav Ovadia of – Rav Ovadia (ca.1445–ca.1550) was a student of the Maharik, and became rabbi of the Italian city of Bartenura. He later moved to Israel and helped rejuvenate the Jewish community of Jerusalem. His commentary to the Mishna gained universal popularity, possibly being the most used commentary on the Mishna to this day.

Be'er Yosef – see Salant, Rav Yosef Zundel

Beit HaLevi – see Soloveitchik, Rav Yosef Dov Halevi

Beit Yisrael – see Alter, Rav Yisrael

Berditchev, Rav Levi Yitzhak of – Rav Levi Yitzhak (1740–1809) was rabbi of several communities, including Pinsk and Berditchev. He was a leading student of Rav Dov Ber, the Maggid of Mezritch, and of Rav Shmuel Shmelke of Nickelsburg. He is often called the *sanaigor* (defense attorney) of Israel, for his insistence on finding the positive qualities of the Jewish people. His *Kedushat Levi*, arranged on the *parasha*, is a primary source of Hassidic thought.

Berezovsky, Rav Shalom Noach – Rav Berezovsky (1911–2000) was born in Baranovitch and studied in the Slonim Yeshiva there. In 1940 he became *rosh yeshiva* of the Lubavitch yeshiva Achei Temimim in Tel Aviv. The following year he opened the Slonim Yeshiva in Jerusalem, which became the focal point for reviving the decimated Slonim community after the Holocaust. He was responsible both before and after the Holocaust for recording the mostly oral teachings of the Slonimer rebbes that preceded him. He succeeded his father-in-law as the Slonimer rebbe in 1981. He was a prolific and influential author, writing on Hassidic thought, *parasha*, the *mo'adim*, education, marriage, and other topics, in his series, *Netivot Shalom*.

Berlin, Rav Naftali Tzvi Yehuda – Known by his acronym, the Netziv, Rav Berlin (1816–1893) authored several works, including *Haamek*

She'ela on the *She'iltot* of Rav Ahai Gaon; *Meishiv Davar*, a collection of responsa; and *Haamek Davar* on the Torah. He ran the famed Volozhin yeshiva for almost forty years. He supported Jewish settlement of Israel and was for a time a member of the *Hovevei Tzion* movement of Rav Tzvi Hirsch Kalisher.

Bernstein, Rav Immanuel – Rav Bernstein was born in London and learned in Yeshivat Ateret Yisrael in Israel, receiving his ordination from Rav Chaim Walkin. He has taught at Yeshivat Ateret Yisrael, Machon Yaakov, and the Michlala College for Women in Jerusalem. He has authored books in Hebrew and English, on the *siddur*, tractate *Berakhot*, the Hagadah, Aggadah, and the *mo'adim*.

Birkat Peretz – see Kanievsky, Rav Yaakov Yisrael

Birkat Yitzhak – see Genack, Rav Menachem

Bnei Yissaskhar – see Spira, Rav Tzvi Elimelekh of Dinov

Daat Torah – see Levovitz, Rav Yeruham

Daat Zekeinim MiBaalei HaTosafot – *Daat Zekeinim* is collection of comments on the Torah attributed to the *Tosafot*. It is unknown who authored the collection, but it may have been a student of one or more of the *Baalei HaTosafot*, since the author mentions the imminent end of the fifth millenia, nearly 800 years ago.

David, Rav Avishai Chaim – Rav David (b. 1949) studied under Rav Yosef Dov Soloveitchik for fourteen years and received his ordination from the R. Isaac Elchanan Theological Seminary of Yeshiva University. He also studied under Rav Nisson Alpert and Rav Aharon Lichtenstein, and is a long-time student of Rav Avigdor Nebenzahl. He is rosh *yeshiva* of Yeshivat Torat Shraga in Jerusalem and a rabbi in Beit Shemesh. He authored *Darosh Darash Yosef* on the weekly *parasha* based on the lessons of Rav Soloveitchik and *Shai LeAvi*.

Dessler, Rav Eliyahu Eliezer – Born in Gomel, Belarus, R. Dessler (1892–1953) learned in the yeshiva of Kelm and later was ordained as a rabbi by his uncle, R. Chaim Ozer Grodzinski. After his father lost his considerable wealth in the Russian Revolution, R. Dessler moved to England, where he helped establish the Gateshead Kollel in the early 1940s, forerunner to the Gateshead Yeshiva. After the war, he became the *mashgiah ruhani*, spiritual guide, of the newly re-founded Ponovezh Yeshiva in Bnei Brak, Israel. The letters and lectures he produced in England and Israel were collected into the five-volume *Michtav Me'Eliyahu*, and have had considerable influence on Jewish thought since its publication.

Dubno Maggid – Rav Yaakov ben Wolf Kranz (1741–1804) was a revered traveling preacher (*maggid*) who left a legacy of teachings on the Torah, holidays, Haggada, *haftarot*, ethics, and Jewish thought, through extensive use of parables. He was an outstanding orator, scholar, and pietist, and a close contemporary of the Vilna Gaon. His teachings were collected in five books, including *Ohel Yaakov*, *Kol Yaakov*, and *Kokhav MiYaakov*.

Dvinsk, Rav Meir Simha of – Rav Meir Simha Hacohen (1843–1926) was rabbi of Dvinsk and authored the *Ohr Sameyah* on the Rambam's Mishneh Torah. He also wrote the *Meshekh Hokhma* on the Torah.

Eileh HaDevarim – see Schlesinger, Rabbi Eliyahu

Elazary, Rav Chaim Moshe Reuven – Rav Elazary (d. 1984, Petach Tikva) learned in Slobodka and later in the Hebron Yeshiva, where two of his brothers were martyred in the pogrom of 1929. He served as a rabbi in the Bronx and later in Canton, Ohio. He wrote *Shevilei Chaim* on the *parasha*.

Eliyahu, Rav Mordekhai Tzemah – Rav Mordekhai Eliyahu (1929–2010) was born in Jerusalem and learned at the Porat Yosef Yeshiva. He studied under both Rav Ezra Attia and the Hazon Ish. After receiving ordination from the chief Sephardic rabbi of Israel, Rav

Yitzhak Nissim, he was asked to join the *beit din* (rabbinical court) of Be'er Sheva. He subsequently formed a close relationship with the Baba Sali. He was asked by Rav Nissim to reinter the remains of the Hida from Livorno, Italy, to Har Menuhot in Jerusalem. He later served at the Jerusalem Regional Beit Din and then the Supreme Rabbinical Court in Jerusalem. In 1983 he was appointed chief Sephardic rabbi. During his tenure and afterwards, he was active not only in the rabbinical court system, but also in Jewish outreach and in encouraging the religious-Zionist population in the settlements. He authored several books on halakha, including responsa and *Darkhei Tahara* (on the laws of *nidda*), and his teachings on the *parasha* have been published as *Divrei Mordekhai*.

Elyashiv, Rav Yosef Shalom – Rav Elyashiv (1910–2012) was considered by many the *posek hador*, preeminent authority of halakha. His responsa were collected in four volumes and his comments on the Talmud in the 18-volume *Haorot* series. He was survived by 1,400 descendants, including two sixth-generation descendants.

Epstein, Rav Barukh Halevi – Rav Epstein (1860–1941) was the son of the rabbi of Novhardok and the author of the *Arukh HaShulhan*, Rav Yechiel Michel Halevi Epstein. He learned under his uncle, the Netziv, at the Yeshiva of Volozhin, and later became a bookkeeper. He is often known as the *Torah Temima* after his commentary on the Torah, in which he cites the explanations of the Sages on the verses and then explains and justifies their exegesis. He wrote the *Torah Temima* as a defense of traditional Jewish scholarship against Biblical Criticism and *Wissenschaft*. He also authored a commentary to the *siddur*, *Barukh She'amar*, and a biography of the Netziv and life at Volozhin, *Mekor Barukh*.

Epstein, Rav Yechiel Michel Halevi – Rav Epstein (1829–1908) was rabbi of Novhardok and authored the most comprehensive work of halakha since the Rambam's *Mishneh Torah*, the *Arukh HaShulhan*. This work follows the *Shulhan Arukh*, starting with its sources in the Talmud and the *Rishonim*, and then addressing the insights of the major commentaries on the *Shulhan Arukh* up to his time.

Feinstein, Rav Moshe – Born near Minsk, Rav Moshe (1895–1986) moved to New York in 1936 where he headed the yeshiva Mesivtha Tifereth Jerusalem. His opinion was sought on thousands of modern-day halakhic issues and his rulings, published as *Iggrot Moshe*, established him as the preeminent *posek* of North America, and one of the most influential in the world. His responsa were often innovative and pioneered Orthodox practice in the modern age. However, he viewed his weekly lessons at the yeshiva, collected as *Dibbrot Moshe*, as his greatest work. His insights on the *parasha* were published as *Dvar Moshe*. Renowned for his gentle nature, he is buried at Har Menuhot in Jerusalem.

Feinstein, Rav Dovid – Rav Dovid Feinstein (b. 1929) is the son of Rav Moshe Feinstein and became *rosh yeshiva* of Mesivtha Tifereth Jerusalem in New York after his father. A *posek* and author, he has written nine books on halakha, the Haggada, and on the *parasha (Kol Dodi).*

Firer, Rav Benzion – Rav Firer (1914–1988) was born in Poland and immigrated to Israel. He authored a five-volume commentary on the Torah called *Panim Hadashot BaTorah.*

Frand, Rav Yissocher – Rav Frand was born in Seattle, Washington, and learned in the Ner Israel Rabbinical College in Baltimore, eventually becoming one of its senior lecturers. His weekly class on the *parasha* has for thirty years been one of the most popular of such lectures, attended by and broadcast to an audience of thousands. He is a popular lecturer, and is involved with the Chofetz Chaim Heritage Foundation. He has authored numerous books on Jewish ideas, the Haggada and the *parasha*, including *Rabbi Frand on the Parasha* (3 volumes), *Rabbi Yissocher Frand in Print,* and *Listen to Your Messages.*

Appendix

Galinsky, Rav Yaakov Yitzhak – Rav Galinsky (1920–2014) learned in the Novhardok yeshiva of Bialystok and immigrated to Israel in 1949. He became a popular *maggid* and many of his sermons are collected in the series *Vehigadeta*.

Genack, Rav Menachem – Rav Genack was a student of Rav Yosef Soloveitchik and is the head of OU Kashrut Division. He is an executive member of the American Israel Public Affairs Committee and helped found NORPAC, a pro-Israel political action committee. He is rabbi of Congregation Shomrei Emunah of Englewood, NJ, and the author of *Gan Shoshanim, Letters to President Clinton,* and *Birkat Yitzhak* on the Humash.

Gifter, Rav Mordechai – Rav Gifter was born in Virginia in 1915 and went to public schools before studying under R. Moshe Soloveitchik at R. Isaac Elchanan Theological Seminary. He later studied in the Telz Yeshiva in Lithuania before WWII. He served as a rabbi in Connecticut and Baltimore, where he also taught at the Ner Israel Rabbinical College. He then moved to Cleveland to teach at the newly re-established Telz Yeshiva, eventually becoming its *rosh yeshiva*. He authored several books and articles (including one on law for the Western Reserve University Law Review), including *Pirkei Torah* on the *parasha*.

Gra – Rav Eliyahu Kramer (1720–1797) became known in his lifetime as the Hassid Rabbenu Eliyahu due to his piety, and later as the Gaon Rabbenu Eliyahu, or simply the Vilna Gaon, for his genius. He was considered the preeminent rabbinic authority in Europe in the latter half of the eighteenth century and consequently received questions from rabbis throughout Europe. He authored numerous works, commenting on the Talmud, Mishna, the *Shulhan Arukh, Tanakh,* and Kabbalistic works. He was known to be proficient in mathematics and the sciences of his day. He produced several very influential students, whom he strongly encouraged to move to Israel, and they became an integral part of the rebirth of the Ashkenazic community in nineteenth-century Israel.

Gross, Meshulam Tzvi – Mr. Gross (1863–1947) was a very learned layman, born in Hungary, who went on to be an inventor and successful businessman in New York. He learned Kabbalah weekly with Rav Yosef Yitzchak Schneerson and retired early from the women's clothing industry to learn full-time. He invented one of the first vending machines and a *pareve* shortening to replace lard. He authored two books on the *parasha*, *Nahalat Tzvi* and *Ateret Tzvi*.

Gustman, Rav Yisrael Zev – Rav Gustman (1908–1991) was the rosh yeshiva of the Ramiles Yeshiva in Vilna, which he re-established as Yeshivat Netzah Israel in Jerusalem in 1971. He had learned with Rav Chaim Shmuelevitz under Rav Shimon Shkop at the Grodno Yeshiva. He was the last dayan of Vilna, and, after losing his son to the Nazis, fled with his family, immigrating to New York.

Gutnick Edition Chumash – see Lubavitcher Rebbe

Haamek Davar – see Berlin, Rav Naftali Tzvi Yehuda

HaDerash VeHaIyun – see Lewin, Rav Aharon

Hafetz Hayim – Rav Yisrael Meir Hacohen (Kagan) (1839–1933) was born in Belarus and eventually moved to Radin, Poland, where he established a yeshiva which achieved significant prominence. Active in numerous Jewish causes, he grew to become one of the leaders of European Jewry through dint of his renowned scholarship and saintliness. Often called by the title of his landmark work on the laws of forbidden types of speech, *Hafetz Hayim*, he wrote numerous books to encourage mitzva observance among his fellow Jews, including those drafted into the Czar's army. His *Mishna Berura* on the *Shulhan Arukh* is one of its most widely read commentaries. He also wrote on laws pertaining to the Temple service and the *kohanim*, a topic for which he tried to rekindle interest among European Jewry.

Hatam Sofer – Commonly referred to by the name of his books (Hatam Sofer is an acronym of *Hiddushei Torah Moshe Sofer*), Rav Moshe Sofer (Schreiber) (1762–1839) was born in Frankfurt and later served as the rabbi of Pressburg, Hungary. One of the outstanding scholars of his generation, he was one of Orthodox Jewry's main representatives in the clash with the Reform Movement. The yeshiva he established in Pressburg became for a while, according to many, the most influential yeshiva in Europe. It lasted until the Holocaust, after which it was re-established in Jerusalem by his great-grandson. His writings were published mostly posthumously, and include over one thousand responsa, biblical commentaries, and insights on the Talmud. His comments to the *Shulhan Arukh* are now standard in every edition of the *Shulhan Arukh*.

Hayei Olam – see Steinsaltz, Rav Adin Even-Israel

Hazon Ish – Rav Yeshaya Karelitz (1878–1953) was born in Russia, where he studied primarily under his father, rabbi of Kosava, and later under R. Chaim Soloveitchik. After moving to Vilna, he became close to R. Chaim Ozer Grodzinki, who, along with R. Avraham Yitzchak Hacohen Kook, encouraged his immigration to Israel. There he wrote his work on halakha, *Hazon Ish*, and quickly rose to be the preeminent *posek*. He also wrote a short book on Jewish thought, *Emunah UBitachon*.

Hida – Rav Chaim Yosef David Azulai, the great-great-grandson of Rav Avraham Azulai, was born in Jerusalem in 1724 and died in Italy in 1806. He was one of the outstanding Sephardic rabbis of his time and was extraordinarily prolific, writing on all areas of Jewish thought and practice. Some of his most famous works are *Yosef Ometz*, *Shem HaGedolim* (short biographies of 1,500 rabbis), and the *Birkei Yosef*, a commentary to the *Shulhan Arukh*. He traveled extensively as representative and fundraiser of the Jewish community in the Land of Israel, and his diaries from those arduous and often harrowing experiences are recorded in his *Maagal Tov*.

Hirsch, Rav Shimshon Refael – Rav Hirsch (1808–1888) was chief rabbi of Moravia and eventually of Franfurt am Main. He was a vocal defendant of Orthodox Jewry in Germany against the Reform Movement, printing articles in his *Jeschurun* magazine on Jewish thought. He formulated the *Torah im derech eretz* approach of Orthodoxy to modernity. He authored books explaining traditional Judaism to the modern, Western-educated Jew of his time, including *18 Letters*, *Horeb*, as well as commentaries to the Torah, *Tehillim*, and the *siddur*.

Hizkuni – Rav Hizkiya ben Manoah was a thirteenth-century French rabbi who wrote a commentary to the Torah, Hizkuni (or Hazekuni) in honor of his father's self-sacrifice for his faith. Based mainly on Rashi, he incorporates several other commentaries that preceded him.

Imrei Barukh – see Simon, Rav Barukh

Isserles, Rav Moshe – The Rama (1520–1572) lived in Cracow, Poland and studied under Rav Shalom Shechna of Lublin. Upon returning to Cracow, he opened a yeshiva which he ran, and became one of the most influential *poskim* of Ashkenazi Jewry. He also studied history, astronomy, and Kabbalah. He authored several works, including responsa, a commentary to the Torah, a commentary to Esther, a philosophical treatise on the Temple and its sacrificial service, and his glosses to Rav Yosef Karo's *Shulhan Arukh* (called the *Mapah*). His *magnum opus* is his commentary to the *Arba Turim*, the *Darkhei Moshe*.

Iturei Torah – This seven-volume collection on the *parasha* draws heavily from the Hassidic and *Musar* teachers. Written by Avraham

Yaakov Greenberg (1900–1963), it was first published as a weekly article for the Hebrew newspaper *Hatzofeh* in Israel. Greenberg immigrated to Mandate Palestine in 1934 and was active with the Poel Mizrachi movement. He later served in four Knessets.

Iyunim BeSefer Bereishit – see Leibowitz, Nechama

Kahaneman, Rav Yosef Shlomo – Rav Kahaneman, known as the Ponovezher Rav (1886–1969), learned in the yeshivas of Telz, Novhardok, and Radin. He became rabbi of Ponovezh, was elected to the Lithuanian parliament, and built three yeshivas, a school, and an orphanage. He fled the Germans in 1940, settling in Bnei Brak, where he rebuilt the Ponovezh Yeshiva and an orphanage.

Kaminetsky, Rav Yaakov – Rav Yaakov (1891–1986) was born in Lithuania and studied for twenty-one years under Rav Nosson Zvi Finkel at the Slabodka Yeshiva. He served as rabbi in Tzitavyan and then immigrated to America in 1937, where he served as rabbi in Seattle and then Toronto. He subsequently became *rosh yeshiva* of Mesivta Torah Vodaath in Brooklyn. He authored a series of volumes called *Emet LeYaakov*, on the Torah, the Talmud, and the Shulhan Arukh.

Kanievsky, Rav Shmaryahu Yosef Chaim – Rav Chaim was born in 1928 in Pinsk to Rav Yaakov Yisrael Kanievsky, the Steipler Gaon, and moved to Israel with his family when he was a child. He learned with his father, his uncle the Chazon Ish, at the Tiferes Tzion Yeshiva of Bnei Brak under Rav Yechiel Michel Lefkowitz, and at the Lomza Yeshiva in Petach Tikva. He is recognized as a leading *posek* and has authored numerous books on halakha, *musar*, and *parasha*, including *Derekh Emuna, Derekh Hokhmah, Orhot Yosher*, and *Taama Dekra*.

Kanievsky, Rav Yaakov Yisrael – Rav Kanievsky (1899–1985) grew up in Hornisteipel, Ukraine, and due to his genius gained the nickname

the Steipler Gaon. He studied under Rav Yosef Yozel Horowitz
of Novhardok and later became *rosh yeshiva* in Pinsk. He moved
to Bnei Brak in 1934 and became a leader of Orthodox Jewry in
Israel, along with his brother-in-law, the Hazon Ish. His insights
on the Talmud were published in several volumes as *Kehillat
Yaakov*, and on the Torah as *Birkat Peretz*.

Karo, Rav Yosef – Fleeing Spain with his family in 1492 at the age of four, R.
Karo (1488–1575) lived in several cities in the Ottoman Empire until
finally settling in Tzfat. He gained eminence as a *posek* and assisted
the city's chief *dayan*, judge, Rav Yaakov Beirav, a position he later
assumed along with R. Moshe Trani. He wrote several works, the
most famous being the *Shulhan Arukh*, a comprehensive guide to
the halakha that gained rapid, widespread acceptance and has since
become the foundation for all Jewish practice. He also authored
the *Maggid Meisharim*, lessons he learned about the *parasha* and
other topics from a *maggid*, a spiritual teacher sent from Heaven.

Kasher, Rav Menachem Mendel – Born in Warsaw, R. Kasher (1895–1983)
moved to Jerusalem under the encouragement of the Gerrer Rebbe.
There he established and ran the Yeshivat Sfat Emet. He authored a
multi-volume compendium of the Oral Torah arranged according
to the *parasha*, called the *Torah Shleima*; thirty-eight volumes were
published in his lifetime and seven more posthumously. He wrote
several other works, including *Tekufa HaGedola*, applications of the
Vilna Gaon's teaching on *mashiach* and redemption.

Kashtiel, Rav Eliezer – Rav Kashtiel is *rosh yeshiva* of the post-army
division of Yeshivat Eli (Bnei David), in the Shomron.

Kedushat Levi – see Berditchev, Rav Levi Yitzhak of

Keli Yakar – See Luntschitz, R. Ephraim Shlomo

Kook, Rav Avraham Yitzhak Hacohen – Rav Kook (1865-1935) was
born in Russia and studied under the Netziv in Volozhin and

under the rabbi of Ponovezh, Rav Eliyahu David Rabinowitz-Teomim (the "Aderet"). He immigrated to the Land of Israel in 1904, where he became the chief rabbi of Yaffo, then Jerusalem, and later of British Mandate Palestine. A world-renowned scholar of Talmud, halakha, and Jewish thought, he became famous for teaching about and promoting the settlement of the Land of Israel and the unique nature of the Jewish people. A prolific author, he wrote on halakha and Jewish thought, including *Orot HaKodesh*, *Ein Aya*, and *Olat Reiya* on the *siddur*.

Kornitzer, Rav Yosef Nehemia – Rav Kornitzer was born in the Ukraine in 1880 and later became the chief rabbi of Cracow (d. 1933). He was a grandson of the Hatam Sofer.

Kotler, Rav Aharon – Rav Aharon (1891–1962) studied in Slobodka and then joined his father-in-law, Rav Isser Zalman Meltzer on the faculty of the yeshiva in Slutsk. He escaped Europe to New York in 1941 with the help of the Vaad Hatzalah, which he then helped run. In 1943 he established the Beth Medrash Govoah in Lakewood, New Jersey, for which he served as *rosh yeshiva* until the end of his life. He held senior positions on both the Moetzes Gedolei HaTorah of Agudath Israel and Torah Umesorah. He was also instrumental in establishing the Chinuch Atzmai school system in Israel. His teachings were published in four volumes as *Mishnat Rabbi Aharon*.

Kotzk, Menachem Mendel of – Rav Menachem Mendel Morgenstern (1787–1859) was one of the preeminent students of Rav Bunim of Peshischa. He greatly influenced the Izbitca Rebbe and Rav Yitzchak Meir Alter of Ger. Renowned for his scholarship at a young age, he became well known for his unwavering commitment to the truth. He burned his numerous manuscripts before his death, but several collections of his teachings have been collected, including *Emet VeEmunah*.

Kuzari – The *Book of the Kuzari* (full title: *The Book of the Refutation and Proof in Support of the Debased Religion*) is the most famous work of the medieval Jewish philosopher and poet, Yehuda Halevi. Finished around 1140, it has become one of the most influential books on Jewish philosophy. It tells of the theological discussions between a rabbi and the pagan Khazar king, who converted based on the force of the rabbi's arguments.

Leibowitz, Nechama – Nechama Leibowitz (1902–1997) earned her PhD in 1930 in Bible Studies from the University of Marburg, Germany, and then moved to Israel where she taught *Tanakh* at a religious-Zionist teachers' college. She later taught at both the University of Tel Aviv and Hebrew University. She gave a popular weekly radio show on the Voice of Israel and garnered a following of thousands through a weekly correspondence in which she sent out questions on the *parasha* that she checked and returned. She was the recipient of both the Israel Prize for her contributions to education and the Bialik Prize for Jewish Thought. Her insights on the *parasha* have been collected in five volumes as *Iyunim BeSefer Bereshit* (*Shemot*, etc.) and translated into English as *Studies in Bereshit: Genesis* (*Shemot*, etc.).

Lehitaneg BeTaanugim – contemporary collection of insights by Rav Y. Greenboim.

Leiner, Rav Mordechai Yosef of Izbitca – Often referred to as the *Mei Shiloah*, a collection of his teachings compiled by his grandson. The Izbitca Rebbe (1801–1854) was a student of Rav Simcha Bunim of Pershischa, and subsequently Rav Menachem Mendel of Kotzk. His students included the grandson of R. Akiva Eiger, Rav Yehuda Leib Eiger, Rav Zadok Hacohen of Lublin, and the Radzyner Rebbe (grandson of the *Mei Shiloah*).

Lekah Tov – The *Pesikta Zutarta* is a commentary on the Torah and the five *megillot*, and was originally called the *Lekah Tov* by its author Tobia ben Eliezer, who was an eleventh-century Talmudist and poet. It provides both translations of words and extensive quotations of *midrashim*.

Appendix

Levenstein, Rav Yehezkel – Rav Hazkel, as he was commonly known, was born in Warsaw in 1895 and learned under the Hafetz Hayim in Radin, from Rav Yeruham Levovitz, and from Rav Nahum Zev Ziv, son of the Alter of Kelm (Rav Simcha Zissel Ziv). He later became the *mashgiah* of the Mir Yeshiva, with which he fled to Shanghai, fleeing the Nazis. He helped re-establish the Mir Yeshiva in Jerusalem after the war, and also taught at the Ponovezh Yeshiva in Bnei Brak, where he died in 1974. His legacy of *musar* teachings are contained in the seven volumes of *Ohr Yehezkel*.

Levovitz, Rav Yeruham – Rav Yeruham (1873–1936) studied under Rav Nosson Tzvi Finkel at Slobodka Yeshiva and under Rav Simcha Zissel Ziv of Kelm. He became a famous teacher of *musar*, mainly as the *mashgiah* at the Mir Yeshiva. His *musar* teachings have been published in *Daat Torah* and *Daat Hokhma U'Musar*.

Lewin, Rav Aharon – Rav Aharon Lewin (1879–1941) was rabbi of Sambor and subsequently Rzeszow. He was a gifted orator and a dedicated communal activist, serving on the Polish Sejm and as a leader of the Agudath Israel. He authored several books, including *HaDerash VeHaIyun* on the Humash and *Avnei Heifetz* (responsa). He was murdered by the Nazis in Lemberg.

Lichtenstein, Rav Aharon – Rav Aharon (1933–2015) was born in Paris and grew up in America, where he studied under Rav Yitzchak Hutner at Yeshiva Chaim Berlin in New York. He then studied at R. Isaac Elchanan Theological Seminary of YU, becoming one of the foremost students and the son-in-law of Rav Yosef Dov Soloveitchik. He received his PhD in English literature from Harvard University. He was invited in 1971 to be one of the *roshei yeshiva* of Yeshivat Har Etzion in Israel, where he taught for over forty years. His lectures have been published in several works, including *By His Light: Character and Values in the Service of God; Leaves of Faith; Varieties of Jewish Experience;* and

Minchat Aviv, Kedushat Aviv, and *Shiurei Harav Aharon Lichten-stein* on the Talmud.

Limudei Nissan – see Alpert, Rav Nissan

Loew, Rav Shmuel Halevi – Rav Shmuel (1720–1806) was *av beis din* (chief justice of the rabbinical court) and *rosh yeshiva* in Boskow-itz, Moravia for sixty years. He wrote an extensive commentary to the *Magen Avraham* on the *Shulhan Arukh* and a less extensive one on the *Taz.* Both are printed in almost all editions of the *Shulhan Arukh* as the *Mahatzit HaShekel.*

LaTorah VeLaMo'adim – see Zevin, Rav Shlomo Yosef

Lubavitcher Rebbe – Rav Menachem Mendel Schneerson was the seventh and last leader (*rebbe*) of Chabad Hassidim. Known widely as "the Rebbe," he was born in 1902 near the Black Sea. He received ordination from the Rugatchover Gaon and the Sridei Aish. He also studied physics and philosophy at the University of Berlin. With the rise of Nazism, he moved to Paris in 1933 and escaped Europe in 1941, immigrating to New York. He pioneered Jewish outreach, initially in America and thereafter the world, establishing 3,600 educational centers in over one hundred countries. Thousands of his letters and lectures have been published. The Rebbe taught insights on Rashi that were published as *Biurim LePeirush Rashi al HaTorah,* some of which are incorporated in the Toras Menachem commentary in *Chumash: The Gutnick Edition.*

Lublin, Rav Tzadok Hacohen of – Rav Tzadok Rabinowitz (1823–1900) was an original thinker and prolific writer of Hassidic thought. A Lithuanian rabbi, he became a follower of the Izbitca Rebbe, Rav Mordechai Yosef Leiner. Although a number of his manuscripts were lost, possibly with the destruction of the Lublin ghetto, several manuscripts were published after his death, including

Takkanat HaShavim, Tzidkat HaTzaddik, and *Pri Tzaddik* on the *parasha*. He also wrote articles on astronomy and mathematics.

Luntschitz, R. Ephraim Shlomo – Rav Luntschitz (1550–1619) was *rosh yeshiva* in Lemberg and later became the rabbi of Prague. He wrote seven books, the most famous being his commentary on the Torah, the *Keli Yakar*. It gained sufficient popularity that it is published as part of the Torah with its classic commentaries, the *Mikraot Gedolot*. He also wrote *Olelot Efraim* on the Jewish lifecycle.

Maayan Beit Hashoeva – see Schwab, Rav Shimon

Maggid Meisharim – see Karo, Rav Yosef

Maharit – Rav Yosef Trani (1538–1639), the son of the Mabit of Tzfat, wrote responsa as well as commentaries on some tractates of Talmud. He left behind unpublished manuscripts on the Rif, the Rambam's *Mishneh Torah*, and R. Natan's *Arukh*.

Malbim – Rav Meir Leibush ben Yechiel Michel Wisser (1809–1879) wrote a commentary on the *Tanakh*, incorporating his mastery of Hebrew grammar. He served as rabbi in several pulpits, and battled in-roads being made by the Reform and Neo-Orthodox movements. His commentary, especially on the Torah, reflects his defense of the Oral Law.

Mekhilta – The Mekhilta is the *midrash halakha* on *Sefer Shemot*, meaning it is the collection of legal explanations and interpretations (exegesis), based on that which Moshe received, of the mitzvot of *Sefer Shemot*. Like the rest of the Oral Law, its *baraitot,* or teachings, were probably written down only in the time of the *Tannaim*. The Gemara refers to the Mekhilta as one of the *Sifrei dibei Rav* (books of the study hall), and it has two parts: the Mekhilta of Rabbi Yishmael and the Mekhilta of Rabbi Shimon (bar Yochai). It is frequently quoted as a primary source in the halakhic discussions of the Gemara.

Mei Shiloah – see Leiner, Rav Mordechai Yosef

Meiri – R. Menachem Meiri (1249–1306) lived in Provence, between the worlds of Ashkenazic Jewry in France and Germany, and Sephardic Jewry in Spain. His comprehensive commentary on the Talmud, *Beit HaBehira*, is a digest of the comments of the *Rishonim* from both. It is considered one of the most lucid of all commentaries on the Talmud. He also wrote an influential work on the laws of writing a *sefer Torah, Kiryat Sefer,* and a commentary to *Avot.*

Melamed, Rav Zalman – Rav Melamed (b. 1937) is the rabbi of Beit El and *rosh yeshiva* of its yeshiva. He helped found the yeshiva of Kerem beYavne and the Arutz 7 radio station. He learned under Rav Tzvi Yehuda Kook at Mercaz HaRav.

Meltzer, Rav Isser Zalman – Rav Isser Zalman (1870–1953) was born in Mir, Belarus, and studied under the city's rabbi, Rav Yom-Tov Lipman, then at the Mir Yeshiva, and subsequently at the Yeshiva of Volozhin, under the Netziv and Rav Chaim Soloveitchik. He then learned under the Hafetz Hayim in Radin. He was a member of the secret Nes Ziona Society (a branch of Hovevei Zion) and contributed to the establishment of Hadera. He taught at the Slabodka Yeshiva and later became rabbi of Slutsk, before immigrating to Mandatory Palestine, where he became an admirer of the Chief Rabbi, Rav Avraham Yitzhak Hacohen Kook. Rav Isser Zalman once said to the famous sage Rabbi Chaim Ozer Grodzinsky, "We are considered Torah giants only up until the point that we reach the door of Rabbi Kook's room." In Jerusalem, he became *rosh yeshiva* of the Etz Chaim Yeshiva, where he taught many of the next generation's Torah leaders (including Rav Shlomo Zalman Auerbach, Rav Yaakov Yisrael Fisher, Rav Eliezer Waldenberg, Rav Shlomo Goren, and the *roshei yeshiva* of Slabodka, Shaalvim, Har Etzion, YU, Etz Chaim, and Ponovezh). He is best remembered for authoring the *Even Ha'ezel* on the Rambam's *Mishne Torah.*

Meshekh Hokhma – see Dvinsk, Rav Meir Simcha of

Appendix

Mikhtav Me'Eliyahu – see Dessler, Rav Eliyahu Eliezer

Mishkan Bezalel – see Rudinsky, Rav Bezalel Yehuda

Moshav Zekeinim – see *Tosafot*

Nahalat Tzvi – see Gross, Meshulam Tzvi

Nebenzahl, Rav Avigdor – Born in Israel in 1935, Rav Nebenzahl teaches at Yeshivat HaKotel and Yeshivat Netiv Aryeh, and is the rabbi of the Ramban Synagogue of the Old City of Jerusalem. He had previously taught at the Mir Yeshiva and for many years served as chief rabbi of the Old City. For forty years he was the study partner of Rav Shlomo Zalman Auerbach. He has written a commentary to the *Mishna Berura* and a series of books on the *mo'adim* and on the Torah.

Neiman, Rav Yaakov Aryeh – Rav Neiman (ca. 1887–1983) learned in the Lomza Yeshiva in Poland and later became a prominent student of the Hafetz Hayim, who appointed him head of the Ohr Yisrael Yeshiva in Lida. In 1935 he moved to Israel and soon thereafter opened up a branch of the Ohr Yisrael Yeshiva in Petach Tikva, which he headed for over forty years. He authored books on *musar*, including *Darkhei Musar* and *Pri Yaakov*.

Netivot Ohr – see Salanter, Rav Yisrael

Netivot Shalom – see Berezovsky, Rav Shalom Noach

Netziv – see Berlin, Rav Naftali Tzvi Yehuda

Olat Re'iya – see Kook, Rav Avraham Yitzhak Hacohen

Onkelos – Onkelos was a high-born Roman convert to Judaism at the end of the first century of the common era. He was the nephew of

Emperor Titus, and may have been Aquila of Sinope (ca. 35–120 CE). He wrote the *Targum Onkeles*, an Aramaic translation of the Torah, written under the supervision of Rabbi Yehoshua ben Hananya and Rabbi Eliezer ben Hyrkanus.

Ohr HaHayim – see Attar, Rav Chaim ibn

Otzrot HaTorah – A recent collection of insights from and stories about famous rabbis, written by Rav Eliyahu Chaim Cohen.

Oznayim LaTorah – see Sorotzkin, Rav Zalman

Pam, Rav Avraham Yaakov – Rav Pam (1913–2001) taught for more than sixty years at Mesivta Torah Vodaath in Brooklyn, NY, eventually serving as its *rosh yeshiva*. He taught mathematics as well, having held a degree from City College of NY. He started the Shuvu organization to provide Jewish education to children who immigrated to Israel from the FSU. Some of his teachings are collected in seven works by his student R. Shalom Smith, including *Rav Pam on Chumash* and *Rav Pam on Pirkei Avos*.

Panim Hadashot BaTorah – see Firer, Rav Benzion

Pincus, Rav Shimshon – Rav Pincus was born in New York (1945) and studied in Beth HaTalmud, before moving to Israel, where he studied at the Yeshiva of Brisk. He became *mashgiah* at the yeshiva in Ofakim, then *rosh yeshiva* in Yerucham, and eventually chief rabbi of Ofakim. He authored a few books in his lifetime about Shabbat and prayer, and since his death in 2001 in a car accident, several books based on his recorded lectures have been published, including *Tiferet Shimshon*.

Pliskin, Rav Zelig – Rav Pliskin is the author of twenty-five books on *musar*, self-esteem, *lashon hara*, *parasha*, and relationships. He was born in Baltimore (1946) and learned at the Telshe Yeshiva of Cleveland, and later at the Brisk Yeshiva in Jerusalem. He taught and counseled at Aish HaTorah. In addition to counseling and writing, he is a master practitioner of NLP.

Peninei HaTorah – Rav David Hadad is the author of *Peninei HaTorah*, a recent collection of insights on the *parasha*, and *Maase Avot* on *Pirkei Avot*.

Ponovezher Rav – see Kahaneman, Rav Yosef Shlomo

Premishlaner, Rav Meir – Rav Meir of Premishlan (1783–1850) was a student of Rav Mordechai of Kremenitz and the Hozeh of Lublin. His grandfather, after whom he was named, was a student of the Baal Shem Tov and a descendant of the *Baal HaTosafot*, Rav Yaakov of Corbeil. His insights on the Torah and *Hassidut* were published in several books, including *Divrei Meir* and *Ohr Meir*.

Raavad – Rabbenu Avraham ben David (ca. 1125–1198), known as the Raavad III, was born in Provence, and died in Posquieres. A preeminent Talmudist, he commented on the Talmud, Rav Yitzhak al-Fasi's *Sefer Halakhot*, and the Rambam's *Mishneh Torah* (which earned him the title *Baal Hasagot*). He is also considered one of the greatest teachers of the Kabbalah of his time.

Rabbenu Yonah – Rav Yonah ben Avraham of Gerona, Spain (d. 1263) was a prominent rabbi of Medieval Spanish Jewry. A cousin of the Ramban (Nahmanides), he was the teacher of the Rashba (Rav Shlomo ben Aderet). Possibly his most famous work, dealing with repentance, is *Shaarei Teshuva*, itself having been written as an act of repentance for Rabbenu Yonah's condemnation of some of the Rambam's writings, an act he deeply regretted. His comments on the Talmud were largely lost, except for those on Bava Batra and Sanhedrin, and to a lesser extent, those mentioned by his students (the Rashba in his commentary to the Talmud, and a commentary to the Rif on *Berakhot* by anonymous students).

Radak – Rav David Kimchi (1160–1235) was born in Narbonne, Provence, and became one of the prominent medieval grammarians, philosophers, and biblical commentators. He wrote a commentary on the Prophets, *Bereshit, Tehillim,* and *Divrei HaYamim,* as well as books on grammar. He was influenced by Avraham ibn Ezra and the Rambam, whom he staunchly supported during the Maimonidean Controversy. He participated in polemics with Christians, and, in an ironic twist of fate, his Bible commentary became the favored of the translators of the King James Bible.

Rambam – Rav Moshe ben Maimon (1135–1204), or Maimonides, fled the Almohod conquest of Cordoba, Spain, with his father, the chief rabbi, and his family. He eventually settled in Fustat, Egypt, where he was doctor to Sultan Saladin. He died there and was buried in Teveria, Israel. Doctor, philosopher, and foremost *posek,* his writings have become classics in all these fields, and he is considered one of the most influential of the *Rishonim.* He wrote a commentary on the Mishna, the *Mishneh Torah* on halakha, and the philosophical work *Moreh Nevuhim,* among other writings.

Ramban – Rav Moshe ben Nahman (1194–1270), or Nahmanides, lived most of his life in Gerona, Spain, and became one of the leading rabbinic figures of his time. Many of the leading Spanish *Rishonim* were either his students or his students' students. He authored works on Talmud, halakha, and Jewish philosophy; but the most influential of his works may be his commentary on the Torah. He defended the Jewish community against the Spanish Church in a number of theological debates. He was also a doctor and regarded by many as the greatest kabbalist of his time. He eventually moved to the Land of Israel and assisted the Jewish community of Jerusalem to rebuild after the ravages of the Crusader Kingdom. He then moved to Akko, where he is buried.

Ramchal – Rav Moshe Chaim Luzzatto (1707–1746) was born in Padua, Italy, and became a student of Rav Yitzhak Lampronti, author of the first talmudic encyclopedia, the Pahad Yitzchak; as well as studying Kabbalah under Rav Moshe Zacuto. He also studied science and literature. Already in his twenties he gathered a following of students and became a prolific author, possibly writing more than forty books and pamphlets in the years 1730–1735. Some contemporaneous rabbis became concerned that he would follow in the footsteps of Shabbtai Tzvi, and he was forced to stop teaching and destroy his writings, many of which were therefore lost. Some of his most influential works, however, survived, including *Derekh Hashem* and *Daat Tevunot*. He then moved to Amsterdam and attempted to live a quiet life as a gem cutter. There he published his most famous work, *Mesillat Yesharim* on *musar*. He moved to Acco in 1943 and died with his wife and child in a plague three years later. The subjects of his writing included Kabbalah, Jewish philosophy, ethics and piety (*musar*), Hebrew grammar, and talmudic logic.

Ran (Rabbenu Nissim) – The Ran was born in 1320 in Barcelona and died in 1376 in Gerona, Spain. He was considered by many the greatest *posek* of Spain at the time, and the end of the influential chain of Medieval Spanish *Rishonim*. His most famous work is his commentary on the Rif, which is printed alongside the Rif in all editions of the Talmud. He also wrote his own commentary on the Talmud, and some of these volumes have recently been printed. Other works include his *Derashot HaRan* (collection of sermons and philosophical treatises), a commentary to the Torah, and a collection of over one thousand responsa.

Rashbam – Rav Shmuel ben Meir (ca. 1085–ca. 1158) was one of the *Baalei HaTosafot* and the grandson of Rashi, under whom he studied. He also studied under the Riva, and taught his younger brother, Rabbenu Tam. His comments on the Talmud appear on several tractates. He authored a commentary on the Torah that focuses on the *peshat*-level of understanding the text, and often disagrees with the commentary of his grandfather.

Rashi – Born in 1040 in Troyes, France, Rav Shlomo Yitzhaki studied in the yeshiva of Worms before returning to Troyes, where he was asked to join the *beit din*. There, he eventually became the head of the *beit din*, answering hundreds of questions from Jews all over Europe. He became most famous, however, for his monumental commentaries on most of the tractates of the Talmud and on the whole of the *Tanakh*. These works continue to be the first commentary traditionally learned in the study of both Talmud and *Tanakh*, the latter commentary being the subject of nearly 300 "super-commentaries." Rashi lived through the First Crusades in 1096 and wrote *selihot* commemorating the personal and communal tragedies that he witnessed. He died in 1105, and his descendants and students included some of the most influential of the *Baalei HaTosafot*, such as Rabbenu Tam and the Rashbam.

Rav Pam on Chumash – see Pam, Rav Avraham Yaakov

Reflections of the Rav – see Soloveitchik, Rav Yosef Dov

Reisman, Rabbi Yisroel – Rabbi Reisman was a student of Rav Avraham Pam and is one of the *roshei yeshiva* of Torah Vodaath. He has a popular lecture series on *Tanakh* and has authored *Pathways of the Prophets*, as well as a book dealing with the prohibition of charging interest, *The Laws of Ribbis*. He is the rabbi of the Agudath Israel of Madison.

Rivlin, Rav Avraham – The former *mashgiah* of Yeshivat Kerem B'Yavneh, Rav Rivlin (b. 1946, Jerusalem) has taught at several institutions in Israel and in Johannesburg. He is the author of seven books on *Tanakh* and the *mo'adim*, including *Iyunei Parasha* on the Torah.

Rosh – Rabbenu Asher (ca. 1250–1327), commonly referred to by the acronym Rosh, was born in Cologne, Germany, and studied under the Maharam of Rottenberg. While he became wealthy as a money-lender, his greatness in piety and scholarship lead him to being one of the preeminent rabbis of Ashkenaz. After his teacher was imprisoned due to religious persecution, Rabbenu Asher himself was forced to flee, eventually settling in Toledo, Spain, where, with the encouragement of the Rashba, he became rabbi of Toledo. He authored a comprehensive digest of the Talmud, incorporating the comments and halakhic decisions of the *Tosafot* who preceded him. This commentary became the basis for the *Arba Turim*, written by his son Rabbenu Yaakov, which in turn was the basis for Rav Yosef Karo's *Shulhan Arukh*.

Ruah Hayim – see Volozhin, Rav Chaim

Rudinsky, Rav Bezlalel Yehuda – Rav Rudinsky learned under Rav Tzvi Kushelevsky at Yeshiva Heichal HaTorah in Jerusalem. He is rabbi of Congregation Ahavat Yitzhak of Monsey, NY, and *rosh yeshiva* of Yeshivas Ohr Reuven. He authored a five-volume work on the Humash, *Mishkan Bezalel,* and *Hilukhei HaDaf* on the Talmud.

Saadia Gaon – Rav Saadia (ca. 882–942) became the *gaon,* or leader of the Babylonian Jewish community under the Abassid Caliphate. He was the first rabbinic figure to write in Arabic as well as Hebrew, and wrote on Hebrew grammar, halakha, and philosophy. His work *Emunot VeDeot* is the first systematic presentation of Jewish philosophy, and served as the basis for the Rambam, R. Yosef Albo, and those who followed. He authored responsa and produced a *siddur* to preserve Jewish liturgical unity.

Sacks, Rav Jonathan – Rabbi Lord Jonathan Sacks (b. 1948) served as Chief Rabbi of Great Britain and the Commonwealth from 1991–2013. He has written over twenty books, including three on the weekly *parasha*: *Covenant and Conversation, Lessons in Leadership,* and *Essays on Ethics.*

Salant, Rav Yosef Zundel of – Rav Yosef (1786–1866), commonly known as Rav Zundel of Salant, studied in Volozhin under Rav Chaim of Volozhin. He became the spiritual mentor for Rav Yisrael Salanter, whom he inspired to create the *Musar* Movement. He moved to Israel in 1839 and became the Ashkenazic rabbi of Jerusalem and the head of its court. He established the Etz Chaim Yeshiva and the Bikur Cholim Hospital in Jerusalem. Some of his teachings were published as *Be'er Yosef.*

Salanter, Rav Yisrael – Rav Yisrael Lipkin (1809–1883) studied in Salant under Rav Hirsch Broda and Rav Zundel of Salant. It was in large part due to the influence of the latter, who stressed ethical refinement and piety, that Rav Yisrael developed his approach to these areas, which he called the study of *musar*, and created the *Musar* Movement among Lithuanian Jewry. He served as *rosh yeshiva* at yeshivas in Vilna and later in Kovno. He spent the last decades of his life in Prussia, Germany, and in Paris, strengthening Jewish observance. His *Igeret HaMusar* was first published in 1858, and a collection of his articles, *Imrei Binah,* in 1878. Many of his letters were published in *Ohr Yisrael* by his student Rav Yitzchak Blazer, who also recorded some of his teacher's deeds and practices in *Netivot Ohr.* Many of his teachings were published by his students as *Even Yisrael* and *Etz Peri.*

Schachter, Rav Hershel – Rav Schachter was a long-time student of Rav Yosef Dov Soloveitchik, from whom he received ordination. He is one of the *roshei yeshiva* at YU's Rabbi Isaac Elchanan Theological Seminary, and its *rosh kollel.* He is a prominent American *posek* and halakhic advisor for the Orthodox Union's *kashrut* division. He has authored two hundred articles of halakha and eleven books, primarily on the teachings of Rav Soloveitchik.

Schlesinger, Rabbi Eliyahu – Rabbi Schlesinger is the rabbi of the Gilo neighborhood in Jerusalem and a prominent *posek.* He authored *Eileh HaDevarim* on the *parasha.*

Schwab, Rav Shimon – Born in Frankfurt am Main in 1908, Rav Schwab studied there as well as in the Telz and Mir yeshivas. After serving as rabbi in Bavaria, he moved to America, eventually becoming the rabbi of Khal Adath Jeshurun, a predominantly German immigrant community in Washington Heights, Manhattan. He was active in the Agudath Israel of America and an outspoken advocate of Rav Shimshon Refael Hirsch's approach of *Torah im derekh eretz* until his passing in 1995. Some of his teachings have been published in *Maayan Beit Hashoeva*.

Sefer HaHinukh – This work was written in thirteenth century Spain for the bar mitzva of the author's son. It describes the 613 commandments and follows the Rambam's *Sefer HaMitzvot*. It is organized by the weekly *parasha* and contains a brief halakhic overview and philosophical insights on each mitzva. There are several theories about its authorship, one being that it was written by Rav Aharon, a student of the Rashba.

Sforno – Rav Ovadia Sforno (1475–1550) of Italy was a scholar of *Tanakh*, Talmud, and Hebrew. He was also well versed in mathematics and philosophy. He is best known for his *peshat*-style commentary on the Torah, which is printed in the standard collection of classical commentaries (the *Mikraot Gedolot*). He also wrote on several books from the Writings (*Kesuvim*), and a work entitled *Ohr Ammim*, against the positions of Aristotle (a Latin translation of which he wrote and sent to King Henry II of France).

Shach, Rav Elazar – Rav Shach (1899–2001) studied in Ponovezh and Slobodka, and taught at and became *rosh yeshiva* of yeshivas in Europe before escaping to Israel in 1940. He became *rosh yeshiva* of Ponovezh Yeshiva in Bnei Brak and started the Degel HaTorah political party in Israel.

Shalhevet Yosef – see Siman-Tov, Rav Yosef Hai

Shemen HaTov al HaTorah – see Weinberger, Rav Dov Zev

Shmuelevitz, Rav Chaim – Born in Kovno, R. Chaim (1902–1972) was a member of the staff of the Mir Yeshiva for forty years, being *rosh yeshiva* most of that time. He followed the yeshiva from Europe, through Shanghai in the war years, and led the yeshiva to preeminence in Jerusalem until his passing. His *musar* lectures on ethics have achieved enduring popularity, some of which are collected in *Sihot Musar*.

Shvilei Hayim – see Elazary, Rav Chaim Moshe Reuven

Siftei Hakhamim – Shabtai Bass (1641–1718) was a printer who lived in Germany and authored a commentary, the *Siftei Hakhamim* on Rashi's commentary to the Torah. Bass, who was not a rabbi (he acquired his surname after singing for the choir of the Alt-neuschule of Prague), dedicated much effort to improving elementary education, and wrote his commentary on Rashi to be used by elementary-age pupils. His work is largely a collection of comments from the fifteen commentaries on Rashi that preceded his.

Siman-Tov, Rav Yosef Hai – Rav Siman-Tov is the *rosh yeshiva* of Yehivas Hamasmidim in Jerusalem and the author of *Kerem Yosef* on the Talmud and *Shalhevet Yosef Hai* on the *parasha*.

Simon, Rav Barukh – Rav Simon is a *rosh yeshiva* at R. Isaac Elchanan Theological Seminary of YU and the author of *Imrei Barukh* on Humash and two volumes on halakha; 4,000 of his classes are posted on the YUTorah.org. He lives in Washington Heights in Manhattan.

Slonimer Rebbe – see Berezovsky, Rav Shalom Noach

Sofer, Rav Avraham Shmuel Binyamin – Rav Sofer (1815–1871) was the son and one of the foremost students of his father Rav Moshe Sofer. He is often referred to as the *Ketav Sofer* after his book.

Soloveichik, Rav Ahron – Rav Ahron (1917–2001) was the son of Rav Moshe Soloveitchik, grandson of Rav Chaim, and younger brother of Rav Yosef Dov. He moved to New York in 1930 and earned his law degree from NYU in 1946. He earned his *semiha* from Rav Moshe Feinstein, who invited him to teach at his yeshiva, Mesivtha Tifereth Jerusalem. In Europe, he was the first student of Rav Yitzchak Hutner, who later invited him to teach at Yeshiva Chaim Berlin. He then taught at Yeshiva University and subsequently became *rosh yeshiva* of the Hebrew Theological College in Skokie. He later established the Brisk Rabbinical College of Chicago.

Soloveitchik, Rav Chaim – Rav Chaim of Brisk (1853–1918) was born in Volozhin but grew up in Slutsk, where his father, R. Yosef Dov HaLevi (the Beit HaLevi) became rabbi. After teaching for years in the Yeshiva of Volozhin, he began to teach in the yeshiva at Brisk, and later became its rabbi after his father's passing. He developed an analytical, dialectic approach to talmudic study and the Rambam that became predominant in many yeshivas thereafter, as his sons and students went on to become prominent *roshei yeshiva* in Europe, Israel, and America. His insights on the Rambam were published as *Hiddushei Rabbeinu Chaim Halevi*.

Soloveitchik, Rav Yitzhak Zev – Rav Soloveitchik (1886–1959) was the son of Rav Chaim, and is commonly referred to as Rav Velvel, the Griz (Gaon Rav Yitzhak Zev), or simply the Brisker Rav. He served as rabbi of Brisk and *rosh yeshiva* there, and after fleeing the Nazis to Mandate Palestine, re-established the Brisk Yeshiva of Jerusalem. In Israel he became a leader of the Haredi community and strongly advocated a position of non-involvement with the government.

Soloveitchik, Rav Yosef Dov – Rav Soloveitchik (1903–1993), known as "the Rav" to many, was widely regarded as the pre-eminent rabbi of Modern Orthodox American Jewry. During his forty-five-year tenure as *rosh yeshiva* of the Rabbi Isaac Elchanan Theological Seminary of Yeshiva University, he ordained over two thousand rabbis and taught thousands of others, both at YU and in Boston, where he lived and acted as rabbi. He combined the rigorous approach of talmudic inquiry popularized by his grandfather, Rav Chaim of Brisk (son of the Beit HaLevi, for whom the Rav was named), with knowledge of contemporary philosophy (having earned his PhD in philosophy from Freidrich Wilhelm University in Berlin before moving to Boston). He authored works on Jewish thought, including *Halakhic Man*, *The Lonely Man of Faith*, and *The Halakhic Mind*. His teachings on Jewish thought, the holidays, and biblical personalities have been collected in over thirty books, including the MeOtzar HoRav series of posthumously published essays, as well as *On Repentance*, *Reflections of the Rav* and *Harerei Kedem*. Many of his insights on Talmud have been published as well.

Soloveitchik, Rav Yosef Dov HaLevi – Commonly known as the Beit HaLevi after his book, Rav Yosef Dov HaLevi (1820–1892) was a grandson of Rav Chaim Volozhin on his mother's side. He served as *rosh yeshiva* in Volozhin for ten years along with the Netziv, and then rabbi in Slutsk. After seeing the poverty of the young children at the local schools, he instituted free lunches paid for by the community. Because of his stance against the local *maskilim*, he was forced to leave Slutsk and became the rabbi of Brisk, a position his son Rav Chaim assumed after his death. His two volumes *of Beit HaLevi* contain responsa and insights on part of the Torah.

Sorotzkin, Rav Zalman – Rav Sorotzkin (1881–1966) studied in Volozhin and Slobodka and then served as rabbi in several communities before escaping from the Nazis to Mandate Palestine. He became active in Agudath Israel's Moetzes Gedolei HaTorah and was chosen to run the new Hinukh Atzmai educational system. He authored *Oznayim LaTorah* on the *parasha*, *Moznayim*

LaTorah on the Jewish holidays, as well as a book of responsa and a collection of sermons.

Spira, Rav Tzvi Elimelch of Dinov – Rav Tzvi Elimelech (ca. 1783–1841) is commonly known as the Bnei Yissaskhar after his book on Hassidic insights on the Jewish calendar. He was a follower of several great Hassidic leaders, including the Hozeh of Lublin, the Apta Rav, and Rav Menachem Mendel of Rimanov. He authored several books in addition to his *Bnei Yissaskhar,* including *Derekh Pikudekha* and a commentary on the Torah, *Igra DeKallah.*

Steinsaltz, Rav Adin Even-Israel – Rav Steinsaltz was born in Israel in 1937. He has written over twenty-five books on the Talmud, Kabbalah, the *Tanya,* Jewish thought, and *Tanakh,* including *Hayei Olam* on the *parasha.* He has lectured widely, including at numerous universities in America and Israel. He opened a network of schools in Israel and the former Soviet Union, inspired by his mentor, the Lubavitcher Rebbe. He received the Israel Prize, and is the *rosh yeshiva* of the Hesder Yeshiva of Tekoa. From 1965 to 2010, he translated the entire Talmud Bavli into Modern Hebrew (also rendered into English as the *Koren Talmud Bavli*), opening Talmud study to a wider public. He also published a similar work on *Tanakh,* the *Tanakh HaMevoar.*

Sternbuch, Rav Moshe – Rav Sternbuch was born in 1928 in London and studied in the yeshiva of Stamford Hill. After the War, he studied in the Hebron Yeshiva in Israel and learned regularly with the Chazon Ish and Rav Yitzchak Zev Soloveitchik. He is the head of the Edah HaHareidit in Jerusalem and rabbi of the Gra Shul in Har Nof. He has authored several books, including *Taam Vedaat* on the Torah.

Taam Vedaat – see Sternbuch, Rav Moshe

Targum Yerushalmi – This is a collection of ancient Western-Aramaic translations of the Torah originating in Israel.

Teichtal, Rabbi Yissacher Shlomo – A rising rabbinic figure in pre-war Hungary, Rav Teichtal (1885–1945) began preparing his responsa at the age of twenty-four and later served as rabbi and *av beit din* of Pishtian, Czechoslovakia. While in hiding to escape the deportations of 1942, he witnessed the harrowing sight of the deportations and vowed that if Hashem spared his life, he would author a book in honor of the Land of Israel, encouraging Jews to emigrate and rebuild the land of their forefathers. He began writing this work, *Eim Habanim Semeiha*, and continued as he fled the Nazis, delivering sermons to congregations to bolster their faith and return to Israel. He completed his book in Hungary in 1943, and in 1944 he and his family were sent to Auschwitz. He died on his way to Mauthausen in 1945, and his works were published by his family after the war.

Teller, Rav Chanoch – Rav Teller was born in Vienna in 1956 and grew up in Connecticut. He studied at Yeshiva University and later at the Mir Yeshiva in Jerusalem, and received his ordination from Rav Yehuda Getz. He has published twenty-eight collections of stories, including one about Rav Shlomo Zalman Auerbach (whose lectures he attended for fourteen years) and Rav Nosson Tzvi Finkel of the Mir (whom he studied with for thirty years). He lectures at numerous schools in Jerusalem and venues around the world, and is a senior guide at Yad Vashem. He has produced two movies, a documentary and a docudrama.

Tiferet Shimshon – see Pincus, Rav Shimshon

Tosafot – The *Tosafot* are the commentaries of the French and German Talmudists of the twelfth and thirteenth centuries (CE). The authors of these commentaries, called the *Baalei HaTosafot* (or simply the *Tosafot*), were often the leading rabbis and heads of the yeshivas of Ashkenaz Jewry. Their style of scholarship and halakhic decisions shaped the traditions of Ashkenazic Jewry and nearly all Talmud study thereafter. The Rambam regarded them highly, and they are systematically quoted in such great Spanish

Rishonim as the Ritva. The *Tosafot* are printed in every addition of the Talmud. A collection of insights on the Torah, attributed to the *Baalei HaTosafot*, was written anonymously and published as *Moshav Zekeinim*.

Tropp, Rav Naftali – Rav Tropp (1871–1928), sometimes referred to by the acronym the Granat, studied in Kelm, Slobodka, Telz, and at the Novhardok Yeshiva of Slonim. In 1903 he was invited by the Hafetz Hayim to be *rosh yeshiva* in Radin. His teachings on Talmud were published as *Hiddushei HaGranat*.

Tur – see Baal Haturim.

VeKarata LeShabbat Oneg – This is a contemporary three-volume set of stories, parables, and thoughts about the weekly *parasha*. It is written by Rav Yisrael Yosef Bornstein, author of *Avnei Gazit* on Tractate Sanhedrin.

Volozhin, Rav Chaim – Rav Chaim of Volozhin (1749–1821) studied under the Shaagat Aryeh, but went on to become one of the foremost students of the Vilna Gaon. He later founded the Yeshiva of Volozhin, the flagship of Lithuanian-style yeshivas. He wrote a Kabbalistic treatise, *Nefesh HaHayim*, partly as a response to the growing Hassidic Movement. He also wrote *Ruah HaHayim* on *Pirkei Avot*.

Wasserman, Rav Elchanan – Rav Elchanan (1874–1941) was a student of R. Shimon Shkop, R. Chaim Soloveitchik, and later the Hafetz Hayim. He served as *rosh yeshiva* of the Novhardok Yeshiva in Baranovitch. He was martyred in 1941 by Lithuanian collaborators at the infamous 4th Fort in Poland. His lessons on the Talmud are collected in *Kovetz He'arot* and *Kovetz Shiurim* (among others), and he authored *Ikveta Demeshikha* about the End of Days.

Weinberger, Rabbi Dov Zev (Bernard) – Rabbi Bernard Weinberger (d. 2018) was the rabbi of the Young Israel of Williamsburg, and the author of *Shemen HaTov al HaTorah* and *Haggadat Shemen HaTov*.

Weiss, Rav Asher – Rav Asher Weiss (b. 1953), is the head of the *Dark-hei Torah* and *Minhat Asher* institutions, where he serves as the *av beit din*. Rav Weiss is also the *posek* of Shaare Zedek Hospital and has authored the *Minhat Asher* series on the *parasha, haggada,* and *mo'adim,* as well as several volumes of responsa dealing with modern halakhic issues. Rav Weiss was one of the leading students of the late Klausenberger Rebbe, and currently resides in Jerusalem, Israel.

Wolbe, Rav Shlomo – Born in Berlin, Rav Wolbe (1914–2005) became observant while studying at the University of Berlin. Afterwards, he went to learn at the Hildesheimer Rabbinical Seminary, and then he learned in Switzerland and the Mir, where he was influenced by Rav Yeruham Levovitz. He spent the war years in Sweden and moved to Israel in 1946, where he taught *musar* as *mashgiah ruhani* in several yeshivas. In addition to his popular lectures, Rav Wolbe ran *vaadim*, or small groups that met regularly to help their members' character-trait refinement and spiritual growth. His two-volume *Alei Shur* is based on these meetings. Rav Wolbe's insights on the *parasha* were collected by his grandson, Rabbi Yitzchok Caplan and published as *Rav Wolbe on Chumash*.

Yagdil Torah – This contemporary collection of insights on the *parasha* was written by Rav Moshe Menachem Ludmir.

Yam Simha – A collection of insights on the Torah and the *mo'adim*, arranged by Rav Yisrael Moshe Freid.

Yonatan ben Uziel – The Talmud states that Yonason ben Uziel was the greatest of Hillel's eighty disciples, who lived one hundred years before the destruction of the Second Temple. He authored an influential Aramaic translation of the *Tanakh*, the *Targum Yonatan*, as well as a work on Kabbalah, the *Megadnim*.

Zevin, Rav Shlomo Yosef – Rav Zevin (1888–1978) received ordination from R. Yosef Yitzchak Schneerson of Chabad, Rav Yosef

Rosen (the Rogatchaver Gaon), and Rav Yechiel Michel Epstein, author of the *Arukh HaShulhan*. He was active in promoting Jewish education and observance in Communist Russia. In 1935 he moved to Israel and taught at the Beis Midrash LaMorim, affiliated with the Mizrachi Movement. He later served on the Israeli Chief Rabbinate and was the editor-in-chief of the *Encyclopedia Talmudit*. He authored *LaTorah VeLaMo'adim*.

Zilberstein, Rav Yitzhak – Rav Zilberstein was born in Poland in 1934 and studied in Jerusalem and later in Yeshivat Slobodka in Bnei Brak. A *posek* in Bnei Brak and head of a *beit din* in Holon, he is a popular lecturer and the author of *Aleinu Leshabe'ah*, a collection of halakhic cases organized according to the *parasha*.

Maggid Books
The best of contemporary Jewish thought from
Koren Publishers Jerusalem Ltd.